Praise for *Building Portals, Intranets, and Corporate Web Sites Using Microsoft Servers*

"This book provides concise information on building a robust and user-friendly site. It highlights the key development issues and guides you through the options for addressing them."

—*Christa Carpentiere*
Program Manager

"Jim Townsend's book provides a highly accurate and comprehensive overview of the portal development process on the Microsoft platform. It should be required reading for anyone engaging in an enterprise portal project."

—*Chris Roberts*
Global Industry Manager, E Government
Microsoft Corporation

"Finally, a holistic approach to building enterprise portal projects using the full combined power of Microsoft's technologies and servers! Jim Townsend's book provides excellent, experience-based advice on understanding, designing, and implementing successful portal solutions."

—*Margery Reynolds*
Microsoft Government Solutions Specialist III
Microsoft Corporation

Building Portals, Intranets, and Corporate Web Sites Using Microsoft Servers

James J. Townsend
Dmitri Riz
Deon Schaffer

✦✦Addison-Wesley

Boston • San Francisco • New York • Toronto • Montreal
London • Munich • Paris • Madrid
Capetown • Sydney • Tokyo • Singapore • Mexico City

The publisher offers discounts on this book when ordered in quantity for bulk purchases and special sales. For more information, please contact:

U.S. Corporate and Government Sales
(800) 382-3419
corpsales@pearsontechgroup.com

For sales outside of the U.S., please contact:

International Sales
(317) 581-3793
international@pearsontechgroup.com

Visit Addison-Wesley on the Web: www.awprofessional.com

Library of Congress Cataloging-in-Publication Data

Townsend, James J.
    Building portals, intranets, and corporate Web sites using Microsoft servers / James J. Townsend.
        p. cm.
    ISBN 0-321-15963-2 (alk. paper)
    1. Web portals--Design. 2. Intranets (Computer networks)--Design and construction. I. Title.

TK5105.888.T69 2004
025.04--dc22

                                                                      2003069633

ISBN: 0-321-15963-2
Text printed on recycled paper
1 2 3 4 5 6 7 8 9 10—CRS—0807060504
First printing, March 2004

For Julia
—Jim

For Irene
—Dmitri

In loving memory of my mother,
Bernice Schaffer
—Deon

Contents

Preface

Not even the implosion of the dot.com bubble was enough to derail the proliferation of Internet technology and the move toward e-business that has extended to nearly every industry in the developed world. Few organizations are content to tolerate the isolation of applications into separate "silos" of information, or poor interoperability among their software solutions. The portal has been held up as a means to achieve better application integration and provide a consistent user interface both inside and outside the enterprise.

Companies and other organizations need to take a broader look at their portal strategy to make the various elements of their architecture work together. This is a pivotal time not only in the emergence of new technology but in the convergence of technologies toward open standards and enhanced interoperability.

Audience and Goals

The portal market is an amorphous and elusive target, with a small number of universal standards and a large population of vendors attempting to define those standards in ways that are most beneficial for their product sales. The first generation of portal books was devoted to explaining why portals were such a good idea, and how they could benefit their users. The bulk of these books were devoted to enterprise portals and to extolling the virtues of extensible markup language (XML). Others were devoted to explaining how to use a single product with "portal" in the name, such as Oracle Portal or Microsoft SharePoint Portal Server; but they covered only a small number of the features that an organization needs in a portal.

While these theoretical portal books were helpful and necessary, they didn't go far enough in explaining how to implement their solutions. Some of the theories they expounded were not borne out by experience in the software market. The single-product books could go no further than the products themselves, leaving administrators with half or less of the solution they had in mind.

This book is a practical guide for developers and information technology managers. It is focused on conveying what elements make up a portal and how to construct these elements using the Microsoft development platform. It is a combination of introductions to key concepts, suggestions for portal planning, and limited detailed technical instruction by way of examples that relate to all the main portal elements. Most chapters describe what to build and then show how to build it.

The most important section for managers is the first five chapters. These chapters address the portal from the perspective of a user and provide valuable background that can help managers form reasonable project expectations. The focus is not on individual products and features. Indeed, portals with the functionality described here could be implemented with a number of different technologies and products, and these are introduced in the second part of the book.

Developers will spend more time with the remainder of the book to understand how to fill the gap between products and where each portal service belongs. They will want to review the early chapters to understand the vision for a .NET portal and to ensure that the IT manager doesn't know something that they don't. These later chapters do not attempt to restate the vast amount of information in help files and product documentation for the products used in our examples. Rather, our goal is to create a higher-level overview that encompasses multiple products and puts each product and feature in its proper place. We also highlight best practices and hints that are not found in the product documentation but can save many hours of work or frustration.

No single product provides the infrastructure and tools needed to build a full-featured portal. Therefore we have had to include a number of server and development products to fill each niche in our portal ecosystem.

Prerequisites

There are no prerequisites for grasping the material in this book, as it explains the anatomy of a portal from the ground up. Our goals are to provide a compelling vision for portals that can be applied to your business requirements and to explain in detail how this vision maps to the Microsoft .NET Framework and web services.

This book does not attempt to teach much of the fundamental knowledge and techniques that are required to be a successful and productive developer. For instance, it does not provide background information on the following fundamental topics:

- Relational database concepts
- Web development technologies other than .NET
- Networking and security
- Object-oriented programming

The source code examples included in this book are not sufficient to learn any of the products that are used for examples, nor is the code presented all that would be needed for a full portal implementation. In other words, we are not going to be eliminating any jobs in the information technology service industry by publishing this book. The code examples are intended to be illustrative and inspirational, a springboard from which you can work out your own solution.

Software Requirements

To work through all the code examples in this book, you need the following products:

- Visual Studio.NET
- Commerce Server 2002
- Content Management Server
- SharePoint Portal Server 2003
- Microsoft Office 2003
- BizTalk Server
- SQL Server 2000
- Windows 2000 or Windows XP
- Windows Server 2003

Although it may possible to configure a single server with all these products, a more practical development environment would be to allocate one server to SQL Server, one as the web server, and one for everything else. The number of servers required for a full implementation is discussed in Chapter 14, "Scalability and the Portal."

There has never been a better time to enrich your organization's web presence. We hope you enjoy learning about portals and putting these ideas into practice.

Acknowledgments

Like a software project or a Hollywood movie, a book is a collaborative venture and depends on the talents of many performers. So it is with this book.

My biggest debt is to my coauthors Dmitri Riz and Deon Schaffer, and contributor Chris Wildgoose. Their hard work and sacrifice made this project possible, and their comments made each chapter better than it was before. Our reviewers Christa Carpentiere and James Edelman gave us tremendous insights and perspectives that were lost to our jaded eyes and made the content much more accurate and accessible.

I would like to thank all the talented team at Information Strategies for their contributions to the effort, including Tim McCaffrey, Jimmy Kuo, Gerald Ellison, Steven Nossal, Robyne Kenton, Mike Chiaramonte, Lauren Adler, Erin Rothman, and Kristina Harrison. Tim has kept the ship on course regardless of my multitasking, and Mike came through in the eleventh hour with significant and thankless technical chores essential to finishing the manuscript.

We had tremendous support from Microsoft both in Redmond and in the Washington, DC, field office. Special thanks are due to Ken Brown, Kathleen Burns, Teresa Carlson, Jim Ferguson, Jason Katz, Carol Kerins, Amy Marchibroda, Margie Reynolds, Chris Roberts, Lisa Ruff, Darryl Schaffer, Candace Sokulski, Nelson Taggart, Jamie Tozzi, Christina Treacy, Jim Treacy, and Cliff Ward.

Thanks go to our clients for entrusting us with their projects and data, including David DiEugenio, Rena Lewis, Mike Easley, Tom Thompson, Tony Bingham, Venus Baines, Silvia Edgar, Bob Blake, David Melton, and Rebecca Danvers. There is only one way to learn the most important lessons of delivering software solutions, and that is to do it. These solutions invariably involve difficult projects, tight deadlines, and limited resources. This book contains many of the lessons we have learned through working closely with our clients.

Most of all, I owe thanks to my wife Marcella, for putting up with me working a second shift all these months and for giving encouragement and insight when they were needed most.

Chapter 1

Introduction to Portals

Rise of the Portal

Few topics are as high on the information technology agenda as web portals. Around the world, organizations of all sizes have pledged their commitment to build and maintain comprehensive portals to serve their customers, employees, trading partners, and constituents. Corporations in all industries, governments at all levels, and nonprofit organizations for all interests have jumped on the portal bandwagon. The number of web sites that consider themselves portals has grown exponentially, as has the number of organizations that are building portals for internal or external use. If you use the web, chances are you are a portal user. If you have a public web site or an intranet, you probably want to include portal features.

Although portals are widely used and widely discussed, they are also misunderstood. There is a wide gulf between the architecture and features of various portals. A public portal geared toward anonymous users, such as a Yahoo or MSN, may not have much in common with the intranet portal you create for your employees to access frequently used business applications. A knowledge management portal has different features from one that targets e-commerce.

Just as there are many types of portals, portal products are targeted at different segments of the portal market and often have little overlap in capabilities. For instance, Microsoft SharePoint Portal Server and IBM WebSphere Portal Server have little more in common than the word "portal" in their product names. They vary in the services they offer, such as content management, application integration, personalization, catalog and shopping basket, document management, search, and other services. At the same time, many critical portal services come from products and technologies that are not labeled as portal products per se.

This chapter introduces key portal concepts and offers portal definitions to help describe the type of portal you would like to build. We will start with the early search portal pioneers and work our way to enterprise portals and other portal technologies designed for intranet and extranet use.

Portal Definitions

Although the desire for portals seems nearly universal, the meaning of the term "portal" is not universally agreed upon. It means different things to different people, and it has been seized on as a marketing mantra by software vendors to mean exactly what they happen to be selling. For instance, SharePoint Portal Server is the only current Microsoft product with "portal" in its name, but document management and a search engine are arguably more prominent than the digital dashboard portal feature in this product. If you are building an outward-facing portal on the Microsoft platform, SharePoint Portal Server is probably not your first choice in the Microsoft product family, as it is geared toward use inside the enterprise. On the other hand, Microsoft Content Management Server plausibly could be the centerpiece for building a public portal because it is scalable, its sites do not require the Internet Explorer browser, and users do not need to purchase client access licenses.

Trying to determine what is and is not a portal can spur quite spirited discussions. Is personalization an inherent feature of a portal? Does a search engine alone constitute a portal? How many portal elements are required for a web site to be considered a portal? Where can we find an intelligible and reliable definition of a portal?

At www.dictionary.com, the most applicable definition of a portal is:

> *A web site considered as an entry point to other web sites, often by being or providing access to a search engine.*

This definition is a good starting point, but it fails to cover some of the ideas that have been packed into the word "portal" by the software industry. That's why vendors have come up with their own definitions. Table 1.1 lists some portal definitions from vendors and web sites.

Table 1.1 Vendor Definitions of Portal

Vendor	Definition	Source
Client Help Desk	A web site offers a great amount of content and services, either on many subjects (a horizontal portal, such as Yahoo! or About.com) or on a specific subject (a vertical portal, or vortal, such as women.com or WebMD).	www.clienthelpdesk.com/dictionary/portal.html
Plumtree	A corporate portal brings together content, applications, and services from incompatible platforms, for employees, partners and customers.	www.plumtree.com/default1.asp
BroadVision	A corporate portal is a personalized self-service application that extends your enterprise's information, resources, and business processes to your constituents (employees, partners, and customers) in a unified and collaborative manner.	www.broadvision.com/OneToOne/SessionMgr/products/products_main.jsp?BV_SessionID=NNNN1630750284.1039196546NNNN&BV_EngineID=ccccadcglgjhgglcefecefedghhdfjl.0&product=Portal&channelName=Enterprise+Portal&channelRuleset=Products+Channels&programName=One-To-One+Portal&programRuleset=Enterprise+Portal+Programs

Continues

Table 1.1 Vendor Definitions of Portal (*Continued*)

Vendor	Definition	Source
Oracle	The portal is the single source of interaction with corporate applications, information, and it is the focal point for conducting day-to-day business. The enterprise portal you choose to deploy must allow you to: ■ Ensure interoperability with an open architecture ■ Scale to meeting changing performance requirements ■ Build and maintain the portal with productive tools ■ Integrate essential applications and content ■ Simplify administration with a flexible management model	Oracle 9iAS Portal Overview www.oracle.com/ip/deploy/ias/ portal/portal_overview.pdf
Traffick	The term "web portal" began to be used to describe megasites such as Yahoo, Excite, MSN, Netscape Netcenter, and AOL because many users used them as a starting point or entry point for their web surfing. The term "search engine" had become inadequate to describe the breadth of the offerings of these leading Internet destinations, although search and navigation are still pivotal to most people's online experience. (AOL is a bit different: it's always been an Internet access provider in addition to being a network of proprietary Internet content and services.)	www.traffick.com/article.asp?aID= 9#what

Table 1.1 Vendor Definitions of Portal (*Continued*)

Vendor	Definition	Source
Webopedia	Web site or service that offers a broad array of resources and services, such as email, forums, search engines, and online shopping malls. The first web portals were online services, such as AOL, that provided access to the web, but by now most of the traditional search engines have transformed themselves into web portals to attract and keep a larger audience. A web portal is commonly referred to as simply a portal.	webopedia.internet.com/TERM/W/Web_portal.html

In the interest of simplification and at the risk of oversimplification, I would like to offer our own working definition of "portal" here. A web portal (or portal for short) is:

> *A web site (Internet or intranet) that combines information from multiple, disparate sources, offering a unified interface with the goal of improving usability and providing powerful search capabilities*

The unified interface that the portal provides may access static content such as web pages, unstructured content such as documents, or applications with structured relational database or other backend content providers. The portals we explore and build in this book are targeted both at casual, anonymous users and at employees performing complicated tasks. Our goal is to provide a broad framework with a superset of the services and functionality that you are seeking for your portal.

Now that we have tackled the question of what a portal is in the broadest sense, let's explore some of the web sites that are characterized as portals to distill the essence of the portal concept as it is used for the balance of this book.

Types of Portals

One way to better understand the portal world is to divide portals into groups based on the purpose of the portal. This section describes several types of portals aimed at different functions for different audiences, and illustrates how portal sites have evolved during the short history of the web.

Web-Searching Portals

The first portals on the web were gateways to content that combined search engines with precompiled lists of related links by topic. Many of these portals were general interest and appealed to a broad audience. For instance, Yahoo is one of the most successful web portals. It combines a search engine with personalization (MyYahoo), news, financial information, shopping, and hundreds of other features to aggregate web content, making it more accessible to users. As it has evolved, Yahoo has added a wide variety of services to compete with other portals and retain its share of users. The revenue model for many web-searching portals is selling web advertisements.

While Yahoo was spawned from a directory of sites and a search engine, other portals have grown from Internet service providers such as the Microsoft Network (MSN) and America Online (AOL). These began as jumping-off points to other web sites and also incorporated powerful search engines and navigational assistance. Even the U.S. government has its own portal called FirstGov (Figure 1.1).

Web-searching portals grew beyond their origins of providing links to other web sites. They expanded to offer value-added services such as virtual communities and hundreds of related sites for shopping, travel, finance, and even free email service, as shown in Figure 1.2. The virtual communities are a highly popular attraction of portals, and you may want to seriously consider newsgroups, chat rooms, and other such features in your portal.

Consumer Portals

Another group of portals has ended up looking quite similar to web-searching portals. These started with consumers as their audience and shopping as the primary goal. Along the way, they added content to inform and guide consumers and to encourage them to spend more time in the portal in hopes of generating greater product sales.

Figure 1.1 FirstGov, a U.S. federal government portal

The main difference between a web-searching portal and a consumer portal is the former is a gateway to other web sites while the latter is a destination in itself (Figure 1.3). Consumer portals must support secure electronic transactions and provide a high level of customer support. While web-searching portals help users reach other destinations and hope that

Figure 1.2 The Microsoft Network (MSN)

Figure 1.3 Amazon.com Home Page (© 2002 Amazon.com, Inc. All rights reserved.)

they return for more searching, consumer portals add content such as product reviews, background information, and buyers' guides to make their sites more "sticky" and keep consumers inside the virtual store. The revenue model for a consumer portal is selling goods, with a secondary revenue stream from advertising and affiliations.

Arguably the most successful e-business story is the consumer portal eBay, which modestly characterizes itself as the world's online marketplace. eBay is a thriving electronic community for buyers and sellers, with its auction catalog at the heart of the action. eBay is also a portal in a less visible sense. It supports integration with other web frontends and client programs, allowing developers to write software to tap the eBay commerce engine in specialized ways to enhance the productivity of end users. These software agents, such as eSnipe, BidRobot, LastMinuteBids, and Auction-Sleuth, provide an alternative frontend to the eBay web pages and apply business rules to bidding behavior. They illustrate how a well-made portal can be extended for customers and business partners.

eBay is such a rich portal in terms of functionality that it offers training at eBay University. Check out pages.ebay.com/university/index.html for online training and courses around the United States.

Web-searching portals have not allowed shopping portals to steal user eyeballs without a fight. Yahoo, MSN (Figure 1.4), and others have added shopping features, such as Yahoo's Shopping section (www.shopping.yahoo.com), blurring the line between web-searching and consumer portals.

Vertical Portals

Portals can be targeted at people with particular interests. These are sometimes called **vertical portals**, or **vortals**. Each industry has spawned its own brood of portal sites, from architecture (www.off-design.com) to zymurgy (www.beerflavor.com). Some of these portals were created by leaders in the industry or consortia of companies. For instance, when I took up fishing last summer, I found a quite attractive site called www.waterworkswonders.org (Figure 1.5). The site is run by the Recreational Boating & Fishing Foundation. It contains articles, hints, and links to hundreds of other sites with fishing reports, weather, and other information for recreational anglers.

Some companies have based their entire business plans on creating profitable portal web sites, driving revenue through advertising or through

Figure 1.4 MSN Shopping

Figure 1.5 A Vertical Portal for Fishing

subscriptions to the portal. Portals are well suited to targeting niche audiences, and the behavior of portal users helps portal operators understand the behavior of consumers. Brick-and-mortar companies have extended their marketing reach and brand awareness through portals. Indeed, there are portals and portal products specifically targeted to traditional companies. The Department of Trade and Industry of the United Kingdom has funded a portal called Beyond Bricks (beyondbricks.ecademy.com) to encourage the growth and success of e-business. New Delhi-based NIIT Limited has created a "brick and portal" model to facilitate transformation to e-business.

Government Portals

Governments have embraced portals to the same, or even a greater, extent than private industry. In some ways, governments have more to gain from portals than businesses, because they have so much farther to go in reaching their constituencies with new channels of communication, and governments need to reach a larger population than all but the largest businesses. Much of the interaction between government and citizens is essentially information sharing, and the web lends itself to opening government to citizens, employees, other governments, and businesses. Many government transactions could be simplified with portals, thereby winning public acceptance and votes for elected officials.

The President of the United States has his own portal at www.whitehouse.gov to share presidential news, policies, speeches, and the history of the White House (Figure 1.6). It has grown dramatically to include content for a wide group of audiences.

State and local governments have made even larger investments in portals than the U.S. federal government. All the states in the United States openly compete for honors as the best state portal, and counties vie with their neighbors to offer the best web-based services. State and local government interact with citizens in dozens of ways, from motor vehicle registration and drivers licenses to property tax and business regulations. So-called e-permitting offers significant opportunities to save time and

Figure 1.6 White House Home Page

money. Perhaps the time normally spent waiting in line for a new vehicle license plate can be redirected to more economically productive use, thereby expanding government tax revenue and allowing for increased services or deficit reduction.

We are now in the second wave of state and local e-government transformation. The first wave coincided with the dotcom boom of the late 1990s and witnessed the construction of government portals by the largest, wealthiest states, counties, and cities. States such as California, Michigan, Washington, and Massachusetts signed deals with major portal software vendors and defined statewide portal architectures.

At the same time, private companies targeted the emerging market of citizen services, offering portals to pay parking tickets or taxes online, with revenue to be derived from convenience fees. The most famous, if tragic, example of this movement was govworks.com. This company's rise and fall was the subject of the documentary film *Startup.com*, which chronicled the entire life of a company based on creating an e-government portal, along with the personalities of the company principals and venture capitalists.

The second wave of government portals built on the lessons of the first, with less grandiose plans and more modest budgets. After the dotcom bubble burst, many of the software companies exclusively focused on the portal market (the "pure plays") were swept into the dustbin of history, and local governments found themselves in an unexpected financial deficit when the 1990s party ended. This hangover eliminated neither the need for government portals nor the real and tangible returns they can produce.

Michael Easley, the chief information officer for Tarrant County, Texas, made his county portal a top priority when he assumed his position in 2001. He succeeded in installing a new portal and migrating dozens of web sites to the platform in about 90 days from the start of the project (Figure 1.7). The county portal not only contains information for citizens but is the basis for web-based services such as online tax payment.

Rare is the government chief information officer (CIO) who doesn't give portals a high profile in his annual report. For instance, the Governor's Office of Technology in the state of West Virginia called for "creating a statewide e-portal in which government is more efficient and cost effective" in its IT strategic plan (www.state.wv.us/got/webITreport.pdf). Having a world-class portal is a valuable asset for a state intent on boosting tourism, business opportunities, and its own image as a technology leader.

Figure 1.7 Home Page of Tarrant County, Texas

Intranets and Enterprise Portals

Just as portals are used to reach out to the public, organizations have rushed to adopt portals to reach their internal users. Enterprise portals, also called corporate portals, information portals, decision portals, and knowledge portals, are devoted to organizing and categorizing information within an enterprise, on the intranet.

Enterprise portals share some of the goals of outward-facing portals. They are designed to provide new ways to push information to readers, improved searching, better navigation, and perhaps personalization. But enterprise portals also have the additional requirements of consolidating multiple applications and information sources and of providing more efficient mechanisms for collaboration. The enterprise portal is deeper than the outward-facing portal, as it typically offers much more sophisticated functionality that requires both support and training (Figure 1.8).

Some enterprise portals are successors to decision support systems (DSS) of earlier decades. They are designed to provide information to "knowledge workers" or "empowered employees"—the latest buzzwords

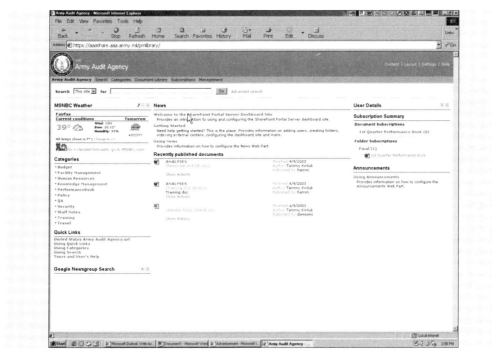

Figure 1.8 Sample Enterprise Portal

for those who manage and make decisions. For instance, one of the metaphors used for enterprise portals is the vehicle dashboard. The digital dashboard in Microsoft SharePoint Portal Server is an example of this approach. The dashboard is a portal that contains elements showing key business indicators such as inventory levels or order status.

While there certainly are valid distinctions to be drawn among the types of uses to which an enterprise portal may be put, for our purposes the commonalities outweigh the differences; and it is more useful to lump these portals and products together and determine the superset of services that makes them tick. Our focus is on the elements that differentiate enterprise portals from public portals, as well as on the common elements shared by both broad portal types.

Knowledge management is a key goal of enterprise portals, and one of the basic tenets of knowledge management is that users need to find data and information when they need it. This is not as easy as it might seem, due to the proliferation of heterogeneous data sources. One approach to enterprise portals is to convert as much data as possible to extensible markup language (XML) to make it easier to search and catalog. For instance, some products convert documents to XML automatically and place them in a special repository for the portal. Because XML is also used for structured data, a common search engine can be used for both structured and unstructured data. The problem with this approach is the labor involved in categorizing unstructured information with XML metatags.

Another common enterprise portal feature is alerts—messages sent to designated users based on events. For instance, department managers might be notified in the event that key metrics fall short of plan, and events relating to inventory might trigger messages to suppliers or to supply clerks. Alerts are also needed for content management, so content owners can participate in the editing and review process for web pages. Both SharePoint Portal Server and Content Management Server have implemented alert features.

The goal of all enterprise portals is to provide a single user interface for as much information and as many applications as possible. Generally companies select a web interface though a proprietary frontend is certainly possible. Some vendors have taken a cross-platform approach so clients can be supported on multiple hardware platforms and operating systems. Others tend toward a single browser or hardware platform.

Enterprise portals often provide access to internal applications, making the portal a replacement for the workstation desktop. Again, the typical portal user interface is a browser, but some vendors also have promoted their own special portal clients that do not run within a browser. With Microsoft Internet Explorer, ActiveX is commonly used to provide controls that access applications within the enterprise.

A common means of providing connectivity to applications is to host controls within the portal user interface that access the application. These controls may be called **gadgets** (Plumtree), **portlets** (Plumtree, BroadVision InfoExchange Portal, and Java Server Pages), **gizmos** (Metadot Portal Server), **web parts** (Microsoft SharePoint Portal Server), or **widgets** (Java Server Pages and others).

Figure 1.9 shows how a personalized page is displayed in a Plumtree portal. This example is for an insurance company to provide information for

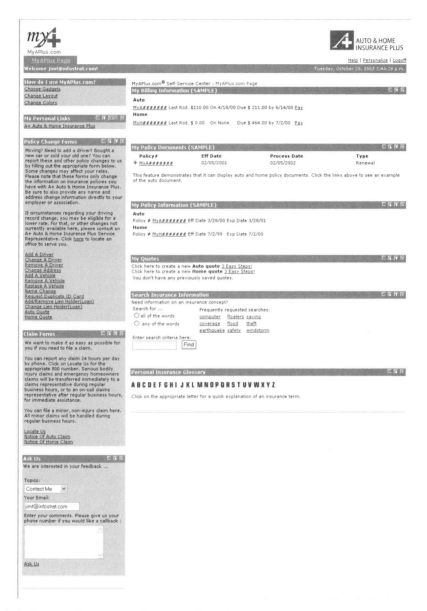

Figure 1.9 Sample Gadgets in Plumtree Portal

its customers. Users can choose the gadgets and determine where they are located on the page by moving them up and down in a columnar layout. In this example you can see separate gadgets for policy information, billing, and searching the portal. The gadgets are rendered on the server and sent to the browser as standard HTML. The gadgets may use data from many different systems and may be spread across multiple servers.

Intranet Self-Service

A key benefit of corporate portals is that they provide a new means of providing services. Creating commerce web sites for internal or external customers can produce significant returns on investment. For instance, routine employee transactions such as expense reimbursement, office supply procurement, travel arrangements, and benefit transaction can be accommodated in a portal.

Self-service may also be targeted at customers, suppliers, business partners, and other constituents. For example, Microsoft offers a portal site for Gold Certified Solution Providers that contains technical and sales resources for companies that provide services and products based on the Microsoft platform. The site offers static content and also integration with transactional systems such as online orders or updates to a partner status form. Microsoft Partners are given accounts on the corporate customer relationship management system (CRM) based on Siebel, allowing them to enter and track business opportunities in conjunction with Microsoft inside and outside account managers.

Another common portal service is event registration. Steps that were once handled through paper forms, faxes, or time-consuming calls to toll-free numbers can now be handled with a few choice mouse clicks. When a user's information is stored for subsequent use, the registration process is shortened further. For instance, on Microsoft's web site, users log in through the Passport service and event registration is prepopulated with the users' profile information such as name and address (Figure 1.10).

Another important service of enterprise portals is in providing the common access point for heterogeneous applications supporting common data. Portals can alleviate the problem of access to multiple legacy and new applications executing on various platforms within disparate operating environments. For instance, Microsoft BizTalk Server makes it easier to design, map, and orchestrate XML data flows among applications.

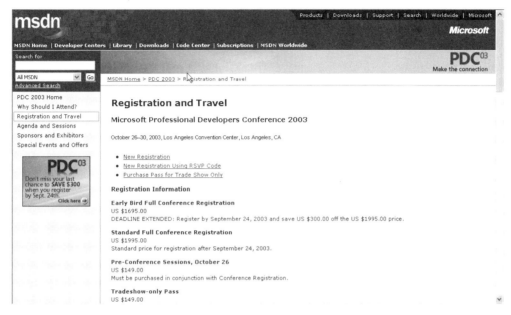

Figure 1.10 Online Event Registration in a Portal

Benefits of Portals

The catalysts for developing portals are as varied as portals themselves. Among other reasons, portals have been developed to:

- Provide better access to information
- Remove barriers to applications
- Create order from the chaos of data in an organization
- Promote reuse of information
- Reduce training time and cost
- Improve information access for decision-making
- Cultivate better relationships with customers
- Reduce overhead costs such as benefits administration
- Speed turnaround for processing such as expense reimbursement
- Allow searches of large volumes of heterogeneous data (documents, pages, database, messages, multimedia)
- Simplify telecommuting

If this sounds like a laundry list of all the benefits of information technology, the web, and automation rolled into one, it is not far from that. Portals have been the inspiration for technology that later finds its way into a broad range of products.

The portal services your organization chooses to deploy are directly related to these business benefits you are trying to achieve. Therefore, you should prioritize your portal efforts to match your business priorities. The following description of portal attributes and the more detailed coverage in Chapter 2 will help you narrow your focus.

Attributes of Portals

Each type of portal offers a unique set of features. Most of this book is devoted to explaining portal architecture and offering practical guidance on how to build portals using Microsoft .NET.

I am proposing a single overarching architecture for all portals, assuming that you may pick and choose the features you would like to include in your portal. This unified architectural approach simplifies application development within the enterprise and shares investments in hardware, software, and security architecture. It also lends itself to Microsoft's portal strategy, which takes a holistic view of the portal in the context of larger information technology (IT) initiatives. These combined portal features include:

- *A consistent user interface for users.* Users should know that they are in the portal, and they should be able to navigate easily. As much as possible, consistent look-and-feel should be enforced in all the nooks and crannies of the portal.
- *Better access to structured and unstructured data.* Portals can unify data access and provide reports, searches, and ad hoc queries. They should allow searching across multiple, heterogeneous sources.
- *A powerful and comprehensive search engine.* Full-text searching is essential, with a wide variety of document formats included such as HTML, text, word processing (Word, WordPerfect), Adobe Acrobat (PDF), and others.

- *Tools to maintain the portal (typically content management).* It is expensive to maintain a portal if all changes must be filtered through a help desk and a programming staff. Content management transfers the burden of updates from programmers to content owners. The net result is timelier refreshing of content and elimination of bottlenecks in the workflow. Content management also allows implementation of review processes to prevent content from being published without one or more reviewers approving it.

- *Improved security and simplified management of security.* Moving applications to a portal framework allows a single security framework to be used in place of the many and incompatible security schemes used by individual applications. Security policies such as password length and expiration can be enforced globally.

- *Personalization at department and individual levels.* The portal lets users and departments create pages with their favorite content and applications to streamline their access and provide a custom window into data they need to manage operations.

- *Shared architecture to support transactions rather than a stovepipe application approach.* The portal provides the transactional backbone for e-commerce transactions, both internal and external. It includes catalogs, shopping carts, payment processing, and other business processes that relate to these transactions.

- *Minimal client footprint and hence reduced cost to deploy and update.* Browser-based applications typically require less desktop configuration than traditional Windows32 client-server applications. This is particularly important when desktop configurations are standardized and "locked down."

- *Accessibility through multiple channels.* The portal can facilitate reuse of content and applications on desktop and laptop computers, Pocket PCs, cell phones, and tablet PCs.

- *Consolidation of multiple applications and data sources.* Ideally the portal would provide one-stop shopping for data and application needs. Instead of connecting many users to many applications, you face the challenge of integrating the applications with the portal.

Summary

For good reasons, portals are high on the information technology priority lists. They offer broad, measurable business benefits for many types of organizations. Now that the technology and products for portals have reached a certain maturity, they have entered the mainstream. With .NET, portal technology is much more affordable than in its first generation. As we will see, the .NET platform offers a richer and more flexible portal platform than many of its competitors.

With the proliferation of portals and portal products, there can be no doubt that portals are a significant phenomenon. They are here to stay and evolve into more sophisticated forms. Indeed, the underlying standards and technologies that make up today's portals are likely to be taken for granted in the future and be incorporated into nearly all web sites.

Rather than propose two distinct and perhaps even incompatible architectures for external and internal portals, this book attempts to offer a single architecture for all portals, united by web services and the Microsoft .NET Framework. I use Microsoft products to illustrate examples as much as possible, although other products or services could be substituted for various components. For instance, I am using SQL Server as the relational database to store structured data such as catalogs, transactions, profiles, and content. Another database management system could be substituted for some or all of these functions.

This book identifies the key elements that define what a portal should offer today, and some predictions of what it will include in the future. I then take a closer look at how to implement a portal to provide those functions, starting with a more detailed description of portal attributes in Chapter 2.

Portal Elements

Although portals are quite diverse, they all contain common elements. This chapter identifies the elements that make up a portal and describes how they look and work from the perspectives of users and portal architects. Not all these elements are present in every portal and some are more important than others, depending on the audience and business objectives of the portal. For instance, a portal geared toward anonymous users, requiring no authentication, would offer only limited support for secure transactions, data entry, or collaboration. A knowledge management portal might focus exclusively on searching and data integration without providing transactional capabilities.

This chapter shows where we are going in terms of the finished portal product. Users cannot usually see which products or technologies are working behind the scenes to provide the functionality they seek, and this is a good thing. What appears as a seamless, consistent user experience relies on several servers running web services, content management, database applications, collaboration tools, and other portal elements. The portal architect must be concerned with making all the pieces fit together. I also compare these elements to pre-web application development, because they illustrate the migration of the web from static documents to dynamic content, web applications, and web services.

The key portal elements are:

- Look-and-feel
- Security
- User profile
- Personalization
- Taxonomy and dynamic navigation
- Application integration
- Database repository

23

- Support for transactions
- Collaboration tools
- Multichannel support
- Search engine

Subsequent chapters show how to create these elements using the Microsoft .NET platform and Microsoft server products.

Look-and-Feel

Like all computer programs that interact with human beings, portals have a look-and-feel or user interface (UI). Indeed, the wellspring of portals is the need for improved user interfaces for content and applications. If organizations used consistent design standards for all their applications, they would already have much of the feel of a portal, just as Microsoft has done with its products. But, alas, most organizations have not taken a consistent approach to user interface over the long term. They have yielded to the desire for progress in interface design for each subsequent application and to the whims of individual developers.

The overriding feeling that users should experience in a portal is unity. That is, the users should always know where they are and how to get to where they want to go. Consistent pages and understandable navigation are essential, and colors, fonts, and other graphical elements should be used to tie all the pages of a portal together. Navigation should never dump an unsuspecting user into a cul-de-sac with no way to return home.

The home page of a portal indicates that it is a portal, either explicitly, with a title containing the word "portal," or implicitly, by hinting at the wealth of information a few clicks away. Users need to be reminded where they are and what they are doing throughout their experience. Figure 2.1 is the home page of GORP.com, a portal devoted to outdoor adventures such as hiking, camping, biking, skiing, and paddling. At the top of the page is the GORP logo, along with navigation tabs for Home, Destinations, Activities, Parks, Close to Home, Gear, Marketplace, Find Trips, and Community. The last three tabs are grouped under "Shop at GORP" to let the user know that these are the e-commerce sections of the site. The others, though plentifully endowed with advertisements, provide information without the ability to buy online.

Figure 2.1 Home Page of GORP Portal

A half-dozen clicks later, I can view a map of a park I'm planning to visit, such as the C&O Canal National Historic Park (Figure 2.2). This page continues the design theme of the home page, repeating the masthead and the tabbed navigation, with additional left navigation choices, more depth to the top navigation, and the obligatory advertisements.

Content management, which is the use of automated tools to create and maintain web page content, is essential for building and sustaining the large, rich sites that we seek, especially if you are not single-handedly attempting to create jobs for all the unemployed coders of the world. Content management is the most important portal tool for defining and maintaining a consistent look and feel throughout the portal. While a site can be maintained by an army of HTML programmers, content management solutions make the process much easier and less labor-intensive, especially when it comes time to update the look of your site.

Content management tools make it unnecessary to write HTML to create pages and put the responsibility for content in the hands of those who write it in the first place. These tools truly separate the content from the presentation, storing content in a relational database and using templates to

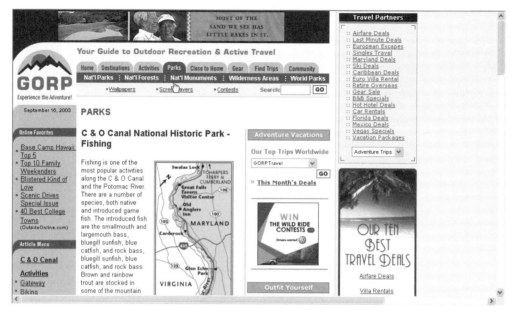

Figure 2.2 Destination Map Page from GORP Portal

display the content as desired. When templates are updated, the appearance of all pages based on those templates is also updated.

These tools also deliver a new discipline to the content creation process. Workflow rules can be enforced, along with an approval process, resulting in less risk of broken or embarrassing web site updates and even less legal risk. Content creators and editors can use a browser or Office application such as Word to create a page, and then route it to the appropriate people to approve the content and make it go live.

Content management provides freshness dating by defining the start and end dates for a page to appear on the site. Content such as a press release can be written, edited, and approved in the content management system in advance of the date it will be made available to the public. Stale content can be set to expire and disappear from the site at a given date.

In Chapter 9, we will see how Microsoft Content Management Server (MCMS) provides all this functionality and more, and learn how it is integrated into other portal elements, such as document management, collaboration, and commerce capabilities. We will examine the content management features of SharePoint Portal Server 2003, as well as the option of building your own custom content management solution.

Security

The walls of our ironclad security fortress are largely invisible to our users, as they should be. There is no reason to publicize our security measures unless we are trying to provoke hackers and crackers. Users notice authentication challenges, such as usernames and passwords, use of encryption (secure sockets layer), and the use of cookies.

There are three general levels of security that apply to portals. For a public portal, the first and loosest level is support for anonymous users. If you are trying to attract new customers, constituents, or other users to your portal, you need to allow them anonymous access. There is little point to improving your search engine results if the first thing users see is a login screen, and they are forced to create an account on your portal. New users need to be able to kick the tires a bit and become comfortable before they divulge personal information or spend money. In fact, the bulk of the portal content may be available to these anonymous users, as it is for many portals. If you support online purchasing, you will have to solicit personal information during the checkout process. At that point you may give customers the choice of simultaneously creating an account for future use and entering the necessary information for the current transaction.

The second level of security is for authenticated portal users. The primary means of authentication at this level is the pair of a username and password. Your portal needs a way to create and maintain these user accounts, performing such tasks as changing passwords and helping users who have lost their passwords. Typically email is used to communicate these administrative actions to users. For instance, Microsoft provides special content for its business partners in the Solution Provider program, such as technical information, sales resources, and downloads. To access this information, the user must log into the Microsoft web site. In this case, Microsoft uses the .NET Passport service, an authentication service that is shared by multiple web sites inside and outside Microsoft, as shown in Figure 2.3.

One of the advantages of .NET Passport is that it reduces the number of passwords that must be maintained. I can use the same password to obtain premium partner content, change my corporate profile on the Gold Partner site, register for Microsoft seminars, and book travel on Expedia.com. You may want to consider using this service as a convenience to your customers. They would need active Internet connections because the public .NET Passport service does not work through an intranet that lacks an outside connection.

Figure 2.3 Members-Only Login Page for Microsoft Partners

All higher forms of security can be lumped into the third level. These measures are more intrusive or demanding than the typical customer might expect, but they are necessary to safeguard proprietary information. For instance, you could implement IP filtering to restrict the range of IP addresses that can access certain pages. This precaution effectively limits the locations from which the page can be accessed. You could add a hardware token to the security mix, such as a smartcard. A customer would need a smartcard reader, along with the card and matching username and password, to be granted access. This is the level at which biometric security, such as fingerprint readers or retinal scans, could be implemented.

User Profile

If you allow users to log into the portal, you need a personal profile for each user. At a minimum, the profile contains the username and password used for authentication. It may also contain data elements such as:

Name
Job Title
Organization Name
Organization Industry

Addresses (Mailing, Shipping, Billing)
Email Address
Interests
Language Preference

Users should have access to their profiles so they can ensure their accuracy and change them as profile information changes. For instance, Figure 2.4 shows the profile-updating page at microsoft.com.

Profiles usually grow over time. It may be too intrusive to ask a user for all the information in the profile at one time. Depending on what actions a user takes in the portal, more information may be needed. There is no point in asking users for dietary preferences until it is time to serve them a meal, such as a meal at a conference. When users travel, you may need to expand their profiles to include seating preferences and next-of-kin contact information.

The profile is a rich source of information about your users. You can combine it with web log usage statistics to better understand who likes what on your portal. The profile may help with directed marketing campaigns through direct mail or email. The profile is also the basis for personalization.

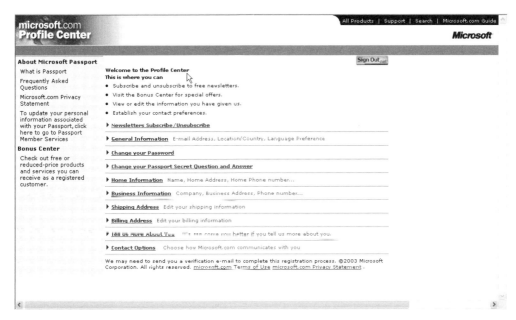

Figure 2.4 Personal Profile Page at microsoft.com

Personalization

Most portals contain thousands or even hundreds of thousands of pages of content, most of which is not of interest to a specific user. Personalization provides a way to cut through the clutter and provide relevant, or at least potentially relevant, information to each user.

The most common form of personalization is to dynamically create pages that vary depending on data in the user's personal profile. For instance, a singles site might display personal ads from individuals who share a user's interests or commentary about issues in which the user is interested.

When I go to amazon.com, I am greeted by "Hello, James J. Townsend," instantly putting me at ease and in the mood to buy books, DVDs, and more. This greeting is just the tip of the Amazon personalization iceberg. From the home page (Figure 2.5), I can see that there are recommendations just for me, special New for You items, messages, and even, buried at

Figure 2.5 Amazon.com Home Page with Personalization (© 2002 Amazon.com, Inc. All rights reserved.)

the bottom of the page, the offer to "Make $345.95 Selling Your Past Purchases at amazon.com Today!" Luckily, times have not been so hard that I must part with my last 25 purchases at amazon.com.

Another aspect of personalization is localization—the ability to cater to users based on their geographic location. For instance, you may want to support multiple languages on your portal. Users would specify the language of choice in their profile, and the personalization engine would dynamically point users to content in the target language. Chapter 8 covers how to use the personalization capabilities of Microsoft Commerce Server 2002 and SharePoint Portal Server 2003 to bring this functionality to your .NET portal.

Taxonomy

A taxonomy is a hierarchy of categories used to simplify navigation and searching. For instance, a standard company brochure web site would have a taxonomy like that shown in Table 2.1.

Table 2.1 Company Brochure Web Site Taxonomy

Home
Company Information
Stockholder Information
Key Personnel Biographies
CEO
President
Director of Research and Development
Vice President of Sales
Human Resources Manager
Products
KnowledgeManager
Collaborama
Product Price List

Continues

Table 2.1 Company Brochure Web Site Taxonomy (*Continued*)

Services
Consulting Services
Support Services
Contact Us

The taxonomy is a powerful tool for creating navigation. For instance, the United States Air Force identified consistent navigation as one of the primary goals of the Air Force portal. When personnel move from base to base, they need the same services for housing, benefits, orientation, and human resource services. Before the portal, each base created its own web site and there was no guarantee that the same content would always be available or that the navigation would be easy to understand. Table 2.2 shows the standard navigation for Air Force base web sites, as defined in the Air Force portal.

Table 2.2 Standard Air Force Base Navigation in the Air Force Portal

Base Common Categories
Base Home
Medical
Services
Personnel
Newcomer's Info
Directives & Policies
Base Common Subcategories Surfaced to Base Home Page
Base Map & Directions
Units
History
Local Community
Base FAQs
Employment Opportunities
Deployment (AEF)
Security
Base News

Table 2.2 Standard Air Force Base Navigation in the Air Force Portal (*Continued*)

Base Common Content Links Surfaced to Base Home Page

    Base-level Announcements; Base Features; Base Spotlight; Threat Condition
    Medical
    Local Hospitals
    Appointments
    Pharmacy
    Local Providers
    Health News
    Self Care

Services

    MWR
    Housing
    Gym
    Library
    Dining
    Child Care
    Movies
    Address
    Mailbox

Personnel

    TMO
    Training
    PCS

Newcomer's Info

    PCS
    Housing
    Community

Directives & Policies

Another way to display a taxonomy is in a site map. Site maps can be displayed as a tree view with branches, which a user can expand or contract as needed. Unfortunately, many portals are so large that site maps of the entire site would be unwieldy. Microsoft.com certainly faces this issue. However, maps of smaller areas, in essence portal neighborhoods, can be quite useful. An example is shown in Figure 2.6.

Figure 2.6 Site Map (MSDN with Navigation Tree on Left)

Loosely connected sites risk losing users when they navigate deep into a site and they cannot find their way back. That's why some portals use **breadcrumbs**, which are listings of the hierarchy of topics traversed by the user. Here is a sample breadcrumb: <u>Home</u> > <u>About Our Company</u> > <u>Executive Biographies</u> > <u>Our CEO</u>. This user, in other words, viewed the home page first and then moved to About Our Company, and so on. Each of the terms in the breadcrumb is a link, which a user could click to go directly to the top page for that topic. Microsoft Content Management Server can automatically create the breadcrumb trail for you (see Chapter 9).

Application Integration

Portals are much more than massive collections of static web pages with nice graphics and clean navigation. To engage users more deeply, they must support web applications, so portals need "hooks" to simplify development of those applications and their integration into the broader portal framework.

Simplified application integration is one of the benefits of choosing .NET as your application architecture. One of the goals of .NET is to embrace open software standards to improve interoperability and to simplify integration tasks (Figure 2.7).

When properly executed, application integration is not visible to end users. Only when integration fails do users see the separate silos of information that underlie a portal. Users often need to fuse data that originates in multiple, often incompatible, sources. Intelligence analysts can pull together an interesting picture from examining bank records, phone calls, and email among suspicious subjects. A portal can integrate customer data in a similar fashion, integrating customer phone calls, transaction records, and timing of promotions and marketing campaigns.

From an architect's point of view, a portal should provide the following features to assist with application integration:

1. *Authentication services.* Individual applications in the portal should not require their own security schemes and authentication. Logging into the portal should be sufficient to provide authentication to all applications hosted in the portal.

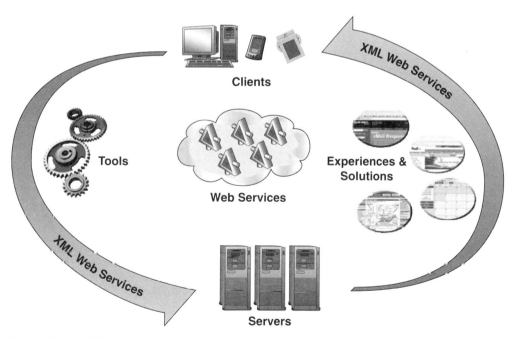

Figure 2.7 .NET Application Integration

2. *Data standards for application data and metadata.* You may choose to publish your data schemas for business partners to access.
3. *Cross-platform integration* using XML as the common data exchange format and enterprise application integration (EAI) tools such as Microsoft BizTalk Server.
4. *Web services* when compatible with consuming applications.
5. *Methods for coordinating and orchestrating distributed transactions*, such as distributed transaction coordinator (DTC).

Database and Other Repositories

Behind the scenes in a portal is a database, usually a relational database. Depending on the portal elements you choose, other repositories will be involved as well, such as a directory service. What does the relational database contain?

- *Structured data for applications that require it*, such as online catalogs, inventory systems, payroll and human resources, and all manner of line-of-business applications. Web pages are used as the frontend for these systems to allow data entry, queries, and reports.
- *Content (text and HTML tags) that is managed by the content management system.* For instance, Microsoft Content Management Server uses SQL Server to store content that is dynamically generated into web pages, and also data needed to generate site navigation.
- *Documents managed by the content management system.* SharePoint Portal Server 2003 stores these documents in SQL Server.
- *User profiles.* This means user information such as name, email address, contact information, and preferences that relate to content that may be used by the personalization engine.
- *Metadata.* The database contains data about the databases (metadata) such as the table structure, relationships among the tables, and data definitions.

I chose SQL Server as the relational database for the examples in this book. It is the standard repository for several servers and services such as Microsoft Content Management Server, Commerce Server, and Windows SharePoint Services. As a result, we can take advantage of all the tools available for SQL Server to manage our portal data and metadata.

Not all portal data ends up in a relational database. Messages, for instance, are stored in Exchange Server, which does not use a relational database as its repository in the current version. SharePoint Portal Server 2001 used the Web Store as its repository rather than storing managed documents in the file system or in SQL Server. SharePoint Portal Server 2003 preserves this storage option but only for backward compatibility with the 2001 version. Figure 2.8 shows the roles of the primary portal repositories.

For the logical and physical planning of portal infrastructure, you as the portal architect must be aware of the repositories that will be used. For instance, scalability considerations will determine how many servers are applied to each of these repositories, and you must prepare failover contingencies.

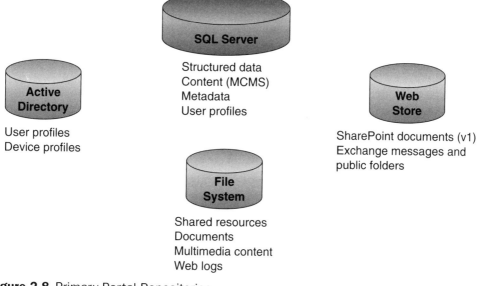

Figure 2.8 Primary Portal Repositories

Support for Transactions

As a corollary to the need for an integration framework, the portal must provide support for transactions. This means the infrastructure allows online commerce, electronic payments, and other transactions.

The difference between the portal approach and standalone applications is that the portal provides common transactional functionality that can be shared across all applications, thereby reducing development time, testing, and support. For instance, there is no point in developing a web-based catalog and payment system for an association's bookstore and then building another, separate system for conference fees and a third system for membership dues.

Commerce Server is the element of the Microsoft .NET portal platform that provides prebuilt objects and tools for a full e-commerce implementation. It includes a catalog, a flexible and extensible payment process, marketing tools, usage statistics, and other utilities. With Commerce Server 2002 comes full integration with the .NET Framework, including web services and use of management of Commerce Server sites as Visual Studio .NET projects.

Catalogs

If you are trying to sell goods or services on the Internet, an online catalog is an obvious place to start. The catalog should be database driven and allow items to be browsed, searched, and viewed in many ways to suit the needs of shoppers. The catalog should be tied into the transactional engine by means of a shopping basket and a checkout process. As you would expect, Commerce Server provides this functionality out of the box and allows us to use .NET to extend the functionality as far as we need to go to meet the needs of our customers.

You may need marketing capabilities within your portal. For instance, users might opt to receive email notification of special promotions or email newsletters. Cross-selling related items can boost revenue and improve customer satisfaction. Customers who purchase winter tents may soon be looking for warm sleeping bags, thicker socks, and parkas. People who read reviews of camp stoves are likely to be shopping for them. By tracking these relationships among products and personalizing the experience of the user, you can enhance the utility of your portal and increase customer satisfaction.

Financial Transactions

Selling online provides one of the easiest cases for calculating return on investment. If you can double your online revenue by upgrading your web site to a portal, the financial return can provide solid justification for the required investment. The portal needs solid, trusted support for financial transactions, including interaction with other parties such as banks and credit card processing facilities. Commerce Server fits this bill nicely. Figure 2.9 shows a recommended environment for a commerce-enabled portal site.

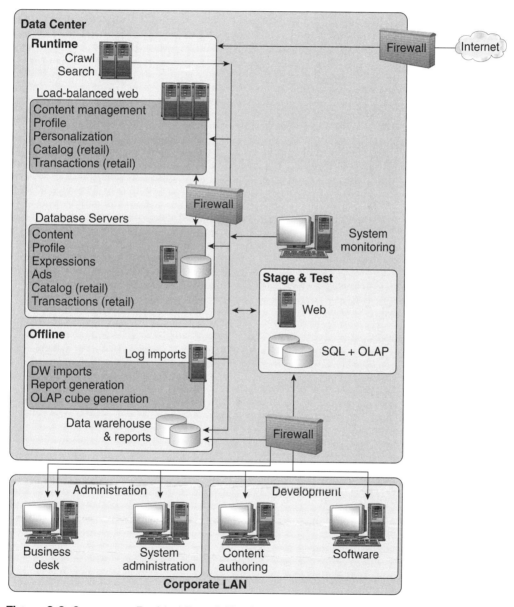

Figure 2.9 Commerce-Enabled Portal Site (Source: Microsoft, Microsoft Solution for Internet Business, Services Guide, version 1, December 2001.)

Collaboration Tools

Today's portals should contain collaborative tools such as online presence awareness, instant messaging, virtual communities, threaded discussion, and user profiles. According to a study cited by IBM, 70% of those implementing a portal desire collaborative features.[1] For interacting with the public, a virtual community can create a sense of belonging and create closer relationships than with a read-only web site. You may want to allow customers to share information and tips with one another, or ask technical support questions in a moderated forum (Figure 2.10).

If you are planning to support collaborative tools for the public, you must beware of abuse of the system. The content will be read by competitors, who may post unflattering or inaccurate information. The forum may become a blank wall for graffiti or even hate mail from people with lots of

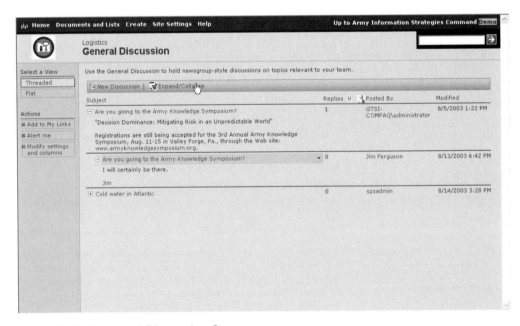

Figure 2.10 Threaded Discussion Group

---

[1] IBM, "A Portal Strategy to Deliver a Complete Portal Solution for E-Business," April 2002, p. 11. ftp:// ftp.software.ibm.com/software/websphere/portal/pdf/G325-5537-00.PDF.

time on their hands. Indeed, you may expose yourself to legal liability for what you show and don't allow to be shown in this forum. People may impersonate others in order to commit fraud. Therefore, be sure to monitor all such content and clearly post the rules of engagement and your liability on the site.

Another constraint for public collaboration is the lack of standardization for hardware, software, and user ability and training. You may find yourself forced to cater to the least common denominator in your user community—old browsers with low bandwidth and limited user patience for learning new software. On the other hand, highly motivated users may overcome these barriers if content is sufficiently compelling.

For internal collaboration, neither of the problems of public collaboration should apply. You will be able to expect or demand standard infrastructure, bandwidth, and even training. In the cloistered environment of a workplace, legal liability is different from on a public web site, and the lack of anonymity may encourage a modicum of civility. Employees are motivated to learn a new system when proficiency is tied to their success in a career. As a result, you can have more sophisticated collaborative offerings in an enterprise portal.

Multichannel Support

Most portals today support computer browsers as the user interface, but web services make it easier to support multiple hardware platforms from the same applications and content. While enterprise portals are great, what if you need to query a database from the airport and you have no Internet connection or PC? What is the simplest way to check or update your calendar or look up a phone number? These applications call for a portable device like the Pocket PC.

The .NET Framework inherently supports additional hardware such as cell phones and personal digital assistants (PDAs) as well as PCs. These new devices are more suitable for mobile and wireless applications, require less power than a PC, and have other advantages such as instant-on. Pocket PCs and tablet PCs may be equipped with biometric security devices to allow authentication with fingerprints rather than with username and password.

With third-party products, you can extend the reach of a portal to allow use by people who do not have computers. This approach to bridging the digital divide is called integrated voice response (IVR). With IVR functionality in a portal, you can access content and applications through any telephone.

For instance, building contractors must apply for permits for construction projects and cannot start the work until the permits are approved. Contractors may have dozens or hundreds of permit applications outstanding at any given time. With IVR, a contractor can inquire from the job site without a laptop and an Internet connection. The contractor would call a number and respond to voice prompts either by speaking or entering numbers on a touchtone phone. For instance, entering a username and password (using the phone pad) would authenticate the user. Next, the contractor would enter the permit number, and the system would respond with the status and approval code for the permit.

If you are starting a new portal project, you may choose a phased approach to supporting multiple devices. Standards are evolving in handheld technology, but few organizations have deployed uniform hardware for their mobile users.

Search Engine

All types of portals require search capabilities, as the extensiveness of content makes it challenging to find what you need by browsing alone. Microsoft provides two search engine choices: Index Server, which ships along with Windows server products, and the search engine that accompanies SharePoint Portal Server. Index Server is a full-text search engine that crawls web pages and provides simple and advanced searches via a web interface.

The SharePoint search engine (Figure 2.11) is the most sophisticated that Microsoft offers, and it is geared toward the knowledge management needs of an enterprise portal. In the likely event that the portal encompasses data sources in addition to static web pages, the search engine is essential for bringing content to users from file shares, databases, Lotus Notes, Exchange public folders, and other sources.

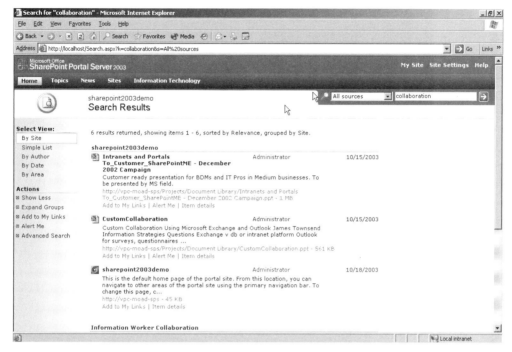

Figure 2.11 SharePoint Portal Server Search Engine Results

Adding powerful and accessible search functionality to your portal can provide immediate returns to users. It is one of the best ways to integrate heterogeneous data sources without requiring additional user training on the specifics of data storage.

Portal Solution Requirements Table

We have surveyed some of the key functions that are required of today's portals, but which ones must you implement in version 1 of your portal? Which are least important? Where do you get started in scoping the hardware and software requirements for the portal? To answer these and other questions, a good place to start is with the following solution requirements table (Table 2.3).

Table 2.3 Portal Requirements Table

Requirements Question	Comments and Suggestions
Who are the intended users of the portal? Will anonymous users be supported? Will any features require authentication?	For example, estimate the number of public (anonymous) portal users, the total number of internal employee users. Content management features will definitely require authentication.
What growth in portal usage is anticipated?	Consider usage statistics for other sites in calculating these numbers.
Does the security and authentication of the portal integrate with any other security scheme? Is it part of a larger domain with single sign-on?	Single sign-on is quite popular, but not easy to implement as it requires trust and changing behavior on the part of system administrators.
What are the roles for the portal users? How will their access to portal elements be controlled?	
What groups must be created and what permissions assigned to each group? For instance, will groups be needed for content authors, editors, administrators, template authors, graphic designers, subscribers, and application developers?	See Chapter 9 and Microsoft Content Management Server documentation for descriptions of typical roles.
Who will administer user accounts in the portal? Is this management centralized or decentralized?	Consider delegation of access administration to those closest to the users. For a large portal, centralized administration can grow to quite a burden.
What is the failover plan? How will the plan be tested and exercised?	This is the most often overlooked part of portal planning.
How will the portal be monitored? Will certain events trigger alerts to administrators?	
What applications need to be integrated with the portal?	Gather detailed information about each of the applications, such as browser and bandwidth requirements, as well as authentication.
How much content will the portal contain when it is launched? How quickly will the content grow?	Be optimistic that content will grow at a significant rate, especially if you are implementing content management.

Table 2.3 Portal Requirements Table (*Continued*)

Requirements Question	Comments and Suggestions
Where is content currently stored? Is it in static HTML files or in a content management system? What formats are used? Which web servers?	Content may require editing and reformatting during the migration.
How will existing content be migrated to the portal? Will content be edited or removed during this process?	Migrating content is one of the most time-consuming tasks in portal development.
What are the business rules for routing and approval of content?	A pilot to test these rules is often useful.
Are commerce capabilities required? What are the commerce requirements for the portal?	The catalog project may be run independently from the static content migration.
What is the estimated transaction volume for portal transactions?	Include average and peak loads.
Will the portal be integrated with third parties such as financial institutions or suppliers? What are the integration points? What standards are these organizations supporting? Are they publishing XML schemas? Do they support web services?	Contact these third parties early in the development process and solicit their rules for integration.
How can you test the integration with outside parties? What failover plans do they offer?	Be sure you can submit test records that will not affect your accounts.
Will source code be controlled with a product such as Visual SourceSafe?	I recommend that you use a tool like this for projects with multiple developers.
How will you test and built iterative versions of your site? Will builds be performed on a daily basis?	A build schedule allows managers to see progress regularly.
What is the graphic design for the portal? Has the necessary artwork and photography been completed?	Keep the group for making these decisions as small as possible.
Are color and font standards set?	

Continues

Table 2.3 Portal Requirements Table (*Continued*)

Requirements Question	Comments and Suggestions
Which accessibility standards will be followed? Will the site comply with section 508 guidelines? If so, how will the site be tested for such compliance?	Automated testing tools are available for this purpose.
Are collaboration tools needed for the site? Which ones? Should any of these be made available to anonymous users?	Consider requirements for moderating these discussions when outsiders are permitted.
Has a taxonomy been developed for the portal? Who is responsible for creating and maintaining the taxonomy?	The earlier you start this process, the better.
Which devices should be supported? What browsers and browser versions will be supported?	New devices are shipping every day. Don't invest too much in devices or technologies that have small numbers of users or are on the edge of obsolescence.
What are the search requirements for the site? Which content will be indexed? Will content outside the portal be indexed?	Typically you will want to support simple and advanced searches.

Putting the .NET Portal Together

Clearly, a full-featured portal provides a wide range of functionality to its users. What is not as obvious is the complexity of the underlying solution. Microsoft has not attempted to pack all the tools you may need into a single product. Based on the results of the portal solution requirements table, we can determine which Microsoft Server components are needed for our portal, as shown in Table 2.4. I omitted .NET, Visual Studio, and Windows Server from this table because they are required for all the portal solutions discussed in this book.

The priorities you assign to these portal elements are up to you. My clients have pointed toward common priorities for external and enterprise portals. The external portal places the highest priority on managing a large volume of HTML web content and creating a consistent and pleasing look-

Table 2.4 Portal Elements and Microsoft Server Products

	CMS	SQL Server	SPS	WSS	Commerce	BizTalk	Active Directory
Look-and-feel	X	X					
Security		X					X
User profile		X					X
Personalization		X			X		X
Taxonomy and dynamic navigation	X						
Application integration						X	
Database repository		X					
Support for transactions		X				X	
Collaboration tools			X	X			
Multichannel support	X	X					
Search engine			X				

and-feel. Anonymous users are the most important customers, and solutions must be simple to use and support low bandwidth and multiple browser versions. Content management is therefore the top goal, which makes Microsoft Content Management Server the center of the portal effort. A taxonomy and search engine are also requirements for this type of portal.

The next priority for a public portal is usually a commerce system. For a retailer, this means an electronic storefront with a catalog, shopping cart, and order fulfillment. For an association, the electronic store might also offer free publications and registration for public events. Government agencies would use the e-commerce capability to support transactions such as tax payments, parking tickets, and permit applications.

The low priorities for the public portal are collaborative tools, such as virtual communities, document management, knowledge management, and line-of-business application integration, as well as support for multiple hardware platforms. All these may ultimately make it into the portal to some extent, but they are usually reserved for subsequent versions.

The priorities for an enterprise portal are quite different. The infrastructure for an enterprise portal is known; you may be able to assume standard hardware and software for each user, high bandwidth, and solid connectivity. You can interview users in person and grill them on their needs, as well as observe how they work.

The enterprise portal starts at the desktop of the knowledge worker. You will not shy from the expense or the training burden of a sophisticated new solution if it will produce return on investment from your employees. This equation is in stark contrast to the least-common-denominator approach you must take with anonymous web users.

The highest priorities are usually integration of line-of-business applications and collaboration. SharePoint Portal Server is a key part of the enterprise portal, although MCMS may be just as important. SharePoint provides document management, threaded discussions, and the advanced search engine for knowledge management solutions. The .NET platform provides a host of tools to make application integration easier. Chapter 4 explains how web services work, and they are the key to application integration, along with standardization on XML for all applications.

To understand how technologies and products fit the portal roadmap, we need to take a broader view of the Microsoft .NET portal platform (see Chapter 3). Then we will take each of the portal elements one at a time and show how it is implemented with .NET and the Microsoft platform. Along the way I will offer suggestions on successful approaches to portal development and share best practices.

Microsoft's Portal Strategy

For several years, Microsoft has marched forward on the long journey from a desktop software company to a provider of enterprise solutions. Despite its dominance of desktop operating system and office productivity software, the company has had an uphill struggle to gain respect and market share in the enterprise software market. Microsoft has played the underdog to Oracle in the database market, the upstart to BEA in the enterprise application integration (EAI) market, and second fiddle to Sun and Unix in e-commerce and web servers. Only with the advent of .NET and the generation of server products that began after Windows 2000 Server has Microsoft boasted a comprehensive enterprise platform and serious competition for IBM, Oracle, Sun, and other market leaders.

Microsoft faces the same struggle to achieve recognition as a portal platform vendor as it faced to become an enterprise software player. It came late to the portal market, and some of its early technology and branding choices did little to improve the image of Microsoft in the portal market. Too much of Microsoft's image for portals was wrapped around a single product—SharePoint Portal Server. If you had searched the Microsoft web site for "portal" in early 2003, most of the pages you would have found would have related to SharePoint Portal Server. Reading reviews of the first version of SharePoint compared to leading enterprise portal products would have made you think that Microsoft's products were not serious contenders against the IBMs or even the Plumtrees of the world and that Microsoft had totally missed the portal boat. What product did Microsoft offer in 2001 or 2003 that compared to those of IBM, BroadVision, Epicentric, or Plumtree? Customers and analysts could have easily concluded that Microsoft was not serious about portals.

This conclusion would be erroneous, however, for two reasons. First, SharePoint Portal Server 2003 is a fundamentally new product, with a scalable, high-performance architecture and a raft of features. Second, and more important, SharePoint is merely the tip of the iceberg of Microsoft's portal platform. Many portal features and services are already provided by other Microsoft servers. Indeed, the misunderstanding of Microsoft's portal approach and the value of .NET as a solid portal platform are key reasons why this book is needed.

This chapter reviews past and present Microsoft portal strategy and emerging elements of its new approach. To maximize the life of your portal investment, you need to know which products and technologies will be supported in the future and which are merely temporary stopgaps or even dead ends.

The Microsoft Portal Perspective

Microsoft takes a different perspective on the portal market than its competitors. Microsoft has not tried to combat the pure play portal companies head-on, with high priced enterprise products that require a long and expensive deployment process. Indeed, Microsoft executives have denigrated the portal perspectives of their competitors. "The cynical description is that it's just a really expensive web site," according to Charles Fitzgerald, general manager of platform strategy at Microsoft .NET. "Fundamentally, we're on a different planet than the big iron, big brother [portal] guys."[1] He was referring to portal efforts that call for centralization of all applications and promote a monolithic software environment, usually based on Unix and Java. Fitzgerald asserts that many competitive portal products are wrongheaded returns to the mainframe mentality, risky and expensive to implement, and lacking in broadly used developer tools.

According to Microsoft, the goal of moving all applications to the browser and consolidating all these applications into a single window is a fool's errand. While this approach might in theory streamline development and reduce administration costs, it is essentially a return to the dumb terminal mainframe past, and it forsakes the huge investment in workstation intelligence already made by organizations and individuals. This processing power is meant to be used to enhance performance, minimize network traffic, and manipulate the user interface in ways that enhance productivity. In the Microsoft view, users will end up spending their time not in one single browser-based application but in three: the portal for application integration, Outlook and Exchange for messaging and calendars, and Windows Explorer to directly access documents and other resources.

---

[1] Jim Ericson, "Microsoft and the Portal," Line56, September 12, 2002.

Most users will spend more time using office productivity suites than a browser because document creation and editing demand as much desktop real estate as is available, as well as the ability to work disconnected from the network and without the inherent delays imposed by Internet latency. I can attest that I spend my workday in a three- or four-window world, albeit with multiple instances of each type of application. I would not be thrilled to give up these rich, multiwindow applications such as Outlook and Word, or similar custom applications.

Some portal concepts take the idea of consolidating user views too far. I once met a customer who was fixated on the idea of having one browser window run all the applications he needed. He started by asking how to make these applications fit within a single window, using a small "dashboard" element to provide some summary information from each application. Next, he asked how one application could expand to use more of the screen and make the others shrink. Finally, he asked for a quick way to switch among applications. Considering that his computer was running Windows 2000, he already had the solution at his fingertips. The value of Alt-Tab should not be underestimated.

Microsoft has a huge investment in the processing power and functionality of workstations, as the majority of its revenue comes from sales of operating systems and end-user productivity tools. If competing portal vendors achieve their vision of making the portal user interface the new desktop, they will create a powerful threat to Microsoft. Therefore it makes sense for the company to oppose a philosophy that minimizes the role of the client, even as many Microsoft products enhance the role of the server. Microsoft is unlikely to concede the battle it has already won, the battle for the desktop, to a portal upstart.

The approach of integrating portals deep in the Windows platform makes sense in light of the markets that Microsoft chooses to pursue. The company has maintained that it is not a vertical solution company and it is not interested in dominating small niches. Instead, it has often waited until a product category reaches critical mass before building or buying a product to bring to market. For instance, Microsoft was one of the last major vendors to come up with a content management offering when it bought the Canadian company NCompass and its Resolution product. Another example is Microsoft's customer relationship management package (Microsoft Business Solutions CRM), which targets the small and medium business market segment. Microsoft waited for the market to consolidate and created an offering at the low end where there is a mass market for its product.

When it does enter a market, Microsoft often offers a price well below competitive offerings in order to further expand the size of the total market. Microsoft knows that market share and a large user base are ultimately its winning formula rather than extracting maximum dollars from a single, small customer base.

Another underlying trend that explains Microsoft's portal strategy is the steady addition of new features to the operating system. Some portal elements will be taken for granted in the operating systems of the future rather than offered as expensive add-ons to be supported by a third-party vendor. For instance, collaboration features such as document sharing, chat, and threaded discussion have been built into end-user suites such as Microsoft Office. Document management itself could plausibly be added to the operating system as well—or at least version control and check-in, check-out functionality. Those of us who remember computing before Windows may recall that version control was an inherent part of the Digital Equipment Corporation's VMS operating system. As the line between the file system and a relational database system continues to blur, storage for documents, structured information, and web content could easily become part of the core operating system.

Portal innovations have come from three distinct groups at Microsoft: the Office product group, the enterprise group, and the online Microsoft properties such as MSN and microsoft.com. By understanding the heritage and destiny of the key portal products, you can make better decisions on where to place your technology "bets."

Microsoft Office Group

In the grassroots of portals, demand comes from knowledge workers or information workers. This is the market served by Microsoft desktop products such as the Office suite. Nearly all activities of such users have a place in the portal. In many instances, Microsoft product literature lumps together portals and intranets, such as in the Microsoft Solution for Intranets (www.microsoft.com/solutions/msi). The target market covers users who need these features:

- *Rich tools to create content and documents.* Despite the hype around network computing and browser-based applications, the browser is not yet the place where these are created. Instead users still rely on rich, 32-bit Windows programs such as Word, PowerPoint, or Excel for much of their work.

- *Interfaces to line-of-business applications, including accounting, customer information, manufacturing, contracting, and more.* Many of these interfaces have already moved to the browser, but the portal can provide additional levels of integration and ease of navigation.
- *Real-time collaboration.* Once they have tasted instant messaging, users are reluctant to give it up. Presence detection is a valuable asset in the corporate portal and is an additional benefit of this technology.
- *Content management.* Content owners should be able to create and maintain their own web content without the bottleneck of HTML programmers and webmasters. This requires a workflow process for editorial review and approval. The user interface should be either a browser or Office application.
- *Messaging and scheduling.* Some workers, especially managers, spend the bulk of their time reading and writing email. While browser-based email is widely used and has its advantages, a rich client such as Outlook supports offline use and offers higher performance than email relying on a network connection.
- *Virtual communities and collaboration.* Teams need virtual locations to store shared documents and work products. These are useful inside an organization but even more critical when a virtual team spans multiple organizations and geographical boundaries.
- *Search tools.* Information is not truly at your fingertips if you cannot find it. Search tools that can reach all repositories of data, information, and knowledge are required. For instance, users need to search against the intranet, external web sites, Internet search engines, documents, other files (such as metadata on images and video), and messages. Advanced search algorithms to improve the success of searches are desirable, as are agents that periodically update search results and notify knowledge workers.

Figure 3.1 shows a vision of a unified view of information from the user perspective.

In the final analysis, end users do not and should not care whether these capabilities are part of the operating system, office productivity suite, or server platform or are custom-built. What they seek is a reasonably pleasant experience that helps them be more productive. IT managers may not

Figure 3.1 Unified User View of Information in the Portal

care where these services reside either, although they will care intensely how much they cost and how much effort is required to design, build, integrate, and test them.

Part of Microsoft's portal offering—in fact, the only Microsoft product with "portal" in its name, SharePoint Portal Server—has grown from the grassroots level of the Office product development team. Rather than start with an enterprise architecture perspective and craft an overarching portal that would replace all the end-user applications that came before it, Microsoft started from the perspective of the end user in a corporate department, and this is how SharePoint was born.

By the late 1990s, several products were on the market that provided a browser-based view into documents and applications. One of the most popular of these was Plumtree, a product originally developed for the Microsoft platform. A Plumtree portal consists of elements called **gadgets** that provide access to content such as HTML or applications such as SAP or Siebel.

Microsoft took a similar approach with SharePoint Portal Server, calling these portal elements **web parts**, based on the digital dashboard feature of Outlook that originally appeared in Outlook 97. The digital dashboard grew out of Outlook Today, a combined view showing calendar and schedule items in a single window. It could be extended and customized with dynamic HTML (DHTML).

SharePoint web parts were based on ActiveX and required Internet Explorer. They can be downloaded and placed where desired within the browser window. Developers can create their own web parts as well, and many are available from third parties that provide access to their applications. For instance, you can install a stock ticker or news web part that receives content from MSNBC.

SharePoint provided a quick fix for the lack of a corporate portal in the Microsoft product family. Version 1 of the product combined the search engine that grew from Site Server version 3.0 with the digital dashboard from Outlook (Figure 3.2) and a document repository borrowed from Exchange 2000. As we will see in Chapters 9 and 12, SharePoint Portal Server has come a long way in its second version.

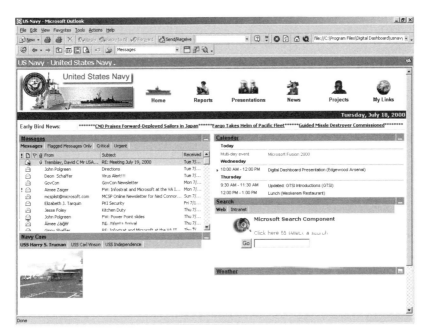

Figure 3.2 Outlook Digital Dashboard: A Precursor of SharePoint Portal Server

The first version of SharePoint Portal Server (SPS) had two main problems. First, it had not been designed as an enterprise product, and it would not scale for large numbers of users or massive repositories of documents and data. The rule of thumb was a maximum of 1,000 users on a single SharePoint server. In version 1, scalability was not a primary design goal. It was impossible to simply add more servers to a SharePoint portal to share the document management load. Instead, you had to create separate SharePoint installations and invent your own creative ways to connect them. This shortcoming was not as limiting as it might first appear, as document collaboration typically occurs at the workgroup level anyway; but customers were concerned with such performance limitations.

Second, SharePoint Portal Server was still a bit more complex and expensive than Microsoft would have liked it to be to reach the mass of its users. With a client access license price of $60–$70 per seat, large organizations were thinking twice before adopting SPS. Therefore Microsoft created a new product in the SharePoint family called SharePoint Team Services. This product has been replaced in the current SharePoint generation with Windows SharePoint Services (WSS).

SharePoint Team Services (STS) solved the problem of price objections to SharePoint Portal Server. It was essentially a free product that came with Office XP and FrontPage 2002. STS version 1 steered clear of the Exchange Web Store repository, relying on a relational database (SQL Server and its variants) as its repository. It was essentially a collaboration web site in a box, providing a document library, threaded discussion, shared calendar, and contacts. Perhaps to justify the difference in pricing, STS was stripped of document management capabilities such as version control and check-in, check-out, as well as the powerful SharePoint Portal Server search engine. In place of the digital dashboard and web parts, STS provided a canned web site design that could be administered through forms and further tweaked with FrontPage 2002. For Windows XP users, STS allowed integration such as drag-and-drop from Outlook contacts.

STS also overcame the licensing issues with SPS to allow easier collaboration with users outside the enterprise, because STS did away with the need for client access licenses. STS is easy to deploy inside and outside the corporate firewall and lends itself to quick, disposable collaboration site creation.

Today, with version 2 of SharePoint, most version 1 shortcomings have been addressed, as described in detail in Chapter 12, "Collaboration in the

Enterprise Portal." SharePoint now scales to support larger numbers of users and can be deployed on multiple servers for this purpose. The attractive features of STS that were lacking in SPS version 1 have been subsumed by the version 2 product. These include the ability to easily generate team collaboration sites, built-in web page templates for threaded discussion, news, calendars, and other popular intranet features. The line between SPS and STS has also been blurred, with WSS gaining version control, for instance. Most important of all, SharePoint has now been migrated to .NET, offering tremendous power and scalability to developers versed in this platform.

The Microsoft Office Product Group is likely to continue its efforts to add more collaboration functionality in Office itself, as well as related desktop products, and some of these technologies will end up in the operating system. Microsoft had already made Windows XP a real-time communications (RTC) platform, supporting voice, video, instant messaging, application sharing, and collaboration. Products such as InfoPath and OneNote extend desktop collaboration capabilities even further than Office alone, and this progress is likely to accelerate as Microsoft turns its pure research into product reality. And don't forget Exchange 2003 Server for extending your portal to support mobile, wireless devices.

Microsoft Enterprise Software Group

While SharePoint became the lightning rod for Microsoft portal criticism, the Enterprise Software Group was quietly assembling the server products that make up a solid part of the portal platform. This part of the company was responsible for Commerce Server 2002, Content Management Server, BizTalk Server, and more.

The Enterprise Software Group is the source of the products used to define a portal framework from the top down rather than starting with individual and workgroup productivity tools. Products from this group lead Microsoft products in terms of security, scalability, and raw performance, as one would expect from an enterprise product team. The team also charted a path to .NET that made the server products more consistent for developers and administrators.

Table 3.1 shows how all the products fit together into the portal roadmap.

Table 3.1 Microsoft Product Map for Portals

Microsoft Product/Feature	Windows 2000 / 2003 / Active Directory	Commerce Server	SPS v2	WSS	CMS	SQL Server	Exchange	BizTalk
Look-and-feel	X		X	X	X			
User profile	X		X				X	
Personalization	X	X	X					
Content management		X	X	X				
Taxonomy		X	X					
Application integration	X		X			X		X
Database repository						X		X
Support for transactions					X			X
Workflow			X	X				
Collaboration tools			X	X			X	
Search engine	X		X				X	

Microsoft Online Properties

An unspoken advantage of Microsoft in the portal marketplace is that Microsoft has itself created many of the web's top portal sites, and it has constructed them largely on Microsoft's own technology. Examples include Expedia for online travel, the online literary salon slate.com, and the sister portal MSNBC for news. This set of web properties has provided an amazing laboratory and proving ground, stress testing web sites, personalization, e-commerce, collaboration, and other user services. Three sites stand out as Microsoft portals that convey best practices: microsoft.com, the Microsoft corporate intranet, and the Microsoft Network (MSN).

Microsoft.com

Microsoft's web site microsoft.com is a portal in its own right, and one of the most popular and successful portals at that. It has been the laboratory for improvements in the successive generations of operating systems, web servers, search engines, and other elements of the web platform.

For instance, Content Management Server has been deployed on microsoft.com, providing valuable real-life input to the product team. The Microsoft intranet has also been the proving ground for Commerce Server, SharePoint Portal Server, SharePoint Team Services, BizTalk, and other elements of the portal platform. For instance, ad hoc teams at Microsoft built hundreds of SharePoint Team Services sites with the version 1 STS product.

Microsoft Intranet

Microsoft has long advocated a policy of using its own tools and products even before they turn them loose on the world. This approach, picturesquely described as "eating your own dog food," means that internal Microsoft users are extensions of the beta software program. The dog food menu includes portals as well as other tasty entrees.

The Microsoft employee portal had a design goal of dramatically cutting the use of paper and consolidating the number of electronic forms as well. Therefore, Microsoft employees use the intranet to order business cards, change payroll tax withholding, check their retirement plans, reserve conference facilities, order conference meals and hotel accommodations, and buy items from the company store.

A part of the Microsoft intranet called MS Expense (www.microsoft.com/technet/treeview/default.asp?url=/technet/itsolutions/MSIT/Finance/MSExpTCS.asp) is an impressive case study in its own right. The intranet-based solution handles all employee expense reports to the tune of about 200,000 reports with expenses of over $210 million per year. The solution is built on the .NET Framework, with a web frontend and an SQL Server backend. It replaces a pastiche of Excel spreadsheets and paper forms, with manual data entry by clerks. Microsoft estimates that the cost per transaction has been cut from $21 to $8 per report, saving the company $4.3 million each year. The system is integrated with American Express data to enhance its reporting capabilities. Another benefit is the employee satisfaction of being reimbursed much more quickly than with a manual system. Employees generally don't enjoy lending money to their employers, and corporate travel expenses can make it difficult to pay credit card bills on time.

The Microsoft Network (MSN)

The behemoth among Microsoft portal properties is one of the world's leading portals, the Microsoft Network (MSN). While MSN has not unseated America Online (AOL) as the dominant home user Internet portal, it has gained a prodigious number of users and proliferated a great deal of content. MSN provides a large-scale testing ground similar to microsoft.com for testing new product innovations and developing best practices for site management, content management, and workflow.

A few years back Microsoft flirted with offering the software used to power MSN, with special enhancements to Microsoft's web server software Internet Information Server (IIS), to its customers, but no such offering exists today. Some of the concepts from this offering live on in the Microsoft Solution for Internet Business (MSIB), a solution offering that combines products with prescriptive architectural guidance and best practices. See www.microsoft.com/solutions/msib/default.asp for more details.

Fundamental Portal Elements

There is a baseline of products and technology that make up the foundation of the Microsoft platform. All of these are discussed in subsequent chapters as they relate to portal services. Figure 3.3 shows the entire Microsoft product "stack."

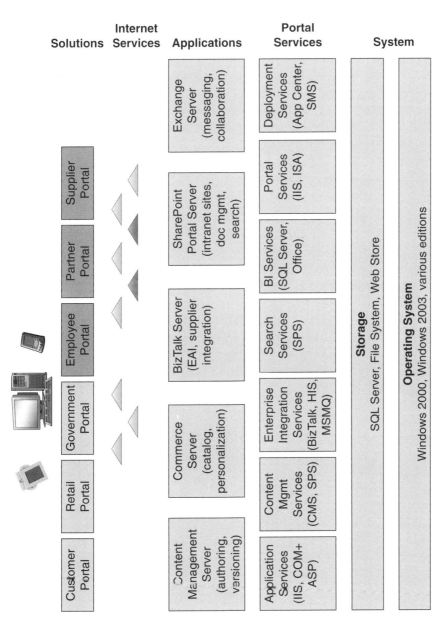

Figure 3.3 The Microsoft Product Stack

At the bottom is the server operating system. Windows 2000, Windows 2003, and subsequent versions provide a wide range of portal functionality, including security services, the HTTP server (Internet Information Server), Active Directory for managing user accounts and other assets, and support for all the server products in the portal.

Chapter 4 defines .NET and explains how it is needed for a portal. Naturally .NET is at the foundation of a .NET portal as well. For now, .NET requires a Microsoft operating system, but this may change in the future. For instance, there are efforts under way to provide .NET support for the Linux operating system. The .NET Framework is built into Windows 2003 and is a free add-on for Windows 2000. The framework is necessary to support .NET applications.

Content Management Server (CMS) is a key element of a .NET portal, to the extent that content management is a core portal function. CMS, SPS, Commerce Server, and BizTalk are tightly integrated with the .NET Framework, web services, and Visual Studio .NET.

SQL Server is a required element of the .NET portal. It is the repository for structured data used by all the portal applications, as well as the store for CMS and SharePoint Portal Server and Windows SharePoint Services. SQL Server 2000 has native support for XML, and future versions of SQL Server will have enhanced support for programming in .NET with Visual Studio .NET in stored procedures.

For an enterprise or corporate portal, you need the capabilities offered in SharePoint Portal Server for document management, collaboration, searching, and portal presentation. With its tight integration with Office, it is a natural for boosting knowledge worker productivity. SPS indexes Exchange public folders, documents in Windows, Novell and Unix files, and internal and external web sites.

Optional Portal Elements

The Microsoft .NET platform offers additional products that further expand the power of your portal beyond the foundation capabilities. For instance, BizTalk makes it easier to create and maintain multiple interfaces to external data sources such as legacy mainframe applications using XML.

Windows SharePoint Services (WSS) offers simple team collaboration web sites, including a document library, group calendar, threaded discussion, and shared contacts. WSS is integrated into Office XP and also FrontPage 2002.

In January 2003, Microsoft announced the formation of the Real Time Collaboration Group business unit, headed by Anoop Gupta, formerly of Microsoft Research and technical advisor to Bill Gates. The group focuses on online communication tools and solutions, including Microsoft Live Meeting, formerly PlaceWare Conference Center. These products and technologies are a natural adjunct to the .NET portal platform.

Support for handheld and wireless devices usually is an optional portal feature, or at least is left until the core portal functionality is fulfilled. Fortunately, the .NET Framework supports such devices without a major redevelopment effort.

Third-Party Portal Elements

With such a comprehensive portal platform, what could be missing from the Microsoft offering? Which third-party products will you need to provide all the functionality your users demand?

Microsoft does not offer vertical software solutions and line-of-business solutions, with the exception of some framework offerings based on packaged platform solutions (such as the BizTalk Accelerator for the Health Insurance Portability and Accountability Act, or HIPAA). If you need a dental office automation package, enterprise resource planning, or convention planning software, you will have to look at vendors other than Microsoft.

There are other gaps in the Microsoft portal offering when it comes to more specialized horizontal niches. For instance, Microsoft does not offer records management software, or software to manage compliance with section 508 web accessibility guidelines. Microsoft depends on partner companies to provide solutions in these areas. For instance, a Microsoft packaged offering called the Solution for Online Accessibility bundles Content Management Server with AccVerify and AccMonitor Server from HiSoftware to help customers meet section 508 requirements.

Future Evolution of Portal Platform to Jupiter and Beyond

There is no constant in the technology business except for change, and the Microsoft portal platform is no exception. While 2003 marked a turning point for .NET with the shipment of a new server operating system and the completion of the first generation of .NET server products, the evolution is never-ending.

A Microsoft project code-named Jupiter is reportedly planned to integrate several of the popular server offerings more completely than the former "glue code" that is available for download under such offerings as the Microsoft Solution for Internet Business (MSIB). The purpose of Jupiter is to stress the integration of portal elements from the perspective of developers and information workers through tighter integration with Visual Studio .NET and Office, integrated security, deployment, management and monitoring across the technologies, and XML web services support.

Paul Flessner, senior vice president of Microsoft .NET Enterprise Servers, and David Kiker, general manager of E-Business Servers, presented Jupiter at the October 2002 Microsoft Exchange Conference. They defined the design goals of Jupiter as:

- *Business process management.* Portal business rules cut across traditional Microsoft product lines. Jupiter will make it easier to follow improved business processes rather than tailoring processes to meet product constraints.
- *Integration.* Developers can be more productive in a single integrated development environment (IDE) than in multiple environments and languages, one for each product or service. Jupiter tools and components will be integrated with one another, primarily through a common and seamless development, deployment, and management experience. Visual Studio .NET will be the common development environment, and server management will take advantage of common management consoles.
- *Interoperability.* Microsoft does not embrace the "rip-and-replace" philosophy of scrapping existing hardware and software investments to make way for a shiny new portal. Instead, the Jupiter vision aims to integrate existing CRM, ERP, and other line-of-business applications that represent serious investments through XML web services and application and technology adapters.

■ *Componentization.* A portal requires a wide range of services, but not every organization needs the same services nor plans to deploy them on day one of the project. Offerings must be flexible, allowing architects to choose a tailored combination of components and incrementally add functionality as the portal evolves. Jupiter will deliver many off-the-shelf components, and XML web services standards will allow enterprises to add the key pieces from other vendors or custom-build them for a complete e-business solution.

An overarching business goal of Jupiter for Microsoft is to counter offerings from vendors such as IBM and Broadvision. Microsoft has not announced the specifics of Jupiter, but press accounts have cited the offering to contain Commerce Server, Content Management Server, Host Integration Server, and BizTalk.[2] The data repository for the portal is likely to change as the next version of SQL Server, codenamed Yukon, ships in 2004. Microsoft has announced that this product will not only replace SQL Server 2000 but will also be the store for future versions of Exchange Server and SharePoint Portal Server.

The current portal platform does not require Active Directory, with the exception of Exchange 2000, which itself is optional for a portal deployment. This approach has the advantage of allowing those who have not taken the Active Directory plunge to embrace the .NET platform, but it also forsakes many of the potential benefits from tighter integration with Active Directory.

A likely direction for .NET portals is tighter integration with Active Directory. In particular, it would make sense for the portal to use Active Directory to store the profile used for personalization. This is the approach used by the Corechange product acquired by Open Text in February 2003.

Portal standards will continue to evolve in the next two years and reach a maturity that will make them more functional and less risky. The growth of interest in web services, and support for this standard from nearly all the major IT vendors, creates a tremendous opportunity for standards that cross both the Java and .NET worlds. Will Microsoft join the Web Services for Remote Portals (WSRP) standard? Will .NET be successfully ported to Linux? Either of these would be a major advance in interoperability.

---

[2] "Microsoft Details Vision for the Connected Business and Unveils 'Jupiter,'" October 8, 2002, at www.microsoft.com/presspass/press/2002/Oct02/10-08JupiterPR.asp.

Migration of Server Products to .NET

Since .NET jelled, Microsoft has been laboring to migrate all its server products to the .NET Framework, support for .NET development tools, and web services where appropriate. While .NET has been used as an overall brand for many Microsoft products, the .NET Framework and object model have been integrated into server products in the 2002/2003 generation. As of late 2003, the following products had shipped .NET versions:

> Windows Server 2003
> Exchange Server 2003
> Content Management Server 2002
> Commerce Server 2002
> SharePoint Portal Server 2003
> BizTalk Server

Now that virtually the entire Microsoft enterprise product line has been adapted to be friendly to .NET, there are strong arguments for buying into this coherent server architecture and development environment. A developer taking this approach has a much larger arsenal of weapons. With a family of desktop applications, servers, and operating systems all built to support the same languages and development approach, Microsoft now has a key differentiator in the portal market. While other vendors have built or acquired products for services such as document management, content management, collaboration, and application integration, they often rely on different programming and scripting languages with limited ability to share code and components among the products.

Conclusion: A Two-Pronged Portal Approach

Portal projects have a checkered reputation for becoming resource sinkholes, leading to cost overruns and unmet user expectations. This reputation is deserved due to the lofty ambitions of most portal projects. The central idea behind the portal is to rein in disparate decentralized applications, creating bold new standards at the highest level of an organization that permeate down to the lowest branches on the corporate tree. Cooperation among groups of users and organizational decision makers is essential to the enterprise portal, and central authority, along with a healthy dose of resolve, are often needed to break through bureaucratic gridlock. The portal may call for rewriting dozens or hundreds of applications and scrapping hardware and software acquired over many years. No wonder that so many portal projects have crashed on the rocks of despair.

Microsoft does not want to risk its position by being caught in an IT train wreck with high-risk implementations that must overcome serious organizational hurdles for its customers. Nor does Microsoft have the large services delivery capability of an IBM to take a major stake in such projects. Microsoft executives would also no doubt want to stay clear of the fate that has befallen the majority of the portal software vendors that have watched their revenue and stock prices slip significantly in the tech bear market. Therefore, Microsoft has adopted a two-pronged strategy to win the portal market. At the end-user level, the strategy is to add enterprise portal tools to office automation products, such as the collaboration and document management enhancements to Office by means of SharePoint technology. This is a subtle way to provide productivity tools to users and defuse the challenge from more specialized knowledge management or collaboration tool vendors.

The second prong of this strategy is targeted at the top of the IT pyramid. By offering .NET as an enterprise architecture standard for driving a standardized server platform and development languages, Microsoft positions itself as a viable contender for the application space now dominated by Java, but with a much larger base of programmers and a rich set of server tools from a single vendor (Microsoft itself). Portals are an excellent proving ground for web services, as I show in the following chapter.

Chapter 4

Web Services

No reference guide on portals or .NET would be complete without thorough coverage of web services. For many people, web services are the core of what .NET offers, and Microsoft indeed does have ambitious plans for weaving web services into its entire platform. Web services are vital to opening your portal to business and government partners. They can link disparate and otherwise incompatible systems and bridge the chasm between Java and .NET. Web services promise to be the foundation for the next generation of the Internet.

This chapter introduces web services from a few different perspectives. First we look at what the world was like before web services. We look at the trends that require systems integration and data exchange within local applications and even across disparate homogeneous (disparate *or* homogenous) systems. After that, we review the strengths and weaknesses of current technologies before defining web services and explaining how they address the shortcomings of other technologies.

Life Before Web Services

Did life exist before web services? Undoubtedly so. Even today, most portals deny themselves the benefits of web services. In the pre–web services architecture, the lack of a standard communications infrastructure was a major hurdle for data exchange within as well as between organizations. Organizations used a number of different hardware and software solutions, there was no common protocol or data format, and there were many proprietary data stores. Although electronic interactions between companies were cumbersome to create and maintain, they have existed for quite some time in various forms. The Internet, and the many technologies that have been developed for the Internet medium, have slowly helped businesses find new ways to cooperate electronically.

Over the last few years some trends in communication have clearly emerged within and between organizations. These trends include business-to-business integration (B2Bi), virtual value chain, software as a service, system integration within the distributed enterprise, and more. All these trends point toward standards for integrating systems across organizational boundaries. And they all represent ways for businesses (or departments within an enterprise) to work together to create more efficient ways of doing business. The data format for such interchanges has been standardized as extensible markup language (XML). While the XML standard has made data exchange easier, something more is needed to enable compatibility among programs—web services.

In the past, the mere thought of integrating disparate systems was frightening. An interface for communication between two platforms was not always available. With no common network mechanism, no common character codes, and therefore no common ways to send data back and forth between disparate systems, integrating these systems seemed like a nightmarish task. Fortunately, with the advent of XML and web services, system administrators no longer dread integrating disparate systems.

Current Technologies

Most of the integration goals that I have discussed can be addressed by current technologies. However, there are some serious limitations with these technologies that continue to make life difficult for developers. Just to clarify this point, developers may be up to taking on challenging projects, but in the past these projects typically have had a high risk factor and therefore had a tendency to fail. To better understand the risks, let's take a look at some of the most popular methods of data exchange in the IT world today.

Data Format

In the past, companies have struggled to exchange data because of the differences in data format preferences. Few tools were available to automate the translation of different formats, and those that did exist were weak solutions that needed a lot of customization. Microsoft's BizTalk Server has emerged in this space within the last two years. (For more about BizTalk Server, see Chapter 11.)

Two well-known solutions for data formatting have prevailed, although each has its own problems and limitations. The ASCII file format, which remains popular today, includes ASCII delimited files and ASCII fixed-width files. There is no standard way to format these files or even the values within the files. The implementation of the file format depends entirely on the business partners who are trying to exchange data. These businesses need to work closely to develop custom applications to load and handle each other's file format.

ASCII delimited files are basically text files, using the ASCII character-set, that have some form of delimiter between each field. The delimiters could be any ASCII character, though the popular delimiters are a comma or a tab. In some cases, text qualifiers like double quotation marks (") are used to specify the beginning and end of textual information. Using text qualifiers prevents textual information from being broken into separate values when a delimiter appears in the text.

In an ASCII fixed-width file, each column of data has a fixed width. A file of this type needs to be accompanied by a **format file** (also known as a **header file**) that describes the width of each column. Again, there is no standard for formatting the fixed-width or format files.

A second solution is the use of specific file formats. Companies can exchange data using file types such as Microsoft Excel, Microsoft Access, IBM DB2 databases, or other proprietary options. A large amount coding is required to create "bridges" between the consuming applications and the application format of choice.

(At the dawn of the Internet age, in 1995, Microsoft was seriously planning to make the Word document a standard Internet format. Luckily for Microsoft, this idea was quickly dropped.)

Communication/Data Transmission

Sending and receiving data between business partners has been complicated by the fact that the available methods are slow, error prone, and typically need human intervention when an error occurs. Many data transmission types exist. Following are a few examples of how companies have exchanged data as well as the problems that they have encountered.

File Transfer Protocol (FTP) is a popular way to transfer files, although it is not highly automated and requires constant human intervention. This solution in not dynamic because it depends on files being sent and received. FTP facilitates the sending and receiving of files, but there is no specific approach to the actual data exchange. FTP also lacks sufficient security, which rules out any transferring of sensitive data.

Electronic Data Interface (EDI) has been around for many years now and has become a somewhat proven solution for data exchange between companies. EDI has its own issues, which include complexity and inflexibility. EDI is relatively expensive to implement, maintain, and deploy. This high cost tends to restrict the use of EDI to big organizations that support large transaction volumes and exclude small or new companies that want to exchange data with large organizations but do not have a budget for the software, hardware, and network connectivity required for EDI. If the implementation of EDI were somewhat easier and less expensive, EDI would allow trading partners, both small and large, to reap the benefits.

Recently, two competing technologies have emerged: Microsoft's Component Object Model (COM) and the Common Object Request Broker Architecture (CORBA). These technologies allow a more object-oriented approach to data exchange. COM and CORBA both support a remote procedure call (RPC) approach in contrast to the file-based transmission process. These technologies are also much less expensive to implement than other methods.

The Distributed Component Object Model (DCOM) enables communication between Microsoft COM-based applications residing on different machines. The DCOM protocol allows this communication to appear as if it were on the same machine. Internet Inter-ORB Protocol (IIOP)/Object Request Broker (ORB)/CORBA standards enable similar communication within Unix-based applications.

These technologies offer their own challenges and limitations. DCOM and CORBA are both platform-specific. To create a DCOM-based data exchange mechanism, you would need to make sure that all of the potential business partners could use the protocol.

Although DCOM and CORBA attempt to solve the same problem, they do not work together. To get systems that have been developed with these competing technologies to communicate, some form of bridging software is needed that allows the systems to understand and respond to messages from the other system. COM–CORBA bridging software packages do exist, but they are far from perfect. There are many difficulties with mapping data types as well as functionality. Underlying technologies are updated periodically, and the resulting changes add to the complexity of the bridging software.

Figure 4.1 shows the conceptual diagram of a COM–CORBA translator. To implement such functionality, the translation utility would need to

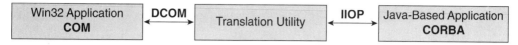

Figure 4.1 Conceptual Diagram of a COM–CORBA Translator

know how to understand the requests and responses of DCOM as well as IIOP and act on them appropriately. Implementation of that "box" would involve a lot of effort and require extensive knowledge of each of the protocols.

DCOM and CORBA also introduce some security risks. Today, most companies use some type of firewall product to protect their networks against security problems. Firewall solutions prevent network communication across certain configurable ports and protocols. They also prevent transmission of certain data types (such as binary executables) into the company's network. Almost all companies allow HyperText Transfer Protocol (HTTP) requests through port 80 in addition to Simple Main Transfer Protocol (SMTP) for email purposes. Typically all of the other ports are "locked down" to prevent malicious activity within the network.

Both DCOM and CORBA require that certain ports be opened in the firewall to accommodate transmission of their messages. Opening a large number of ports in the firewall would turn it into nothing more than a "fire-fence." By defining the height of the fence, you dictate what you will be able to keep out (or in). As with fences, the fewer ports you have open in a firewall, the higher hackers will have to "jump" to exploit a hole. Numerous open ports give hackers more opportunities to intercept messages and, in the worst-case scenario, bring down a system or even a network. Although most network administrators advise against opening ports in a network firewall, many companies still open ports to allow protocols to communicate. Without business, what good would a network be?

Finding a Better Solution

The title of this chapter points to a better solution for integrating and communicating between systems than the current technologies we just explored. Because the trends in e-business require the integration of distributed and often disparate systems, a technology that can bridge these systems is required. This technology must interface easily with legacy systems without posing a security risk. The technology must also be relatively inexpensive, easy to implement, and easy to maintain, and it must take advantage of existing technologies such as protocols, network access, hardware, and software. One of the most important criteria is that the technology must allow companies to leverage knowledge and existing resources.

The goal is to transfer information across platform boundaries and between companies on different networks to provide services to other businesses on the Internet. Simple Object Access Protocol (SOAP) fits the bill perfectly as it can be easily integrated into existing systems and it meets all of the requirements for a solution.

SOAP is a specification that is used to define the structure of an XML message. These messages can be sent over the Internet to call and return results from an application. Web services is the technology that relies on SOAP as its protocol and makes SOAP-callable methods available. Web services can be created by any software or operating system manufacturer and do not have to use SOAP to send messages, although web services and SOAP often seem to be synonymous terms.

SOAP is covered in greater detail later in this chapter, but let's look now at one of the main reasons why SOAP is so easy to integrate into disparate systems. Take a retail chain that sells thousands of products. Many models exist for inventory management, from the retailer ordering more stock, to supplier representatives monitoring the inventory and reordering stock as necessary to maintain a minimum count per product. The antiquated methods of inventory management include electronic methods as well. Most of these reside on proprietary systems and require suppliers to implement these methods of inventory management as well. Small businesses will not be able to afford to develop or implement this type of system. Here is where SOAP steps in. The retailer can implement a web service using SOAP as a mechanism for allowing suppliers to monitor the inventory of their products. Listing 4.3 shows a sample implementation of an Inventory Monitor that automates the task of inventory management.

Figure 4.2 shows a diagram of an application with multiple distributed clients using DCOM over the Internet. As you can see, many ports need to be open in the corporate network firewall to allow consuming clients to interact with the application by using DCOM. In fact, the more concurrent client connections the application might have, the more ports need to be opened in the firewall. As a result, the firewall is no longer able to function as a solid barrier and looks more like a sieve.

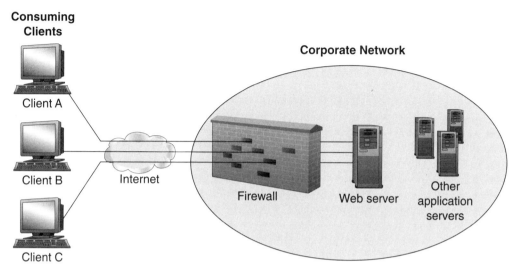

Figure 4.2 Distributed Disparate Systems Using DCOM

Figure 4.3 shows an application with multiple distributed clients using SOAP over the Internet. In contrast to DCOM, only one brick is missing from the wall because SOAP uses port 80 for communication. No additional ports need to be opened, even when more consuming clients are added.

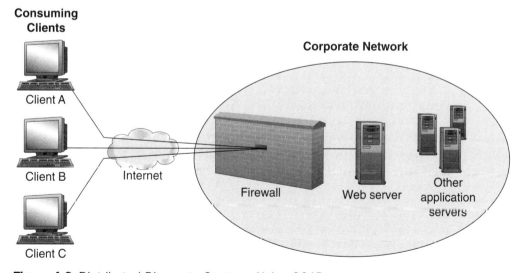

Figure 4.3 Distributed Disparate Systems Using SOAP

Defining Web Services

The World Wide Web Consortium (W3C), which is responsible for the development of interoperable technologies (specifications, guidelines, software, and tools) to lead the web to its full potential, defines web services as:

> *A Web Service is a software system identified by a Uniform Resource Identifier (URI), whose public interfaces and bindings are defined and described using XML. Its definition can be discovered by other software systems. These systems may then interact with the Web service in a manner prescribed by its definition, using XML based messages conveyed by Internet protocols.*

A web service is a programmable entity that provides a particular element of functionality, such as application logic, and is accessible to any number of potentially disparate systems using ubiquitous Internet standards, such as XML and HTTP. Web services depend heavily on the broad acceptance of XML and other Internet standards to create an infrastructure that supports application interoperability at a level that solves many of the problems that previously hindered such attempts.

A web service can be used internally by a single application or exposed externally over the Internet for use by any number of applications. Because it is accessible through a standard interface, a web service allows heterogeneous systems to work together as a single web of computation.

With the introduction of XML, data exchange between systems residing in different environments was made much easier. Web services then added an entirely new dimension. Instead of pursuing the generic capabilities of code portability, web services provide a viable solution for enabling data and system interoperability. Web services use XML-based messaging as a fundamental means of data communication to help bridge differences between systems that use dissimilar component models, operating systems, and programming languages. Developers can create applications that weave together XML web services from a variety of sources in much the same way that developers traditionally use components when creating a distributed application.

One of the core characteristics of a web service is a high degree of abstraction between the implementation and the consumption of a service. By using XML-based messaging as the mechanism by which the service is created and accessed, both the web service client and the XML web service provider are freed from needing any knowledge of each other beyond inputs, outputs, and location.

XML web services are enabling a new era of distributed application development. It is no longer a matter of object model wars or which programming is better than the next. By tightly coupling systems using proprietary infrastructures, you limit application interoperability. Web services deliver interoperability on an entirely new level that negates such counterproductive rivalries. As the next revolutionary advancement of the Internet, web services will become the fundamental structure that links together all computing devices.

The architectural design of web services seems to be a natural evolution from the previous generation of object-oriented design (OOD) and the components developed to match that design. Web services implement fundamental concepts from OOD, including encapsulation, dynamic binding, message passing, and service description and querying. The concept of providing functionality as a service lies at the heart of web services. The API is published for use by other systems and the implementation is encapsulated within the web service's logic.

In addition to interoperability and extensibility, the real power of web services is the ability to combine multiple web services to achieve a more complex solution. A web service that provides a simple service can interact with another web service to deliver a more complex service. Simply put, a web service allows one system to call a function in another system and pass data through as XML without regard for the platforms or implementation details of either system.

Understanding Web Services

To really understand web services, you need a basic understanding of what makes the technology tick. Web services combine the best aspects of component-based development and the web. Just as components represent black-box functionality that can be reused without worrying about how the logic is implemented, web services can be reused and the implementation of the logic is encapsulated within the service.

Unlike almost all current component technologies, web services are not accessed via object model–specific protocols such as DCOM or RMI. DCOM, for example, is a binary protocol that consists of a method request layer that resides on top of a proprietary communication protocol. Such protocols are not conducive to creating highly interoperable applications.

One of the major drawbacks of using a protocol such as DCOM is that its dependence on a specific archtecture of underlying systems limits the spectrum of potential clients. Instead, web services are accessed via universal web protocols and data formats, such as HTTP, XML, and SOAP. Furthermore, a web service interface is defined strictly in terms of the messages that the web service accepts and generates. Consumers of the web service can be implemented on any platform in any programming language, as long as they can create and consume the messages defined for the web service interface.

There are a few key specifications and technologies you are likely to encounter when building or consuming web services. The following sections discuss the five main specifications and technologies required for service-based development.

XML for Data Representation: A Standard Way to Represent Data

XML is a meta-markup language that provides a format for describing structured data. The ability to describe structured data from within the data structure itself makes it possible to describe content more precisely. Because XML is a standard that is based on ASCII strings, XML can be used across multiple platforms as well.

XML is the understandable choice for a standard way to represent data. Web service–related specifications use XML for data representation as well as XML schemas to describe data types. Developers must master XML as a prerequisite to building web services.

Listing 4.1 shows an example of a simple XML document containing information pertaining to a purchase order.

Listing 4.1 Example of a Simple XML Document

```
<?xml version="1.0" encoding="utf-8"?>
  <ORDER ID="012593">
    <CUSTOMER ID="85783">
      <DELIVERYADDRESS>
        <ADDRESS1>4301 Conn. Ave, NW</ADDRESS1>
        <ADDRESS2>Suite #135</ADDRESS2>
        <CITY>Washington</CITY>
        <STATE>Washington</STATE>
        <ZIPCODE>20008</ZIPCODE>
      </DELIVERYADDRESS>
```

```
  </CUSTOMER>
  <ITEM ID="123654">
    <QUANTITY>7000</QUANTITY>
    <DISCOUNT>25</DISCOUNT>
    <PRICEPERUNIT>1.99</PRICEPERUNIT>
  </ITEM>
  <ITEM ID="987123">
    <QUANTITY>100</QUANTITY>
    <DISCOUNT>2</DISCOUNT>
    <PRICEPERUNIT>7.50</PRICEPERUNIT>
  </ITEM>
</ORDER>
```

This example shows that, by using XML, you could write an entire purchase order in a single document that outlines customer information, delivery information, and order information. It also demonstrates the use of XML elements and attributes. Line 2 of the example displays the order number in the following format: `<ORDER ID="012593">`. The order identifier (`ID="012593"`) within the order element is an attribute. Further down, `<QUANTITY>7000</QUANTITY>` is an example of a value that is defined as an element.

Of course this is just one of many ways to describe a purchase order; but with that in mind, you can see the power of the XML standard. The ability to describe the same data in many different forms allows XML to be used in many different scenarios. One of these scenarios is web services.

SOAP As a Messaging Protocol: A Common, Extensible, Message Format

Web services require a messaging protocol that can invoke a web service and exchange data with it. SOAP is a lightweight, XML-based protocol for exchanging structured information in a decentralized, distributed environment. It is a network protocol, with no underlying explicit programming model. The main design goal of SOAP was to keep it as simple as possible and to provide as little functionality as possible. Because SOAP does not mandate the technology used to implement the client or server applications, it requires no application programming interface (API) or object model. As such, SOAP provides an open methodology—XML web services—for application-to-application communication. The protocol defines a messaging framework and does not contain any application or transport semantics. As a result, SOAP is an extremely extensible framework.

Because SOAP uses standard transport protocols, it can leverage the open architecture of the Internet and gain easy acceptance by almost all systems that support the basic Internet standards. SOAP adds very little to the existing infrastructure of the Internet. The fact that SOAP uses the simple infrastructure of the Internet, thus facilitating universal access to web services built on this platform, demonstrates how powerful the protocol really is.

The SOAP specification consists of four main parts:

- An extensible envelope for encapsulating data. The SOAP envelope defines a SOAP message and is the basic unit of exchange between SOAP message processors. This part is the only mandatory part of the specification.
- Data-encoding rules for representation of data types defined in the application, directed graphs, and a uniform model for serializing nonsyntactic data models. This part of the specification is optional.
- An RPC-style (request/response) message exchange pattern. Each SOAP message is a one-way transmission. The fact that SOAP's origin lies in RPC does not limit it to being a request/response mechanism. XML Service often combines SOAP messages to implement such patterns, but SOAP does not mandate a message exchange pattern. This part of the specification is optional.
- A definition of the SOAP and HTTP binding. SOAP can potentially be used in combination with any transportation protocol or mechanism. This part of the specification is optional.

To read more about the SOAP specification, look on the W3C web site at www.w3.org/TR/SOAP/.

WSDL as a Contract Language: A Common, Extensible Service Description Language

The infrastructure of web services is based on communication by means of XML-based messages that abide by a published service description. To support this design, Microsoft and IBM jointly developed a standard for describing web services, called Web Services Description Language (WSDL). WSDL defines the XML grammar used as a standard mechanism for creating and interpreting web service contracts. WSDL is an XML format for describing network services as a set of endpoints operating on messages containing either document-oriented or procedure-oriented information. The operations and messages are described abstractly and then bound to a concrete network protocol and message format to define an endpoint. Related concrete endpoints are combined into abstract endpoints (services). WSDL is used to create a file that identifies the services and the set of operations within each service that the server supports. The WSDL file also describes the format that the client must follow in requesting an operation.

The services description serves as a contract between the web service provider and the clients and defines the behavior of a web service. The "contract" includes instructions on how clients interact with the web service, including the messaging patterns (the messages that it accepts and generates) that the service defines and supports. For example, the request/response pattern associated with a remove procedure call style service would define which SOAP message schema to use for invoking specific methods. This pattern would also define the format that the resulting response SOAP message should follow.

Another example of a messaging pattern represents unidirectional interactions. This pattern is implemented when one-way communication is to take place. In this situation, the sender does not receive any messages from the XML web service. If the one-way communication is established using a protocol that is traditionally request/response, however, a fault message might be returned.

SOAP message schemas can be defined internally, within the actual service description, or they can be defined externally and imported into the service description. The service description can contain the address that is associated with each of the entry points within the web service. The format of the address is appropriate to the protocol used to access the service. Examples include URL (Uniform Resource Locator) for HTTP or an email address from SMTP.

To read more about the WSDL specification, look on the W3C web site at www.w3.org/TR/WSDL/.

DISCO: A Way to Discover Services Located on a Particular Web Site

XML web service discovery is the process of locating, or discovering, one or more related documents that describe a particular XML web service using WSDL. Through the discovery process, XML web service clients learn that an XML web service exists and identify where to find the service's description document. A published Discovery Protocol (DISCO) file, which is an XML document that contains links to other resources that describe the XML web service, enables programmatic discovery of an XML web service.

Listing 4.2 shows the structure of a discovery document for a Task Tracker web service:

Listing 4.2 Example DISCOvery Document

```
<?xml version="1.0" encoding="utf-8"?>
  <discovery   xmlns:xsd="http://www.w3.org/2001/XMLSchema"
    xmlns:xsi="http://www.w3.org/2001/XMLSchema-instance"
    xmlns="http://schemas.xmlsoap.org/disco/">
    <contractRef ref="http://www.infostrat.com/TaskTracker/ _
    svc Task.asmx?wsdl"
      docRef="http://www.infostrat.com/TaskTracker/svcTask.asmx"
      xmlns="http://schemas.xmlsoap.org/disco/scl/" />
   <soap         address="http:// www.infostrat.com /TaskTracker/ _
    svcTask.asmx"
      xmlns:q1="http://tempuri.org/"
      binding="q1:svcTaskSoap"
      xmlns="http://schemas.xmlsoap.org/disco/soap/" />
  </discovery>
```

The document shown in this listing is basically a container for elements that contain links (URLs) to the resources that provide discovery information for a web service. It is good practice to fully qualify the URLs; but if the specified URLs are relative, they are assumed to be relative to the location of the discovery document.

A web site that implements a web service does not need to support discovery. The discovery and description of the web service can be implemented on an alternative web site such as a web service directory. On the other hand, a web service may not have any means of being discovered, such as when the implementation is intended for private use.

A Way to Discover Service Providers

Like companies that consume commercial services, consumers of web services need to know about a service. As with any other resource on the

Internet, these consumers would not be able to find a particular web service without some means of searching for it. The DISCO specification defines a discovery document format based on XML and a protocol for retrieving the discovery document, enabling developers to discover services at a known URL.

However, in many cases, developers who need to consume the web service in their code, do not know the URLs at which services can be found. Web services directories provide central locations at which web service providers can publish information about their available services. Such directories can even be web services themselves, accessible programmatically and providing search results in response to queries from potential web service clients. It might be necessary to use a web services directory to locate an organization that provides a web service for a particular purpose, or to determine what web services that particular organizations provide. The Universal Description, Discovery, and Integration (UDDI) specifications define an advertising mechanism for web service providers and a location device for web service consumers. UDDI, in other words, serves as the yellow pages of web services.

UDDI defines how to register business data as well as how to advertise the existence and location of XML web services. Developers and users of web services typically interact with UDDI either by registering their web service or by looking for web services that serve particular needs. When using UDDI, you need to understand how to discover what you need.

The UDDI specifications define a standard way to publish and discover information about web services. The XML schemas associated with UDDI define four types of information that enable a developer to use a published XML web service. These are business information, service information, binding information, and information about specifications for services. A core component of the UDDI project, the UDDI Business Registry, allows businesses to programmatically locate information about XML web services exposed by other organizations. Developers can use the UDDI Business Registry to locate discovery documents and service descriptions.

To read more on UDDI, look on the Organization for the Advancement of Structured Information Standards (OASIS) web site at www.UDDI.org/ or on Microsoft's site at UDDI.microsoft.com/.

Choosing to Deploy a Web Service

Before diving in and turning all new products and functionality into web services, you should realize that web services are not the solution to all problems. This section outlines the factors you should consider before choosing to develop a given functionality as a web service.

Type of functionality. Is the function needed for internal use or for external business partners and customers? For internal use and a homogeneous target environment, a web service does not really make sense. Interdepartmental data exchange may warrant the development of web services, but there are other technologies that make more sense, including COM+ or .NET Remoting.

Deployment. Does the deployment of the function require a complex installation procedure or a complicated hardware configuration? If so, you can free business partners and customers from this onerous requirement by deploying as a web service. There would then be no need to deploy the software locally.

Access to proprietary data. Does the function need to access data that is proprietary, not available to the public, or located exclusively within your organization? If so, a web service would be an appropriate way to expose this data to consumers. A web service would also let you keep certain information private and away from the public eye. This is clearly a much better method than sending data files.

Frequency of data change. Does the data on which the function relies change frequently? If so, a web service would be a perfect fit. Using a web service would ensure that consumers had up-to-date data while also supporting data updates behind the scenes. As a result, consumers would not have to be constantly supplied with data files, and consumers would not have to spend time handling these files.

Version release frequency. Do you expect incremental or periodic releases to the function? Using a web service would reduce the amount of maintenance needed for code updates and release of new versions. There would be no need to perform installations on any of the consuming machines because the deployment would be performed on the web server hosting the web service.

You must ensure that the interface to each function remains the same so the consuming code will not need to be changed. A change to a function call can break code that is expecting a different function interface.

Performance. Is performance of the function of utmost importance? Web services consume time in the transport of data. Calling a web service within a loop would result in a significant performance impact. Functions of this type would be better implemented as functionality exposed by local compiled libraries (DLLs).

Availability. Is 24/7 availability required? If so, you should probably not use a web service. Web services are taken offline for maintenance. In other cases web servers go down or network troubles arise. Even well-protected and well-maintained networks need to undergo maintenance and therefore will have some downtime during the year. A web service that runs on someone else's infrastructure will never be as dependable as a service running on your own servers.

Fitting Web Services into the Portal

Web services and portals can fit together like hand and glove. After all, both web services and a portal have a fundamental goal of systems integration. They both allow users to connect to disparate data sources, yet hide complexities of this connection such as protocol and syntax.

Web services can be vital as a means of content syndication, which means the repackaging of content that is created or managed elsewhere. Portals are often made up of components that extract information from many different sources. These information sources can be on the same machine, within the local area network, within a wide area network, or (thanks to web services) on the other side of the planet! Web services allow developers to create programmatic interfaces for any type of information and then expose these interfaces over the Internet. Portal developers can then consume these web services within a portal without having to establish direct contact with the data source itself. For instance, you might want to establish subscriptions to news services, yet make the news articles conform to your web site's look and feel.

Another promising use of web services in a portal is to provide support for transactions. Through web services, you can connect to an e-commerce system for order entry or inventory management. For instance, you could requisition office supplies by filling in a form, then route the transactions to a supplier for fulfillment. A similar example is travel and lodging services.

You could link your portal to Expedia or another travel site and get flights and hotel rooms as you are planning a meeting.

Sample Web Service

This section demonstrates a simple web service for retrieving an inventory level. This sample web service is created with the Microsoft .NET Framework and Microsoft Visual Studio .NET. You can apply this example to many other scenarios in which you need to consume a web service that makes an inquiry into a relational database table.

To begin, you need a computer that meets the prerequisites for creating an ASP.NET application. For more information about these prerequisites, see the Visual Studio documentation. You also need access to the Northwind demo database that is installed with SQL Server.

To create the web service:

1. Open Visual Studio .NET.
2. Select **New Project** from the **File** menu.
3. In the New Project dialog box, make the following selections (Figure 4.4) and click OK.

   - Project Types: **Visual Basic Projects**
   - Templates: **ASP.NEW Web Service**
   - Location: **http://localhost/PortalServices**
   - Name: PortalServices (this entry should appear automatically)

The Visual Studio .NET IDE creates a web application on your local machine and generates all of the files necessary for the creation and execution of the web service. You may want to give the Service1 class (Service1.asmx) that is created a more meaningful name. To do so, delete the file and create a new file with the name of your choice. Select the file from within the Solution Explorer, right-click, and select Delete from the popup menu. To then create a web service file:

1. Select **Add Web Service** from the **Project** menu.
2. In the Add New Item dialog box, name the web service **InventoryService.asmx**, and click OK.

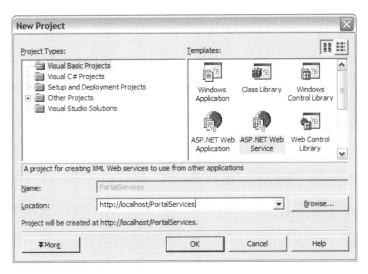

Figure 4.4 Creating a Web Service Project

Next, open the class, add the code for the sample web service, and build the project:

1. Select the ASMX file from within the Solution Explorer pane. Right-click and select **View Code** from the popup menu.
2. Add the code shown in Listing 4.3 to the class, below the HelloWorld web service example.
3. Select **Build** from the **Build** menu.

Listing 4.3 Sample Web Service

```
01:  <WebMethod()> Public Function GetInventoryLevel _
02:      (ByVal SupplierID As Integer, _
03:       ByVal CriticalLevel As Integer) As DataSet
04:    Dim ds As New DataSet()
05:    Dim cn As New SqlConnection( _
06:      "User ID=sa;Data Source=.;Initial Catalog=Northwind;")
07:    Dim com As New SqlCommand()
08:    Dim stbSQL As New System.Text.StringBuilder("")
09:    Try
```

Continues

Listing 4.3 Sample Web Service (*Continued*)

```
10:     stbSQL.Append("SELECT ProductID, ProductName, UnitsInStock _
        FROM Products ")
11:     stbSQL.AppendFormat("WHERE SupplierID = {0}", _
        SupplierID.ToString)
12:     stbSQL.AppendFormat("  AND UnitsInStock <= {0}", _
        CriticalLevel.ToString)
13:     com.CommandType = CommandType.Text
14:     com.CommandText = stbSQL.ToString
15:     com.Connection = cn
16:     Dim ad As New SqlDataAdapter(com)
17:     ad.Fill(ds, "InventoryItems")
18:   Catch ex As Exception
19:     Diagnostics.Debug.WriteLine(ex.ToString)
20:   End Try
21:   Return ds
22: End Function
```

In lines 01 to 03 of the code you added, you can find the function definition, which is divided into four parts:

1. Function attributes, which are new to the .NET languages, allow developers to define certain attributes before the definition of classes, member variables, and methods. In this case, the attribute <WebMethod()> defines the GetInventoryLevel() function as a web method. When the Common Language Runtime (CLR) sees this attribute while loading and compiling the ASMX file, it knows that this function needs to be exposed as part of a web service.
2. Function Name is the name that will be used to call the function/web service.
3. Variable/parameters are passed to the function.
4. A return variable, used to return the outcome of the function. In the case of web service development, it is important to make sure that the variable type can be serialized. In the sample web service, that variable type returned is a dataset, which is a serializable variable. Although the .NET framework will do most of the plumbing when it comes to serializable variables, there are numerous variable types that are not serializable and can therefore not be used to return values from a web service.

The remainder of the function is a call to the database to retrieve a dataset containing the products that currently have an inventory level equal to or lower than that specified in the function's parameters. Lines 04 to 08 define a number of variables that will be used during the function. Note that the connection string, defined on lines 05 and 06, may need to be modified depending on the configuration of SQL Server on your machine. The SQL statement is prepared on lines 10 to 12 by using a String Builder object. (The String Builder object is used to concatenate strings and has been optimized to perform this action.) Lines 13–15 define the command that will be used to extract the data from the database and lines 16 and 17 make the call to the database and fill the dataset with the records that are returned from the database. On line 21, you can see that the function returns the dataset without having to perform any special handling of the dataset variable.

To run the sample web service, open Internet Explorer and navigate to localhost/PortalServices/InventoryService.asmx. Figure 4.5 shows the window that opens, which is generated automatically by ASP.NET using .NET reflection APIs. No work is required on the part of the developer.

On the generated page, there is a link to the GetInventoryLevel web service. Clicking that link opens a page from which you can call the Get-InventoryLevel function, shown in Figure 4.6. This page, too, is automatically generated by ASP.NET and creates an impromptu user interface for

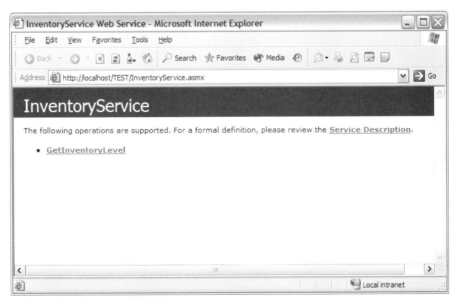

Figure 4.5 Automatically Generated Function Listing

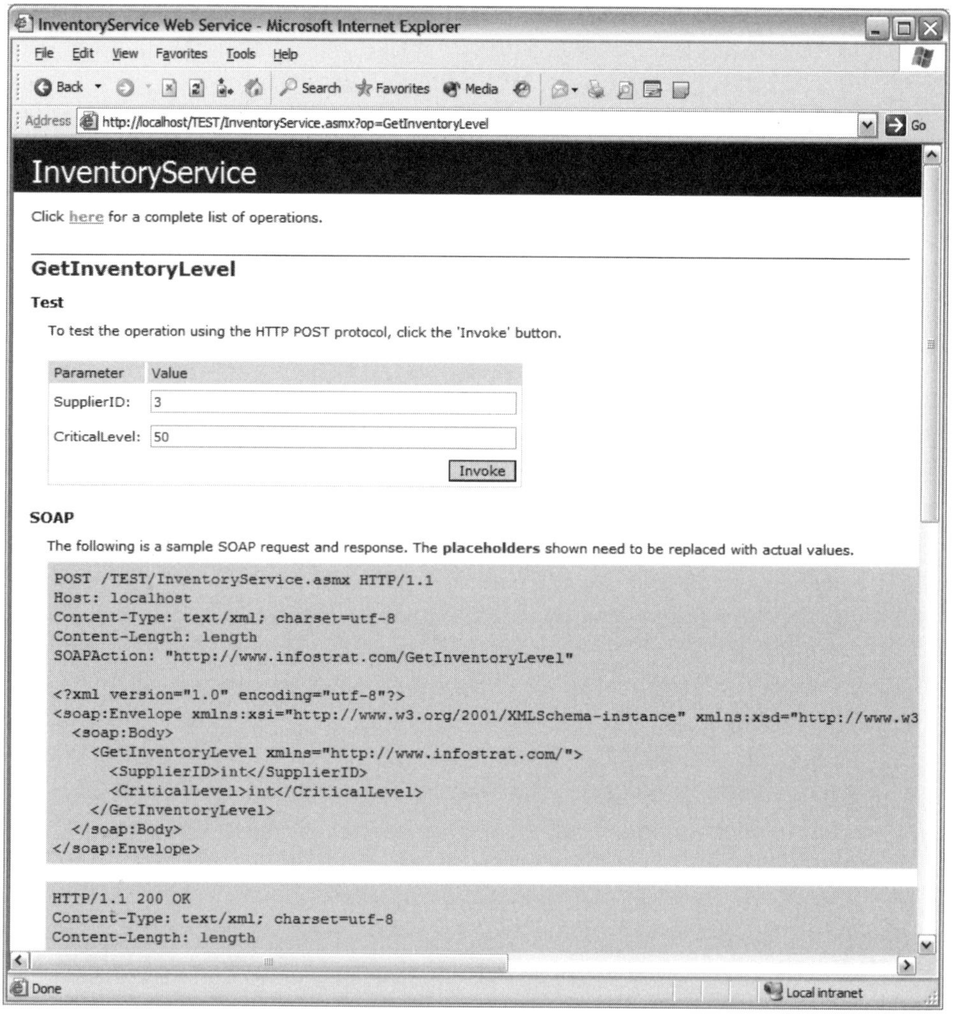

Figure 4.6 GetInventoryLevel Test Interface

testing the GetInventoryLevel web service. It outlines how to call the function using SOAP, HTTP/GET, and HTTP/POST, and it displays a general format of the message exchange so you know what to send and what to expect in return.

To test the GetInventoryLevel web service, set values for each of the variables and click the Invoke button to open a new browser window with the function's results (Figure 4.7).

The results from the service are in the format of a dataset serialized to XML format. These results can be consumed by any environment on any

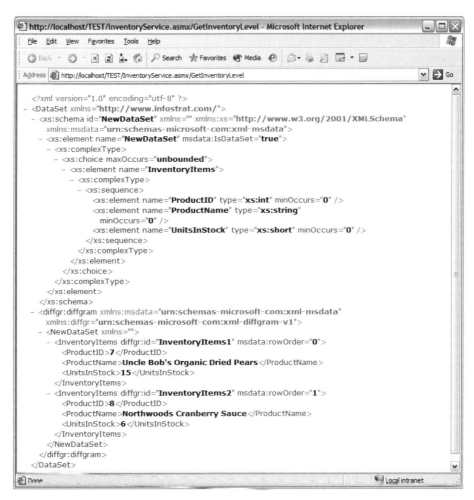

Figure 4.7 GetInventoryLevel Web Service Results

platform. For example, this web service could be included on a B2B (business-to-business) portal where users are identified as representatives of the supplier. A "portlet" within the portal could be configured to take the user's supplier identification and an inventory level, thus allowing the portal to display the current inventory level of products that are below the preset critical value.

Web Service Benefits

With all the effort it takes to learn web services and change your programming paradigm, what is the upside for making the switch? How can you get a return from your web services investment? Web services yield significant benefits for many kinds of applications. We can break these benefits into the categories outlined here.

Platform independence. Web services are platform independent and not intimately tied to proprietary hardware or operating system software. Because they rely on SOAP and SOAP is really just XML, web services can be used on any platform that supports SOAP and can be invoked from any such platform. Finally, the obstacle that has prevented heterogeneous RPC-based systems from interacting has been eliminated.

Ease of integrating disparate systems. This is the key benefit of web services. Integration of a web service that sends and receives SOAP messages is easy to implement and a few orders of magnitude less complex than translating from or into a message format that is specific to a given application or platform.

Reduced security risk. Some forms of application integration carry security risks with them as well. Because web services with SOAP are really just XML, the same port (port 80) typically configured for HTTP can be used. As a result, web services can pass through firewalls without additional ports being opened, thereby significantly reducing the risk of potential security breaches.

Conclusion

Web services are the next stage of evolution for e-business and are the result of viewing systems from a perspective that everything is a service, dynamically discovered and orchestrated, using messaging on the network. Microsoft recognizes the importance of web services, which lie at the center of the .NET paradigm. Indeed, .NET is sometimes characterized as simply a means of creating web services.

In a web services architecture, each component is regarded as a service, encapsulating behavior and providing the behavior through an API available for invocation over a network (usually the Internet). This is the logical evolution of object-oriented techniques (encapsulation, messaging, dynamic binding, and reflection) in e-business. Many product vendors can be expected to jump on this bandwagon, providing ERP, CRM, and other solutions delivered through web services.

The web services architecture provides several benefits, including:

- Promoting interoperability by minimizing the requirements for shared understanding
- Enabling just-in-time integration
- Reducing complexity by encapsulation
- Enabling interoperability of legacy applications

For a portal, web services may be both provided and consumed. If you are an information provider, you may want to create a web service that pushes information to your subscribers and opens up your applications to their access. You may want to consume web services in the form of subscriptions for content and leverage sophisticated transactional systems that would be far too expensive to build for your enterprise alone.

Web services provide extensibility to the capabilities that are built into the off-the-shelf Microsoft server products such as Content Management Server, SharePoint Portal Server, and Commerce Server. They can serve as glue for integration with customers, suppliers, and government agencies.

Chapter 5

Portal Framework—.NET

Just as a building needs a foundation, walls, and a roof, an application or a web site needs a framework. Indeed, a portal is essentially a combination of a web site and one or more applications. A framework is required to coordinate programming activities and maximize consistency and object reuse.

I have found that building .NET applications on a common framework shortens development time and reduces the number of software errors. As we have built one .NET solution after another, we have improved and extended the framework. We have also brought the framework to our clients as a way of transferring .NET knowledge and speeding up projects.

The most fortunate aspect of Microsoft's portal platform is that the current generation of server products is all marching to the beat of the .NET drummer. Whether you are creating a user control in Content Management Server, a web part in SharePoint Portal Server, or a class in Commerce Server, you build objects in .NET using Visual Studio .NET. This commonality is a tremendous step forward for the Microsoft portal platform, offering advantages over competitive solutions based on a hodgepodge of tools and languages.

This chapter explains what a framework should do, the key elements of the framework, and how you can build your own portal framework with .NET. There is not room to print all the code for a complete framework in this chapter. My goal is to illustrate the elements of the framework and suggest ways that you can implement a framework that meets your special requirements.

The Fundamentals of .NET

Despite heroic communication efforts undertaken by Microsoft, there still is a lot of confusion as to what exactly .NET is. .NET is actually three different but interrelated things:

- .NET is a broad vision of the future of computing where services will be developed and then sold or leased to consumers by software providers. In this context, the core of the .NET brand is web services.
- .NET is a set of development tools, primarily the .NET Framework and Visual Studio .NET. For developers, this is the central meaning of .NET.
- .NET is a group of products: Visual Studio, Exchange, BizTalk, Commerce Server, SQL Server, and others. For a while, Microsoft was extending the .NET brand to promote these server products. Indeed, the original product name for Windows 2003 Server was Windows .NET Server. More recently, the .NET brand has retrenched a bit and the name has been removed from products except for Visual Studio.

For our purposes, we will focus on the second meaning of .NET. While web services are also important to the framework, much can be done in .NET that is not a web service. Let's explore what a .NET portal framework is all about and how it can help your portal.

What Is a Framework?

Here are two commonly used definitions of a framework:

- "A framework is a partially complete software system that is intended to be instantiated. It defines the architecture for a family of systems and provides the basic building blocks to create them. It also defines the places were adaptations for specific functionality should be made."[1]

---

[1]   F. Buschmann et al. *Pattern-Oriented Software Architecture*, John Wiley & Sons, Ltd., England, 1996.

- "A framework is a set of classes that embodies an abstract design for solutions to a family of related problems."[2]

A developer builds a complete application by instantiating and inheriting from components in the framework. The framework therefore contains a set of objects that serve as examples for other objects to be created or as parent objects from which new objects inherit methods and properties. A more colorful analogy is to look at a framework as a Noah's Ark, with one or two examples of each type of object that needs to be created in order to populate the application.

We are discussing two frameworks here. One is the out-of-the-box .NET Framework. I will explain how .NET provides benefits to developers and can be used to create our second framework, the one you create specifically for your portal requirements. It is at this stage that you will determine how server products such as SharePoint, Content Management Server (CMS), BizTalk, and Commerce Server dovetail with your custom .NET code.

.NET Framework Benefits

The .NET application development framework offers many benefits to developers. These benefits carry over into portal development. They include:

- *Object-oriented programming (OOP).* The .NET Framework was written from the ground up with OOP ideology in mind. This is the most dramatic departure from the "spaghetti code" era of Active Server Pages (ASP). It is also the biggest challenge for veteran Visual Basic 6 programmers. Many habits must be broken and lessons unlearned to make the transition to .NET.
- *Base class library.* The .NET Framework exposes a rich set of classes to use with various development tasks. An additional benefit is a set of wrapper classes to use instead of the Windows API.
- *Garbage collection and automatic memory management.* Various memory related bugs very common to C++ development are no more in the .NET Framework. The garbage collection mechanism is responsible for controlling the lifetime of the objects and their proper disposal.

---

[2] Ralph Johnson and Porian Foote. "Designing Reusable Classes," *Journal of Object-Oriented Programming,* Volume 1, Number 2, June/July 1988.

- *Increased performance.* Several new caching techniques and just-in-time (JIT) compilation make .NET-based applications perform significantly faster, especially when compared with old ASP-based code.
- *New advanced security options.* These include code access security, which allows the assignment of security rights to an executing block of code.
- *Native support for XML and web services development.* This brings .NET in line with industry standards.
- *Interoperability with existing applications.* The .NET Framework includes an interoperability layer that makes it very easy to consume existing COM components from .NET modules and also to use .NET objects from unmanaged (not .NET) code.
- *Increased productivity of the development team.* Visual Studio .NET includes many new tools to boost developer productivity and, without any doubt, is the best integrated development environment (IDE) to come from Microsoft so far.
- *Simple, copy-based deployment model.* Installation of ASP applications can be quite interesting, especially if, as is typically the case, that installation is not well documented. Self-referenced assemblies and a simplified deployment model eliminate the "DLL hell" problem so common with traditional Windows development.

Building Blocks of the .NET Framework

The .NET Framework consists of several elements. Together they provide the integrated development environment we need for developing many types of applications.

Common Language Runtime

The Common Language Runtime (CLR) is the foundation of the .NET Framework. There are quite a few languages in which developers could write .NET code. Microsoft has taken the approach of supporting many old and new languages. Visual Studio .NET is shipped with Visual Basic .NET, C#, and managed extensions for C++. In addition, many other languages are available now in .NET flavors: Java, FORTRAN, COBOL, and others.

The CLR supports a high degree of language interoperability: Modules written in different languages can coexist within the same project, call each other's methods, and also inherit from classes written in a different language without any additional effort from the developer. This integration is achieved through the use of a common underlying language, Microsoft Intermediate Language (MSIL). All .NET-based code compiles to MSIL, which serves as a common denominator for all higher-level languages. Other important services performed by CLR are memory management, error-handling services, and security management and type safety enforcement.

Compiled .NET Framework is packaged differently from familiar unmanaged executable files. After your .NET source code is compiled, the framework creates an assembly containing compiled code and metadata. One of the differences is that each assembly can contain several compiled managed modules and several resource files. Besides metadata used to describe classes and types, each assembly contains a manifest that describes the contents of the assembly itself. This approach allows developers to simplify deployment, versioning, and maintenance tasks by creating a single assembly file instead of multiple DLL modules.

A simplified deployment model allows .NET-based applications to be distributed and installed by copying the application directory to the target computer. No additional registration is required, which is another important .NET benefit. This model is achieved by storing metadata describing an assembly within the assembly itself along with MSIL instructions (code). The metadata included in an assembly makes assembly self-describing. There is no need for additional registration information stored in the system Registry or any other data source. When the assembly is loaded into memory, its metadata provides all the information needed by calling code to instantiate and use objects stored within the assembly. Metadata contains the following information:

- Full information about classes within the assembly, including class attributes and information about class methods and properties
- Information about referenced assemblies

Assemblies

Assemblies in .NET are basic units of execution, versioning, and deployment. Traditional languages, like Visual Basic or C++, compile their code to a native executable format, EXE or DLL, which can be directly loaded by the system loader. .NET compilers produce MSIL code that, along with the metadata information and assembly manifest, forms the assembly. Just like a regular EXE or DLL, each assembly has only one main entry point.

Assemblies resolve an important versioning problem: In a large application consisting of many separate executable modules, it is very hard to ensure the version consistency of all application parts. An assembly allows developers to treat such a large application as a single unit.

Each assembly contains type metadata that describes fully all objects contained within the assembly, resource files, the compiled code (in MSIL format), and assembly manifest. The assembly manifest describes the composition of the assembly.

An assembly is installed by simply copying all files constituting that assembly to a directory on a target computer. The code that uses assembly types will try to locate the assembly in the application directory, in a subdirectory of an application directory, or in the global assembly cache (GAC). The GAC provides a way to share a single assembly among multiple applications just as a single registered COM component can be reused by multiple clients. The .NET Framework comes with a command-line tool, gacutil.exe, which can be used to copy an assembly to GAC, to remove an assembly from GAC, or to view GAC contents.

Base Class Library

.NET Framework class library or Base Class Library (BCL) consists of a set of classes representing the prepackaged functionality tightly integrated with the CLR. The framework classes greatly simplify and speed up many common development tasks and also allow developers to extend the library by inheriting from Base Class Library types.

The framework class library is organized in a number of namespaces, each of which contains a set of logically related classes. All namespaces in BCL derive from the common base namespace called **System**. .NET uses dot syntax convention to organize its types into a hierarchy. To denote the full type name, it concatenates the namespaces to which that type belongs with the type name. For example, the **DataSet** type (representing an in-memory cache of data) belongs to the **Data** namespace, which in turn belongs to the root **System** namespace. The full name of the **DataSet** type is therefore **System.Data.DataSet**.

Some of the most important namespaces are:

- *System.Web* provides a rich programming framework for building web-based applications and services using .NET Active Server Pages (ASP.NET).
- *System.Windows.Forms* contains functionality used to build client user interface applications.
- *System.Data* contains ADO.NET classes used to connect applications to databases and other data sources.
- *System.Xml* contains classes used when developers are working with XML data.
- *System.IO* is used to perform stream-based input/output operations and also work with files and directories.
- *System.Security* provides several mechanisms for controlling access to the resources and code. See Chapter 6 for an overview of various security mechanisms in the .NET Framework.

Figure 5.1 shows a conceptual overview of the .NET Framework architecture.

Running Managed Code

Developers can write code using any of the compilers that target the .NET runtime. After code is written, it is compiled to a set of MSIL instructions. MSIL is platform and CPU independent. Before the managed code is executed, it is converted from MSIL to a CPU- and platform-specific native code using the JIT compiler. .NET compilers produce MSIL together with metadata describing type information.

When MSIL code is compiled to the native code, it undergoes a type safety verification process. Type safety primarily ensures that the code is only accessing authorized memory locations. When an MSIL-compiled method is called during execution for the first time, it is JIT-compiled to the native code and then the new native code is executed. All subsequent execution requests will refer to the previously compiled code.

The operating system loader recognizes a managed code module by examining a special bit in the Common Object File Format (COFF) header. If the managed module is detected, the loader changes the entry point to the CLR entry point.

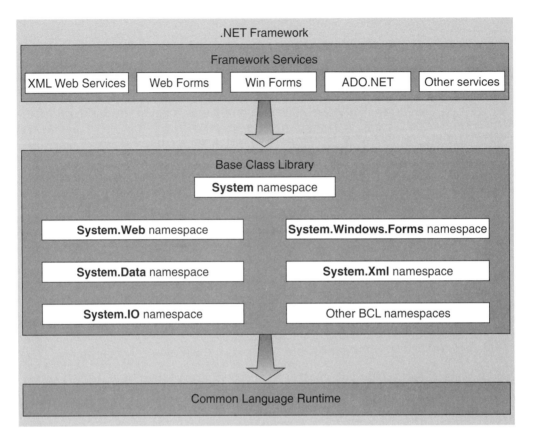

Figure 5.1 Overall .NET Framework Architecture

Garbage Collection and Automatic Memory Management

Garbage collector (GC) is the .NET mechanism responsible for the allocation and release of memory for all objects in the managed code. Garbage collector uses managed heap (a contiguous area of memory allocated for a managed process during its startup) to allocate memory for an object created using the **new** operator. Garbage collector contains a set of optimizer algorithms that keep track of the allocated memory and decide when the collection is being performed. During the garbage collection, unused objects are deallocated and destroyed.

The concept of garbage collection represents a significant paradigm shift for COM and C++ developers. COM developers are used to controlling the lifetime of an object using reference counting (through the **IUknown** interface). Reference-counting bugs are notoriously tricky to find and are the source of many COM development hardships.

Memory management is one of the most important tasks of a C++ developer. In C++, every object created on the heap using the **new** operator must be explicitly deleted by using the **delete** operator. The tasks of writing proper destructors that release all dynamic memory and of keeping track of all heap-based objects are the source of many bugs in C++ applications.

Garbage collection allows developers to concentrate on the application logic and relegate mundane memory management tasks to the framework. When the first object is created using the new operator, it is allocated at the base of the managed heap. The next object created by the code is allocated in the address space immediately following the first object. This process continues while there is available address space in the managed heap.

The garbage collector keeps track of all allocated objects. It checks periodically to see whether there are any objects that are not being used by the application anymore. If unused objects are found, they are destroyed and the memory space they had occupied is returned to the managed heap.

The tracking process employs a set of application roots, which are reference type pointers. The application roots include:

- Global and static pointers
- Local reference type variables on a stack
- CPU registers

The JIT compiler and CLR together maintain the list of application roots. The garbage collector scans the set of roots to determine the set of objects that are reachable from the application roots. After GC finds an unreachable object, it considers this object to be garbage. Each garbage object is destroyed and its memory is freed. When garbage objects have been destroyed, the garbage collection process compacts the managed heap by copying memory allocated by objects to the new locations and then updating the application roots.

The GC process contains a number of optimizations, the most important of which is the generations-based approach to the garbage collection.

The main idea behind this approach is that newer objects tend to have shorter lifetimes and should be collected first.

All objects on the heap belong to generation 0, 1, or 2. Every time a new object is created, it is assigned to generation 0. When address space belonging to generation 0 fills up, the garbage collection process is triggered. The GC algorithm tries to find garbage objects only in generation 0, thus optimizing performance. After the garbage in generation 0 is collected, its unused memory space is reclaimed and it is compacted. All generation 0 objects that survive this collection are considered to have longer lifetimes and are reassigned to generation 1. Various GC algorithms decide when to look at and compact generations 1 and 2 (for example, when insufficient memory has been freed from generation 0).

C++ and Visual Basic developers have traditionally freed object resources explicitly upon the object's destruction using class destructor methods in C++ and class terminate events in Visual Basic. In .NET, the exact moment when an object will be destroyed is not deterministic. Instead, the garbage collector calls a **Finalize** method on the object. This method performs an implicit cleanup; it is never called directly. To allow the consumer of an object to perform an explicit cleanup, you should implement the **IDisposable** interface. This interface exposes a **Dispose** method. Object consumers can call this method directly to clean up expensive resources without waiting for the CLR to perform a garbage collection.

.NET Common Type System

Common Type System (CTS) plays a crucial role in providing type safety, cross-language integration, and cross-language inheritance features. The CTS defines all data types that a language targeting .NET runtime can use. Each .NET language must implement at least a subset of types specified by CTS. The CTS resolves multiple cross-language integration issues, all of which are very familiar to anyone who has had to develop software systems incorporating, for example, COM components written using Active Template Library (ATL) C++ classes in conjunction with a Visual Basic frontend.

CTS compliance means that not only the compiler implements CTS types but also that it adheres to the common set of rules dictating how these types are created and used by the code. The following section describes the primary concepts and the most important features of the Common Type System.

Common Root for All Types

Each type in a language that targets CLR must inherit from the **System.Object** type, which provides a common set of services including support for .NET garbage collector. This inheritance is implied; you do not have to explicitly derive your type from **System.Object**. The following two class definitions are identical:

Using Visual Basic .NET:

```
Class C
End Class
Class C
    Inherits System.Object
End Class
```

Using C#:

```
class C
{
}

class C : System.Object
{
}
```

Value Types and Reference Types

Every type in CLS belongs to one of two broad categories: **value types** and **reference types**. Value types inherit from CLR class **ValueType** (which derives from **Object**). Value types are allocated on the stack and contain the value itself. Most of the primitive types like **System.Int32**, **System.Boolean**, and **System.Single** are built-in value types. Structure in .NET is a value type as well, which might come as a surprise to C++ developers accustomed to treating classes (which are reference types in .NET) and structures similarly. Because value types are not allocated on the managed heap, they are not garbage-collected. The lifetime of a value type is determined by its scope. For example, all value types declared within a function are destroyed when the function exits. When the value type object is created, it is zeroed by default. The **Copy** operation on the value type object copies its value.

Reference types resemble C++ pointers: They contain the reference to the value contained in the object. Reference types are created on the managed heap and derive from the **System.Object** class (when a reference type is instantiated, the value itself is allocated on the heap and the reference to the value is placed on the managed stack). When the reference type object is created, its default value is null. The Copy operation on the reference type object copies the reference only.

The following reference types are supported by the CLS:

- *Classes* form the basis of object-oriented features of a language. A class contains a set of fields holding data defining its state and a set of methods, properties, and events, which define the class's behavior. An object is the running instance of a class. A class can inherit from other classes. Abstract classes are classes that cannot be instantiated and whose members are not implemented. Abstract classes are primarily used in inheritance chains as base classes. A class can directly inherit from only one base class.
- *Interfaces* resemble classes: They too can have methods, properties, and events (but not fields). All interface members must be abstract. Interfaces are used to declare the common functionality without providing the implementation. A class can implement one or many interfaces by inheriting from these interfaces and providing the implementation for each method of each interface.
- *Delegates* build on the idea of C++ function pointers. While regular pointers point to the memory addresses where objects are located, function pointers point to the location of the function. Unlike C++ function pointers, delegates are actual objects implementing a lot of useful behavior. Delegates can reference both static and instance methods (while function pointers can only deal with static functions). Delegates support an invocation list, which allows for the execution of multiple methods when the single delegate is invoked. CLR supports the asynchronous execution of the delegates. Delegates inherit from the **System.Delegate** class and are widely used in .NET development to program callbacks and event handlers.
- *Arrays* should be familiar to developers with both C++ and Visual Basic backgrounds. .NET arrays inherit from the **System.Array** type. .NET arrays are type safe: Each element in the array belongs to the same type.

- *Strings* in .NET are reference type values and are immutable. After a string is created, it cannot be modified. When string operations occur, the original string object is destroyed and a new string is created. The BCL provides the **System.Text.StringBuilder** class to optimize string operations. This class contains various fast string-handling methods and is preferred when intensive string manipulations are required.

Boxing and Unboxing

There are cases in which the translation between value and reference types is required. The process of conversion of the value type to the reference type is called **boxing**. The process of conversion of the reference type to the value type is called **unboxing**. Generally, the value types are treated like the primitive types in C++: They reside on the stack, are not garbage-collected, and have predictable lifetimes. The ability to sometimes treat value types as if they were reference types allows for great flexibility in the code and provides for a unified way to treat all variables without sacrificing the performance benefits of the value types.

Following is a C# example of boxing and unboxing in action.

```
// Boxing
Int32 n = 10;      // create and assign value to a value type
                   // object
Object obj = n;// allocate memory on the heap to store the value
           // of variable n
           // copy the value of n to the heap and copy the
           // value of the reference to the heap address to
           // the memory allocated on the stack for object
           // obj Unboxing
Int32 m = (Int32)obj;    // take the value reference to by obj
                         // from the managed heap and copy it
                         // on the stack
```

Many CLR collection classes store **Object** types as collection members, which means that they expect reference type objects. You can easily store both value and reference types in .NET collections due to the automatic boxing/unboxing process: When a value type object is added to the collection, it is automatically converted to the reference type that could be stored as a collection member.

Application Domains

Application isolation is one of the most crucial tasks of any computer system. The infamous instability of the old 16-bit version of Windows was due to the fact that the application isolation level was low: All processes shared a common memory space. Any misbehaving application could corrupt other running processes, including system processes.

The level of application isolation in Windows currently is the process. Each application running under Windows is loaded into its own process with its own independent memory space protected from the memory used by the other processes. The .NET Framework provides more control over the application isolation level by introducing a concept of application domains. In a nutshell, just like an operating system allows you to run multiple processes simultaneously, you can run several application domains within a single CLR process. The isolation level between different application domains within a process is similar to the isolation between different processes.

Just as with processes, code in one application domain cannot directly access code in a different application domain. To pass an object from one application domain to another, either an object is marshaled (local copy of the object is created in a second application domain) or the object is accessed through a proxy using remoting technology.

Application domains have several important advantages:

- When code crosses a process boundary, a context switch occurs. This resource-intensive operation is not required during cross-domain calls.
- You can start and stop individual application domains without stopping the whole processes. A misbehaving application in one application domain will not affect other application domains within the same process.
- A server application can perform dynamic updates without restarting by monitoring for assembly updates. When a new assembly is detected, a server can unload a single application domain and restart it with the updated assembly.

■ Application domains provide a unit of security and configuration. Each application domain can have its own security policy and its own configuration file.

The **System.AppDomain** class is used to control application domains programmatically. It allows developers to create an application domain, load an assembly into or unload an assembly from the domain, and shut down the domain.

Runtime Hosts

.NET Framework allows you create multiple types of applications, from console applications, web server applications, and web services to Windows GUI-based applications. Even though these applications might be packaged as familiar EXE and DLL files, they are not native Windows applications. Each .NET-based application must be hosted by a special Windows process called Runtime Host. The task of the Runtime Host is to create a native Win32 process, load CLR into this process, create .NET application domains, and finally load the code from the application's assembly into the application domains.

The following runtime hosts are included with the .NET Framework: ASP.NET, Microsoft Internet Explorer, and Windows Shell executables. The .NET Framework ships with an unmanaged API that allows developers to create custom Runtime Hosts.

.NET Versus Other Approaches

As in life, there is no single ultimate truth in software development. The choice of the software development tool depends perhaps to a larger degree on personal preferences and past experiences of the members of the development team. How many times have you met a weathered COBOL developer whose credo is, "Why learn new tools when everything I need could be done in COBOL?"

Despite the inevitable bias creeping into any technology comparison discussion, side-by-side technology analysis can reveal many interesting facts and make the task of selecting an appropriate technology easier. In this section we take a look at several competing web application development technologies, including legacy technology from Microsoft (ASP) and competing development environments from Sun (J2EE) and IBM (WebSphere).

ASP

ASP gained great popularity by allowing developers to easily build dynamic web applications by mixing HTML with script-based code (VBScript or JScript). In ASP, the code was interspersed with HTML, and the way ASP was implemented prevented the developers from using object-oriented principles. The absence of the clear separation of presentation (HTML) code and application logic (script) and inadequate support for object-oriented features often led to the creation of spaghetti code with its usual problems: high cost of debugging and maintenance and low level of code reuse. Because ASP uses interpreted scripting language, its performance is lackluster. ASP developers had to use other technologies, usually COM, to implement application components that required high performance. The ASP/COM connection was based on late binding, a technology that resolves references to COM objects at runtime. This by itself led to multiple issues with both performance and debugging.

ASP.NET, even though it shares a name with ASP, was completely rewritten to address all of ASP's shortcomings. ASP.NET produces compiled code and provides well-rounded object-oriented technology. Because ASP.NET is part of the .NET Framework, it can easily use all of the services provided by the framework and the Base Class Library. This feature—the ability to stay completely within a single technology—is one of the biggest advantages of .NET. Indeed, all pieces of a multitier distributed application, including web application components, Window GUI applications, Windows services, and others, can be developed using only .NET. With the release of the next version of Microsoft SQL Server, this advantage will be even more pronounced due to the ability to develop SQL Server stored procedures using any CLR-compliant language.

The **WebForms** introduced by ASP.NET represent a major step away from the structure-based spaghetti code of the old ASP. **WebForms** allow developers to physically separate the HTML presentation code of the web page from the processing logic implemented by any .NET language and employ many new language features, including built-in authentication support, support for various caching techniques, and others. The new mode of web application development is then very similar to traditional wizard-based Windows application development in which a GUI is built using graphical designers and developers write event-handling and business logic code.

ASP.NET delivers additional great benefits for a web site's administrators: The simple copy-based mode of application deployment and the ability to update web applications without stopping them or restarting the server can run circles around the old ASP installation scenario. Prior to ASP.NET, administrators had to use complex installation scripts that would stop the running application and the server, unregister the COM components, and perform the installation and registration of updated modules.

Even though the ASP.NET designers did not try to reach full backwards compatibility with ASP, many familiar ASP features have made it into ASP.NET. For example, the core ASP objects **Request**, **Response**, and **Server** are available in ASP.NET. The similarity between the two technologies eases the learning curve for ASP developers and makes the transition process smoother. The process of conversion of ASP applications to ASP.NET could be aided by the possibility of the coexistence of both ASP and ASP.NET modules on the same server. In fact, it is possible to have web applications composed of both ASP and ASP.NET parts.

Simply put, there's no competition: ASP.NET is the clear winner over ASP. For more details on differences and similarities between ASP and ASP.NET, refer to the "Migrating to ASP.NET: Key Considerations" article available on MSDN at http://msdn.microsoft.com/library/default.asp?url=/library/en-us/dnaspp/html/aspnetmigrissues.asp.

Personal Home Pages (PHP) is another script-based technology that is very similar in its ideology and development practice to older versions of ASP. Much of the previous discussion applies to the PHP versus ASP.NET comparison as well.

Java (Sun J2EE and IBM WebSphere)

Years of marketing wars between Microsoft and various companies representing the Java development camp have led to a wide chasm between Java- and Microsoft-oriented developers. Multiple discussions comparing tools and products from Microsoft with the ones from Sun, IBM, Oracle, BEA, and others achieve almost religious fervor. Time and again, industry pundits publish articles promoting their preferred provider under the guise of neutrality.

The truth is that there's no apparent winner. You should take prior experiences of the development team, personal preferences and prejudices, the targeted platform, licensing agreements with software and hardware vendors, and many other factors into account when you make the choice between .NET and its competitors.

Both J2EE and the .NET Framework offer similar services, especially when it comes to creating XML web services. In fact, the standards underpinning web services—Simple Object Access Protocol (SOAP), Universal Description, Discovery and Integration (UDDI), and Web Services Description Language (WSDI)—have been developed jointly by Microsoft and IBM. Both .NET Framework and IBM WebSphere therefore adhere to the same set of standards.

The difference comes in a core design philosophy. J2EE-based offerings all are language-centric: Java is the only supported language. J2EE is supported on multiple platforms and a wide range of hardware. The cost of this versatility is the multitude of vendors, which results in a multitude of tools typically employed in a J2EE-centric development. A typical scenario would be, for example, using IBM WebSphere Studio Application Developer to build web applications and web services in conjunction with an Oracle database server. A J2EE-based development team must include members with expertise in various software development tools, each with its own architecture and development methodology.

Microsoft historically has been an underdog in the enterprise tools and servers market. Even though the latest batch of Microsoft servers, primarily Microsoft SQL Server 2000, have proven worthy of competition with established enterprise products like the Oracle 9i database server and IBM's DB2, the impression that Microsoft's server products are designed to target low-end markets still lingers.

While J2EE is centered on a single language, the .NET Framework is built on a concept of multiple languages all targeting a unified execution environment represented by CLR. Even though at the moment .NET Framework development is centered around Windows, this is not a built-in limitation. While Microsoft has not indicated what it plans for .NET beyond the Windows platform, third-party developers are already shipping development environments that claim to run .NET on other operating systems, including Linux. We might expect additional platforms to be supported when more MSIL-to-native code compilers are developed.

When it comes to developer productivity, the .NET Framework with its unified development model and single integrated development environment

(IDE) incorporating revolutionary productivity tools like Intellisense has a definite advantage. .NET and other Microsoft products tightly integrate with web services, allowing for a generic approach to a host of software development tasks.

Microsoft's competitive pricing policy of offering its server products at a fraction of the cost of analogous products from Oracle and IBM can be very attractive if your development effort is starting from scratch, without the burden of prior investment in software and hardware. The actual costs of implementation and deployment could vary widely, especially if your selected configuration involves purchasing client access licenses (CALs).

After the release of the .NET Framework, Microsoft implemented Sun's Java Pet Store blueprint J2EE application using .NET Framework and published the comparison between the two implementations. Later, Microsoft published another study comparing the process of building XML web services using .NET Framework versus IBM Websphere Studio Application Developer, and it made available a .NET versus Websphere 4.0 benchmark kit. Whitepapers, source code, and comparison tables are available at the following Microsoft site: gotdotnet.com/team/compare/.

Portal Architecture

Before we can drill down into the portal framework, we need to take a look at how an application of this kind is architected. The portal architecture is based on a classic n-tiered architecture that relies on .NET as the underlying technology. As shown in Figure 5.2, the classic n-tiered architecture includes a presentation services layer, a business services layer, a data services layer, and the database layer.

A logical architecture explicitly defines the boundaries of application processes without regard to the physical deployment of the system. Its scalability is primarily gained by enabling the distribution of an application's processing across all the available processors in a given physical environment. Logically dividing an application into well-defined tiers allows us to exercise a high degree of control over the system's performance. This modularization promotes tighter security and supports easy tailoring of the application according to the specific performance and scalability requirements of the system.

For example, if the development team learns through load testing that the heavy processing in one of the tiers is overtaxing that server's CPU, they can focus their efforts on optimizing the code for that specific tier. If the code is already fully optimized, an additional server or servers can be added to the tier to address the processing shortfall directly.

Figure 5.2 displays a sample distributed portal architecture.

The following sections discuss each of the layers that appear in the figure in more detail.

Presentation Services Layer

The presentation services layer is responsible for:

- Gathering information from the user
- Sending the user information to the business services layer for processing
- Receiving the results of the business services layer processing
- Presenting those results to the user
- Application workflow
- Module workflow
- Implementation

A Web application uses the following technologies in the presentation services layer:

- .NET Active Server Pages is a rich programming framework for building web-based applications and is the foundation of the web application. ASP.NET is part of the .NET Framework and is a compiled environment for generating HTML pages.
- Web-user controls are components used to create modular pieces of code. ASP.NET web user controls are similar to server-side include directives that were used to leverage the reuse of code modules. One main difference is that web-user controls are full-blown classes that fit into the object-oriented realm.
- Code-behind is used to provide a separation between the user interface and the programming logic necessary for the page or control. This concept separates the interface designers from the application developers and affords each with an opportunity to work on an application without interfering with each other.

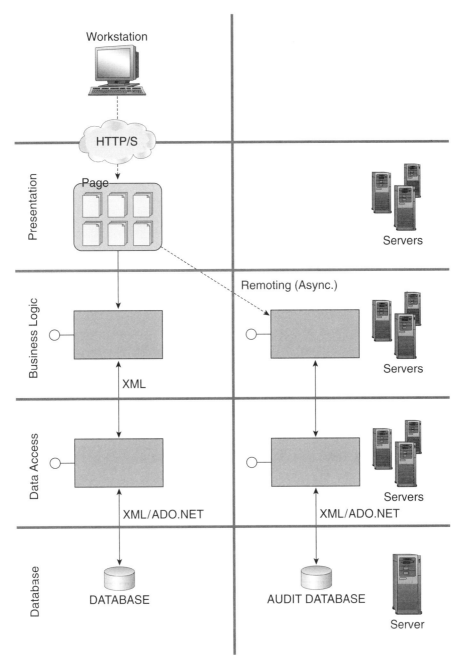

Figure 5.2 Sample Portal Architecture Diagram

- Cascading style sheets (CSS) are used for defining and using styles for elements that are used repeatedly in the application.
- Dynamic HTML (DHTML) allows a web page to change in appearance and functionality without a roundtrip to the server to refresh the page.
- Extensible markup language (XML) is a platform-neutral markup language that allows the system to exchange data in the form of structured text documents. It provides a mechanism by which the system can store data on the client, avoiding unnecessary hits to the business and data layers.
- JavaScript is an interpreted scripting language used to manipulate information on the client browser.

Inheritance is a relationship between classes in which one class is the parent class of another. Sometimes people refer to the parent class as a base class, superclass, or ancestor. When a subclass inherits from a base class, it's a "is-a-kind-of" relationship. For example, suppose we have a base class named Cat with a subclass named Lion. A Lion is-a-kind-of Cat. Inheritance is used extensively throughout the framework to create a class that reuses methods, properties, events, and variables from another class. We can create a class with some basic functionality, and then use that class as a base from which to create other, more detailed, classes. All these classes will have the same common functionality from the base class, along with new, enhanced, or even completely changed functionality.

Business Services Layer (Business Logic Layer)

The business services layer (BLL) contains the business logic for the application. This layer is stateless; meaning it does not hold any data between method calls. This design simplifies resource sharing and promotes scalability by allowing a single BLL instance to be shared by multiple presentation services.

The business services layer is responsible for:

- Receiving input from the presentation layer
- Interacting with the data services layer to send/receive information
- Sending the processed results to the presentation services layer
- Enforcing business rules

Data Services Layer (Data Access Layer)

The data services layer contains the data access logic. This layer is responsible for the storage and retrieval of data. To get optimal performance, minimal business rules are included within this tier. Moving data back and forth from the SQL Server 2000 database and the data access layer is handled through objects using ADO.NET. ADO.NET is used to make calls directly to SQL Server to run the SQL stored procedures that provide the data needed by the business logic layer.

The data services layer is responsible for:

- Receiving input from the business logic layer
- Interacting with the SQL Server database to send/receive data
- Sending the results to the business logic layer

Database

All of the local content for the portal is stored in a SQL Server database. This allows server administrators to farm the frontend of the portal across a number of servers, each pulling from a single unique data store. This section provides an overview of the database used in the portal.

The database is responsible for:

- Storing structured data
- Indexing data
- Retrieving data

Portal Framework

The need for a structured framework is not something new. Over the years, departments in many companies have been developing their own home-grown solutions to problems they encountered. They purchased off-the-shelf software to solve other problems they had. Although these applications solved most of the problems that they were intended to solve, they also introduced other problems into the workplace. The homegrown solutions became harder and harder to maintain and, with all of the independent solutions within the company, almost none of them knew how to "talk" to each other.

Many companies started implementing IT departments, and many of the smaller solutions were turned over to the IT department for continued development and maintenance. Purchasing of applications moved from a per-department basis to a company-wide basis. Nevertheless, the advent of the IT department did not solve one of the most important problems—communication between the applications. The IT departments began to see the power in consolidating many of the singleton applications into larger company-wide systems and so a new trend began. Although consolidation of these small applications was seen as a positive step in the right direction, not all applications can or should be consolidated. For off-the-shelf products and for applications that could not be included in the consolidated systems, the IT departments began to develop application integration solutions. This allowed more applications to be able to communicate with each other.

Define Portal Framework Goals

A portal in general and specifically a portal framework can be looked upon as the natural evolution of the consolidation and integration of disparate enterprise systems. One of the main goals of the portal framework is to achieve a high degree of organizational integration. Here is a more complete listing:

- *Extensibility.* During the design phase of a portal framework, extensibility is the principal goal. Allowing users to build and use individual portal modules to view, manage, and manipulate data is the basis for the extensibility of the framework.
- *Common infrastructure.* The portal framework needs to act as a common infrastructure for all of the modules that make up the portal. While each module may extract data from a different source, this common infrastructure should act as the plumbing for the portal. Users should not need to have to think about implementation of the infrastructure and should be able to focus on the design and development of the specific portal modules.
- *Security.* Security is of utmost importance within the portal and therefore the portal's framework needs to incorporate a security layer

that will deal with authentication and authorization of the end user. Authentication is the process of obtaining credential information from a user, and then validating those credentials against some sort of authority. The process ensures that users are who they say they are. Authorization is the process of validating permissions using a user's credentials and either granting or denying access to operations or resources.

■ *Authentication.* This task needs to be done at the time of initial login, while authorization can occur throughout the system, depending on user roles and the type of action that they are attempting to perform.

■ *Scalability and performance.* Without the ability to scale to the required number of users, the portal would be useless. Performance is also a factor that comes into play because a portal, or any web application, that performs poorly will produce a bad user experience and thereby discourage users from returning to the portal. The scalability and performance factors need to be taken into account from day one of the portal framework design.

Identify Framework Benefits

There are numerous benefits associated with using a portal framework. This list summarizes the benefits gained by using the portal framework:

■ *Shorter development schedule/shorter time to market:* Development projects no longer have to solve the many problems related to web applications. They simply reuse the code provided by the framework. Project developers don't have to design, develop, or test these framework services; they take them for granted.

■ *Reduced development risk.* With a complex programming model like .NET, the risk of project failure is initially high. The portal framework significantly reduces the risk by serving as a reliable proven base.

■ *Consistent application architectures:* Using a framework results in all applications having similar application architectures, which makes them easier to learn, support, and maintain.

These benefits boil down to design savings, code savings, and test savings.

Figure 5.3 shows a conceptual view of a portal page, which consists of multiple regions known as **panes**. Each pane has a specific location within the page. While some panes, like the header, footer, and navigation panes, are only intended to host a single module, all panes can contain zero or more modules. Portal modules provide the actual content of the portal and allow users to customize the portal depending on their preferences.

Define the Portal Module Object Model

Portal modules provide the actual content for the portal. The modules are ASP.NET user controls that inherit from the **ModuleControl** base class. The **ModuleControl** class provides functionality common to all modules,

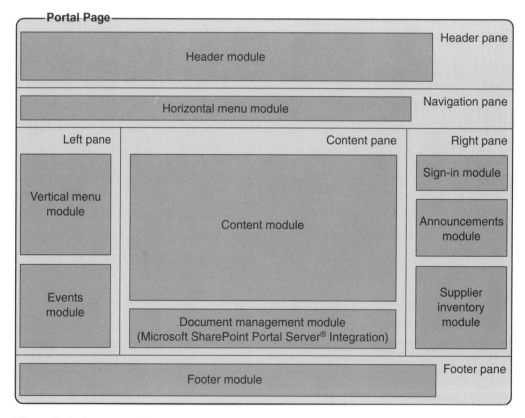

Figure 5.3 Conceptual View of a Portal Page

enforces behavior common to all modules, creates hooks necessary to control and position each **ModuleControl** from the portal page, and provides communication between the module and the underlying portal framework.

The **ModuleControl** itself inherits from the **UserControl** class that is part of the .NET Framework. While this second generation of inheritance gives the module functionality shared by all portal modules, it also gives the module all of the functionality exposed by the **UserControl** class.

Figure 5.4 shows a partial object model for the **ModuleControl** base class as well as modules that inherit from the **ModuleControl**. The portal module object model has been designed in such a way that each module type inherits the exact amount of code needed for the implementation of a control of this type. In the diagram you can see that **ModuleControl** inherits from the System.Web.UI.UserControl, which means that the **ModuleControl** is a type of UserControl.

Figure 5.5 demonstrates a potential design for a portal module. The portal page controls the modules through two interfaces implemented by each module: **IPlacement** and **ITheme**. **IPlacement interface** contains methods used by the page to position a module in a required location on the selected pane. The **ITheme interface** contains methods used to control the appearance of each module. The mode of inheritance used in this scenario is called **implementation inheritance**, which allows each module to use the default implementation of both interfaces implemented in a BaseModule control or to override the default implementation with control-specific implementation.

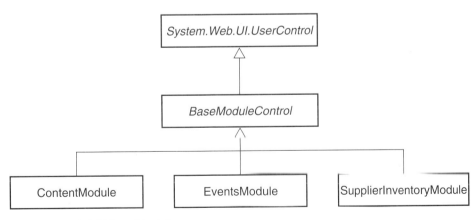

Figure 5.4 Partial Object Model

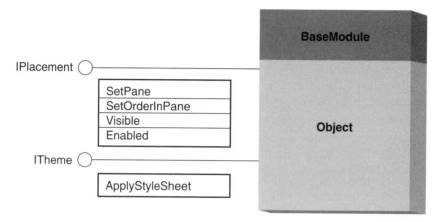

Figure 5.5 BaseModule with Interfaces

The portal framework exposes a set of objects that build on the .NET functionality and offer a set of services consumed by portal modules. The portal framework consists of the following services:

- Security
- Encryption
- Data
- SharePoint connector service
- Commerce Server Catalog connector
- BizTalk 2002 WebService connector

Figure 5.6 illustrates the relationship between portal modules, the portal framework, and .NET Framework.

Develop the Data Model

Now, after we have familiarized ourselves with the .NET Framework and with the design goals and practices of portal framework architecture, let's roll up our sleeves and develop a minimal portal framework. Our ultimate goal is to make the framework extensible, easily manageable, and dynamic. To achieve this goal, we first develop the data model for the object that will comprise the portal framework. The data model will provide necessary containers and operations to enable the creation of the dynamic page shown in Figure 5.3.

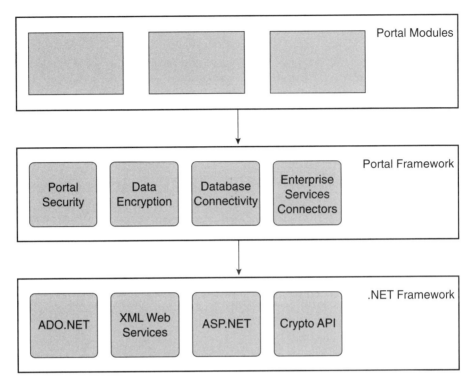

Figure 5.6 Portal Framework Layers

This section describes the tables, their use, and descriptions for each of the fields. The data structure is designed to give the framework a high degree of extensibility. In Figure 5.7, you can see the framework's data model. This diagram shows the tables that make up the data model as well as the relationships between each of the tables. The data model consists of four "nouns" that can be seen as the main entities of the framework: Page, Template, Control, and Area.

As you will see later in the chapter, a template is made up of a number of areas and each page is a specific instance of a template. A common analogy used within object-oriented design can be seen here within the data model. If you think of a template as a blueprint for a house, then a page can be seen as a finished house. In other words, a template defines the structure of the page and each page can be seen as a concrete, implemented instance of that template. Each page can contain one or more controls within each of its areas. For a visual example of the page layout, see Figure 5.3.

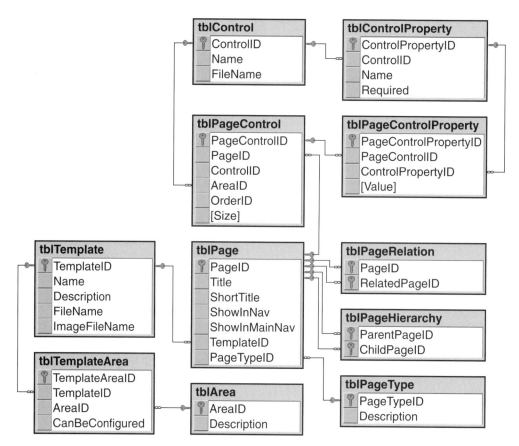

Figure 5.7 Portal Framework Data Model

Template

tblTemplate contains data that is used to define a template. The template is used to define a page layout. Table 5.1 briefly explains the data that is stored in the tblTemplate table.

Table 5.1 Structure of the tblTemplate Table

Field Name	Data Type	Description
TemplateID	Integer	Identity column for the table
Name	Alphanumeric (25)	A descriptive name for the template
Description	Alphanumeric (100)	A description of the purpose of the template
FileName	Alphanumeric (100)	The fully qualified filename of the template file (ASPX file)
ImageFileName	Alphanumeric (100)	The fully qualified filename of a graphic image that will be used to display what the template will look like

Area

tblArea contains data that is used to describe an area, which is a section of page used to hold one or more controls. Table 5.2 briefly describes the data that is stored in the tblArea table.

Table 5.2 Structure of the tblArea Table

Field Name	Data Type	Description
AreaID	Integer	Identity column for the table
Description	Alphanumeric (100)	A description of the area

Template Areas

tblTemplateArea contains data that is used to define the relationships between a template and an area. A collection of template-area records, grouped by a single template identifier, defines the areas that make up a single template. Table 5.3 briefly explains the data that is stored in the tblTemplateArea table.

Table 5.3 Structure of the tblTemplateArea Table

Field Name	Data Type	Description
TemplateAreaID	Integer	Identity column for the table
TemplateID	Integer	A template identifier—this is a reference to the template that will contain the area
AreaID	Integer	An area identifier
CanBeConfigured	Bit	Flag used to denote if the template area configuration can be over-ridden within a page

Page

tblPage contains data that is used to define each page within the portal. The page table is the central table of the data model. Table 5.4 briefly explains the data that is stored in the tblPage table.

Table 5.4 Structure of the tblPage table

Field Name	Data Type	Description
PageID	Integer	Identity column for the table
Title	Alphanumeric (255)	A descriptive title for the page
ShortTitle	Alphanumeric (100)	A shortened version of the page title; this data is used in various situations in which screen real estate is expensive

Table 5.4 Structure of the tblPage table (*Continued*)

Field Name	Data Type	Description
ShowInNav	Boolean	A Boolean used to indicate whether this page should be shown within any of the navigation mechanisms
ShowInMainNav	Boolean	A Boolean used to indicate whether this page should be shown within the main navigation mechanism
TemplateID	Integer	A template identifier; this is a reference to the template that defines this page
PageTypeID	Integer	A page type identifier; this is a reference to the page type that specifies what type of page this is

Page Type

tblPageType contains data that is used to define each page within the portal. The page table is the central table of the data model. Table 5.5 briefly explains the data that is stored in the tblPage table.

Table 5.5 Structure of the tblPageType Table

Field Name	Data Type	Description
PageTypeID	Integer	Identity column for the table
Description	Alphanumeric (50)	A description of the page type
		The page types that can exist within the portal are:
		■ Portal page
		■ External page (a page belonging to an external application or web site)
		■ External page–new browser (this is similar to an external page, but the page is opened in a separate browser window)

Page Relations

tblPageRelation contains data that is used to define relationships between pages. By maintaining relationship information, the framework can expose functionality that will provide dynamic links between these pages, thus allowing the end users to navigate between them.

The extraction of data from this table should take into account that relationships between pages are bidirectional; therefore, there should not be a need to store links in both directions for each of the pages in question. Table 5.6 briefly explains the data that is stored in the tblPageRelation table.

Table 5.6 Structure of the tblPageRelation Table

Field Name	Data Type	Description
PageID	Integer	Identity of the page
RelatedPageID	Integer	Identity of the related page

Page Hierarchy

tblPageHeirarchy contains data that is used to define the hierarchy of pages within the portal. The navigation within the portal is generated by recursively "walking" the page hierarchy programmatically and thus building a site map. Table 5.7 briefly explains the data that is stored in the tblPage-Hierarchy table.

Table 5.7 Structure of the tblPageHierarchy Table

Field Name	Data Type	Description
ParentPageID	Integer	Identity of the parent page
ChildPageID	Integer	Identity of the child page

Control

tblControl contains data that is used to describe controls, which are modular pieces of code that are used to define a specific set of functionality. A control can be placed into any of the areas on one or more pages. Table 5.8 briefly explains the data that is stored in the tblControl table.

Table 5.8 Structure of the tblControl Table

Field Name	Data Type	Description
TemplateID	Integer	Identity column for the table
Name	Alphanumeric (25)	A descriptive name for the control
FileName	Alphanumeric (100)	The fully qualified filename of the control file (ASCX file)

Page Controls

tblPageControl contains data that is used to describe the relationship between a page and a control. The page-control relationship defines more than just the appearance of a control on a page; it also defines the location of the control and how it should appear in that location.

A collection of page-control records, grouped by a single page identifier, defines the controls that will appear on a single page. Table 5.9 briefly explains the data that is stored in the tblPageControl table.

Table 5.9 Structure of the tblPageControl Table

Field Name	Data Type	Description
PageControlID	Integer	Identity column for the table
PageID	Integer	A page identifier; this is a reference to the page being defined
ControlID	Integer	A control identifier; this is a reference to the control being defined
AreaID	Integer	An area identifier; this is a reference to the area in which the control will be placed
OrderID	Integer	The order in which the control will be placed within the area, used for instances in which more than one control will be placed in the same area
Size	Integer	An optional value used to indicate the requested maximum height for the control

Control Properties

tblControlProperty contains data that is used to describe a property that will be exposed by a control. Control properties are used to dynamically configure a control. By describing each of a control's exposed properties, the framework can change the properties based on the specific instance of a control. Table 5.10 briefly explains the data that is stored in the tblControl-Property table.

Table 5.10 Structure of the tblControlProperty Table

Field Name	Data Type	Description
ContolPropertyID	Integer	Identity column for the table
ControlID	Integer	A control identifier; this is a reference to the control to which this property belongs
Name	Alphanumeric (100)	A descriptive name for the property
Required	Bit	A Boolean field used to indicate whether the specific property must have a corresponding value for each instance of the control

Page Control Properties

tblPageControlProperty contains data that is used to define a control property's value. A single page-control-property specifies the value of a property for an instance of a control property where it appears on a specific page. Table 5.11 briefly explains the data that is stored in the tblPageControl-Property table.

Table 5.11 Structure of the tblPageControlProperty Table

Field Name	Data Type	Description
ContolPropertyID	Integer	Identity column for the table
ControlID	Integer	The identifier of the control to which this property belongs
ContolPropertyID	Integer	A control property identifier; this is a reference to the control property whose value is being set by this record
Value	Alphanumeric (255)	The value for the specified control property

Create SQL Server Stored Procedures

With the data model in place, we can now proceed to defining the data retrieval operations. We create SQL Server stored procedures to retrieve the information necessary to display the hierarchy within a site and to create a page based on a page template and sets of controls contained within its panes.

SQL Server stored procedures represent a compiled SQL code stored within the SQL Server. Stored procedures offer the benefits of additional speed, security and code encapsulation, and reuse, and they are always preferable to the inline SQL statements.

The first stored procedure retrieves the information about the page. Because each page is a specialized page template, we return the template and template area information in this stored procedure as well.

Listing 5.1 Complete Code Listing for the Stored Procedure Page Data

```
/*
 Purpose:  Stored procedure for retrieving portal page data
 Inputs:   @PageID - numeric ID of the page for which the data is _
           retrieved
*/

Create  PROCEDURE spFetchPageInformation
   @PageID INT
 AS

SET NOCOUNT ON

Select P.PageID, P.Title, P.ShortTitle,
       P.ShowInNav, P.ShowInMainNav,
       P.TemplateID, P.PageTypeID,
       PT.Description as PageTypeDescription,
       T.Name as TemplateName,
       T.Description as TemplateDescription,
       T.FileName, T.ImageFileName
FROM      tblPage P
       INNER JOIN tblPageType PT
          ON P.PageTypeID = PT.PageTypeID
       INNER JOIN tblTemplate T
          ON P.TemplateID = T.TemplateID
WHERE
   P.PageID = @PageID

RETURN @@ERROR

SET NOCOUNT OFF
```

With the stored procedure in Listing 5.1, we can now retrieve the page information. The next stored procedure tells us which controls to load into each pane defined for the page. Because we are allowing each control to persist its properties in a table in SQL Server, the same stored procedure retrieves the list of properties for each control and the list of values set for these properties (if any) as well.

Listing 5.2 Complete Code Listing for the Stored Procedure Retrieving Control Data for All Controls Within a Page

```
/*
 Purpose:  Stored procedure for retrieving control data for all _
           controls within a page
 Inputs: @PageID - numeric ID of the page for which the data is _
         retrieved
         @ControlID - ID of the control whose information we retrieve
*/
CREATE    PROCEDURE spFetchPageControlInformation
    @PageID INT,
    @ControlID INT = NULL
 AS

SET NOCOUNT ON

SELECT  PC.PageControlID, PC.PageID, PC.ControlID,
    PC.AreaID, PC.OrderID, PC.[Size],
    C.[Name] as ControlName, C.[FileName]
FROM    tblPageControl PC
    INNER JOIN tblControl C
        ON PC.ControlID = C.ControlID
WHERE
    PC.PageID = @PageID
    AND PC.ControlID = CASE WHEN IsNull(@ControlID, 0) = 0
                THEN PC.ControlID
                ELSE @ControlID
                END
ORDER BY
    PC.AreaID, PC.OrderID

RETURN @@ERROR

SET NOCOUNT OFF
```

The last stored procedure required for our framework implementation retrieves values for all control properties saved in the database based on the PageControlID parameter.

Listing 5.3 Complete Code Listing for the Stored Procedure Retrieving Control Data for All Controls Within a Page

```
/*
 Purpose:  Stored procedure for retrieving the properties, stored in _
           the database, for a specific instance of a control within a _
           page.
 Inputs:   @ControlID - ID of the control whose information we retrieve
*/
CREATE    PROCEDURE spFetchControlProperties
    @PageControlID INT
 AS

SET NOCOUNT ON

SELECT
    CP.ControlPropertyID,
    CP.[Name] as ControlPropertyName, CP.Required,
    PCP.Value
FROM   tblPageControl PC
   INNER JOIN tblControlProperty CP
      ON PC.ControlID = CP.ControlID
   INNER JOIN tblPageControlProperty PCP
      ON PC.PageControlID = PCP.PageControlID
         and CP.ControlPropertyID = PCP.ControlPropertyID
WHERE
   PC.PageControlID = @PageControlID
ORDER BY
   CP.[Name]

RETURN @@ERROR

SET NOCOUNT OFF
```

Create Code for Minimal Portal Framework

Armed with these stored procedures, we can finally start creating the code for the minimal portal framework. In this example, we omit such advanced portal features as authentication, maintenance of user profiles, personalization, and advanced caching techniques.

Here are the steps:

1. Open Visual Studio .NET and create a Visual Basic web project called **PortalFramework**. Visual Studio creates a project and adds a new blank page to the project.
2. Rename the page **TemplatePage.aspx**. This page will serve as our main framework template page.
3. With the page opened in design mode, add a few HTML elements to the page. Provide container areas for left, right, top, and bottom portions of the page according to the layout shown in Figure 5.3. For the purposes of this example, we use an HTML table to break our portal page in the required area. Listing 5.4 shows the HTML for the prototype portal page.

Listing 5.4 HTML for the Portal Page Showing Portal Page Panes and Navigation Control Placement

```
<%@ Page Language="vb" AutoEventWireup="false"
Codebehind="TemplatePage.aspx.vb"
    Inherits="PF.TemplatePage"%>
<HTML>
  <HEAD>
    <TITLE id="PageTitle" runat="server">
      Portal Framework Template Page
    </TITLE>
    <LINK href="Portal.css" type="text/css" rel="stylesheet">
  </HEAD>
  <BODY style="margin:1px">
    <FORM id="Form1" method="post" runat="server">
      <TABLE width="800" cellspacing="0" cellpadding="0" border="0">
        <TR valign="top">
          <TD id="TopPane" visible="False" runat="server" align="center">
          </TD>
        </TR>
        <TR valign="top" height="20">
          <TD id="NavPane" visible="False" runat="server">
          </TD>
        </TR>
```

Continues

Listing 5.4 HTML for the Portal Page Showing Portal Page Panes and Navigation Control Placement (*Continued*)

```
<TR>
  <TD>
    <TABLE width="100%" cellspacing="0" cellpadding="4" _
    border="0">
      <TR height="*" valign="top">
        <TD id="LeftPane" Visible="false" Width="150" _
        runat="server">
        </TD>
        <TD id="ContentPane" Visible="false" Width="*" _
        runat="server">
        </TD>
        <TD id="RightPane" Visible="false" Width="150" _
        runat="server">
        </TD>
      </TR>
    </TABLE>
  </TD>
</TR>
<TR>
  <TD id="BottomPane" visible="False" runat="server" _
  align="center">
  </TD>
</TR>
</TABLE>
</FORM>
</BODY>
</HTML>
```

The page consists of the HTML table containing four user controls: header, top breadcrumb menu control, left menu control, and the footer control. These standard controls will be used to display site navigation, page information, and general site information. If you were to try to run the solution, now it would fail because we have included forward declarations for our standard controls but have not defined the controls themselves.

The next step is to create four standard controls:

1. Using Visual Studio Solution Explorer, right-click your solution and select **Add New Folder** from the popup menu.
2. Name the new folder **Controls**. All our user controls will be grouped together in this folder.

3. To create the header control, right-click the Controls folder and select **Add Web User Control** from the popup menu.
4. Name the new control **ctrlHeader.ascx**. Visual Studio creates a control and opens it in design mode.
5. Add the ASP.NET Label control with the ID of **Header** and the text **Basic Portal Framework Demonstration** in the design area.
6. Repeat this process three more times to create the breadcrumb, left menu, and footer controls. Name them, respectively, **ctrlBreadcrumb.ascx**, **ctrlMenu.ascx**, and **ctrlFooter.ascx**.
7. Set the text of the label of the footer control to **Building Portals with .NET_Basic Portal Framework Demonstration**.

We will use these four controls on the majority of the portal pages. To make a page dynamic, we will need to complete these steps:

1. Store the database connection information in the Web.config file.
2. Create a base page object; make it responsible for retrieving page-level information, and inherit all portal pages from the base page.
3. Create a base control object and derive all portal user controls from the base control. The base control will be responsible for the common operations such as reading control properties during the base control's Load event.
4. Implement code in the menu and breadcrumb controls to display, respectively, the site menu and the current breadcrumb trail.
5. Add code to the Page Load event of the portal page. In this code, call the stored procedure **spFetchPageInformation**, which indicates which controls should be loaded into the page and which areas on the page should contain these controls.
6. Enter template and page information in SQL Server tables.
7. Create a generic content control and configure control-related data in SQL Server tables.

Store and Read the Database Connection Information

We need to keep the database connection string in a safe but easily reachable place. One good option is to store it in the Web.config file. Let's add the entry shown in Listing 5.5 to the Web.config file:

Listing 5.5 Storing the Database Connection String in the Web.config File

```
<appSettings>
      <add key="ConnectionString" value="Persist Security _
      Info=True;User ID=sa;Password=password;Initial _
      Catalog=Northwind;Data Source=."/>
<appSettings>
```

Note that you will have to modify the connection string to specify a valid user for your database.

Create the Base Page Object

To create this object:

1. Create a new ASP.NET page and name it **BasePage.aspx**.
2. Add the function shown in Listing 5.6 to the code-behind module of the base page.

Listing 5.6 Executing Stored Procedure in Base Page Object

```
' GetDataTable() function executes a stored procedure
' and returns a first ADO.NET DataTable object from the
' resulting DataSet
Protected Function GetDataTable(ByVal StoredProcName As String, _
                       ByVal ParamName As String, _
                       ByVal ParamValue As Integer) As DataTable
    Dim ds As DataSet, dt As DataTable
    Dim SQLParams(1) As SqlClient.SqlParameter
    Dim strConn As String = AppSettings("ConnectionString")
    Try
        SQLParams(0) = New SqlClient.SqlParameter("@ReturnValue", 0)
        SQLParams(0).DbType = DbType.Int32
        SQLParams(0).Direction = ParameterDirection.ReturnValue
        SQLParams(1) = New SqlClient.SqlParameter("@" & ParamName, _
                 ParamValue)

        ds = SqlHelper.ExecuteDataset(strConn, _
            CommandType.StoredProcedure, StoredProcName, SQLParams)
        If ds.Tables.Count > 0 Then dt = ds.Tables(0)
    Catch ex As Exception
        System.Diagnostics.Debug.Write(ex.ToString)
```

```
        Finally
            ds = Nothing
        End Try
        Return dt
    End Function
```

This function will be used by all derived template pages to run stored procedures in order to retrieve page-level data. The function uses ADO.NET objects to execute the stored procedure and return the result as the **DataTable** object.

3. Change the definition of the template page by modifying its Inherits statement to read: **Inherits BasePage**. Now all functionality of the base page object will be available to the derived template object.

Create the Base Control Object and Derive All User Controls from the Base Control

Complete these steps:

1. Add a user control to the Controls folder.
2. Name the new control **BaseControl.ascx**.
3. Add the code shown in Listing 5.7 to the code-behind module of the base control:

Listing 5.7 Root Object for the User Controls Hierarchy. BaseControl.ascx

```
    Inherits System.Web.UI.UserControl

    Protected _PageControlID As Integer = 0
    Protected _dtProperties As DataTable

    Public Property PageControlID() As Integer
        Get
            Return _PageControlID
        End Get
        Set(ByVal Value As Integer)
            _PageControlID = Value
        End Set
    End Property
```

Continues

Listing 5.7 Root Object for the User Controls Hierarchy. BaseControl.ascx (*Continued*)

```
' Load the values of the control properties during the Page Load _
event
Private Sub Page_Load(ByVal sender As System.Object, ByVal e As _
        System.EventArgs) Handles MyBase.Load
    Try
        _dtProperties = GetControlProperties()
    Catch ex As Exception
        Debug.WriteLine(ex.Message)
    End Try
End Sub

' Executes a stored procedure which loads all propeties
' for the given control and the given page.
' Returns the properties as ADO.NET DataTable
Protected Function GetControlProperties() As DataTable
    Dim ds As DataSet, dt As DataTable
    Dim SQLParams(1) As SqlClient.SqlParameter
    Dim strConn As String = AppSettings("ConnectionString")
    Try
        SQLParams(0) = New SqlClient.SqlParameter("@ReturnValue", 0)
        SQLParams(0).DbType = DbType.Int32
        SQLParams(0).Direction = ParameterDirection.ReturnValue
        SQLParams(1) = New SqlClient.SqlParameter("@PageControlID", _
                _PageControlID)

        ds = SqlHelper.ExecuteDataset(strConn, _
            CommandType.StoredProcedure, _
            "spFetchControlProperties", _
            SQLParams)
        If ds.Tables.Count > 0 AndAlso _
            ds.Tables(0).Rows.Count > 0 Then dt = ds.Tables(0)
    Catch ex As Exception
        System.Diagnostics.Debug.Write(ex.ToString)
    Finally
        ds = Nothing
    End Try
    Return dt
End Function
```

First, we defined two member variables, **_PageControlID** and **_dtProperties**, to hold, respectively, the ID of this control as it appears on the current page and the ADO.NET **DataTable** object to hold all properties for the current control. Next we defined a public property, **PageControlID**, which will be used by the parent page to set the page control ID value for the given control. And finally we created a function, **GetControlProperties**(), executed during the Page Load event of the base control. This function uses a stored procedure to query the database for the values of all properties defined for the current control.

4. Now modify the definitions for all four standard controls to make them children of the base control. Open the code-behind modules for the menu, breadcrumb, header, and footer controls and replace the **Inherits System.Web.UI.UserControl** line with a **Inherits BaseControl** line. The new barebones code-behind for the header control should now look like that in Listing 5.8:

Listing 5.8 Header User Control Deriving from the Base Control. ctrlHeader.ascx

```
Public MustInherit Class ctrlHeader
    Inherits BaseControl

    Private Sub Page_Load(ByVal sender As System.Object, ByVal e As _
    System.EventArgs) Handles MyBase.Load
        'Put user code to initialize the page here
    End Sub
End Class
```

Implement Breadcrumb and Menu Controls

Easy and convenient navigation is one of the primary objectives of a good portal. Our portal framework will provide two means of navigation: using the site menu displayed on the left side of the page and implemented in the menu control and the breadcrumb trail implemented in the breadcrumb control that shows the user the path traversed to the current page from the top page of the site.

The data for the menu control will be generated in XML format by the SQL Server stored procedure and pushed to the Load event of the menu control, where it will be transformed into the HTML format suitable for the display on a page using an XSL style sheet. Due to space limitations, it is impossible to discuss here in detail the usage of XML and XSL with SQL Server and .NET Framework. Refer to the MSDN site for extensive documentation and code samples for these technologies at http://msdn.microsoft.com.

1. Create the stored procedure shown in Listing 5.9 to read the site menu information:

Listing 5.9 Site Menu Stored Procedure. spFetchMenu.sql

```
CREATE   PROCEDURE spFetchMenu
   @ROOTPAGEID int = 1,
   @PAGEID int = 2
 AS

SET NOCOUNT ON

   Select          ROOT.PageID
      ,PAGE.PageID
      ,PAGE.Title
      ,PAGE.ShortTitle
      ,PAGE.URL
      ,CASE WHEN PAGE.PageID = @PageID THEN 1 ELSE 0 END as _
      PAGESELECTED
      ,SUBPAGE.PageID
      ,SUBPAGE.Title
      ,SUBPAGE.ShortTitle
      ,SUBPAGE.URL
      ,CASE WHEN SUBPAGE.PageID = @PageID THEN 1 ELSE 0 END as _
      SUBPAGESELECTED
   From vwPages ROOT
      LEFT OUTER JOIN vwPages PAGE
         ON PAGE.ParentPageID = ROOT.PageID
      LEFT OUTER JOIN vwPages SUBPAGE
         ON SUBPAGE.ParentPageID = PAGE.PageID
   WHERE ROOT.PageID = @ROOTPAGEID
      AND PAGE.ShowInMainNav = 1
      AND SUBPAGE.ShowInMainNav = 1
   FOR XML AUTO

RETURN @@ERROR

SET NOCOUNT OFF
```

The **spFetchMenu** stored procedure uses the FOR XML AUTO clause to produce the output in the form of the XML document. Refer to the Microsoft SQL Server documentation for the detailed explanation of this feature.

2. Implement the **Page_Load** event handler of the control responsible for the creation of the portal menu. Listing 5.10 shows how the menu control uses the stored procedure **spFetchMenu** to build and display the portal menu. The stored procedure is being called during the Load event of the control using a .NET XMLReader object.

Listing 5.10 Page Load Event of the Menu User

```
Private Sub Page_Load(ByVal sender As System.Object, _
                      ByVal e As System.EventArgs) Handles _
                      MyBase.Load
 Dim strXMLMainMenuInfo As String = ""
 Dim strHTMLMainMenuInfo As String = ""
 Dim m_ConnectionString As String

 '-- RECEIVE THE PAGE ID
 If Not Request.Params("PageID") Is Nothing Then _
         _PageID = Int32.Parse(Request.Params("PageID"))

 Dim CacheKey As String = "MainMenuInfo_" & _PageID.ToString

 Dim sbXML As New System.Text.StringBuilder("")
 Dim xrReader As System.Xml.XmlReader

 Dim oStringWriter As New System.IO.StringWriter
 Dim oXMLDoc As New System.Xml.XmlDocument
 Dim oXslTransform As New System.Xml.Xsl.XslTransform

 strHTMLMainMenuInfo = Cache.Item(CacheKey)

 If strHTMLMainMenuInfo Is Nothing OrElse _
 strHTMLMainMenuInfo.Length = 0 Then
   Try
     '-- GET THE CONNECTION STRING
     m_ConnectionString = ConfigurationSettings.AppSettings _
     ("ConnectionString")
     Dim con As New SqlClient.SqlConnection(m_ConnectionString)

     '   PACKAGE PARAMETERS
     Dim Params(1) As SqlClient.SqlParameter
     Params(0) = New SqlClient.SqlParameter("@RootPageID", 1)
     Params(0).DbType = DbType.Int32
```

Continues

Listing 5.10 Page Load Event of the Menu User (*Continued*)

```
    Params(1) = New SqlClient.SqlParameter("@PageID", _PageID)
    Params(1).DbType = DbType.Int32

    Try
      '-- FETCH THE DATA FROM THE DATABASE
      con.Open()
      xrReader = SqlHelper.ExecuteXmlReader(con, _
               CommandType.StoredProcedure, "spFetchMenu", _
               Params)
      ' READ THE CONTENTS OF XML READER
      xrReader.MoveToContent()
      While Not xrReader.EOF
         sbXML.Append(xrReader.ReadOuterXml & vbCrLf)
      End While
       strXMLMainMenuInfo = sbXML.ToString
       xrReader.Close()
       con.Close()
    Catch ex1 As Exception
      System.Diagnostics.Debug.WriteLine(ex1.ToString)
      Throw New Exception(ex1.Message)
    Finally
      xrReader = Nothing
      con = Nothing
      sbXML = Nothing
    End Try
     oXMLDoc.LoadXml(strXMLMainMenuInfo)
     oXslTransform.Load(Server.MapPath("~/Controls/xslMenu.xsl"))
     oXslTransform.Transform(oXMLDoc, Nothing, oStringWriter, _
     Nothing)

     strHTMLMainMenuInfo = oStringWriter.ToString

     Page.Cache.Add(CacheKey, strHTMLMainMenuInfo, Nothing, _
                  DateTime.MaxValue, TimeSpan.FromMinutes(60), _
                  Caching.CacheItemPriority.High, Nothing)
    Catch ex As Exception
      'HANDLE ERROR
    Finally
      oStringWriter = Nothing
      oXMLDoc = Nothing
      oXslTransform = Nothing
    End Try
  End If
```

```
    If strHTMLMainMenuInfo.Length > 0 Then
      ctrlLiteral.Text = strHTMLMainMenuInfo
    Else
      ctrlLiteral.Text = "An error occurred while attempting to _
      retrieve the Main Menu"
    End If

End Sub
```

As you can see in Listing 5.10, because the **Menu** control data is retrieved from the database in XML format, it needs to be transformed into HTML. Once this step is complete, the data is cached for subsequent requests using the ASP.NET cache object. This reduces the processing time when additional requests are made to the same page.

3. Create an XSL file used to transform the data returned from the SQL Server into the HTML required to render the actual menu. Detailed explanation of XSL is beyond the scope of this chapter. Listing 5.11 demonstrates the finished XSL file used to transform the Menu data.

Listing 5.11 XSL File Used to Transform the Menu from Raw XML into HTML

```
<?xml version="1.0" ?>
<xsl:stylesheet xmlns:xsl="http://www.w3.org/1999/XSL/Transform" _
version="1.0">
  <xsl:output method="html" indent="yes" />
  <xsl:template match="PAGE">
    <xsl:choose>
        <xsl:when test="@PAGESELECTED='1'">
          <DIV class="SelectedPage">
            <B><xsl:value-of select="@Title" /></B>
          </DIV>
        </xsl:when>
        <xsl:otherwise>
          <DIV class="NonSelectedPage">
              <A class="MenuItem">
                <xsl:attribute name="href">
                  <xsl:value-of select="@URL" />
                  ?PAGEID=<xsl:value-of select="@PageID" />
                </xsl:attribute>
```

Continues

Listing 5.11 XSL File Used to Transform the Menu from Raw XML into HTML (*Continued*)

```
                <xsl:value-of select="@Title" />
                <xsl:attribute name="alt">
                  Go to the "<xsl:value-of select="@Title" />" page
                </xsl:attribute>
                <xsl:choose>
                  <xsl:when test="@Target">
                    <xsl:attribute name="target">_Blank</xsl:attribute>
                  </xsl:when>
                </xsl:choose>
              </A>
            </DIV>
          </xsl:otherwise>
        </xsl:choose>
        <xsl:apply-templates select="./SUBPAGE" />
  </xsl:template>

  <xsl:template match="SUBPAGE">
    <xsl:choose>
        <xsl:when test="@SUBPAGESELECTED='1'">
          <DIV class="SelectedPage">
            <B>  <xsl:value-of select="@Title" /></B>
          </DIV>
        </xsl:when>
        <xsl:otherwise>
          <DIV class="NonSelectedPage">
                <A class="MenuItem">
                <xsl:attribute name="href">
                  <xsl:value-of select="@URL" />
                  ?PAGEID=<xsl:value-of select="@PageID" />
                </xsl:attribute>
                <xsl:value-of select="@Title" />
                <xsl:attribute name="alt">
                  Go to the "<xsl:value-of select="@Title" />" page
                </xsl:attribute>
                <xsl:choose>
                  <xsl:when test="@Target">
                    <xsl:attribute name="target">_Blank</xsl:attribute>
                  </xsl:when>
                </xsl:choose>
              </A>
          </DIV>
        </xsl:otherwise>
      </xsl:choose>
  </xsl:template>
</xsl:stylesheet>
```

4. Next we will create the functionality needed to produce the bread-crumb trail user control to enable the display of the breadcrumb trail navigation bar. Create the stored procedure shown in Listing 5.12 to read the page hierarchy data and create the navigation path from the database.

Listing 5.12 Breadcrumb Trail Stored Procedure. spFetchBreadCrumbTrail.sql

```
CREATE PROCEDURE spFetchBreadcrumbTrail
   @PageID int
 AS

SET NOCOUNT ON

DECLARE  @tmpPages TABLE
   (
     [Order]        int,
     [PageID]       int,
     [ParentPageID]        int,
     [Title]        nvarchar(255),
     [ShortTitle]   nvarchar(100),
     [URL]                  varchar(150) ,
     [Selected]     bit
   )

DECLARE @Order int
SET @Order = 1

DECLARE @Title          nvarchar(255)
DECLARE @ShortTitle     nvarchar(100)
DECLARE @URL            nvarchar(150)
DECLARE @ParentPageID   int
DECLARE @CurrentPageID  int
DECLARE @PageType  int
DECLARE @PageEntity     nvarchar(300)
DECLARE @ParentFound    bit


INSERT INTO @tmpPages
Select 1, PageID, ParentPageID, Title, ShortTitle, URL, 1
FROM   vwPages WHERE  PageID - @PageID

Select @ParentPageID = ISNULL(ParentPageID,0) from vwPages where _
PageID = @PageID and ShowInNav = 1
```

Continues

Listing 5.12 Breadcrumb Trail Stored Procedure. spFetchBreadCrumbTrail.sql
    (*Continued*)

```
WHILE (@ParentPageID <> 0)
    BEGIN
    Set @Order = @Order + 1
    INSERT INTO @tmpPages
    SELECT @Order, PageID, ParentPageID, Title, ShortTitle, URL, 0
        FROM vwPages WHERE PageID = @ParentPageID and ShowInNav = 1

    Set @CurrentPageID = @ParentPageID
    Set @ParentPageID = 0
    Select @ParentPageID = ISNULL(ParentPageID,0)
        FROM vwPages WHERE PageID = @CurrentPageID and ShowInNav = 1
    END

SELECT PageID, Title, ShortTitle, URL, Selected
FROM @tmpPages PAGE ORDER BY [Order] DESC FOR XML AUTO

RETURN @@ERROR

SET NOCOUNT OFF
```

5. Implement the code consuming the breadcrumb data retrieved by the stored procedure. The code for the **Page Load** event of the breadcrumb control displayed in Listing 5.13 is similar to the Page Load event of the Menu control. The data, in XML format, is being loaded from the database using the **spFetchBreadCrumbTrail** stored procedure. When the data received from the SQL Server is loaded into the XML document, XSL (extensible stylesheet language) transformation is applied using the style sheet stored in the file xslBreadCrumbTrail.xsl. To optimize server load and execution time, the breadcrumb trail XML data is loaded into the .NET cache object.

Listing 5.13 Breadcrumb Trail User Control

```
Private Sub Page_Load(ByVal sender As System.Object, _
                    ByVal e As System.EventArgs) Handles MyBase.Load
    Dim strXMLBreadCrumbTrailInfo As String = ""
    Dim strHTMLBreadCrumbTrailInfo As String = ""
    Dim m_ConnectionString As String
```

```
'-- RECEIVE THE PAGE ID
If Not Request.Params("PAGEID") Is Nothing Then _
        _PageID = Int32.Parse(Request.Params("PAGEID"))

Dim CacheKey As String = "BreadCrumbTrailInfo_" & _PageID.ToString

Dim sbXML As New System.Text.StringBuilder("<ROOT>")
Dim xrReader As System.Xml.XmlReader

Dim oStringWriter As New System.IO.StringWriter
Dim oXMLDoc As New System.Xml.XmlDocument
Dim oXslTransform As New System.Xml.Xsl.XslTransform

strHTMLBreadCrumbTrailInfo = Cache.Item(CacheKey)

If strHTMLBreadCrumbTrailInfo Is Nothing _
    OrElse strHTMLBreadCrumbTrailInfo.Length = 0 Then
  Try
    '-- GET THE CONNECTION STRING
    m_ConnectionString = ConfigurationSettings.AppSettings _
    ("ConnectionString")
    Dim con As New SqlClient.SqlConnection(m_ConnectionString)

    '-- PACKAGE PARAMETERS
    Dim Params(0) As SqlClient.SqlParameter
    Params(0) = New SqlClient.SqlParameter("@PageID", _PageID)
    Params(0).DbType = DbType.Int32

    Try
      '-- FETCH THE DATA FROM THE DATABASE
      con.Open()
      xrReader = SqlHelper.ExecuteXmlReader(con, _
      CommandType.StoredProcedure, _
              "spFetchBreadCrumbTrail", Params)
      ' READ THE CONTENTS OF XML READER
      xrReader.MoveToContent()
      While Not xrReader.EOF
        sbXML.Append(xrReader.ReadOuterXml & vbCrLf)
      End While
      sbXML.Append("</ROOT>")
      strXMLBreadCrumbTrailInfo = sbXML.ToString
      xrReader.Close()
      con.Close()
```

Continues

Listing 5.13 Breadcrumb Trail User Control (*Continued*)

```
        Catch ex1 As Exception
          System.Diagnostics.Debug.WriteLine(ex1.ToString)
          Throw New Exception(ex1.Message)
        Finally
          xrReader = Nothing
          con = Nothing
          sbXML = Nothing
        End Try
        oXMLDoc.LoadXml(strXMLBreadCrumbTrailInfo)
        oXslTransform.Load(Server.MapPath("~/Controls/ _
        xslBreadCrumbTrail.xsl"))
        oXslTransform.Transform(oXMLDoc, Nothing, oStringWriter, _
        Nothing)

        strHTMLBreadCrumbTrailInfo = oStringWriter.ToString

        Page.Cache.Add(CacheKey, strHTMLBreadCrumbTrailInfo, Nothing, _
                       DateTime.MaxValue, TimeSpan.FromMinutes(60),  _
                       Caching.CacheItemPriority.High, Nothing)
      Catch ex As Exception
        'HANDLE ERROR
      Finally
        oStringWriter = Nothing
        oXMLDoc = Nothing
        oXslTransform = Nothing
      End Try
    End If

    If strHTMLBreadCrumbTrailInfo.Length > 0 Then
      ctrlLiteral.Text = strHTMLBreadCrumbTrailInfo
    Else
      ctrlLiteral.Text = "An error occurred while attempting to _
      retrieve the Bread Crumb Trail"
    End If

  End Sub
```

      6. Use the XSL transformation to create HTML presentation code from the data retrieved from the SQL Server. Listing 5.14 demonstrates an XSL file used to transform the breadcrumb data.

Listing 5.14 XSL File Used to Transform the Breadcrumb Trail from Raw XML
into HTML

```
<?xml version="1.0" ?>
<xsl:stylesheet xmlns:xsl="http://www.w3.org/1999/XSL/Transform" _
version="1.0">
  <xsl:output method="html" indent="yes" />
  <xsl:template match="PAGE">
    <xsl:choose>
        <xsl:when test="@Selected='1'">
            <SPAN class="SelectedPage"><xsl:value-of select="@Title" _
            /></SPAN>
        </xsl:when>
        <xsl:otherwise>
            <SPAN class="NonSelectedPage">
              <A>
                <xsl:attribute name="href">
                  <xsl:value-of select="@URL" />
                  ?PAGEID=<xsl:value-of select="@PageID" />
                </xsl:attribute>
                <xsl:value-of select="@Title" />
                <xsl:attribute name="alt">
                  Go to the "<xsl:value-of select="@Title" />" page
                </xsl:attribute>
              </A> >
            </SPAN>
        </xsl:otherwise>
    </xsl:choose>
    <xsl:apply-templates select="./PAGE" />
  </xsl:template>
</xsl:stylesheet>
```

Dynamically Load User Controls

Notice that our template page is blank; it does not contain any design-time
controls. We will load controls dynamically during the template page's Page
Load event by querying the database for the list of all controls belonging to
the current page and the area into which the controls should be placed. Our
stored procedure will return both the file name of the control and the area
name that should contain the control.

1. Modify the code-behind module of the portal page to read the list of controls belonging to the current page.
2. Position the controls within the panes on the page.

Listing 5.15 below shows the complete text of the code-behind module of the portal page implementing these two steps.

Listing 5.15 Dynamically Creating User Controls in the Portal Page

```
Inherits BasePage ' Inherit template from BasePage

' Define template page's containing area controls
Protected PageTitle As HtmlControls.HtmlGenericControl
Protected TopPane As System.Web.UI.HtmlControls.HtmlTableCell
Protected NavPane As System.Web.UI.HtmlControls.HtmlTableCell
Protected LeftPane As System.Web.UI.HtmlControls.HtmlTableCell
Protected ContentPane As System.Web.UI.HtmlControls.HtmlTableCell
Protected RightPane As System.Web.UI.HtmlControls.HtmlTableCell
Protected BottomPane As System.Web.UI.HtmlControls.HtmlTableCell

' define enumerator corresponding to the page areas
Enum Pane As Integer
    TopPane = 1
    NavPane = 2
    LeftPane = 3
    ContentPane = 4
    RightPane = 5
    BottomPane = 6
End Enum

' define a class member to hold the database-received ID of
' the current page. Default it to Zero. Actual value will
' be retrieved in the Page Load event handler
Private _PageID As Integer = 0

' Page load event handler will:
' - Receive the ID of the current page from the parameter list
' - Retrieve page information using FetchPageInformation() function
' - Load all controls on the page using LoadPageControls() function
Private Sub Page_Load(ByVal sender As System.Object, ByVal e As _
                    System.EventArgs) Handles MyBase.Load
    If Not Request.Params("PageID") Is Nothing Then
        _PageID = CType(Request.Params("PageID"), Integer)
```

```vbnet
        Else
            _PageID = 2        ' Assume the first page with data (ignore _
                             Root page)
        End If

        Dim strTitle As String = "", strShortTitle As String = ""
        If FetchPageInformation(strTitle, strShortTitle) Then _
                             PageTitle.InnerText = strTitle


        LoadPageControls()
End Sub

' FetchPageInformation() function will call GetDataTable() function
' defined in the BasePage class to receive page's title and short
' title.
' Data is returned as ADO.NET DataTable.
Private Function FetchPageInformation(ByRef Title As String, _
ByRef _
            ShortTitle As String) As Boolean
    Dim retVal As Boolean = False        'ASSUME FAILURE
    Dim dt As DataTable
    Try
        dt = GetDataTable("spFetchPageInformation", "PageID", _
        _PageID)
        Title = CType(dt.Rows(0).Item("Title"), String)
        ShortTitle = CType(dt.Rows(0).Item("ShortTitle"), String)
        retVal = True
    Catch ex As Exception
        retVal = False
    Finally
        dt = Nothing
    End Try


    Return retVal
End Function

' LoadPageControls() function will:
' - call GetDataTable() function to execute a stored procedure
'   which returns the data about controls belonging to the
'   current page
' - iterate through the resulting data table; dynamically
'   load each control and assign it to the specified area on
'   the page
Private Function LoadPageControls() As Boolean
    Dim retVal As Boolean = False        'ASSUME FAILURE
```

Continues

Listing 5.15 Dynamically Creating User Controls in the Portal Page (*Continued*)

```
Dim dt As DataTable, dr As DataRow
Dim ctrl As String = "", intArea As Pane = 0
Dim intOrder As Integer = 0, strFileName As String = ""
Dim theControl As BaseControl

Try
    dt = GetDataTable("spFetchPageControlInformation", _
    "PageID", _
                    _PageID)
  For Each dr In dt.Rows
        ctrl = dr.Item("ControlName")
        intArea = dr.Item("AreaID")
        intOrder = dr.Item("OrderID")
        strFileName = dr.Item("FileName")

        ' Find the containing area control
        Dim ParentTableCell As HtmlControls.HtmlTableCell
         ParentTableCell = Page.FindControl(intArea.GetName( _
                            intArea.GetType, intArea))
        If ParentTableCell.Controls.Count > 0 Then
            Dim ctrlLiteral As New WebControls.Literal
            ctrlLiteral.Text = "<BR>"
            ParentTableCell.Controls.Add(ctrlLiteral)
        End If
        ' Dynamically load new control
         theControl = Page.LoadControl("~/" & strFileName)
         theControl.PageControlID = _
        CType(dr.Item("PageControlID"), Int32)
        ParentTableCell.Controls.Add(theControl)
        ParentTableCell.Visible = True
    Next
    retVal = True
Catch ex As Exception
    retVal = False
Finally
    dt = Nothing
End Try

Return retVal
End Function
```

In the code fragment in Listing 5.15, we have defined a set of controls corresponding to the containing panes on the form. We have used a member variable **Pane** of the **Enum** data type for easier access to the area controls. Enumerators (**Enum** in .NET Framework) let developers supply alternate human-readable names for the underlying primitive types.

The Page Load event handler executes a function to load main page–level information and another function to retrieve the list of controls, instantiate and position each control within its target area, and populate control properties.

Add Template and Page Information to the Database

Our framework is database-driven; but at this point, the database is empty. Let's add the page area definitions and create one generic template and a few pages based on this template. We don't have an administrative module yet, so we will enter the data by hand using SQL Server Enterprise Manager. Note that we need a root page to enable the functioning of the menu and breadcrumb controls. The root page only serves as root of the page hierarchy; it doesn't contain any controls and is never shown to the user. To populate the data, open all portal tables in Enterprise Manager and type in the values for all fields, referring to Figure 5.8. After populating the Area, Template, Template Area, Page, and Page Hierarchy tables, you should see the data as shown in Figure 5.8.

We have defined a single template, Framework Template, which contains all six possible areas. We then created three pages; all based on this template, and we created a simple hierarchy with one page, Home Page, at the root of the hierarchy and two sibling pages, Content Page 1 and Content Page 2, one level below the Home Page.

The framework reads the page definition data and loads and displays the page hierarchy. This is great, but the crucial part of any portal—the content—is still missing. To display the content, we create a simple content control derived from the base control and we con the framework into displaying it in the content pane of each page.

Create the Content Control

To create this control:

1. Using Visual Studio .NET, add a new control to the Controls folder.
2. Name the new control **ctrlContent.ascx**.

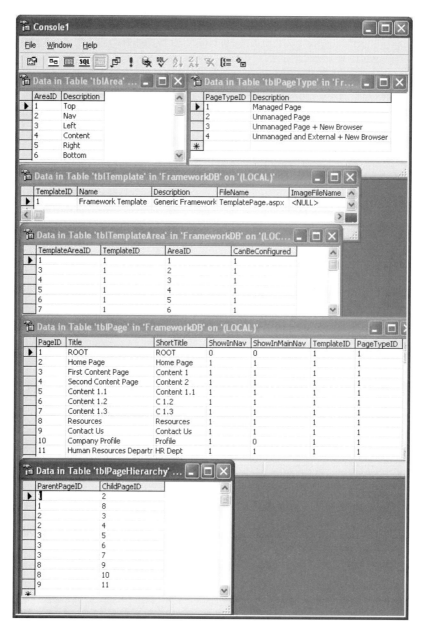

Figure 5.8 Adding Page and Template Definitions to the Database

3. Change the **Inherits** statement at the top of the code-behind module to inherit the new content control from the base control.

The Content control works by reading the list of its properties for a given page and displaying them using ASP.NET Label controls. Each of the properties for the control is populated by the content creator and may consist of text, HTML data, or image data. The values and names of the properties are contained in the ADO.NET **DataTable** object **_dtProperties** inherited from the **BaseControl**.

4. To display the values of the properties, create two label controls, **Header** and **Content**. Later we configure the database to match these content properties. Add the code shown in Listing 5.16 to ctrl-Content.ascx:

Listing 5.16 ctrlContent.ascx

```
<asp:Label id="Header" runat="server" Font-Size=16 _
Font-Bold=True>Header for content control</asp:Label>
<br>
<asp:Label id="Content" runat="server" >Content data</asp:Label>
```

5. Add the code shown in Listing 5.17 to the code-behind module of the **ctrlContent** object:

Listing 5.17 Code Module for the Content Control ctrlContent.ascx.vb

```
Protected Header As System.Web.UI.WebControls.Label
Protected Content As System.Web.UI.WebControls.Label

' Go through all properties for the Content control
' and load them
Private Sub Page_Load(ByVal sender As System.Object, ByVal e As _
        System.EventArgs) Handles MyBase.Load
    If _dtProperties Is Nothing Then Exit Sub
    Dim i As Integer, DisplayControl As Label

    With _dtProperties
        For i = 0 To .Rows.Count - 1
            Select Case .Rows(i).Item("ControlPropertyName")
                Case "Content"
                    Content.Text = .Rows(i).Item("Value")
```

Continues

Listing 5.17 Code Module for the Content Control ctrlContent.ascx.vb (*Continued*)

```
            Case "Header"
                Header.Text = .Rows(i).Item("Value")
        End Select
    Next
End With

End Sub
```

We have defined two label objects and have implemented a Page Load handler event that uses the DataTable object inherited from the parent BaseControl object to loop through the list of property names and property values and populate both label controls with the values defined for them.

Finally we can configure our three portal pages to display the content control in its content areas. In a full-blown portal framework implementation, this data is entered by using Administration and Content Management modules. In this stripped-down version, you enter the data by hand using SQL Server Enterprise Manager. If you follow along, you can enter the data shown in Figure 5.9 or create your own content.

Let's review the steps completed so far. We have associated header, breadcrumb trail, menu, footer, and content controls with the header, top, left, footer, and content areas, respectively, on each of our three portal pages using **tblPageControl**. Next we created two properties, Content and Header, for the content control (ControlID = 2) and a single property, Content, for the inventory control (ControlID = 6) using the **tblControlProperty** table. Finally we set up some content to be displayed by the content and inventory controls on each of the three portal pages using the **tblPageControlProperty** table.

Run the Portal

If you have followed this exercise closely, you should be able now to successfully compile and run the project. With control content specified as shown in Figure 5.8 and Figure 5.9, the first page of the portal should look like that shown in Figure 5.10.

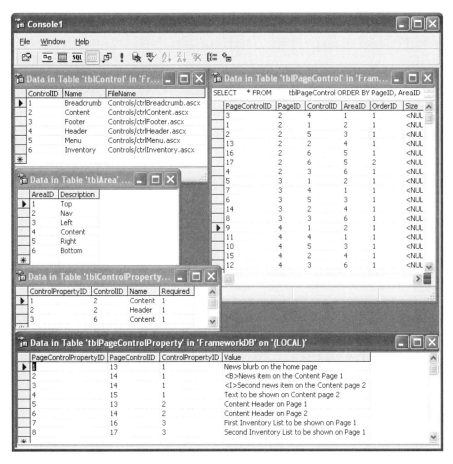

Figure 5.9 Adding Control Definitions and Content to the Database

Where to Go from Here

At this point we have a functioning (albeit rather simple) site. We can navigate the site using menu and the breadcrumb trail controls; and we can modify data in SQL Server tables to change the page composition as well as add or delete pages or change control placement within the page.

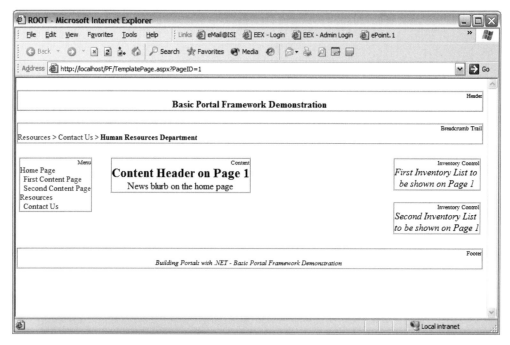

Figure 5.10 First Portal Page

Follow these steps to take your work in this exercise closer to a full-blown portal framework implementation:

1. Add the administration module to allow portal administrators to manage user, page, and content information.
2. Add login, logout, and authentication mechanisms.
3. Add the authorization mechanism to provide the ability to restrict content based on the current login (refer to Chapter 6 for a detailed review of .NET-related security, authentication, and authorization options).
4. Add the logging and usage statistics gathering and management modules.
5. Add caching to support better performance.
6. Add the content management module to allow content authors to create, edit, and manage portal content.

Conclusion

This chapter defines frameworks, discusses the basics of the .NET Framework, and shows how to build a simple portal framework. Frameworks offer significant benefits for developers and for businesses that rely on portals. They can reduce development time, technical risks, and maintenance costs. If you plan on developing multiple portals, the savings are even greater for the incremental portals that are developed.

The framework is the basis for coding custom modules and also provides integration points for other software products that may be included in the portal, whether they come from Microsoft or other vendors. It also simplifies team development by providing a common reference point and a set of standard objects and methods that can be reused by the entire project team.

While off-the-shelf products can get you started on your .NET portal, there are few businesses that don't need the tight connections with their line-of-business applications that the portal framework can provide. Many of these applications are custom and they often come from multiple vendors and are based on multiple technologies and products.

As you choose the features of your portal, consider how they fit into the framework that you are developing. As your framework grows in richness and functionality, you will find it more and more important to the success of your projects—so much so that you wonder what you did without it.

Chapter 6

Security Services

It has become a truism that we live in a dangerous interconnected world. Malicious users, hackers, worms, and viruses are abundant in the open world of the Internet. With the advent of massively multiuser online applications, the importance of implementing solid, unbreakable security solutions while building scalable high-performance online applications cannot be overestimated.

Portals are usually built to provide access to a multitude of disparate corporate applications and data sources. Users of a portal site demand secure and reliable access without sacrificing the features that make the portal attractive such as single sign-on and smooth access to heterogeneous enterprise applications. The scope of a large enterprise portal combined with usability demands increases the role of the security implementation. A portal site with overbearing security features will turn off many users, and the lack of solid security implementation might allow a determined hacker to gain access to many applications on a corporate network.

This chapter introduces basic security concepts and explains how new .NET Framework security features combined with the features of other backend products help you design and build impregnable yet easy-to-maintain online applications.

Building Blocks of Secure Applications

Most web sites and portals require the ability to identify users and protect the resources kept on the site. Even when allowing anonymous users to browse the information on your portal site, you still have to guard against intruders trying to take control of the internal resources of your site.

Building secure sites requires careful up-front planning and a clear understanding of the available options. The good news is that ASP.NET, in conjunction with Internet Information Server (IIS) and SQL Server, provides many out-of-the-box security features that require little or no coding and are easily configurable by administrators using wizards. The .NET Framework security model provides the ability to have low-level control on all security features without impeding the application's scalability or performance characteristics.

Four primary concepts underlie any security implementation:

- Authentication
- Authorization
- Impersonation
- Principals

Authentication

Authentication commonly refers to a process that verifies that the user is who the user claims to be. There are two sides to the process of authentication: gathering user credentials and validating these credentials against a chosen credentials authority. The types of credentials vary and may include a username and password collected using a login dialog box, a cookie saved on a user's computer, or credentials established by another credential authority—for example, a Windows authentication mechanism.

The credentials authority could be represented by a custom validation process implemented by SQL Server, in the case of a massive online application, or by the Windows Kerberos or NTLM mechanisms, which authenticate users logging on to Windows NT, 2000, or later computers. When credentials are validated against some trusted authority, the user's identity is considered to be proven true.

Authorization

Authorization is another key security safeguard for building secure web applications. Authorization is the process of limiting access of authenticated users to only the resources these users are allowed to see. If your portal contains a document library, the process of authorization guarantees that each user will be able to access only the documents for which he or she has permissions. Almost all resources and objects in Windows are associated with access control lists (ACLs), which control who can access the resource and what that user can do with the resource (in other words, read, write, execute, delete). Each access control list consists of an ordered set of entries called access control entries (ACEs) that connect a security principal with a set of permissions (read, delete, and so on).

Impersonation

Impersonation enables the .NET code modules to change execution context based on the currently authenticated user. As a result, your application starts executing with privileges of the user account it impersonates. Impersonation is commonly used when an ASP.NET module receives the credentials of the authenticated user from IIS. Both IIS and ASP.NET perform an authentication and authorization process. By choosing to implement authentication at the IIS level and turn impersonation on in the ASP.NET application configuration file, you can avoid having to resolve authentication issues at the ASP.NET level. By default, impersonation is turned off.

Principals

A principal represents an authenticated user and carries the user's identity information. When dealing with security issues programmatically, .NET developers use **principal** objects. Principals are key elements in implementing .NET Framework role-based security.

There are three kinds of principals in .NET:

- Windows principals represent Windows users and groups. Windows principals can impersonate other Windows principals by assuming their identities.
- Generic principals represent users without connection with an existing Windows account.
- Custom principals are objects created by applications to implement specialized role-based security rules.

Authentication and Authorization Flow

The security features of IIS, .NET Framework, and SQL Server work together to establish the flow of the authentication and authorization process. A client submits a request for an ASP.NET page. The request is first received by IIS, which works with the Windows operating system to initiate the security process. IIS analyzes the request and, based on selected IIS authentication options, validates it. If IIS authentication fails, the request is rejected and the appropriate error message is displayed in the client's browser.

If IIS successfully validates the incoming request, the request is passed to ASP.NET. The Windows operating system then looks at the properties of the file containing the ASP.NET page and decides whether the read request on the file is authorized. If the Windows validation is successful, the request reaches the ASP.NET application, which can implement additional custom steps to authenticate the request and to authorize the resources for the request. The ASP.NET application often works in conjunction with SQL Server to implement custom credentials validation.

The sample portal implementation code example at the end of this chapter demonstrates these steps. Figure 6.1 illustrates the authentication and authorization flow.

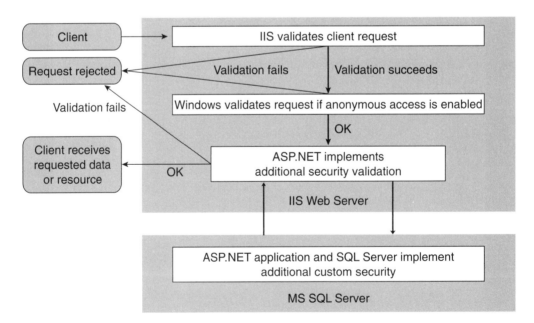

Figure 6.1 IIS, ASP.NET, and SQL Server Authenticate a Request

IIS Authentication Methods

IIS plays a crucial part in online application security by serving as the first checkpoint on a request's path into your system. IIS tightly integrates with the Windows operating system and can authenticate user requests based on local machine or domain Windows accounts associated with the request.

You configure IIS authentication methods and other security-related parameters by using the IIS management plug-in located in Administrative Tools in the Control Panel. To view available IIS authentication methods, open the Properties dialog box for your web site using the IIS plug-in and click the Directory Security tab, as shown in Figure 6.2.

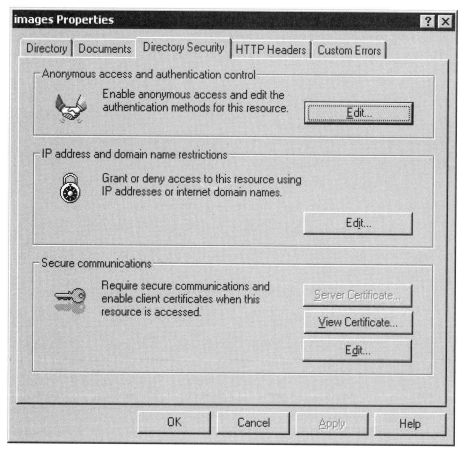

Figure 6.2 Configuring Site Security

IIS can authenticate user requests through one of five different approaches:

- Anonymous authentication
- Basic authentication
- Digest authentication
- Integrated Windows authentication
- Certificate authentication

The IIS dialog box shown in Figure 6.3 allows administrators to select and configure IIS authentication.

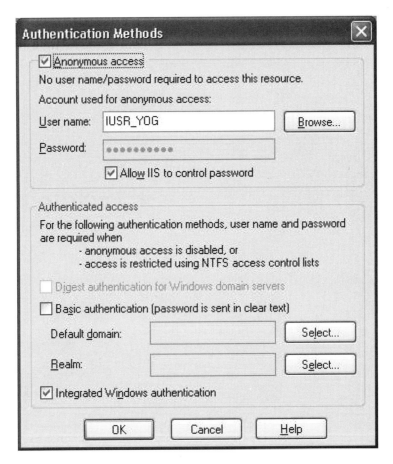

Figure 6.3 IIS Authentication Methods Dialog Box

If you disable Anonymous authentication and enable all other authentication methods, IIS will try to authenticate each incoming user request by using the most secure authentication methods. It will start with Integrated Windows authentication and, if that fails, will work its way up to Basic authentication.

Anonymous Authentication

If you select this mode (which is enabled by default), anyone can access your site. IIS can still restrict anonymous user access by filtering out certain IP addresses. If this mode is selected, user credentials are not requested and the same Windows account is used to execute on behalf of the connecting user. By default, this account, called IUSR_<MACHINE NAME>, is controlled by IIS. If you override the default settings by supplying a different account for anonymous access or by modifying the password used by IUSR_<MACHINE NAME>, be sure to enter the changes in the Authentication Methods dialog box shown in Figure 6.3. Otherwise, connections will fail.

Selection of the account used for an anonymous access is very important for your portal's security. The IUSR_<MACHINE NAME> account belongs to the GUESTS group and its access rights are fairly limited. If you select a different account, do not give it wide access. Using an account belonging to the Administrators group would be a poor choice security-wise for anonymous access.

Anonymous access does not provide any security restrictions and is recommended for public areas of web sites or portals. If you are trying to encourage casual visitors to access your content, you do not want to ask them to log in. Many users click the Back button when faced with a logon screen. There are no client browser limitations for this type of authentication, so all browsers are supported for anonymous access.

Basic Authentication

Basic authentication uses the browser logon features. When a user tries to connect to a site protected by Basic authentication, the user's browser opens a Login dialog box. IIS uses the credentials gathered from a login dialog box to match user information with an existing Windows domain account. If the account is found, IIS uses Windows security features to check the account privileges and access rights.

Because a Windows domain account list is used for user validation, using Basic as your authentication method means that each user of your site must have a valid Windows domain account. The general rule of thumb for granting rights to these Windows accounts is to be minimalist: Administrators should grant the smallest subset of privileges that would allow users to perform their tasks. Each account must be granted Log On Locally rights.

The Basic authentication method derives its name from the fact that both username and password are passed to IIS in base64-encoded form. Base64 encoding is not an encryption method and is easily decoded with simple code. Both username and password therefore are passed in the equivalent of plaintext—a gigantic security risk. If the data stream were intercepted, the hacker would have little trouble cracking the username and password. In fact, IIS informs you that you are taking chances when you enable this form of authentication.

To alleviate this problem, you can use **secure sockets layer (SSL)**, a technology for encrypting and protecting the whole channel of communication. With SSL, all communication between the server and client is encrypted. Basic authentication with SSL is recommended for use on an intranet or when the usage of a portal is limited to a well-defined and relatively static group of users.

Digest Authentication

Digest authentication resembles Basic authentication, but it is augmented to make it significantly more secure. As with Basic authentication, the client browser prompts the user for a username and password. The browser then combines the user's responses and some other information available on the client (requested URL) to create a hash or digest of this information, which then is passed to the IIS. IIS takes this hash value and decrypts the password portion, which is then used to perform a network logon. For it to function, the server must store a copy of each such digest.

By default Windows does not store user passwords anywhere. Windows uses an ingenious technology that creates an encrypted value using both the username and password; this value and not the password is stored internally and used to validate user credentials. Windows is therefore a very secure system because even administrators do not have a way to obtain users' passwords. As a result, enabling Digest authentication would weaken Windows security by storing actual password values (albeit encrypted) on a server.

Another potential problem with Digest authentication is its susceptibility to replay attacks: If a hacker manages to snoop on a channel while a client browser and IIS are exchanging authentication data, he could record the user's digest and then use it to impersonate the user. While the chances of this kind of attack happening are very low, it is theoretically possible.

In spite of these issues, Digest authentication provides a reasonably high level of security. It also requires a valid Windows account for each user. Currently only Internet Explorer 5.0 or later supports Digest authentication, which is usable when access across proxy servers and a firewall are required.

Integrated Windows Authentication

Integrated Windows authentication uses Kerberos (an advanced authentication mechanism that appeared first in Windows 2000 and is used whenever both the client and server are running a Windows 2000 operating system or later). Pre–Windows 2000 systems use NTLM, an authentication mechanism used by NT4. While Integrated Windows authentication uses a hashing algorithm to pass and validate user credentials and is a very secure technology, it does have an important limitation: Many firewalls will block it so it is useful primarily on intranets. Like Digest authentication, Integrated Windows authentication requires each portal user to have a valid domain account.

Integrated Windows authentication has several attractive advantages: It provides a high degree of user identity protection while tightly integrating with the rest of the client/server pieces in the Microsoft world, thus requiring minimum additional effort to implement. It allows seamless hidden authentication: After users have been authenticated by NTLM or Kerberos as they log in to Windows, they can log in to sites protected by Windows authentication without being prompted to log in again. This **single sign-on** is a highly desirable portal feature.

Internet Explorer is the required browser for applications employing Integrated Windows authentication.

Certificate Authentication

Digital certificates form a part of the SSL implementation of IIS and work as a means of identifying the certificate owner. Certificates are used by both clients and servers to identify each other and contain encryption keys. Client certificate and server certificate encryption keys form a key pair used by SSL to facilitate data encryption and decryption and to establish a secure communication channel. Client certificates contain information required by the server to identify each client, and server certificates contain data allowing each client to verify the server's identity.

To enable Certificate authentication, you must obtain and install a valid server certificate on your web server. Generally, server certificates can be obtained from an accepted third-party certification authority (CA) such as Verisign. Such organizations are trusted to validate the identification information contained in a server certificate. If you are building an internal portal, you can use Microsoft Certificate Server to create and distribute certificates internally without using outside CA organizations.

You should use the IIS snap-in to install security certificates:

1. Open the Properties dialog box for your site.
2. Click the **Directory Security** tab.
3. Click **Server Certificate** to launch the Web Server Certificate wizard (see Figure 6.4).
4. Enter your organization parameters, select one of the CA organizations, and send the certificate request to the certification authority.

When the certificate authority gives you the file containing the server certificate, you use the same wizard to apply the certificate to your server.

Certificates let you create mappings between client certificates and user accounts. Certificate mapping is very flexible: You can map multiple user accounts to a single certificate or a single user account to multiple certificates using wildcard pattern matching; you can also create one-to-one mapping. For example, a many-to-one mapping strategy can be helpful in very large networks. For a network on which it is easier to allow each user to obtain a client certificate than to maintain separate Windows accounts, a portal administrator can set up special Windows accounts according to the roles established for the portal users and then set up several matching rules to establish a client certificates–Windows account connection.

Certificate authentication is a very secure authentication method. It works with both Internet Explorer and Netscape Navigator browsers and requires SSL. Certificate authentication is the widely accepted authentication mechanism for protecting online transactions. You can find more about client and server certificates on the MSDN site at www.microsoft.com/windows2000/en/advanced/iis/htm/core/iicerts.htm?id=90.

Figure 6.4 Request Server Certificate

IP Address and Domain Name Restrictions

Although IP Address and Domain Name Restrictions is not an authentication method, it often serves as the first barrier to prevent unauthorized traffic. This security mechanism uses rules to block traffic from certain originating IP addresses. These restrictions only allow access to users from a specified domain or network. For instance, you could block intranet access to anyone with an IP address that falls outside the range you specify.

To set up IP address restriction rules:

1. Using IIS Manager, open the Properties dialog box of your web site by right-clicking the web site name and selecting **Properties**.
2. Click the **Directory Security** tab.
3. Click **Edit** in the IP Address and Domain Name Restrictions section of the tab.
4. In the IP Address Restrictions dialog box, grant or deny site access based on incoming IP addresses or domain names. Figure 6.5 shows how to configure IIS to grant access to all callers except those coming from 192.168.0.1.

IP address restrictions rules are available on Windows servers beginning with NT4 (NT4, Windows 2000, Windows XP, Windows 2003 server families) and are not available on the NT4 workstation, Windows 2000 Professional, or Windows XP Professional.

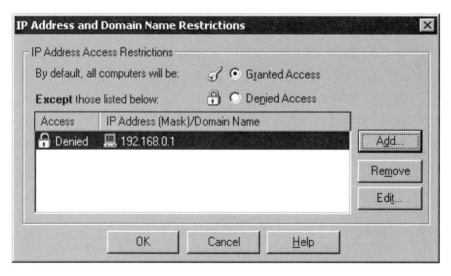

Figure 6.5 IP Address and Domain Name Restrictions Dialog Box

ASP.NET Authentication Methods

ASP.NET provides its own authentication mechanism that comes into play after a request clears IIS (see Figure 6.1). ASP.NET authentication lets you add more flexibility and protection to your security implementation through four authentication and authorization options:

- Windows authentication
- Passport authentication
- Forms authentication
- No authentication (also called default or IIS authentication)

As with many other parameters in ASP.NET, you configure the authentication method by editing the Web.config application configuration file that resides in the application root folder. The code excerpt from this file included in Figure 6.6 displays the selected authentication options.

```
<configuration>
    <system.web>
      <identity impersonate="true"/>

    <!--  This section sets the authentication policies of the application.
        Possible modes are "Windows",
        "Forms", "Passport" and "None"      -->
        <authentication mode="Windows"/>

        <!--  This section sets the authorization policies of the application
            You can allow or deny access
            to application resources by user or role. Wildcards: "*" mean
            everyone, "?" means anonymous (unauthenticated) users.      -->
        <authorization>
            <allow users="*"/> <!-- Allow all users -->
            <!--  <allow      users="[comma separated list of users]"
                             roles="[comma separated list of roles]"/>
                   <deny       users="[comma separated list of users]"
                             roles="[comma separated list of roles]"/>  -->
        </authorization>
    ...
```

Figure 6.6 Choosing ASP.NET Authentication Options

Windows Authentication

When you select Windows authentication mode, ASP.NET relies on IIS to authenticate a request. IIS employs one of the authentication methods described earlier in this chapter and creates a Windows access token, which ASP.NET receives from IIS and uses later when user identity is requested.

After IIS authenticates a user, ASP.NET executes in the context of the user. The portal site administrator can authorize user access to various objects and resources using the following two approaches:

- By configuring access permissions using ACLs
- By modifying the <authorization> section of the Web.config file to grant or deny resource access to users and roles

Windows authentication works best in intranet portals or when the user base is not large and administrators can create a Windows account for each portal user. The code excerpt displayed in Figure 6.6 shows an application configured for Windows authentication. Note that identity impersonation has been turned on in this scenario. Identity impersonation was on by default in older versions of ASP; but in ASP.NET, it is not turned on by default.

Using identity impersonation ensures that ASP.NET code will access the portal resources requested by a user executing under the context of the user's account. That allows the administrator to define resource usage rules based on a Windows user account.

Imagine that your portal contains a document named Sensitive.doc. As a site administrator, you allow user Bob to read the document and deny any access to Alice. When Bob logs in to the portal using ASP.NET Windows authentication with identity impersonation turned on, ASP.NET code trying to read the Sensitive.doc will run as if it were Bob and will successfully retrieve the document. When Alice logs in, the code will execute with the privileges and access permissions associated with Alice's account and she will be denied read access to the document. If identity impersonation had been turned off, the code would have executed under the same account and the desired permission-granting granularity would have been lost.

Passport Authentication

Passport authentication uses the authentication service called Microsoft Passport. Microsoft keeps databases of user information and allows users to consume a centralized login service that authenticates the user and creates encrypted cookies containing user validation information on the client's machine. Microsoft Passport provides several services that can be used separately or within the same application, including:

- *Passport Single Sign-In.* This is an authentication service allowing a single set of user credentials (username and password) to be used to authenticate an access to any Passport-enabled web site.
- *Passport Express Purchase using Passport wallet.* This service allows users to securely store their credit card information with Passport and then use a Passport wallet in transactions on sites employing Passport Express Purchase.

Perhaps the most important advantage of using Passport authentication is that it supports a single pass-through login for multiple Passport-enabled sites or applications. This is a very elegant solution for a scenario in which you need to give a single login to a set of related applications or sites. With a Passport wallet, users can store their sensitive information in fewer locations. In addition, all web sites employing Passport services are required to comply with the standard privacy policy.

The single sign-in process starts when a previously unauthenticated user tries to access a Passport-enabled site. Code on the protected page uses the Passport **Manager** object (in the .NET Framework, the **PassportIdentity** class) to redirect to a Microsoft Passport site where authentication occurs. Passport servers use the user's credentials along with the information about a Passport-enabled site during the authentication process. After this authentication process is finished, the user's browser is redirected back to the original site. Cookies are used to store user profile data and the Passport authentication ticket. Subsequent authentication requests would be based on the Passport cookies.

To use passport authentication, site developers must write additional code using the Microsoft Passport Software Development Kit (SDK). Most of the .NET Passport functionality is exposed in code in the **PassportIdentity** class from the **System.Web.Security** namespace. The Passport SDK, which is available from Microsoft, must be installed on each server that uses Passport authentication. Passport service requires a subscription, but at present these subscriptions are free.

Detailed discussion of the Passport SDK is beyond the scope of this chapter. To add Passport Single Sign-in to an ASP.NET application:

1. Obtain a Passport account. You can get free .NET passport here: www.passport.net.
2. Download the latest Passport SDK (version 2.5 at the time of writing) at tmsdn.microsoft.com/library/default.asp?url=/downloads/list/websrvpass.asp.
3. Sign the .NET Services agreement with Microsoft and create and configure a .NET Passport application by following steps on the Microsoft .NET My Services manager site:
   www.netservicesmanager.com/wizard/default.aspx.
4. Configure the local application using the Passport .NET Administration utility installed with the Passport SDK (select **Programs-> Microsoft Passport->Passport Administration** Utility).
5. Configure the authentication element of the site configuration file Web.config to specify Passport authentication mode: <authentication mode="Passport"/>.
6. In your ASP.NET code, access Passport information using PassportIdentity class: Dim MyPassport as System.Web.Security.PassportIdentity = Page.User.Identity.
7. Use the **PassportIdentity.LogoTag2** method to display sign-in and sign-out buttons on your page. The **LogoTag2** method returns correct HTML to display Passport buttons along with the hyperlink to the Passport authentication server.
8. Use the **Passport.IsAuthenticated** method to determine the outcome of the .NET Passport authentication process.

You can read more about Microsoft Passport at msdn.microsoft.com/library/default.asp?url=/downloads/list/websrvpass.asp. Passport integration is one of the new features of Windows Server 2003. By mapping Passport identity to an Active Directory identity, you can support an IIS-based authentication and authorization process without users having to log on to a Windows network.

Forms Authentication

The Forms authentication method should be familiar to anyone who has ever built a custom authentication mechanism with pre-.NET versions of Active Server Pages (ASP). In those days, you would develop a simple HTML form to gather the username and password and then send it off to a middle-tier component for validation—for example, by matching username and password against values stored in a database table.

.NET Forms authentication uses a technology called HTTP client-side redirection. When an unauthenticated request comes in, it is redirected to a specified page where the user can enter his or her credentials. If these credentials are authenticated, an authentication token is created (typically a cookie). This token is reused during the same session whenever user identity information is requested because it is passed in the request header. The authentication cookie can also contain a list of roles for the authenticated user.

It is important to keep in mind that Forms authentication does not provide any protection for user credentials when they are passed from an HTML form to the server. The best practice when using Forms authentication is to secure the channel used to pass credentials at all times by using SSL.

Setting up Forms authentication does not require much coding. This form of authentication is configured in the application configuration file Web.config (see Figure 6.7). The code snippet in Figure 6.7 redirects all

```
<authentication mode="forms">
    <forms forms="401kApp"
            loginurl="/login.aspx"
            decryptionkey="1!#$$*13^">
        <credentials passwordFormat=SHA1>
            <user name="Kim" password="9G11E4F94EC497£D5A537EA28C65F85AD28E5B3b"/>
            <user name="John" password="BA7157A99DFE9DD70A94D89844A4B4993B10168F"/>
        </credentials>
    </forms>
</authentication>
```

Figure 6.7 Configuring Forms Authentication

unauthorized requests to the Login.aspx page, which you can easily create by customizing the example page installed with Visual Studio.NET.

Forms authentication is customarily used when security requirements are not extremely stringent. In this case, IIS authentication is often turned off (anonymous access is allowed), and user's credentials are requested by ASP.NET when it discovers that a valid session token is not present in the request header. The HTML form specified in the Forms section of the Web.config file is sent to the user's browser and is used to collect the user's credentials, which are then sent to ASP.NET for authentication. Figure 6.8 illustrates this process.

No Authentication

This option is usually selected when no authentication is required on the ASP.NET side or when authentication is implemented completely outside of the built-in ASP.NET authentication method. The context under which the code will execute and the resources will be accessed depends on whether impersonation is turned on or off.

If impersonation is enabled, the execution context is IUSR-<Machine Name>. If it is disabled, the Local System account will be used. ASP.NET is somewhat shielded from this issue because its worker process aspnet_wp is running by default as a special username ASPNET that is created automatically when you install the .NET Framework.

Web Services Authentication

Web services are hailed as one of the most important recent communication standards. Web services allow users to easily create and consume applications remotely using regular HTTP channels without any hindrance from firewalls. There are three general approaches to creating secure Web services: HTTP security mechanism, custom SOAP-based security schemas, or WS-security.

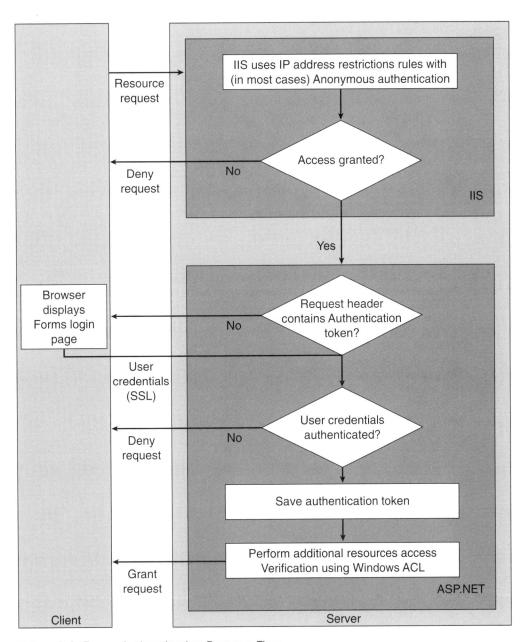

Figure 6.8 Forms Authentication Process Flow

HTTP (Transport) Security

This method lets you implement familiar authentication methods available from the combination of IIS and ASP.NET. Basic, Digest, and Certificate authentication options are available. This mode is often used when you can control both channel and platform configurations on both ends, typically in an intranet scenario. This mechanism is based on Windows platform features and provides point-to-point security. SSL is often used to ensure packet protection.

SOAP-Based Custom Security Implementation on Application Level

In this scenario none of the standard methods is used. Instead, a customized Simple Object Access Protocol (SOAP) message carries the required set of credentials with every call. This approach is often used when it's necessary to integrate a web service implementation with other non-Microsoft products.

You can put user credentials either in the SOAP message header or in the message body. These credentials are analyzed by the custom security mechanism on the backend. If credentials encryption is required, you must implement custom code using .NET cryptography providers.

The natural difficulties with implementing this security scenario stem from not using built-in security mechanisms. In this case, the user's browser cannot maintain identity information automatically and the backend has to perform additional work when validating user credentials. Maintenance costs may rise due to the custom development work required to implement this option.

WS-Security

WS-security is a set of specifications describing how to implement message security by using digital signatures and storing authentication tokens in SOAP message headers. It enhances SOAP by providing message integrity, confidentiality, and additional authentication. The WS-security specification was developed jointly by Microsoft, IBM, and Verisign, and it was published in 2002. To learn more about WS-security, read a white paper on the subject from IBM and Microsoft at msdn.microsoft.com/library/en-us/dnwssecur/html/securitywhitepaper.asp?frame=true&_r=1.

This mode of security is useful in highly heterogeneous environments and when abstraction from the transport channel implementation is required.

ASP.NET Process Identity

ASP.NET uses a special worker process implemented in aspnet_wp.exe. You can enhance the overall security of your portal by carefully choosing an identity (essentially a Windows user account) under which this ASP.NET worker process executes.

If your other security measures fail and an intruding hacker gains control of your site, he or she will probably receive the access privileges of the ASP.NET worker process. You can diminish this risk by reducing the privileges associated with this account to a minimum. Running under the identity of a Local System account or an account from the Administrators group will significantly compromise your overall security. Initial releases of the .NET Framework defaulted this account to a Local System account, though later releases changed this default setting to a special local account named ASPNET, which has significantly fewer privileges.

To set the ASP.NET process identity, you have to modify the values in the processModel element in the machine.config file. This file sits at the top of the XML-based application configuration tree and can be found in the CONFIG subfolder of the Framework folder tree. On Windows XP the path is C:\WINDOWS\Microsoft.NET\Framework\v[FrameworkVersion]\CONFIG.

Figure 6.9 shows a portion of the .NET system configuration file machine.config dealing with default process attributes.

```
<configuration>
    ...
    <system.web>
        ...
        <processModel
            userName="machine" password="AutoGenerate"
            comAuthenticationLevel="Connect" comImpersonationLevel="Impersonate"
            enable="true" timeout="Infinite" idleTimeout="Infinite"
            shutdownTimeout="0:00:05" requestLimit="Infinite"
            requestQueueLimit="5000" restartQueueLimit="10"
            memoryLimit="60" webGarden="false"
            cpuMask="0xffffffff"
            logLevel="Errors" clientConnectedCheck="0:00:05"
            responseRestartDeadlockInterval="00:09:00" responseDeadlockInterval="00:03:00"
            maxWorkerThreads="25" maxIoThreads="25"/>
```

Figure 6.9 Setting ASP.NET Process Identity

The userName element of processModel recognizes two predefined values. If `userName="machine"` (the default in recent releases), the worker process will run under the ASPNET account. If `userName="system"`, the default identity will be the Local System account. The latter option is sometimes employed by developers to facilitate debugging. Don't forget to change it when your product goes live! And note that if you are using machine or system values, you must set the value of the password attribute to AutoGenerate.

You can also create a special account solely for the worker process. This account might have more restrictions on your network than the default ASPNET account. To specify this account, set the userName attribute to the account name in [Domain Name]\[Windows Account Name] format (for example, ACCOUNTING\BSMITH) and the value of password elements to this account's password. If you use a custom account, give it the following access rights:

- Read for the .NET Framework install folder and its subfolders and for the application folder
- Read/write for the Windows Temp folder and for the Temporary ASP.NET Files subfolder located under the .NET Framework install folder

ASP.NET achieves additional levels of security because its worker process by default runs in a separate process. If, however, you change this default setting by specifying `enable="false"` in the processModel element, it will run in-process with IIS. In this case, all settings in processModel will be ignored.

Code Access Security and the .NET Framework

The security mechanisms discussed so far in this chapter all validate users by gathering and checking user credentials against trusted credential authorities. Just as there are users who might damage or compromise data, either intentionally or by accident, there are malicious or poorly written code fragments that, if executed unchecked, could violate the security of your portal site.

These code fragments can come from many sources: Internet pages, email messages, downloads by users, and so on. When Windows executes the code, in most cases it trusts the code implicitly (many script-based languages, like JavaScript and VBScript, have built-in restrictions on what they can do that limits their access to underlying operating system resources). Imagine that there is a middle-tier component on your site that contains the DeleteFile method. When executed properly within the context of your application, this method is responsible for cleaning temp files. If a malicious user were to gain control of the assembly containing this method, Delete-File could be executed and some vital files on your servers could be destroyed. Without Code Access Security (CAS), your only protection lies in the restrictions on the user account under which the code executes. Because in many cases this would be the Local System account, the protection is ephemeral.

To enable protection from malicious code running on your servers and from legitimate code performing undesired actions (as the result of bugs in the code), Microsoft has created an additional security mechanism in .NET called CAS. It allows you to explicitly describe what the code executing on your server can do based on the code origination and some other code properties.

User-based security and code-based security complement each other in securing sites. When determining whether to grant or deny resource access, both security mechanisms run their permission checks, granting access only when both have succeeded.

This section briefly outlines the main ideas and usage patterns of CAS. At the foundation of CAS is the idea of analyzing the source of the code and assigning different trust levels based on the code origination. The code installed by your network administrator would have a higher trust level than the code downloaded from a web site. Because you can have code from disparate sources executing together within the context of your application, it is possible for code with a lower trust level to execute code with a higher trust level and acquire the execution results (returned data or system resources) from the higher trust level code, thus breaking the trust boundary. To prevent this from happening, CAS scans the call stack and tries to match the permissions granted to each caller in the stack to the requested set of permissions. If it encounters a caller with insufficient permissions, it throws a security exception and the resource is not accessed.

With this foundation, we are ready to discuss the two most important concepts of the CAS mechanism:

- Code evidence
- Code permissions

Code Evidence

The unit of code as it is analyzed by CAS and the .NET Framework is an assembly. CAS collects information about an assembly, which is known as evidence. Different assemblies carry different sets of evidence data. Generally, the following data is collected together as assembly evidence:

- URL of assembly origin
- Site of assembly origin
- Application root folder
- Cryptographic value (hash) associated with the assembly
- Authenticode signature of the assembly created by its author
- Strong name of the assembly (strong names provide a unique identity for an assembly and consist of the assembly text name, version number, culture information, public key, and a digital signature)

CAS assigns various weight parameters to different evidence values. The authenticode value, for example, is more important than the site name. Evidence is calculated dynamically when the assembly executes, and it is not cached.

Code Permissions

While code evidence allows CAS to authenticate running code (assembly), code permissions are employed in the implementation of the authorization mechanism. CAS authenticates an assembly using assembly evidence and authorizes resource requests by using code permissions. Permissions define exactly what your assembly can and cannot do.

The **System.Security.Permissions** namespace contains a fairly granular set of classes that control permission sets for various areas. Some of the classes include:

- *FileIOPermission*. Controls the ability to access files and folders.

- *UIPermission*. Controls the permissions related to user interfaces and the Clipboard.
- *RegistryPermission*. Controls the ability to access registry variables.

Once the evidence set is created from the executing assembly, CAS can look at the hierarchical set of existing security policies and apply the evidence. When this process is complete, CAS assigns the resultant access rights to the assembly.

To administratively configure CAS, use the .NET configuration Microsoft Management Console (MMC) plug-in. To start MMC:

1. Select **Run** from the Start menu and enter MMC to open a blank MMC console window.
2. Select **Add/Remove Snap-in** from the **File** menu.
3. In the Add Snap-in dialog box, click **Add**.
4. Select the **.NET Configuration** snap-in.

There are three different sets of security policies installed with the framework (enterprise, machine, and user) and several built-in permissions (FullTrust, SkipVerification, and so on). Both policy sets and permissions can be created or modified by administrators or through code. Figure 6.10 shows the MMC CAS snap-in displaying the CAS settings for the local machine.

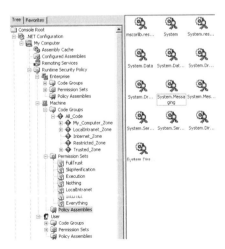

Figure 6.10 MMC Snap-in for CAS Configuration

In addition to permissions determined for your assembly when it executes based on configured policy set and assembly evidence, you can also demand permissions programmatically in code. There are two kinds of permission demands, declarative and imperative. The names refer to the way you try to acquire permissions in code. With a declarative permission demand, you use standard code attributes (stored in the metadata of your assembly); with an imperative demand, you use classes from the System.Security.Permissions namespace.

Listing 6.1 demonstrates both concepts with a simple DeleteFile function.

Listing 6.1 Using Permission Demands in Code

```
' Import the Permissions namespace
Imports System.Security.Permissions

' Example of using Declarative permission demand
<FileIOPermission(SecurityAction.Demand)>
Public Function DeleteFile(byval strFileToDelete as string) as boolean
  try

    System.IO.File.Delete(strFileToDelete)

catch SecException as SecurityException
  ... code to process exception thrown by CAS
  catch GeneralException as Exception
  ... code to process generic exception
  end try
End Sub


' Example of using Imperative permission demand

Public Function DeleteFile(byval strFileToDelete as string) as boolean
  try

    Dim DeletePerm as New FileIOPermission(FileIOPermissionAccess. _
    AllAccess, _
                  strFileToDelete)
    DeletePerm.Demand()

    System.IO.File.Delete(strFileToDelete)
  catch SecException as SecurityException
  ... code to process exception thrown by CAS
  catch GeneralException as Exception
  ... code to process generic exception
  end try
End Sub
```

For a detailed discussion of CAS, refer to MSDN at msdn.microsoft.com/library/en-us/cpguide/html/cpconcodeaccesssecurity.asp.

Microsoft SQL Server Security

Microsoft SQL Server 2000 is used by many portal implementations as data storage for personalization and user profile information. Many portals incorporate enterprise data residing in SQL Server databases. A detailed discussion of Microsoft SQL Server features is beyond the scope of this chapter, but this section does briefly cover the main points on SQL Server security.

SQL Server 2000 security is based on Windows security. SQL Server provides two authentication modes:

- Windows authentication mode
- Mixed authentication mode

Windows Authentication Mode

Windows authentication mode is the default and most secure authentication mode. As its name implies, it bases SQL Server security on existing Windows user or group accounts. In this mode, if a user wants to access the SQL Server database, the network administrator must first create a valid domain user account. After a Windows account has been created, the SQL Server administrator creates an SQL Server account mapped to the Windows account and grants access to some of the databases contained within the SQL Server to this Windows account. The walkthrough at the end of this chapter shows in detail how to create a SQL Server account using Windows authentication mode.

Windows authentication is the recommended authentication mode. It is more secure than the Mixed mode and allows for transparent login to SQL Server after Windows has authenticated the user. Figure 6.11 displays the SQL Server Enterprise Manager interface for creating SQL Server logins. You open this dialog box by expanding the Security node of the selected server, right-clicking the Logins item, and selecting New Login. In Figure 6.11, user Alice from the Windows domain Proto is being given access to the Nwind database. This mode of communication is known as trusted mode.

Figure 6.11 Creating SQL Server Login

Mixed Authentication Mode

In Mixed authentication mode, users requesting a connection to an SQL Server database can be authenticated either by Windows or by SQL Server. If an administrator were to click the SQL Server Authentication radio button during login creation (as was done for Alice in Figure 6.11), SQL Server would store an encrypted username and password internally. When Windows cannot authenticate the user, SQL Server would require explicit user credentials, which then would be compared to those stored internally. This mode of connection is called nontrusted.

Microsoft recommends using Mixed mode when you are dealing with legacy applications that cannot support Windows authentication or when you are working with SQL Server installations on the Windows 98 family of operating systems, which do not support NTLM or Kerberos.

Microsoft Internet Security and Acceleration (ISA) Server 2000

ISA Server 2000 (formerly known as Proxy server) is a product designed to provide two services. It can function as a multilayer firewall providing packet filtering on packet, circuit, and application layers; access policy control; virtual private network (VPN); stateful inspection; and traffic routing. It can also serve as a web cache server. ISA Server tightly integrates with Windows security features and can be deployed as a firewall, as a cache server, or in integrated mode combining both features. ISA Server fits into an overall portal security strategy by providing a necessary level of physical security. You should always include firewalls in online enterprise architectures as the first line of defense against potential attacks. They work by examining all incoming traffic and blocking packets that are deemed dangerous.

The RAM and disk-based caching functionality of the ISA Server can benefit any portal site. Data caching is important for high-performance, high-volume sites. Caching, when implemented correctly, can significantly reduce network traffic, dramatically reduce response time, and therefore improve the user experience.

ISA Server allows administrators to define rules that control the visibility of internal resources to external portal users. These rules, which make up a publishing policy, work by analyzing each request coming into your site from outside and matching request parameters with existing rules to decide whether the targeted server should be allowed to serve the request.

ISA Server can also provide necessary protection by working in the opposite direction. You can establish a set of access policy rules that control how internal users can access external Internet sites. ISA Server then analyzes each outgoing request, looking at its originator's username or IP address and matching it with an established set of access policy rules. Access policy can be applied to individual users or Windows groups, thereby giving administrators wide powers in controlling Internet access rules for your internal users.

You can install ISA Server as a VPN solution, which provides a secure channel of communication across an insecure medium (the Internet). A typical scenario would involve two offices that were geographically separated (see Figure 6.12). ISA Server would be installed in each office and serve as a gateway providing interoffice secure connections over the Internet.

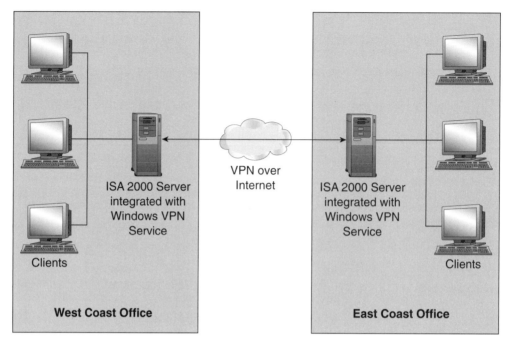

Figure 6.12 ISA 2000 Deployment

Designing a Security Strategy

Designing robust and impenetrable strategy for your portal is one of the most important and often overlooked design goals. While no one can predict all possible attacks and security risks for your site, the security options are well understood and rather straightforward to implement.

There is a widespread misconception that establishing solid security is extremely complicated. This idea stems from the fact that many security requirements are fairly new, and there is a certain latency in the way designers and developers accept and act upon changing requirements. Very often security is treated as an add-on feature of an application, to be applied after core functionality is in place. This approach is very dangerous and leads to potential security holes or delivery slides when your business logic has to be uprooted to incorporate security features.

By carefully choosing appropriate security options on the physical and application levels, you can mitigate almost all security risks. The security features of the .NET Framework combined with the security features of IIS, SQL Server, and other backend products provide many desirable security characteristics out of the box. Every time you plan the security strategy for a site, you should answer these key questions:

- What is the application scope?
- Where does authentication occur?
- What mechanism provides authentication implementation?
- How and where are authorization rules stored and how are they applied?
- What resources should be protected?
- How do user identities relate to protected resources?

Determining Application Scope

Most applications have a well-defined scope and are deployed and used on the Internet or on an extranet or intranet. Internet scenarios assume a wide and disparate user base. Typically you cannot make any assumptions concerning the type of browser or operating system that your users have installed.

In an intranet or extranet scenario, you typically have greater control over your user base and the types of operating systems installed on both client computers and servers. In this scenario, browsers and transport channels are known and well defined. The tighter administrative control over the environment allows you to reduce development costs by relying on out-of-the-box security features.

Selecting Authentication Implementation

Your goal should be to select the most secure authentication possible for a given scenario. Windows authentication using Windows users is very secure but requires a domain account for each user of your system. A lot of work is done for you if you choose this authentication mechanism because Windows manages credentials automatically.

If you choose to identify and manage credentials outside of Windows, you can use a custom security implementation using SQL Server or choose to use the personalization and user management features of Commerce Server.

It's important to evaluate the types of browsers used by your clients. Some authentication features are available only for clients using Internet Explorer. If you need to support Internet users, you should steer clear of relying on the browser-specific security techniques.

After resolving these issues, consider where the authentication will occur. Based on the degree to which you want to use impersonation and flow user credentials into the lower levels of the system, you can choose one or a combination of several authentication methods. If you need to have access to user credentials at the level of method execution, you should turn impersonation and .NET authentication on so user context flows downstream.

Authorization, Resources Protection, and Identities

You have to have a clear idea concerning which resources you want to secure and the desired protection granularity. By using impersonation and flowing each user identity down, you can have different permission sets for different users. On the other hand, you can use the same identity to access all resources: By default, it is the ASPNET account, though you can specify your own account instead of this account.

If you choose to use impersonation, you will have caller identity at your fingertips at all times. You can use Windows access control lists (ACLs) to specify various levels of access for each of the users to each protected resource. On the other hand, you can define a set of application roles. As a part of your authentication process, users will be mapped to a particular role. This role membership determines the types of operations a user can perform and the code access resources using the same trusted account and therefore is referred to as a trusted model.

In some cases these two modes can be mixed: You can protect access to files stored on your server using ACLs and protect database access using roles. Generally, you would choose the trusted model over the impersonation model because the former is usually easier to implement and naturally results in higher performance. The impersonation model might be required if you need extremely granular access and to allow users to access resources directly.

Selecting Types of Roles to Use

If you have ever worked with SQL Server or COM+, you know that both of these products let you define roles and group various entities into roles. While you can use both COM+ and/or SQL Server roles in your portal implementation, a discussion of these options is beyond the scope of this book. .NET roles are a new and very powerful concept and deserve a brief overview.

If you select Windows authentication, .NET automatically creates a **WindowsPrincipal** object representing the .NET role. You use WindowsPrincipal in your code to gain access to a protected resource. .NET principals are flexible and let you protect both "physical" resources such as files and also code. If you have ever dealt with authentication and authorization issues using previous versions of Microsoft development tools (such as Visual C++ 6.0 and earlier), you will appreciate the tremendous amount of work the framework objects do for you out of the box.

The code snippet in Listing 6.2 shows how easily .NET roles can be used to authorize resource access. Let's assume that we have turned on both Windows authentication and impersonation. We have to make sure that only the users Bob and Alice can access our protected resource. The user must belong to the Manager role to be able to modify the resource or to the User role to be able to view it.

Listing 6.2 Using the WindowsPrincipal Object to Authorize Resource Access

```
Imports System.Threading
Imports System.Security
...
  '  get principal object from the current thread

Dim CurrentPrincipal As Principal.IPrincipal = Thread.CurrentPrincipal

 If CurrentPrincipal.Identity.Name <> "Alice" And _
 CurrentPrincipal.Identity.Name <> "Bob" Then
   ' only Alice or Bob can access this resource
```

Continues

Listing 6.2 Using the WindowsPrincipal Object to Authorize Resource
Access (*Continued*)

```
   Throw New SecurityException(String.Format("User {0} cannot access _
   protected resource", _
                        CurrentPrincipal.Identity.Name))
End If

If CurrentPrincipal.IsInRole("Manager") Then

   ReturnModifyableResource()

ElseIf CurrentPrincipal.IsInRole("User") Then

  ReturnReadOnlyResource()

Else

   Throw New SecurityException(String.Format("User {0} cannot access _
   protected resource", _
                        CurrentPrincipal.Identity.Name))
End If
```

There are many different scenarios describing the best approach for designing the optimal security strategy based on a combination of the various factors described in this section. To review these options, consider using Microsoft's *Building Secure ASP.NET Applications Guide*. This bible-sized manual carefully explores various permutations of factors and suggests an ideal solution for each situation. To get this guide, go to MSDN at msdn.microsoft.com/library/en-us/dnnetsec/html/secnetlpMSDN.asp?frame= true&_r=1.

Security Model Changes in Windows Server 2003

Windows Server 2003 contains numerous enhancements and modifications compared to the older members of Windows server family. Built-in .NET Framework support, hot-add memory, updated kernel and UI APIs, improved heap management, vectored exception handling, and many other features make it a significant improvement over Windows 2000 servers; and each of these features merits a discussion beyond the scope of this chapter. In this section I focus on changes in the Windows Server 2003 security model.

Changes in Internet Information Server Security

The following list introduces some of the most important changes in the Windows security model.

- Windows Server 2003 comes with the new version of IIS: IIS version 6.0. Except with Web Server Edition of Windows Server 2003, IIS 6.0 is not installed by default.
- IIS 6.0 is installed in a "locked-down" mode. In the default configuration, IIS 6.0 will serve only static content. An attempt to serve a dynamic file (such as ASP, ASP.NET, or server-side includes (SSI)) results in a "file not found" error. All files with dynamic extensions must be added to the web service extensions list using IIS Manager.
- When IIS 6.0 is installed, its worker processes run under a Network Service user account. This account, new to Windows Server 2003, is associated with limited privileges and provides a more secure execution environment.
- The new implementation of SSL offers a 35% increase in performance over the previous one. The SSL session cache can now be shared by multiple processes, which reduces overall load on the authentication modules.
- IIS comes with a new mode of authorization, URL authorization, which works in conjunction with a new tool called Authorization Manager. Authorization Manager and URL authorization allow administrators to control access to URLs based on the user's role and provide a very powerful tool for enhancing server security.
- Advanced digest authentication is a new authentication mechanism introduced with IIS 6.0. The user's credentials are stored on a domain controller as an MD5 hash. This authentication mechanism requires IE 5 or later and provides enhanced security compared to the original digest authentication.

Changes to the Default Permission Settings

Windows Server 2003 demonstrates Microsoft's shift of focus from access as the top priority to security. This shift is most visible in the changes made to the default access rights. In the previous versions of Windows, members of the Everyone group had Full Control access to shares and NTFS permissions. The locked-down default settings of Server 2003 give Everyone group members only noninheritable read and execute permissions to the drive roots. When new files are created, the permissions are not inherited from the parent and must be set manually. New shares give by default only read permission to the Everyone group.

Another new access restriction in Windows Server 2003 applies to the anonymous users. They do not receive a membership in the Everyone group and instead belong to the new built-in Anonymous Logon group.

To find out more about these and other new Windows Server 2003 features, use the numerous resources available on the following Microsoft site: www.microsoft.com/windowsserver2003/default.mspx.

Example: Securing an Intranet or Extranet Portal

To illustrate the ideas outlines in this chapter, let's create a small demo portal site that demonstrates the following:

- Authenticating users with Windows authentication turned on in all tiers on our system
- Flowing user identity through the system layers
- Authorizing users and protecting system resources based on the caller's role
- Personalizing the portal based on caller identity and user profiles stored in the SQL Server database

Because it will be an intranet/extranet portal, we have good control over the user base and the environment. We can use Windows authentication in IIS, the ASP.NET application, and SQL Server. This option provides tight security and comes to us at no cost. With Windows authentication and impersonation turned on, code in all layers of our system executes under the caller identity, giving us constant access to identity information. Based on user identity and group membership, our system will grant or deny over-all access and will give different access rights to our protected resources.

We are storing user profile information in a table in the SQL Server database. The key to this table is the username. The profile data is used by the ASP.NET application to customize the portal. Figure 6.13 illustrates this approach.

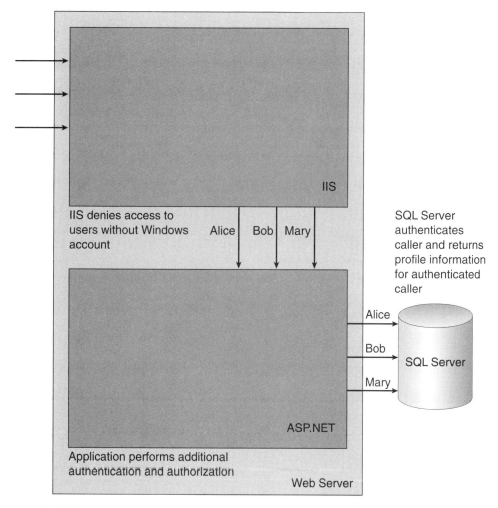

Figure 6.13 Portal Identity Flow

Let's outline our portal design goals:

- Every user of your network can access the portal site except for members of the NoPortalForYou Windows group.
- Our protected resource is the text file stored on the server. The file contains a memo from the management. Every authenticated user can read the file, which is displayed in a text box on the portal page. Members of the Managers Windows group can also modify contents of the text box and save it back to the memo file. We protect the file by configuring ACL for the file and hiding the Save command button if the caller does not belong to the Managers group.
- SQL Server queries the tblUserProfile table based on the authenticated user's identity and returns two bits of information to the ASP.NET application: your preferred stock symbol and the background color you have selected for the page. ASP.NET personalizes the page by displaying the greeting with your name, showing the value of your preferred stock and painting the page background in the color of your choosing.

Now let's roll up our sleeves and start writing the code.

Step 1. Create Users and Groups

We start with creating three accounts for testing the application (Alice, Bob, and Mary) and two groups, **NoPortalForYou** and **Managers**. We also assign Mary to the NoPortalForYou group and Alice to the Managers group. To manage groups and users:

1. Open **Administrative Tools** under Control Panel.
2. Launch the Computer Management utility, and go to **Local Users and Groups**.
3. Create these three users by selecting the **New User** option under Users (Figure 6.14).

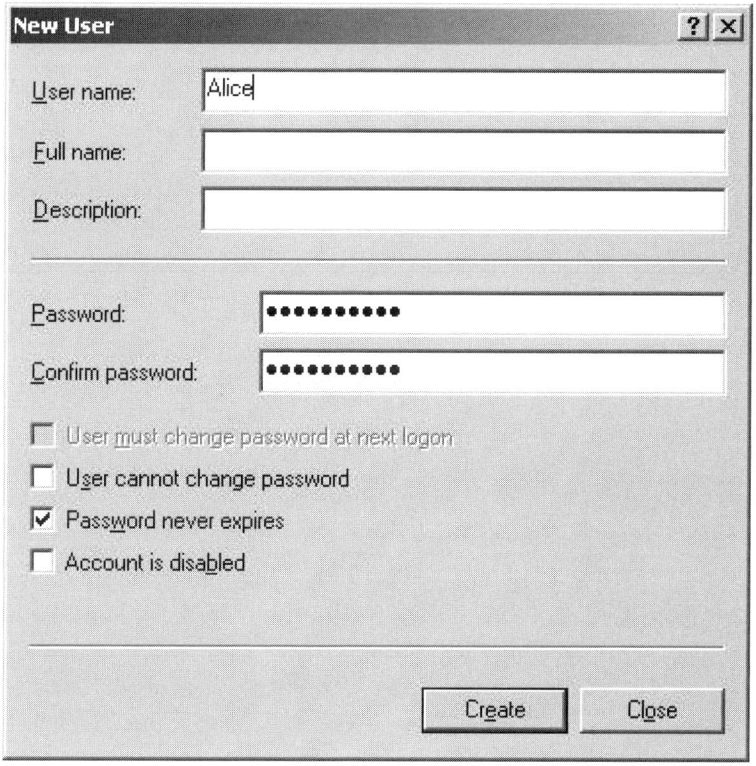

Figure 6.14 New User Dialog Box

4. Create two groups and set the groups' membership.

Figure 6.15 shows New Group dialog box where the group and its members' list are created.

Figure 6.15 New Group Dialog Box

Step 2. Create the SQL Server Profile Storage

The next step is to create our user profile storage in SQL Server:

1. Open SQL Server Enterprise Manager and create a new SQL Server database called **PortalDB** with all default options.
2. Right-click the **Tables** node under PortalDB and create a new table with three columns:

   - **UserName**; key field containing user's login name
   - **FavoriteStock** to hold the user's stock symbol
   - **BackgroundColor**

3. Save the table as **tblUserProfile**.

Figure 6.16 displays the SQL Enterprise Manager interface used to design and save a new table.

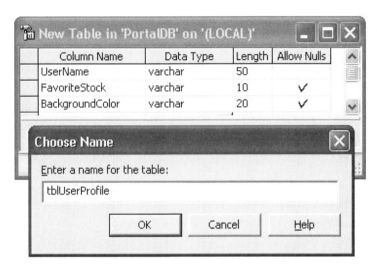

Figure 6.16 Create New Group

4. Next open the table in Enterprise Manager and enter some test data as shown in Figure 6.17. Note that each **UserName** value contains the Domain Name prefix, which is likely to be different on your machine.
5. Create three SQL Server logins for Alice, Bob, and Mary specifying Windows as the authentication option and giving each new login a Public access to the **PortalDB** database (see Figure 6.11).
6. None of the new SQL Server users has an access to tblProfileData table. To verify that, right-click the table, select **Properties**, and click **Permissions** (Figure 6.18). Because none of the check boxes is checked, even if the user is successfully authenticated and given database access, read/write on the table is prohibited.

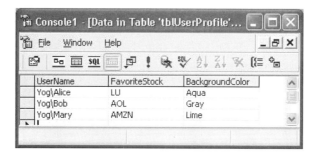

Figure 6.17 Populate tblUserProfile

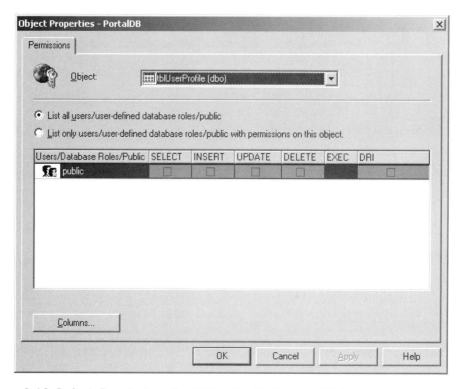

Figure 6.18 Default Permissions for **tblUserProfile** Prevent All Access

7. To give authenticated users access to profile data, we create the view **vwProfileData**, which restricts table access to records owned by the user. Views are like predefined queries stored in SQL Server and are often used to customize or restrict data access. Create the view as shown in Listing 6.3.

Listing 6.3 Create a View to Provide Access to Profile Data

```
CREATE VIEW vwProfileData
as
SELECT * FROM tblUserProfile
WHERE UserName = SYSTEM_USER
```

The SYSTEM_USER function resolves to the Windows Login name of the authenticated user; if Alice were to execute this view, she would be able to see only her profile data. Profile data of other users of the system is protected. This approach provides modularity and code reuse because other applications on your network might consume user profile data without having to worry about reimplementing security.

8. Grant all users SELECT access to the view. Open the view's **Properties** dialog box, click **Permissions**, and check the **SELECT** box (Figure 6.19).

Step 3. Create the ASP.NET Application

Finally we can create our portal application:

1. Start Visual Studio .NET and create a new ASP.NET project called **MiniPortal** (Figure 6.20).
2. As part of its magic, .NET creates a new IIS site for us. In IIS, open the **Properties** dialog box for the MiniPortal site, and click the **Directory Security** tab.
3. Configure the site to use Windows authentication only (see Figure 6.3).

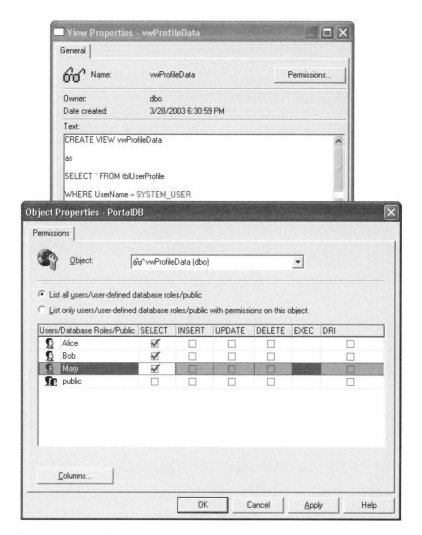

Figure 6.19 Grant View Select Permission

4. Next we configure our ASP.NET application to use Windows authentication and impersonation. Locate and open the **Web.config** file in Solution Explorer in Visual Studio.
5. Make sure that Windows authentication mode is selected and impersonation is on (see Figure 6.6).

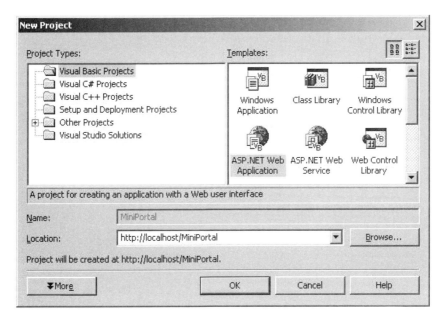

Figure 6.20 Create an ASP.NET Project in Visual Studio

6. Visual Studio creates a default page for you. Rename it **Portal-Page.aspx** and open it in design mode.

7. Drop the following web controls on the default page:

- Panel **Panel1** to serve as a container for other controls
- Label **lblPortalName** displaying the name of your portal site
- Label **lblGreeting**, which holds personalized greetings
- **lblStock**, which displays the value of your favorite stock
- Text box **txtMemo**, which displays the contents of your protected resource—the text file with the memo from management
- Command button **cmdSave**, which allows members of the Managers group to save the memo

8. Create a text file called **C:\MEMO.TXT** and write some fictitious memo to it.

9. To configure ACL protection on this file, right-click it in Windows Explorer, select **Properties**, click the **Security** tab, and make sure that only the Managers group has Full Control access to the file.

10. Return to Visual Studio and double-click the **cmdSave** command button to open the code-behind module of your page.
11. Paste the code shown in Listing 6.4 there.

Listing 6.4 Complete Code Listing for Portal Page

```
' Imports keyword allows us to add selected namespaces
Imports System.Security.Principal
Imports System.Threading
Imports System.Data.SqlClient

Public Class WebForm1
 Inherits System.Web.UI.Page
 Protected WithEvents txtMemo As System.Web.UI.WebControls.TextBox
 Protected WithEvents lblStock As System.Web.UI.WebControls.Label
 Protected WithEvents lblGreeting As System.Web.UI.WebControls.Label
 Protected WithEvents cmdSave As System.Web.UI.WebControls.Button
 Protected WithEvents lblPortalName As System.Web.UI.WebControls.Label
 Protected WithEvents Panel1 As System.Web.UI.WebControls.Panel

#Region "Web Form Designer Generated Code"
 'This call is required by the Web Form Designer.
 <System.Diagnostics.DebuggerStepThrough()> Private Sub _
 InitializeComponent()

 End Sub
 Private Sub Page_Init(ByVal sender As System.Object, ByVal e As _
 System.EventArgs) _
 Handles MyBase.Init
  'CODEGEN: This method call is required by the Web Form Designer
  'Do not modify it using the code editor.
  InitializeComponent()
 End Sub
#End Region

 Private Sub Page_Load(ByVal sender As System.Object, ByVal e As _
 System.EventArgs) _
   Handles MyBase.Load
  Try
   '*** Here's our authorization and personalization rules:
   '*** 1. Everyone except members of NoPortalForYou group can access _
   the portal
   '*** 2. Only members of Managers group can save memo text
```

```
'*** 3. Upon successful authentication, the portal site is _
personalized by
'***    - displaying your name
'***    - displaying the value of your favorite stock
'***    - paint the page background using your preferred color

'*** Since we have turned only Windows authentication on for IIS
'*** and Windows authentication and Impersonation for ASP.NET, only
'*** authenticated users can get here

'*** Determine the caller's identity:

If IsPostBack Then Exit Sub

Dim CurrentPrincipal As WindowsPrincipal = CType(context.User, _
WindowsPrincipal)
Dim strCallerIdentity As String = CurrentPrincipal.Identity.Name

'*** If the caller belongs to NoPortalForYou group, deny all access
If CurrentPrincipal.IsInRole("YOG\NoPortalForYou") Then
 lblGreeting.Text = "System Access Denied"
 lblStock.Visible = False
 txtMemo.Visible = False
 cmdSave.Visible = False
 Exit Sub
End If

'*** If caller does not belong to Managers group, Save button _
should be hidden
If Not CurrentPrincipal.IsInRole("YOG\Managers") Then
 txtMemo.ReadOnly = True
 cmdSave.Visible = False
End If

'*** Now read user profile data from SQL Server table tblUserProfile
'*** since we configured SQL Server for Windows Authentication, we
'*** can use trusted connection which does not require explicit
'*** username or password

'*** Initial Catalog parameter of the connection string is the _
database name
'*** Data Source parameter of the connection string is the SQL
Server name
```

Continues

Listing 6.4 Complete Code Listing for Portal Page (*Continued*)

```
Dim strConnectionString As String, strSQLQuery As String
strConnectionString = _
"Persist Security Info=True;trusted_connection=true;Initial _
Catalog=PortalDB;Data Source=."

strSQLQuery = "SELECT FavoriteStock, BackgroundColor FROM _
vwProfileData"

'*** connect to SQL Server
Dim DBConnection As New SqlConnection(strConnectionString)
DBConnection.Open()

'*** read user profile data
Dim Reader As SqlClient.SqlDataReader
Dim Command As New SqlCommand(strSQLQuery, DBConnection)
Reader = Command.ExecuteReader(CommandBehavior.SingleRow)

Dim strFavoriteStockSymbol As String = "", _
    strBackgroundColor As String = ""

If Reader.Read() Then
 strFavoriteStockSymbol = Reader.GetString(0)
 strBackgroundColor = Reader.GetString(1)
End If
Reader.Close()
DBConnection.Close()

'*** Customize portal using profile data retrieved from database
If strFavoriteStockSymbol.Length > 0 Then _
ShowStockValue(strFavoriteStockSymbol)

If strBackgroundColor.Length > 0 Then
 Dim MyColorConverter As New System.Drawing.ColorConverter()
 Panel1.BackColor =
MyColorConverter.ConvertFromString(strBackgroundColor)
End If

lblGreeting.Text = "Welcome " & strCallerIdentity

'*** Read memo from text file on the server
Dim FileReader As System.IO.StreamReader = _
System.IO.Filc.OpenText("C:\MEMO.TXT")
txtMemo.Text = FileReader.ReadToEnd()
FileReader.Close()
```

```
Catch ex As Exception
 ' if error occurs put error description in the memo box and _
 disable Save button
 txtMemo.Text = ex.Message
 cmdSave.Visible = False
End Try
End Sub

Private Sub ShowStockValue(ByVal strFavoriteStockSymbol As String)
  If strFavoriteStockSymbol.Length = 0 Then
    lblStock.Text = ""
  Else
    '*** In a real portal Web Service would get life stock value
    '*** In this sample we generate it randomly (which by the way
    '*** reflects my opinion of stock markets)
    Randomize()
    lblStock.Text = strFavoriteStockSymbol & _
        " is at " & CInt(Int((100 * Rnd()) + 1)) ' random value _
        between 1 and 100
  End If
End Sub

Private Sub cmdSave_Click(ByVal sender As System.Object, ByVal e As _
System.EventArgs) _
Handles cmdSave.Click
  Try
    '*** save the contents of the text box back to the memo file
    Dim FileWriter As New System.IO.StreamWriter _
    (System.IO.File.OpenWrite("C:\MEMO.TXT"))
    FileWriter.Write(txtMemo.Text)
    FileWriter.Close()
  Catch
  End Try
End Sub
End Class
```

In the Load event of our page, we:

- Make sure that members of the **NoPortalForYou** group cannot use the portal.
- Hide the Save button and make the text box read only if the caller is not in **Managers**.
- Use **SQLDataReader** to query the SQL Server database **PortalDB**.

- Display the value of your stock, display your name, and paint the background in your preferred color.
- Use the **StreamReader** object to read contents of the C:\MEMO.TXT file and display it in the **txtMemo** text box.

The Click event of the **cmdSave** command button is available only to members of the Managers group. There we use the **StreamWriter** object to save the memo from the text box back to the file.

12. Compile the application and test it logging out and logging in as Alice, Bob, and Mary. Using Mary's login, you cannot see portal data. When logging in as Alice, you have full access and can modify the memo. Logging in as Bob (shown in Figure 6.21), you still can use the personalized portal, but you can only read the memo.

Be aware of a bug fixed in .NET Framework Service Pack 2: If you are a member of too many groups, the **IsInRole** function may fail and return false every time incorrectly. The bug, which has been confirmed by Microsoft, happens due to incorrect buffer allocation when you create a group list. If you log in as an administrator, you will belong to all groups and have a good chance of encountering this bug.

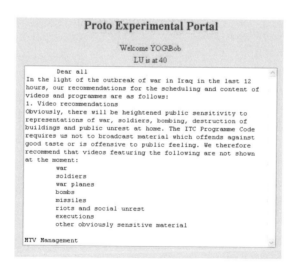

Figure 6.21 Portal Page for Bob

Conclusion

Designing portal security should be high on your list of priorities. There are many types of illegal, harmful, or dangerous access attempts that could be undertaken against your site, and the safety your portal provides is directly proportional to the security of the various software and hardware pieces that together comprise the portal. This chapter demonstrates .NET security features and explains how they integrate with the security features of other mainstream Microsoft products.

Chapter 7

User Profiles

Portals are designed to serve many types of users and to provide an experience for each audience that best matches their expectations and needs. Portal audiences include anonymous Internet users, employees, system administrators, developers, webmasters, content creators, editors, trading partners, and many others. It is much easier to meet the needs of your users when you know who they are and can make educated guesses about what they might need from your portal. As a result, user profiles are essential for nearly every portal.

User profiles are records containing two kinds of data:

- Information about the user such as name, address, interests, demographic information, and a host of other data relevant to the portal
- Data concerning the user's activities in the portal, such as authentication details and past behavior on your portal

In most cases, personal information is gathered by users filling out online forms such as registration forms, order forms, and others. The web log, which tracks which pages were visited and in which order, is the key source for data about user activity on the site. You may want to merge data from both these sources into a data warehouse for reporting and analysis purposes. User profiles are essential for securing your site, providing personalization, and tracking user activity. You can use them for targeted emails, mailings, and marketing and advertising campaigns. Figure 7.1 shows the overall architecture for a profile within a portal.

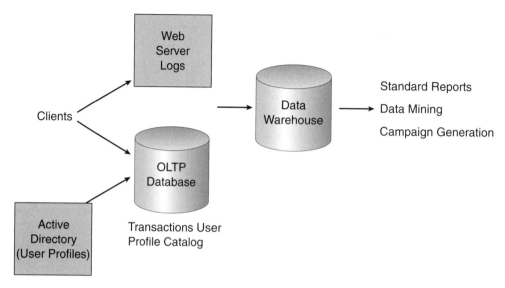

Figure 7.1 Portal Profile Architecture

You can store profile data in a directory service such as Microsoft Active Directory or a Lightweight Directory Access Protocol (LDAP) directory, in a relational database, or both. For an enterprise portal, Active Directory is a likely choice for authentication because the portal is only available to internal users; and if you are using Active Directory for network and email authentication, you know every user already has an Active Directory entry. A commerce site, on the other hand, is more likely to use a relational database such as SQL Server to track orders, which in turn provide vital data for the profile. SharePoint Portal Server and Commerce Server both store profile information in the database.

This chapter explains how to determine the user profiles you will need, where the data should be stored in the overall portal architecture, and how that data might be used for enhancing the user experience and increasing the effectiveness of your portal in reaching your audience. I also discuss how profiles can be helpful for anonymous users, and the differences between profiles in Internet, intranet, and extranet scenarios.

Identifying Key User Groups

Most portals have several types of users, each with different needs. Every portal has administrators whose requirements differ from those of the bulk of the user population. You have to decide which user groups to target. For instance, if you were building an enterprise portal, you would optimize for the needs of your employees and not consider anonymous Internet users, suppliers, or outside groups. Similarly, you could build an Internet portal targeted to anonymous users, at least up until the point that they cross a threshold, such as by making a purchase, which redefines the relationship. In the latter case, you could use techniques to personalize content on the fly so you meet these users' apparent preferences as exhibited through prior navigation or searching during the current session. To implement persistent personalization, which lasts from one session to another, you must prompt users to register with the site or use techniques such as cookies to identify users on subsequent visits.

The first step in determining the roles you will profile is to ask some questions about the business goals of the portal:

- Who will be using the portal? Will anonymous users be allowed access?
- What are the key business goals? Increasing sales, delivering a message to constituents? Providing a forum for online collaboration? Increasing employee productivity?
- For each of the business goals, what are the metrics that will measure success?
- How does each group currently do business? Is there an existing procedure that can or should be copied? How would users benefit from new approaches?
- Will additional groups be brought into the fold, now or in the future? What about suppliers, employees, or customers?

You use the answers to these questions to identify key user groups along with their business goals and associated metrics, such as is shown in Table 7.1.

Table 7.1 User Groups and Business Goals

User Group	Business Goal	Key Metrics
Anonymous users	Provide easy access to company information and catalog.	Page views, searches, shopping basket activity.
Suppliers	Reduce cost of goods. Generate orders to maintain optimum inventory. Streamline orders and payments.	Inventory levels, out-of-stock situations.
Employees	Simplify access to benefits and corporate services.	Page views, transactions entered on site rather than on paper, employee satisfaction surveys.
Customers	Create high customer satisfaction and repeat business. Allow quick and easy ordering. Target campaigns based on past purchases. Allow customers to check on order status.	Customer satisfaction surveys, repeat business, average revenue per customer, returned orders, on-time order delivery.
Customer care representatives	Allow representatives to check on order status. Provide quick correction of order errors. Handle returns expeditiously.	Customer satisfaction with customer service representatives, time per call, call productivity.
Webmasters	Streamline site and content administration.	Reduce time spent on routine maintenance. Increase uptime of site. Minimize overtime of webmasters.

Now that you have defined these groups, you can take a closer look at the information you need to track in their profiles. Tie the information you select to the business goals of your organization. For instance, a consulting firm places a great deal of value on the knowledge and skills of its people; therefore, storing the areas of expertise for each employee in the portal profile would be important so users could search for colleagues based on their areas of expertise. In addition, companies with a small number of large clients may need to gather more detailed profiles than a mass market company with a broader customer base but lower average sales per customer. The latter type of company typically cannot afford the investment of getting to know each and every customer really well.

To start the ball rolling, you must prompt the user to register. This section describes alternatives for user registration.

NOTE *On public web sites, users are reluctant to provide personal data. You must provide compelling reasons, such as exclusive content or quicker transactions, to persuade them to share this information with your site.*

Registration Methods

An outward-facing web site can either create its own user accounts or rely on a third party such as the Microsoft Passport service to provide authentication services (see Chapter 6). The most common scenario is to have users register and provide their own username and password for use on the portal. This approach is described in detail later in this chapter. A large number of users will remain anonymous for a public web site and therefore never register.

An intranet begins with a set of known users who already have accounts. If these accounts are mapped to the enterprise portal to enable single sign-on, the starting place for the profile already exists in Active Directory. You can tap into that information so users do not have to enter their name, phone number, or other contact information twice. SharePoint Portal Server allows you to add a group of users from Active Directory en masse rather than create each account individually. In this enterprise portal scenario, there are no anonymous users, and in many cases all users belong to the same domain.

An extranet could start with either of these approaches. You could treat the extranet portal as an independent entity and have members of your organization maintain accounts on the portal separate from their network accounts. This approach makes sense, especially when the extranet is open to a broader group of users such as suppliers, vendors, and customers who constitute the bulk of the user population. By keeping the systems separate, you eliminate security vulnerabilities that might arise from sharing authentication information. If the internal users outnumber those on the outside, you might want to take the intranet approach, adding accounts for the additional users and providing access to the system through network firewalls.

Creating User Profiles with Self-Registration

From the user's perspective, the first step in personalization is to obtain a username and password through the registration process. This step, which creates the personal profile later used for personalization, may occur the first time a customer makes a purchase from an online business. At that point, they are required to provide personal information to complete the transaction.

Profile creation may occur when a user requests premium content that is only available to registered users. For instance, a service called Bitpipe KnowledgeAlert serves as a clearinghouse for white papers and studies published by knowledge management vendors. Anonymous users may search and browse these papers, but they are required to create accounts and log in to download a paper. Bitpipe also uses that profile information to send email notification when new items are published based on the topics chosen by the user.

Let's look at another example. Users are required to create a personal profile in order to file an aircraft accident report with the National Transportation Safety Board in Washington, DC. Aircraft operators must file a report whenever an accident occurs to one of their aircraft, including minor incidents such as a flat tire on the runway or a dent in the wing from a luggage-handling vehicle. This solution replaces paper forms, which were printed from PDF files, filled out, and mailed to the NTSB. After the forms were received, an accident investigator had to enter the data by hand.

A new user clicks the link to register on the logon page (Figure 7.2). The personal profile page opens (Figure 7.3), which prompts the user to enter the minimum information necessary to create the account. You can always add to the profile later, and a long profile screen is daunting to new users. In this example, the user can choose his own password. You may want to specify the minimum password length to encourage stronger passwords. You can also have the system generate a password.

After entering the requested information, the pilot clicks Submit. The system displays a message that the request is being processed and that an email will be sent to the new user (Figure 7.4).

Next, the system generates an email notification to the user containing a link to the NTSB site (Figure 7.5). This is created as a plain text message with an SMTP mail server. You should not assume that a customer's email system can handle formatting such as HTML or rich text.

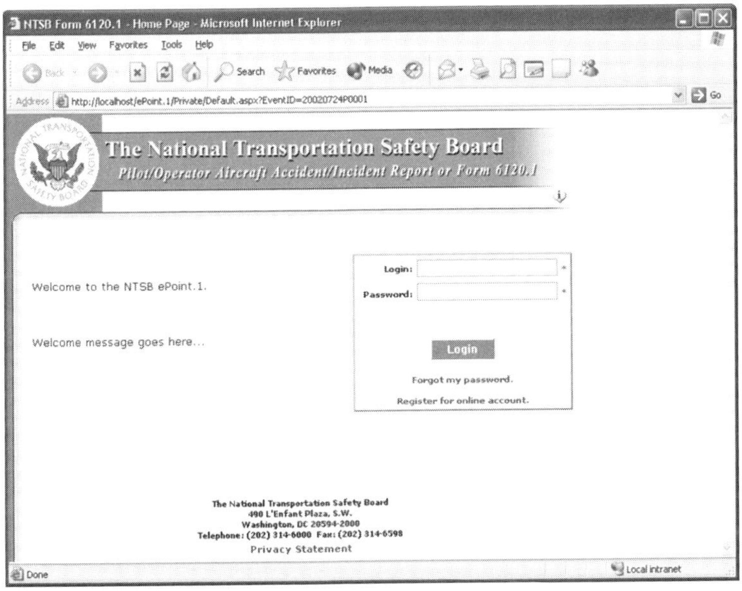

Figure 7.2 Logon Page

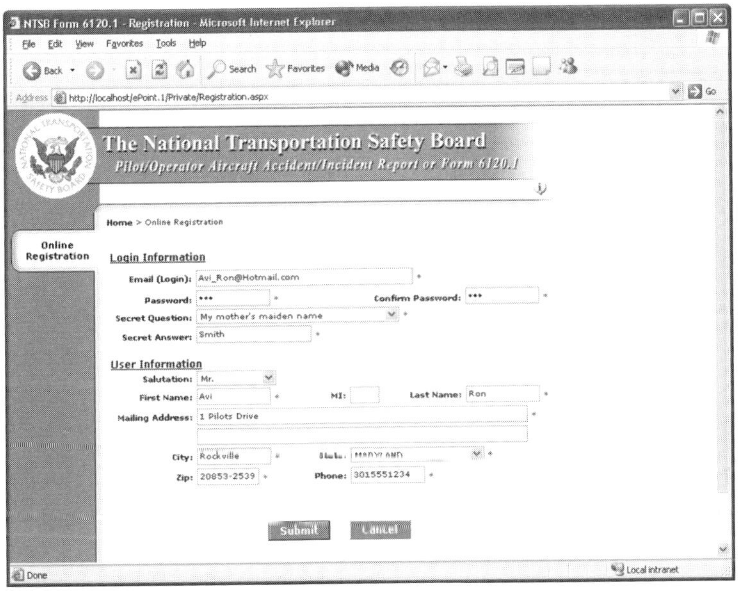

Figure 7.3 Creating an Online Account

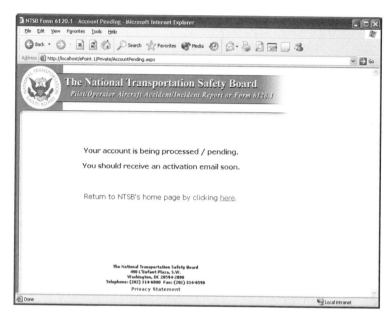

Figure 7.4 Account Processing Notification

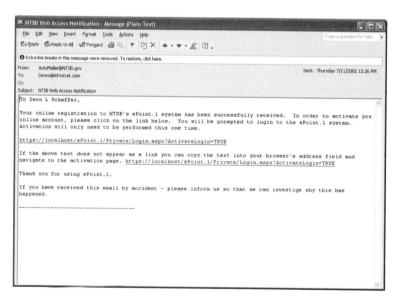

Figure 7.5 Online Registration Email

By following the link provided in the notification email, the user can log in to start filling out the accident report (Figure 7.6).

Figure 7.6 Login Screen for Account Activation

You are likely to have a similar set of steps for account creation. Sometimes all you need to gather is a valid email address and the password chosen by the user. Be sure to check on the legal privacy implications of gathering personal information. If you were to compromise personal information provided by users, you would make your company a target of lawsuits and decrease customer satisfaction. The need to keep customer data safe underscores the importance of security on your site. See Chapter 6 for more details on how to secure your site. As always, don't put confidential information online unless absolutely necessary.

You should have a process for handling forgotten passwords. Some sites allow users to enter their email addresses and send them their passwords as email messages. Others provide a second path for authentication by prompting users to answer a question to identify themselves. Such sites ask users to answer a personal question, such as their place of birth or mother's maiden name, as part of registration. When a user clicks the "Forgot my password" link on the logon page (see Figure 7.2), he is asked to answer that question (Figure 7.7). If the same answer is provided as the user entered at registration, the system sends the password in an email. Sending the password in an email message provides an additional level of security, because it requires the requester to have access to the email account used during registration.

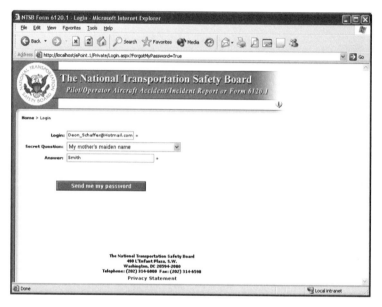

Figure 7.7 Question Asked and Answered

You may want to provide a telephone number on your registration and logon pages to allow users to contact customer support. If they encounter problems trying to access personalized content, this may be your last chance to communicate with them.

Self-Registration with Commerce Server 2002

Commerce Server 2002 ships with a sample site called the Supplier Solution site (also known as the SupplierAD site) that includes code for implementing self-registration. The sample site provides a good way to see this self-registration functionality in action and take a closer look at the objects and code.

1. Follow the instructions in the Commerce Server 2002 Enterprise Edition online help to install the sample site. The site requires two computers to demonstrate all its functionality.
2. Stop the IIS service while you modify the ASP files.
3. Open the SupplierAD site in Commerce Server Manager. Expand **Site Resources**.
4. Click **App Default Config**.
5. In the Commerce Server Resource pane, right-click **Site Registration Options**, then select **Properties**.
6. Change the **Selected Property Value** to 1 in the Site Registration Options Properties and then click **OK**. Additional property values and their meanings are shown in Table 7.2.
7. Create the registration page **newuser.asp** in the www.root/supplierAD/ Authfiles directory.
8. Cut and paste the sample code from the online help file.
9. Edit the **global_siteconfig_lib.asp** file to correctly reference the newuser.asp file you created. Replace the line with the text string **dictPages.NewUser** with **dictPages.NewUser = "authfiles/ newuser.asp"**.
10. Update the **login.asp** code to provide a link to newuser.asp.
11. Restart IIS.

Table 7.2 Site Registration Options Properties

Login Option	Value	Description
FORM_LOGIN_NOT_SUPPORTED	0	Login is not supported.
FORCE_LOGIN_ON_ENTRANCE	1	Login is required to enter the site.
LOGIN_OPTIONAL_ON_ENTRANCE	2	Login is optional on entering the site.
FORCE_LOGIN_ON_PURCHASE	5	Login is required at the time of purchase.

Continues

Table 7.2 Site Registration Options Properties (*Continued*)

Login Option	Value	Description
LOGIN_OPTIONAL_ANY_TIME	6	Login is optional at any time. This is the default for the Retail site.
USE_IIS_AUTH	7	Authentication is through Internet Information Services (IIS) using basic or integrated Windows authentication.

Profile Information

The information provided by a user when creating an account is the basis of the profile. You add to that profile by explicitly querying the user and by observing his behavior on the portal. Table 7.3 lists some of the elements you might want to add to a profile.

Table 7.3 Representative Profile Data Elements

Data Elements	Means of Gathering	Comments
Username	Explicit during registration	Often email address is used
Email address	Explicit during registration	
Secret question	Explicit during registration	
Name	Explicit during purchase	
Address	Explicit during purchase	
Phone number	Explicit during purchase	Do no solicit from user unless needed for purchase as phone number not readily provided until relationship with portal is trusted

Table 7.3 Representative Profile Data Elements (*Continued*)

Data Elements	Means of Gathering	Comments
Interests	May be explicit on subscriptions page; implicit based on pages viewed and search behavior, or both	Use taxonomy to categorize user interests
Product likes and dislikes	Explicit and implicit	Purchases and returned purchases, comparing searching versus purchases and questionnaires
Usage frequency	Implicit	Based on site statistics

Commerce Server 2002 contains a quite rich data model right out of the box. You are likely to find that the information you need to track is already in the database. Many of the fields you will need for user registration are in the Commerce Server 2002 user object, as shown in Figure 7.8.

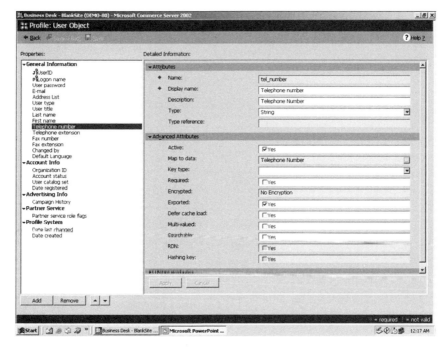

Figure 7.8 User Object Viewed in Commerce Server Business Desk

To add new properties here, click the Add button at the lower left-hand corner of the window. A dialog box opens, prompting you to add either a new property or a new property group (Figure 7.9). Select the property groups to organize properties such as general information and account information so they may be more easily found. When you click OK, a new property called New Property 1 is added to the current section.

You can change the group's property name and other attributes, as shown in Figure 7.10.

This user object shows only a fraction of what Commerce Server tracks regarding the profile, as several tables are involved in storing this data. As you build a commerce site, you can save yourself time by printing a large version of the Commerce Server 2002 schema (Figure 7.11) and hanging it on your wall. The schema shows the structure of the SQL Server database repository for Commerce Server, color coded to indicate the type of data stored in each of the tables. To download the schema, go to www.microsoft.com/commerceserver/techinfo/productdoc/2002/dwschema.asp.

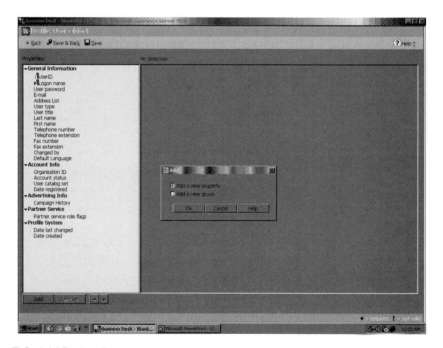

Figure 7.9 Add Dialog Box

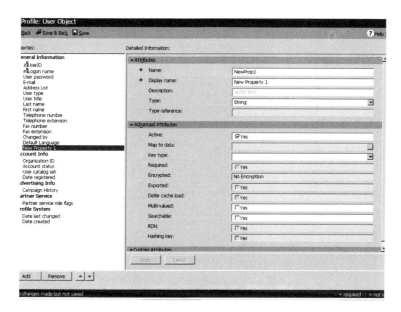

Figure 7.10 Changing Attributes for a New Property

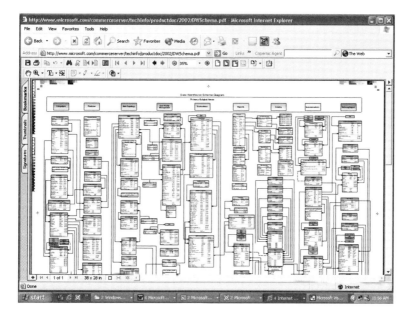

Figure 7.11 Commerce Server 2002 Database Schema

Let's take a closer look at the section of the data model concerned with the profile (Figure 7.12). The RegisteredUser table stores profile data elements such as name, email, and organization.

RegisteredUser		
Column	Logical	Physical
UserId	WSTR	nvarchar
AccountClass	LONG	int
AccountStatus	LONG	int
ApprovalLimit	LONG	int
ApprovalLimitCurrency	WSTR	nvarchar
ApprovingManagerID	LONG	int
AuthType	SHORT	smallint
DateCreated	FILETIME	datetime
DateLastChanged	FILETIME	datetime
DateRegistered	FILETIME	datetime
DefaultBlanketPONumber	WSTR	nvarchar
DefaultBlanketPOProfileID	LONG	int
DefaultCostCenterNumber	WSTR	nvarchar
DefaultCostCenterProfileID	LONG	int
Email	WSTR	nvarchar
EmployeeClassID	LONG	int
FaxNumber	WSTR	nvarchar
FirstName	WSTR	nvarchar
IDCode	WSTR	nvarchar
IDCodeQualifier	WSTR	nvarchar
LastName	WSTR	nvarchar
LocationID	LONG	int
Logon_Name	WSTR	nvarchar
Name	WSTR	nvarchar
OrgID	WSTR	nvarchar
ShipToID	LONG	int
ShipToMethodCode	LONG	int
TelephoneNumber	WSTR	nvarchar
UserIDChangedBy	WSTR	nvarchar
UserTitle	WSTR	nvarchar
UserType	LONG	int
RegisteredUserID		binary(6)
AddressID		binary(6)
RegisteredUserInternalFlag		smallint
Id	UUID	
SiteName	WSTR	
SiteTermKey	WSTR48	

Figure 7.12 RegisteredUser Table from Commerce Server 2002

The RegisteredUser table is related to other tables, including Address, SiteTerm, SiteVisit, Order, and others. The Address table stores multiple addresses for users, such as home address, billing address, and shipping address (Figure 7.13).

NOTE *If you are using Active Directory, usernames are restricted to no more than 20 characters.*

Extending the Basic Profile

While Commerce Server profiles contain quite a few fields right out of the box, you may need additional ones. You can add an arbitrary number of fields to the user profile to make it as detailed and complex as necessary to accomplish your business goals. A hotel, for instance, might want to take note of room, food, and beverage requests as well as a user's preferences for special services. Based on their profiles, a guest who resents the intrusion of

Address

Column	Logical	Physical
Id	**UUID**	**uniqueidentifier**
AddressName	WSTR	nvarchar
AddressType	LONG	int
City	WSTR	nvarchar
CountryCode	WSTR	nvarchar
CountryName	WSTR	nvarchar
DateCreated	FILETIME	datetime
DateLastChanged	FILETIME	datetime
FirstName	WSTR	nvarchar
LastName	WSTR	nvarchar
PostalCode	WSTR	nvarchar
RegionCode	WSTR	nvarchar
RegionName	WSTR	nvarchar
TelephoneExtension	WSTR	nvarchar
TelephoneNumber	WSTR	nvarchar
AddressID		**binary(6)**
AddressInternalFlag		smallint
SiteName	WSTR	

Figure 7.13 Address Table

the nightly bed turndown might then be spared this service, while another guest could be given a local newspaper at check-in.

The first step in extending the profile is to add new fields or tables to the Commerce Server database. For instance, to add a new database that stores your users' areas of expertise as well as a self-assessment of their skill levels, you would follow these steps:

1. Use SQL Server Enterprise Manager to create the database called **SkillTracking**.
2. Create the tables for **Skills** and **UserSkills**.
3. Add the necessary columns to the new tables.
4. Use the Profiles resource in Commerce Server to map to the new data source.
5. Create a data object and map it to the profile definition.
6. Add a site term to the profile definition.

You can also extend a user profile in an LDAP directory rather than in SQL Server. The steps are roughly the same, but you add LDAP classes and attributes rather than database tables and fields. While the Retail Solution site that accompanies Commerce Server uses SQL Server 2000 to store its profiles, the Supplier Solution site uses Active Directory.

The Commerce Server predictor resource attempts to fill in missing bits of the user profile by making inferences based on the behavior of the general population of your portal. For instance, this resource can be used for cross-selling. Customers who purchase fly rods are likely to need new line and flies sooner or later.

Administering the Profile

Many sites allow users to maintain their own profiles or at least to edit the data they provided through online forms. Commerce Server 2002 uses a feature called Customer Services to allow registered users to view and modify their profiles.

Another approach to managing users is central administration by one or more administrators. Users communicate changes through phone calls or emails, and the administrators dutifully update the profiles. This approach eliminates the possibility of incorrect data entry on the part of users and it creates jobs for administrators.

A third path is to set up decentralized administration delegated through a user hierarchy. For instance, a membership organization could designate a primary contact within a member company and give that user the power to administer all users within that organization. Commerce Server calls this feature Partner Services. In this scenario the site administrator creates the Organization profile and the UserObject profile for the delegated administrator, who in turn creates the individual user accounts. This is a similar approach to that used by the Microsoft Solution Provider program. When applying to the program, an organization names the administrator for the partners-only web site. That administrator subsequently grants permissions to other company personnel who need access to the site.

The sample sites contain a number of pages used to access profiles. Users have direct interaction with the profiling system through the following files (Table 7.4):

Table 7.4 Profiling System Pages

Page	Function
addrbook.asp	Views and edits the user's address book (Address profiles).
newaddr.asp	Adds a new address to the user's address book.
login_guest.asp	Enters the site as an anonymous user and creates an associated anonymous profile.
login\newuser.asp	Allows the user to register with the site. If the user has an anonymous profile, it is changed to a registered profile. If the user does not have an anonymous profile, a new registered profile is created.

Table 7.4 Profiling System Pages (*Continued*)

Page	Function
services\customer\account.asp	Views and changes user's profile through Customer Services.
services\partner\account.asp	Allows delegated administrators to view and modify the profile of their organization using the Partner Services feature.
services\partner\users.asp	Provides a list of users who are members of an organization. Delegated administrators can select profiles to view, modify, or delete from this list, or create new member profiles.
services\partner\edit_user.asp	Allows delegated administrators to manage the profiles of members of their organization.

The self-service of user profile data gives users a feeling of control over this information and provides the opportunity for them to keep it up to date. The same capabilities are used by administrators when they have the appropriate permissions.

Tracking Anonymous Users

While registered users are easier to track, the behavior of anonymous users is no less important to the owners of a site. After all, for a public commerce site, registered users start as anonymous users.

Commerce Server tracks both anonymous and authenticated users. During each session, a unique identifier is assigned to the user that persists during the course of the session so the behavior of the user during the session can be tracked. If you enable cookies, you can keep track of each anonymous user from one session to the next. In this way, for example, you can determine how many visits to the site the user made before completing her first purchase.

Global variables are used to store information about the user. These values are recorded on the web logs that will be analyzed later for usage statistics. Table 7.5 summarizes the user information tracked in the log file. Of course for authenticated users you can extend your analysis to include fields that are in their profiles.

Table 7.5 Global Variables for Anonymous Users

User Variable	User/Access Type	Value	Description
m_userID		unique	Unique numeric value assigned to each user.
m_UserType	ANON_USER	1	An anonymous user. The user is unidentified, does not have a ticket, and is not tracked (is not recognized on return visits).
	GUEST_USER	2	An anonymous user. The user has not registered but has a GUEST_TICKET. The user may have a profile, depending on site options. The user is tracked during the current session and, if cookies are enabled on the client and the site, the user is tracked between sessions.
	AUTH_USER	4	An authenticated user. The user is registered, authenticated (access type equals either IIS_AUTH or TICKET_AUTH), and is tracked.
	ANON_VISIT	5	A visit by an ANON_USER.

Table 7.5 Global Variables for Anonymous Users (*Continued*)

User Variable	User/Access Type	Value	Description
m_UserAccessType	GUEST_VISIT	1	A visit by a GUEST_USER authenticated using the AuthManager object and a GUEST_TICKET.
	IIS_AUTH	2	A visit by an AUTH_USER authenticated to Internet Information Services (i_FormLoginOptions = USE_IIS_AUTH) using either Basic or Integrated Windows authentication.
	TICKET_AUTH	3	A visit by an AUTH_USER authenticated using the AuthManager object and an AUTH_TICKET.

User IDs can be stored in cookies or as part of the URL (URL mode). The user ID is also stored in the profile if the user is authenticated. You can configure Commerce Server to use cookies or URL mode in the Application Default Configuration resource.

Defining SPS Profiles

User profiles in SharePoint help track the interests and expertise of your knowledge workers. In an external portal, profiles are not usually shown to other users, and they are chiefly of interest to site administrators. In the enterprise portal, on the other hand, profiles contain interesting information and can be valuable to users as well, who can use the profiles as a means of connecting to people with similar interests.

As an administrator, you can create user profiles for other members of your online community. You control the properties for profiles and the access granted to property profiles for various groups of users. For instance, users can have private and public property values in the same profile.

SharePoint can import a user profile directly from Active Directory. To do so:

1. From the portal home page, click **Site Settings** in the top navigation.
2. In the User Profile, Audiences and Personal Sites section of the Site Settings page, click **Manage Profile Database**.
3. On the Manage Profile Database page (see Figure 7.14), schedule the import to synchronize SharePoint with Active Directory with either a full or incremental import. For an enterprise portal, you may already be storing helpful attributes about users in Active Directory, such as job titles, departments, or locations. By importing from Active Directory, you make these part of your SharePoint profile.

By making this part of the portal profile, you can use the data to target content and help users build communities of interest by finding others based on profile attributes. Alternatively from this page, you can add user profiles one at a time, although this is not usually an efficient option.

In the most likely scenario for a public web site, users can enter and edit their own profile information, as shown in Figure 7.15. They open this page by selecting Edit Profile from the Actions menu on the My Site page.

Users can view one another's shared profile information, as in Figure 7.16. This figure shows the public view of the profile with private fields hidden.

You can change the user profile template—for example, by adding additional properties. On the Manage Profile Database page, click Add Profile Property in the Profile Properties section of the page (Figures 7.17 and 7.18).

After you add fields to the profile, you may notice that finding the field you want is harder. Profile sections let you group fields to make profile properties easier to find (Figure 7.19).

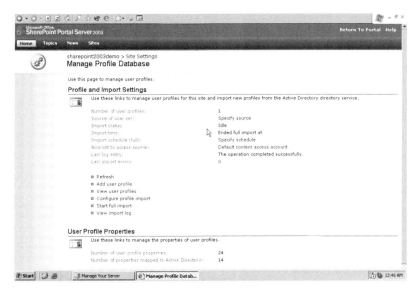

Figure 7.14 Manage Profile Database Page

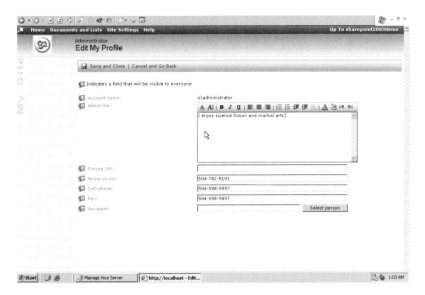

Figure 7.15 SharePoint User Profile

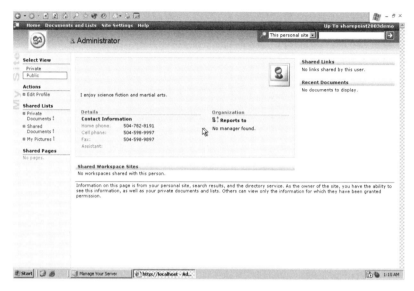

Figure 7.16 Public Profile in SharePoint Portal Server

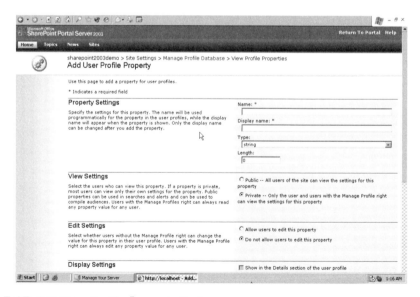

Figure 7.17 Add User Profile Property Page

Figure 7.18 View Profile Properties Page

Figure 7.19 User Profile with New Field Added

Note that the public fields are indicated on the profile page with a special icon. In the example, I made the Hire Date visible to everyone.

SharePoint Audiences

One of the values of profiles is to understand your users so you can fulfill their needs. SharePoint Portal Server takes this an extra step with the concept of audiences. Users can belong to one or more audiences so they can receive targeted content. Web parts and content can be mapped to audiences. For instance, your company might have offices in 16 cities. You could use audiences to refine the company news section to highlight items of interest to local offices.

SPS uses rules to assign profiles to an audience and provides two ways to map people to rules. First, you can link an audience to a Windows security group. This approach makes it quite easy to segment users with the information already contained in their Windows profiles. For instance, you might have a Windows security group called "HR" and therefore want to create a corresponding audience. The second approach is to create a rule for an audience based on a property in the SPS user profile. You can extend these user profile properties as you see fit.

The first step in audience management is to create a new audience:

1. Click **Site Settings** from the portal home page top navigation.
2. Select **Manage Audiences** in the User Profile, Audiences and Personal Sites section . The Manage Audiences page opens (Figure 7.20).
3. Click **Create audience** to create a new audience on the Create Audience page (Figure 7.21). Click **OK**.
4. Create a rule that determines when a person belongs to the audience (Figure 7.22). Click **OK**.

Chapter 8 also covers SharePoint audiences as a means of providing personalized content to your portal users. When you combine the ability to target content based on the judgment of the SharePoint administrator (through audiences) with the ability of the users to choose their own content via subscriptions, you end up with a powerful engine for personalization.

Figure 7.20 Manage Audiences Page

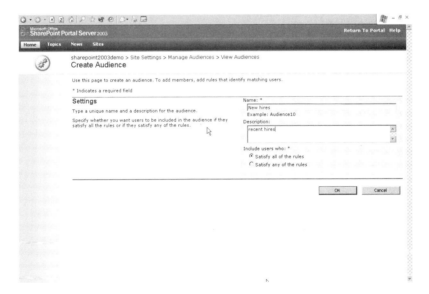

Figure 7.21 Create Audience Page

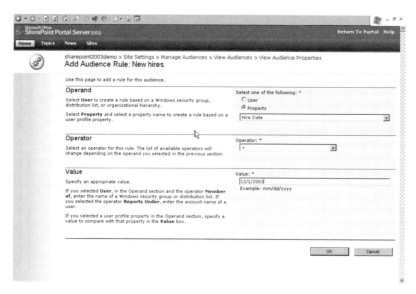

Figure 7.22 Add Audience Rule Page

SharePoint Single Sign-On

SharePoint Portal Server offers a single sign-on service that makes it easier for users to access their applications within the portal. If you embed an expense-tracking or project management system in your portal that requires a separate login, you can configure SharePoint to store user credentials and map them to their SharePoint account. Users can move from one application to another without signing into each one separately.

Single sign-on maps authentication to the individual web parts. You could, for example, design a portal page with three different web parts requiring three different usernames and passwords. The single sign-on service would map all these to the appropriate credentials without prompting the user to log in again.

To implement single sign-on, you must configure the single sign-on service, create a base system key, and then add application definitions for each of the applications to be integrated. Here are more detailed steps:

1. Start the Microsoft Single Sign-On service. From the Start menu, select **Programs**, then the **Administrative Tools** program group, and click **Services**.

2. In the Services console, select **Microsoft Single Sign-On service**. Right-click and select **Start**.
3. Run the SharePoint Portal Server Single Sign-On Administration by selecting it from the SharePoint Portal Server program group on the Start menu. The management console appears, as shown in Figure 7.23.
4. Select **Manage server settings** for single sign-on and enterprise application definitions.
5. Enter the account name, server name, and other information for the account that can manage the single sign-on service (Figure 7.24). You can choose the location of the database that contains this information on this page as well. The account you choose must be a member of the local Administrators group or a member of the STS_WPG local group.
6. Create the base system key, which is the encryption key used to decrypt the credentials stored in the database. SharePoint automatically generates the base system key. You can regenerate the key if the previous credentials were compromised.

Figure 7.23 Manage Settings for Single Sign-On Page

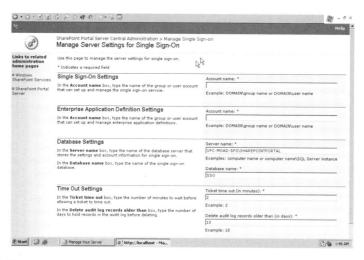

Figure 7.24 Manage Server Settings for Single Sign-On Page

> **NOTE** *You cannot manage the base system key remotely. You must access the job server and specify the settings locally. This may be a long-running process, so take care to perform it at off-peak periods.*

The development interface for SharePoint single sign-on is extensible, so developers can add custom functionality. These changes can make the SharePoint Portal Server user interface a useful part of an enterprise portal even if you are not relying on out-of-the-box functionality.

Analyzing Profile and Data

Now that we have all these profiles, what should we do with them? Can users take advantage of profiles or are they only tools for webmasters and marketing professionals? Which tools can be used to mine the profiles?

Commerce Server Analysis Tools

Commerce Server 2002 offers the richest set of profile analytical tools in the Microsoft portal platform, as befits this flagship e-business product.

The Commerce Server Business Desk is the user interface framework that supports analysis of profiles and other site data. It is a web interface that is separate from the commerce site and exists for the benefit of the "back office" rather than shoppers. The Business Desk consists largely of Active Server Pages along with shared modules. It is designed to be extended by developers and customized for the needs of a particular business. A Harley-Davidson dealership handles its customers and products in a different way from a haberdasher or a food emporium, for instance. Therefore, each instance of Commerce Server has it own Business Desk.

The Business Desk is organized into list pages and edit pages. Because Commerce Server is largely parameter-driven by data from SQL Server, Business Desk provides a user interface to access both global and module-specific settings. For instance, user profiles can be accessed through the Business Desk. You can search for users in the Users module based on fields in the profile such as logon name, email address, first name, last name, and custom properties.

> **NOTE** *The profiles are a rich source of information on the users of the portal, as well as the basis of analysis and decisions relating to content, marketing, and outreach. Before you unleash this data for all to see, however, you need to be aware of the confidentiality of some profile information. Be sure to follow advice of your legal counsel and to adhere to your site's privacy guidelines.*

Commerce Server 2002 comes with 35 preconfigured reports covering such areas as sales, web usage, advertising, and user reports. User reports include distinct users by time, new registered users, user days to register, and user trends. You can customize these reports or add new reports of your own design. The reports are run from a data warehouse that is generated from site data, including web logs. The data is stored in online analytical processing (OLAP) cubes, a format that dramatically improves performance for aggregations. You can also build your own custom reports against the OLAP cubes from your Commerce site, with tools such as Excel pivot tables.

You can also create your own custom reports using Commerce Server data. These reports come from the OLAP cube created by Commerce Server. Table 7.6 lists the Commerce Server Data Warehouse cubes and associated dimensions, along with the source tables that contain that data.

Table 7.6   Commerce Server Cubes and Dimensions

Cube	Dimensions	Source tables	Reports
Bandwidth	DateHour Day of Week Hour of Day Site	HitsByHour	Bandwidth Summary Bandwidth Trends
Basket Events	DateHour Events ProductCategory Site UserType	csdw_BasketEventsFactView	Shopping Basket Events
Buyer Visits	BuyerVisits Site UserType	UserBrowsingtoPurchaseFactView	Buyer Browse to Purchase
Entry Pages	Date Site URI	FirstUriByDate	Entry Pages
Exit Pages	Date Site URI	LastUriByDate	Exit Pages
mscsCampaign	Advertiser DateHour Events Page Group Site UserType	mscsCampaignEvents mscsOrderedImpressions	Ad Reach and Frequency by Date Ad Reach and Frequency per Advertiser Campaign Event Summary Campaign Item Summary

Table 7.6   Commerce Server Cubes and Dimensions (*Continued*)

Cube	Dimensions	Source tables	Reports
mscsCampaignEvents	Advertiser DateHour Events Page Group Site User Type	dbo.csdw_CampaignEventsFactView	
mscsDateIntersect	Date Hour of Day Day of Week Week of Year	csdw_DateFactView	
mscsOrderedImpressions	Advertiser Site	dbo.csdw_OrderedImpressionsFactView	
mscsSales	Address Currency Date ProductCategory Site UserType	dbo.csdw_SalesFactView	Product Sales

Continues

Table 7.6   Commerce Server Cubes and Dimensions *(Continued)*

Cube	Dimensions	Source tables	Reports
mscsVisitInfo	BrowserOS BrowserType Date DateHour Day of Week Hour of Day Referrer Site UserType Week of Year	dbo.csdw_VisitInfoFactView	
mscsWebUsage	BrowserOS BrowserType Date DateHour Day of Week Hour of Day Referrer Site UserType Week of Year	mscsDateIntersect mscsVisitInfo	Activity by Browser Distinct Users By Time General Activity Statistics Top Referring Domains by Request Usage Summary by Day of Week Usage Summary by Hour of Day Usage Summary by Week of Year Usage Trends User Trends User Visit Trends

Table 7.6 Commerce Server Cubes and Dimensions (*Continued*)

Cube	Dimensions	Source tables	Reports
OrderEvents	DateHour Day of Week Events Hour of Day Site UserType Week of Year	Order	Order Events
Page Usage	Date HTTP Status Is Request Level Directory Site URI Win32Status	HitsInfo	Directories Hits by HTTP Status Hits by Win32 Status Top Requested Pages

SharePoint and SQL Server Profile Analysis

If you choose to develop a custom profile in SQL Server, you will not have the benefit of the canned reports or the off-the-shelf data warehouse capabilities of Commerce Server, but you can still write your own reports against the SQL Server database. This is also true for SharePoint Portal Server. Because it stores its profile data in SQL Server, you can use your favorite SQL Server reporting and data-mining tools to extract this data.

Conclusion: Taking the Next Step with Profiles

Now that you have implemented profiles for your portal users, it is time to put them to even better use. Chapter 8 demonstrates how you can use personalization to display information to users when they need it, thereby increasing the popularity and effectiveness of your site. While you can have user profiles without personalization, it is difficult to have personalization without user profiles.

Personalization

Personalization refers to a group of features that tailor the user experience to the preferences of the user. It results in the delivery of custom content to the user when the user needs it, and it improves the online experience of the user. Personalization is important both for public portals and for enterprise portals. Users of public portals, whether commerce portals, membership portals, or government portals, need a sense of belonging to encourage them to keep coming back to the portal. For enterprise portals, personalization can "push" information to users based on their interests, conveying information that can help them but that they might not otherwise have found. Personalization is an essential element for digital dashboards, as the roles played by individuals are different and each role has different information needs.

Personalization builds on the user profile (see Chapter 7). This chapter introduces the personalization techniques most often used in a portal and outlines instructions for implementing these techniques on the Microsoft .NET portal platform. It also describes the integration of personalization with user profiles, web parts, subscriptions, and commerce features.

Personalization Cycle

Personalization is one of the steps in creating an online virtual community. It provides a means for users to express their preferences and mold the content and appearance of the portal. Portal administrators can monitor usage patterns and identify further opportunities to enhance the user experience, thus increasing user satisfaction. This virtuous cycle can be repeated endlessly during the life of the portal (Figure 8.1).

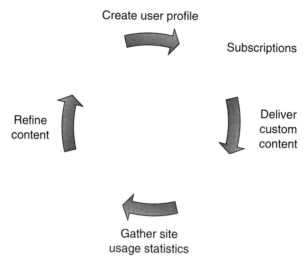

Figure 8.1 Personalization Cycle

The web is an ideal environment for delivering personalization because it lends itself to tracking user behavior and categorizing content based on categories and metadata. Most importantly, personalization of information is virtually free on the web. It is easy to gather user profiles both explicitly and implicitly, based on the behavior of the user. It is simple to deliver custom content. In contrast, allowing a higher degree of customization for each order in other industries, such as the automobile industry, would introduce complications in the design and manufacturing process and hence add cost to the product.

Creating Content for Personalization

What is it that makes personalized content different from other content? How can the same content be used for all users and also in a personalized view? The key to supporting personalization is to create content with the necessary data or metadata that allows it to be dovetailed with user preferences. For instance, many web sites offer weather information. This data is linked to a specific geographic area and to a time period. To allow personalization of weather forecasts, you would need to ensure that the user profile could be matched to those forecasts, such as by associating a set of postal codes with a weather map. Similarly, if you wanted to allow personalization of photographs, you would need to apply the appropriate metadata when the photographs were filed (for example, golf, environment, or state government).

The portal taxonomy is a natural place to turn as you start to map users to content. You can use the taxonomy to categorize content and also link the taxonomy to the user profile. For instance, you could ask users to prioritize the top three taxonomy entries in which they are interested. The site could send email notification when new content is posted in any of these three areas.

Personalizing Home Page Content

When most people think of personalization, they think of My Yahoo or My MSN, which are web pages that allow individuals to control the content they see. When a portal contains a plethora of information, users appreciate anything you can offer to narrow the items displayed to those that match their interests. The user profile provides clues for personalization, such as the user's address, age, job title, or industry. The behavior of users provides even better ideas of what interests them. Watching how my Internet Explorer favorites have evolved over the years is a reminder of how my interests have waxed and waned. One year I was searching for a car and perusing online reviews, used car sites, and consumer ratings. The next year I took up hiking and spent time at outdoor magazine web sites, the National Park Service, and of course gear sites galore. Although I live in Washington, D.C., I am interested in the weather in Florida and Seattle because I have family there.

For personalization in our portal we will explore the various tools provided in the Microsoft platform to customize the appearance and content in the portal, as well as push content to users based on subscriptions. Our primary tools will be SharePoint Portal Server and Commerce Server, but we will also examine how you can take advantage of SQL Server Notification Services and custom coding to provide personalization.

SharePoint Personal Pages

SharePoint Portal Server can deliver personalized pages through the My Site feature. Clicking My Site on the portal home page opens a page on which you can customize content and settings, view a summary of alerts and recent documents, and even access private file storage (Figure 8.2).

The My Site page takes full advantage of the web part architecture. Web parts are the building blocks that make up a SharePoint web part page or dashboard. They are analogous to controls on a page, and they are derived from web form controls. In the first version of SharePoint Portal Server, web parts were ActiveX controls, but the 2003 version uses different functionality to overcome browser compatibility and security concerns.

Web parts are used not only on the My Site page but on all web part pages in SharePoint, including the portal home page. You can create new

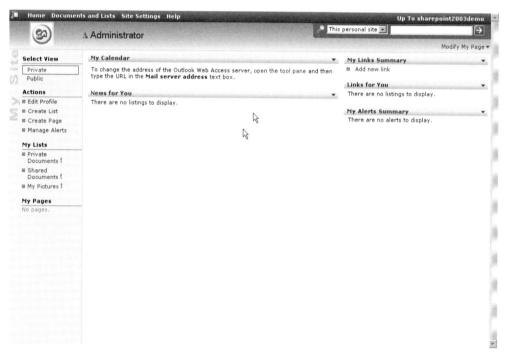

Figure 8.2 My Site Page

web part pages and provide links to them wherever you wish in the portal. These pages provide a number of benefits to a SharePoint portal, including:

- Allowing fusion of data from many sources and formats in a common place
- Facilitating the creation of management dashboards with key metrics displayed in text and graphical formats
- Linking to other web part pages to allow multiple views of the same information
- Customization options in FrontPage 2003
- Reusability, sharing, and easy deployment

SharePoint comes with many types of web parts, such as the List View web part, the Image web part, and the News web part. A web part can consist of web content, such as the contents of a web page, or an interface to an application, such as a view of your Outlook calendar or even the Windows performance monitor. The My Site architecture allows users to add any number of web parts to the page and arrange them as they see fit.

Web parts support integration of applications by consolidating views into multiple applications in a single browser window. They also can integrate applications more deeply by connecting web parts to one another. For instance, you could have a web part retrieve data from your Outlook contacts folder, which would then pass the name of a person to a web part from your customer relationship management system and display the most recent phone calls and orders from that person. Similarly, you could link inventory with supplier data and a web part displaying the home page of the supplier based on its URL in the supplier database.

To modify the web parts displayed on My Site:

1. Click the **Modify My Page** dropdown arrow.
2. Select **Design this Page** from the dropdown menu (Figure 8.3).
3. View the My Site page in edit view (Figure 8.4). The page is divided into areas called zones where you can place web parts. Only the administrator can edit the header, footer, and left navigation menu of the page.

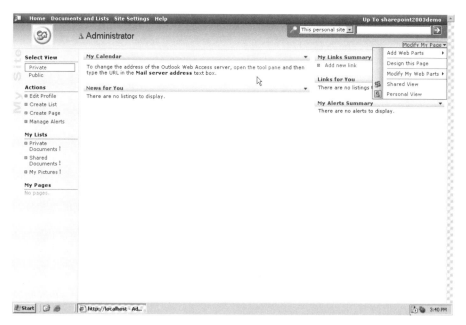

Figure 8.3 Modify My Page Menu

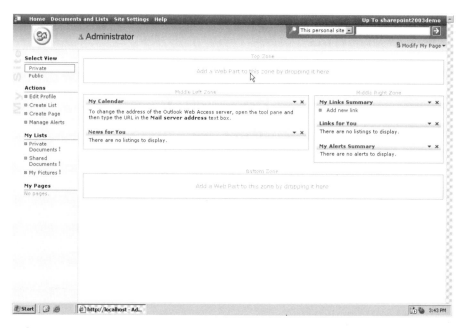

Figure 8.4 My Site in Design View

4. Identify how the body of the page is divided into sections (Figure 8.5).
5. To move a web part, move the cursor over the web part until it becomes a movement indicator (vertical and horizontal arrows). Click and drag the web part to the desired position. For instance, Figure 8.6 shows how the page would look if I dragged the My Alerts web part to the upper zone where it would occupy the full width of the page.
6. To save your changes, navigate away from the page. Clicking **Home** in the top navigation returns you to My Site in view mode.

To add web parts to My Site:

1. Select **Add Web Parts** from the Modify My Page menu.
2. Click **Browse** to display the Add Web Parts menu listing available web parts, as shown in Figure 8.7.

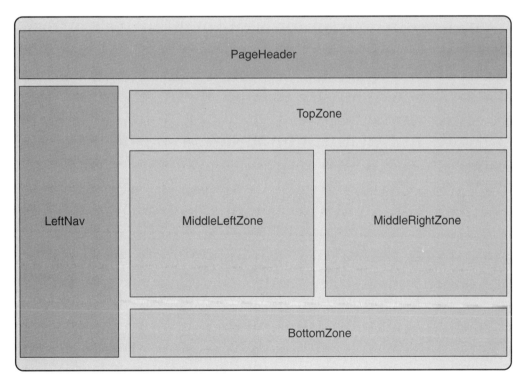

Figure 8.5 Web Part Zones on My Site Page

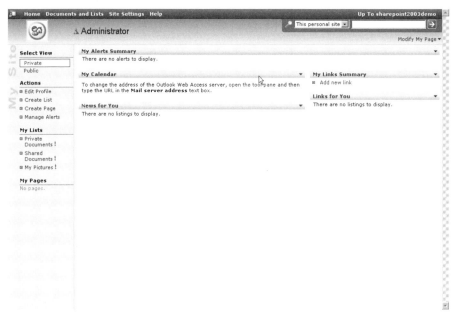

Figure 8.6 My Site Page after Layout Change

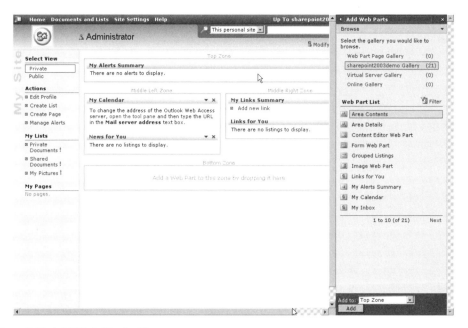

Figure 8.7 Add Web Parts Menu

3. Browse through the web parts in the libraries shown in the upper half of the menu.

4. Select a web part.

5. At the bottom of the Add Web Parts menu, select a zone from the **Add to** dropdown list to determine where the part will be added.

6. Click the **Add** button.

Figure 8.8 shows the My Site page after I added the Image web part to the middle left zone and closed the Add Web Parts menu.

SharePoint lets users share their personal pages using a public view of the My Site page. This public view may differ from the private view, depending on the properties of the web parts.

Personalization Within a SharePoint Web Part

Through My Page personalization, a user can choose content to view and arrange it on the page. Web parts themselves provide another level of personalization, as they can be targeted to provide content mapped to a user's

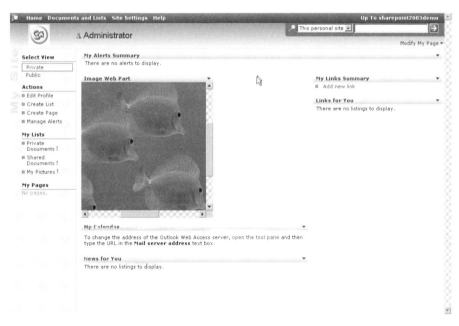

Figure 8.8 Adding the Category Search Web Part to the Middle Left Zone

profile or preferences. For instance, you could send a graph of current sales to the vice president of sales and a summary of personnel changes to users in the human resources department.

Some SharePoint web parts are inherently personalized. For instance, the Outlook web parts display the inbox or calendar of the current user. These web parts are available for Exchange 2003, Exchange 2000, and Exchange 5.5.

SharePoint "Publicization" of Personal Data

Many products and platforms offer personalization, but few allow individual users to determine what they want to share and with whom. SharePoint turns personalization on its ear to offer an important capability for the enterprise portal. I doubt that the neologism "publicization" will get traction, but the idea is to take personal information and make it public selectively. SharePoint Portal Server empowers users to do exactly that in a couple of ways. First, individual fields in a personal profile can be selectively displayed or hidden by the user from public view.

Second, and more importantly, SharePoint allows users to create a special view into their personal web pages for the public. In the left-hand navigation of My Site, there is a toggle between private and public views. Users can design a shared view to show whichever web parts they desire to the outside world.

Personalization with Content Management Server

You can personalize pages for specific users or groups of users in Content Management Server. You can create templates tailored to a specific user, such as a welcome greeting on the home page like the one on Expedia.com or Amazon.com. You enable this feature through ASP.NET output caching. When you do so, the appropriate page is generated and stored in memory.

You can implement output caching at a page or a user control level. To enable role caching on a page level, follow these steps with the template file:

1. Change the inheritance syntax of the Global class in the **global.asax.cs** file to: **public class Global : Cmshttpapplication**.
2. Add the following to the template file: `<%@ OutputCache Duration="300" Location="Server" VaryByParam="None" VaryByCustom="CMSPosting;CMSRole" %>`.

The standard predefined roles in CMS are subscriber, author, editor, moderator, template designer, resource manager, channel manager, and administrator. You can create personalized content for each these roles, such as by hiding or showing selective fields depending on the role.

To enable caching of personalized information for each user on a user control, follow these steps:

1. Change the inheritance syntax of the Global class in the **global.asax.cs** file to: **public class Global : Cmshttpapplication**.
2. Add the following to the template file: `<%@ OutputCache Duration="300" VaryByParam="None" VaryByCustom="CMSPosting;CMSControl;CMSUser" %>`.

Subscriptions, Notifications, and Alerts

Users not only need to be able to find information when they need it, but they want information to be delivered to them before they know they need it. Subscriptions, notifications, and alerts are valuable tools to achieve this capability. The .NET platform provides a number of ways to create and manage these types of personalization. The key concepts to understand are:

- *Subscriber*. The person or application that receives notifications.
- *Subscription*. Request for content or information, such as newsletter subscription, notification of news items, or updates to content in the portal.
- *Event*. A change that triggers a notification, such as a sports score, product delivery, stock price change, or nearly any occurrence that is tracked in your database.
- *Notification*. A message transmitted to the subscriber. This may take the form of an email message, an XML document sent to a subscribing application, or an update to a web page viewed by a user.

In the simplest form of subscriptions, users can subscribe to one or more online publications that are delivered via email. For instance, Microsoft provides many subscriptions to cater to different interests such as home computing, enterprise computing, operating systems, and general corporate news. You create a subscription by entering information in a web form. In the case of microsoft.com, your identity is managed with the Passport service. You may want to create your own similar newsletter and use your web site to gather email addresses from subscribers.

If you provide subscriptions, be sure to provide a page on which users can change their email newsletter subscriptions. Microsoft.com uses the page displayed in Figure 8.9 to allow users to add, edit, or delete subscriptions. You may also want to provide a link in the body of the newsletter itself to allow a user to change or cancel a subscription.

Subscriptions can generate alerts when the content changes in ways that are even more targeted than for a newsletter. For instance, bidders on government contracts might want to subscribe to changes in documents relating to requests for proposals. With the high volume of contracts, users would not want their mailboxes flooded with every possible bid opportunity. Instead, they would prefer to choose their industry and products so they receive the appropriate bids.

For instance, the U.S. government posts requests for bids on a site called FedBizOpps. Through browsing or search, a user could find an opportunity such as the Coast Guard procurement request shown in Figure 8.10.

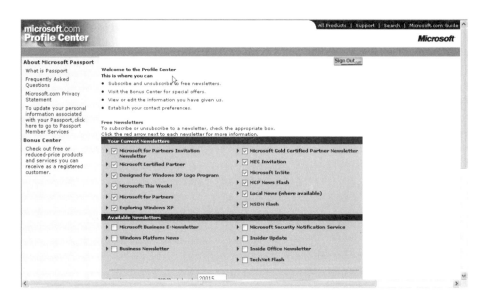

Figure 8.9 Maintaining Subscriptions in the Microsoft Profile Center of microsoft.com

Figure 8.10 Coast Guard Procurement on FedBizOpps

Procurements consist of a number of documents. They start with a synopsis along with key dates in the procurement. The solicitation is in a separate document, and it may be accompanied by additional documents such as a bidders list, amendments, and background information. Bidders need to keep track of the procurement as it moves through the process. At the bottom of the page is a link to subscribe to the procurement. Clicking this link opens the page shown in Figure 8.11.

The government contract or enters an email address and clicks Subscribe to Mailing List to receive notification whenever a new document is posted on the site. Federal Business Opportunities sends an email such as that shown in Figure 8.12 containing updates and links to the appropriate documents to which the contractor has subscribed.

Finally, in a more sophisticated form, notifications can be event-driven, which means they are triggered when an event is reported to the system or

Figure 8.11 Acquisition Notification Service Subscription Form

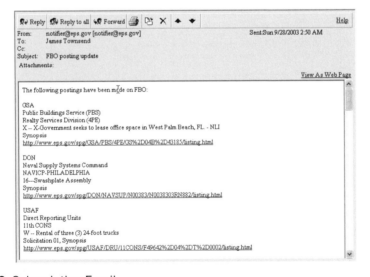

Figure 8.12 Subscription Email

scheduled. Events can come from inside a database or from another source. For instance, an investor might request a message when a stock price hits a certain level or when it varies more than 10% from its opening price in a single day. This is what SQL Server Notification Services calls a notification.

Notifications can be sent to a range of devices and programs. For instance, Microsoft Windows Messenger includes a notification service called Microsoft .NET alerts. You can receive popup messages based on your alert subscriptions. Similarly, notifications can be sent as email to any device that can receive email and also to cellular phones, personal digital assistants, and other devices. Anyone who owns a device such as a Pocket PC would probably appreciate receiving these notifications.

Both external and internal customers can benefit from notification services. They provide a rapid and automated means of reaching out to interested parties. The notification may contain a URL of a page that provides additional information. Imagine the value of letting customers and employees know when an order is running late or when a product has been recalled by its manufacturer.

In sum, subscriptions, alerts, and notifications can bring users back to your portal again and again and foster a stronger sense of community. They are also more targeted than a blanket email because they contain content that subscribers actively requested. This section introduces several approaches to integrating these capabilities into your portal.

SharePoint Subscriptions and Alerts

SharePoint provides similar subscription and alert functionality to that shown for FedBizOpps in the previous section. It applies to many portal elements: lists and list items, people, documents and folders, categories and news, sites and searches. Users can create their own subscriptions or they can be set by administrators. From a user perspective, starting a subscription is as easy as clicking Alert Me on a content page. For instance, Figure 8.13 shows the Alert Me link in the Actions menu of the News page.

By creating an alert (see Figure 8.14), users receive email notification whenever new items are added to the News page.

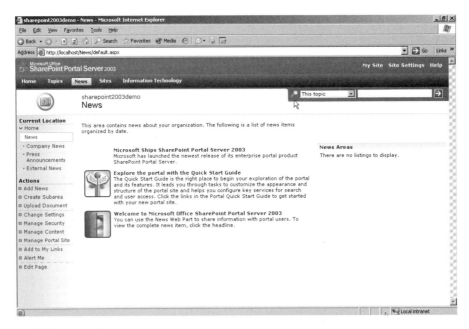

Figure 8.13 News Page

Figure 8.14 Adding a News Alert

Users can elect to have alerts displayed in the My Alerts web part or receive email notification of new content (or both). Clicking the Advanced options link on the Add Area Alert page reveals options for filtering the results of the alert based on criteria provided and determines whether updates or new items appear in the alerts (see Figure 8.15). The discussion group alert does not have an option to show the alert on the web page.

Not all the SharePoint alerts behave in exactly the same way. For instance, when you subscribe to a threaded discussion, you get additional options, as shown in Figure 8.16. These let you receive an aggregated email containing multiple alerts on an immediate, daily, or weekly basis.

Alerts are an excellent way to bring users back to the portal. For many of us, we belong to so many virtual communities that it is easy to forget to check in without a gentle reminder, such as an alert email.

SharePoint Audiences

The audiences feature of SharePoint Portal Server allows the administrator to target content to users based on attributes in their personal profiles.

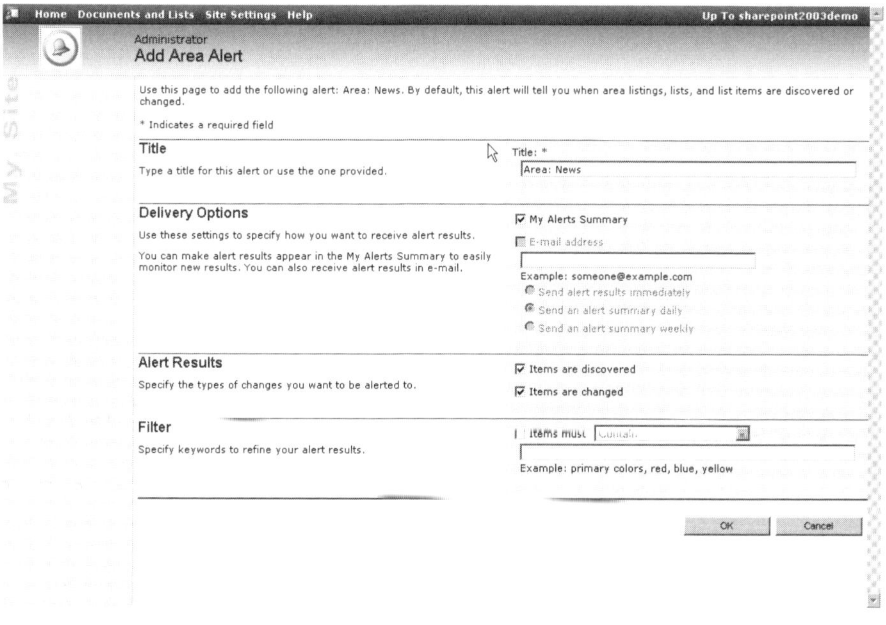

Figure 8.15 Add News Alert Advanced Options

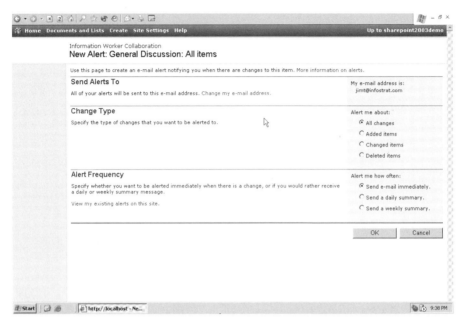

Figure 8.16 Alert for Discussion Group

Users can belong to one or more audiences used to target content. For details on creating an audience and an audience rule, see Chapter 7.

Subscriptions and Alerts with SQL Server 2000 Notification Services

For the most advanced notification capabilities on the Microsoft platform, the place to turn is SQL Server Notification Services (NS). This product is a highly scalable solution integrated with SQL Server and .NET, allowing application developers to add notification capabilities to an SQL Server database. Notification Services shipped in 2002 as an add-on for SQL Server 2000. It is covered by a customer's SQL Server licensing and is available as a free download. For customers licensing SQL Server on a per processor basis, there is no limit to the number of users who can receive notifications under the license. These users need proper server and client licenses for SQL Server but no special license for Notification Services.

Notification Services is essentially a database application devoted to providing scheduled and event-driven notification. It uses the familiar

Transact-SQL, XML, and .NET programming environment you used to create the application in the first place.

The Notification Services architecture consists of the following elements (Figure 8.17):

- *SQL Server databases.* Provide the repository for subscriber and subscription data. There are at least two databases involved: One holds instance data (subscribers, delivery channels) and one is created for each notification application to contain the subscriptions, events, and notifications for that application.
- *Notification Services application programming interface (API).* Provides standard programming interfaces for Notification Services. For instance, subscription management objects are referenced by the developer to create a Notification Services application.
- *Event providers.* Watch for events to occur, such as a new record being written to a database table, or a file being modified in the file system. May run in the event provider host or independently. The event provider writes to the database, like the subscription management application does. The generator then matches information in

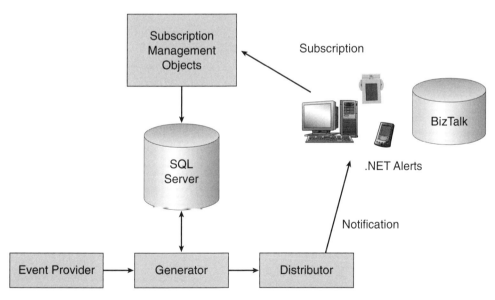

Figure 8.17 SQL Server Notification Services Conceptual Architecture

the event and subscriptions tables based on Transact-SQL rules specified by the developer.

- *Generator.* Periodically runs to check events against subscriptions and generate notifications, forwarding them to the distributor component.
- *Distributors.* Formats using a content formatter and transmits notifications to subscribers using one or more delivery services, such as SMTP email.

Notification Services provides control over the types of subscriptions and how notifications are delivered. The first step in designing a notification solution is to determine what subscriptions you want to provide to your users. The two types of subscriptions are scheduled subscriptions and event-driven subscriptions. Notifications for scheduled subscriptions are sent at a predetermined time, such as a daily email newsletter, or stock prices at market closing time. Notifications for event-driven subscriptions are triggered by an event. A change in a flight time, for example, could trigger notification to all passengers with reservations.

The subscription schema is the database structure for storing subscription information. While some fields, such as the subscriber ID, are required for all subscriptions, others are optional depending on the functionality of the subscription. You would need a field for subscriber device name to allow subscribers to receive notification on more than one device. Similarly, you would need locale information or target language to personalize a notification for the subscriber's region or language. Finally, you would need to specify the proper device to generate the notification. You do not have to store this content in the subscription necessarily, but you do have to get it from somewhere. Storing the information in the subscription record is the most common choice.

The next step in notification planning is to determine the content of the notification. For scheduled notifications, the content may be the same for all subscribers. Event-driven subscriptions tend to be more personalized and may contain data that is unique to the subscriber. For instance, order shipment confirmation could be sent as a notification based on the update to the shipped date field in a commerce database. In other words, the notification can consist of whatever content you choose, but it usually contains some static text combined with fields from the database and URLs for additional information. The optional fields are defined in the application definition file (ADF), as shown in Listing 8.1.

Table 8.1 Common Fields for Subscription Schema

Field	Type	Comments
SubscriptionID	Bigint	Required
SubscriberID	Nvarchar(255)	Required
Enabled	Boolean	Included automatically; default is true
SubscriberDeviceName	Nvarchar(255)	Allows multiple notifications per subscriber
SubscriberLocale	Nvarchar(255)	Allows localization

Listing 8.1 Application Definition File

```
<Schema>
   <Field>
      <FieldName>OrderNumber</FieldName>
      <FieldType>char(10)</FieldType>
      <FieldTypeMods>NOT NULL</FieldTypeMods>
   </Field>
   <Field>
      <FieldName>OrderPrice</FieldName>
      <FieldType>money</FieldType>
      <FieldTypeMods>NOT NULL DEFAULT 10</FieldTypeMods>
   </Field>
</Schema>
```

You can design the format for the notification in pseudocode. For instance, you may want to use HTML tags to highlight certain information, and combine data from database fields with boilerplate text as in Listing 8.2.

Listing 8.2 Boilerplate Text in Customer Service Letter

```
Dear [customer salutation]:

I am pleased to inform you that your order number [order number]
shipped as of [shipdate] via [shipping method]. We appreciate your
business and look forward to serving you in the future.

Best wishes,
Customer Service
1-800-555-1212
```

You need to determine the triggers for the notification, which means you need to build the event schema, event source, and notification rules. SQL Notification Services can obtain event information from XML data files, from SQL Server database tables, or somewhere else. You can build a custom provider to get data from almost anywhere. You could subscribe to a news ticker, for instance, and store the contents of the ticker in an XML file. Whenever a headline arrived that contained a keyword specified by the user and stored in a SQL Server database table, the event would be triggered. If I were to subscribe to "Tiger Woods" as a keyword, for example, that character string would create an event.

The notification generation rules compare the event with the subscription conditions to determine whether a notification should be sent. If the event information fulfills the subscription conditions, a notification is generated. The events are often recorded in a chronicle using an SQL Server database table for future reference. The notification generation rule is expressed as an SQL query such as Listing 8.3.

Listing 8.3 SQL Query

```
SELECT i.ProductCode, i.Inventory
FROM Inventory i, InventorySubscriptions s
WHERE i.Inventory < s.InventoryTriggerValue
AND i.ProductCode = s.ProductCode
```

This query would send a notification to a subscriber whenever the inventory of a specified product fell below the inventory threshold specified in the subscription. The notification generation rule must contain a notification function—a plain SELECT statement won't work. The Notification Service documentation for additional details.

The notification formatting is handled using an XSLT file, which gives the developer maximum flexibility in designing and formatting the notification. As a result, the notification is generated appropriately regardless of the target device.

Developers can deliver notifications through Simple Mail Transfer Protocol (SMTP) or a custom HTTP-based delivery protocol. Notification Services provides two interfaces for developing the custom protocol, implemented as a class in a managed code assembly. The custom protocol can use HTTP (using the IHttpProtocolProvider interface) or any other protocol (using the IDeliveryProtocol interface).

Advertising Based on Profiles

As we have shown, personalization can take many forms. One of the more powerful is to create marketing campaigns based on user profiles. You may want to consider this an involuntary form of the subscriptions and notifications discussed in the previous section. The Microsoft Commerce Server Business Desk lets you display advertisements to users based on values in their user profiles. The ads can be placed in the banner section of the page header.

You can use complex criteria to determine ad display. The criteria are used as the basis of a calculation for determining which, if any, ad will appear. For instance, you may be trying to sell an exciting new model of men's hip waders. The first criteria are that the user is a man and enjoys fishing. You may want to exclude customers who have purchased hip waders in the past six months. Special priority should be giving to customers who have expressed an interest in fly fishing, as waders are more often used for fly fishing than for bass or saltwater fishing.

You can also target people who are not customers. For instance, you might want to provide an incentive for visitors to your site to place their first orders. You could create an ad that would only be visible to new users and that would offer free shipping or a discount on their first order from the store.

Advertising online with Commerce Server is powerful and flexible. The ad campaigns can:

- Calculate product discounts
- Target ads based on profile information
- Schedule campaigns
- Coordinate multiple advertisers
- Calculate billing for advertisers based on clicks or page views
- Charge advertisers based on location where ad appears

If you are running an e-commerce web site, you will need no convincing of the benefits of advertising both as a source of revenue and as a way to drive sales on your site. If you are running a government or nonprofit site, advertising can be just as valuable, albeit in a less blatantly capitalistic way. You could create the online equivalent of public service ads to give users information that they need. An association could promote its annual meeting or use an ad to announce a new publication. County government could promote its latest online service such as tax payment or employment assistance. You determine the look of ads, and you can make them as subtle or jolting as you want.

Advertising is also valuable for an enterprise portal. A human resources department could promote new company benefits and encourage people who have not set up their retirement plan to do so. Management might want to target advertising to new employees or by department. Training and education could be promoted through advertisements targeted to the people who are most likely to take a certain class.

The Commerce Server Business Desk contains a Campaign Manager module to enter details surrounding an advertising campaign (Figure 8.18). You enter a list of your advertising customers, and then each of the campaigns, including a link to the ad itself. For Commerce Server, a campaign consists of the activity around a single ad.

You can control the duration and placement for each ad as well as many other factors (Figure 8.19).

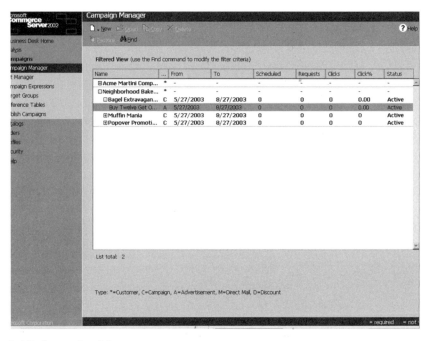

Figure 8.18 Campaign Manager

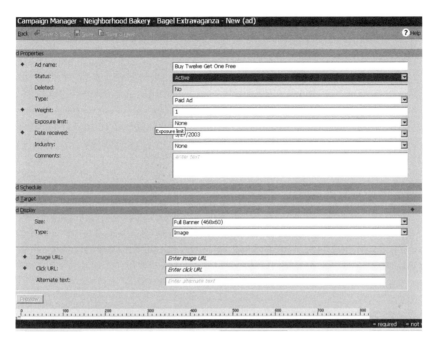

Figure 8.19 New Campaign

Commerce Server employs a concept called **expression-based targeting** to deliver personalized content to users. The expressions are conditions that determine whether content is suitable for a customer. For instance, if the expression "preferred music=jazz" is true for a user, that user might be targeted to receive news of a special sale on Blue Note recordings or a new album from Wynton Marsalis.

You obtain values to test the expression directly from the user or by monitoring user behavior. Users who choose jazz as their favorite music might appreciate music suggestions for this genre. You could also infer that a user was a jazz fan if 80% of the compact discs they have purchased from your site are jazz.

You can create two types of expressions, target expressions and catalog expressions. Target expressions relate to the targeted audience for the campaign, while catalog expressions are tied to catalog items. You could use a target expression of "purchases in last month > 5" to provide a discount to frequent shoppers or a catalog expression of "item type=sleeping bag and price > $200" to offer an early season discount for high-end sleeping bags. Catalog expressions are used for cross-selling, such as promoting hot dog buns to customers who purchase hot dogs.

You can combine these expression types to create richer and more interesting marketing initiatives. You could offer discounts on certain items to specified groups of customers, for example. The expressions could be weighted so one criterion overruled others or the evaluated expressions were added together to determine whether content passed or failed the test.

The Commerce Server Business Desk provides an Expression Builder tool (Figure 8.20) to craft these expressions. It is based on dynamic HTML (DHTML) to allow the style sheets of the parent site to cascade to the Expression Builder. The site manager would typically provide the Expression Builder tool to users who create marketing campaigns within a web interface (Figure 8.20).

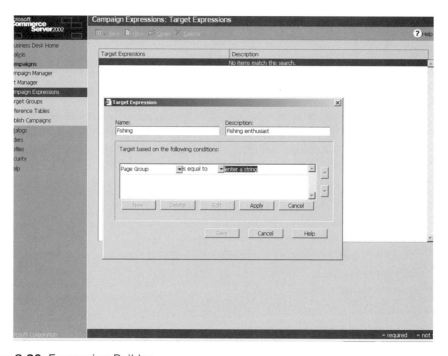

Figure 8.20 Expression Builder

One or more expressions are used to target groups that will view the ads. These expressions may be mandatory for the target group, and you can even enter expressions that cause a user to be excluded.

You use the ContentSelector objects to select the proper content for the user based on profile information (Listing 8.4).

Listing 8.4 Using ContentSelector Objects

```
<%
    ' Create a ContentSelector object.
    Set CSO = Server.CreateObject("Commerce.ContentSelector")

    ' Use the GetContent method to get some content. Use the dictionary
    ' previously created in the Global.asa file and referenced through _
      the
    ' Application collection.
    Set Ads = CSO.GetContent(Application("CSFAdsContext"))
    ' Ads is a SimpleList containing the selected content.
    ' Write the content to the page, if any.
    For Each Ad in Ads
        Response.Write(Ad)
    Next
%>
```

Source: Commerce Server Help File (books online)

When you create an ad, you determine when, where, and to whom it is displayed.

Commerce Server uses the following parameters to place the ad:

- *Exposure limit*. The number of times an ad may be shown to a user within a session.
- *Weight*. In an ad campaign, the weight determines how many times an ad is displayed to a targeted customer relative to the other ads for that customer. If three ads have weights of 1, 2, and 3, the third ad would be displayed half the time.
- *Page groups*. A set of related pages where the targeted ads will appear. For instance, you can specify that training ads appear in the help wanted section of your site.
- *Target groups*. The group of people who will view the ad, based on expressions.

■ *Schedule*. Specifies the start date, end date, start time, end time, and days of the week the ad will run.

You may want to target the content with localization, such as the appropriate language for the content. If you want to deliver an ad in multiple languages, you must recreate the ad in each target language and enter the ad variables for the ad.

If all these ads are not sufficient for reaching your customers, employees, members, or constituents, Commerce Server gives you the ultimate "personalization" weapon. You can extend the campaigns from web ad campaigns to direct mail campaigns by importing mailing lists and generating email or paper mail.

Conclusion: Getting More Out of Personalization

We have seen that several techniques can bring you closer to your users through personalization. Most of these are appropriate for both public portals and enterprise portals. How you employ them is up to you and your portal goals.

To get the most out of personalization, you need to establish metrics and create a feedback loop to continuously improve your portal. If you are an online business, you may use metrics such as total sales, number of customers, number of repeat customers, average dollar value per sale, and number of site visits per purchase. For a nonprofit, you may want to consider the number of unique visitors to your site, the number of registered users, and the number of times that your free publications are downloaded or viewed.

Be sure to monitor your web site statistics and take remedial action when necessary. You cannot take customers or readers for granted, so spare no effort to keep your virtual community interested. If you choose Commerce Server, the business analytics system will provide a wealth of site usage data from both built-in and custom reports. SharePoint Portal Server, on the other hand, provides little in the way of usage analysis tools, although you can write reports against the SQL Server database tables.

Adding personalization features to your portal is a way to stir up new interest in users who have become accustomed to your site's content and features. Slowly adding more features can build up anticipation of what is coming next.

Chapter 9

Content Management

Without content, a portal would be a lonely place. The volume and richness of web content are what brings users back to a portal again and again, whether it is an internal portal for knowledge management or an external portal to create a virtual community and a market for goods and services. While portal content could be created as most web sites are created, one page at a time through authoring tools such as Microsoft FrontPage or Macromedia Dreamweaver or through HTML coding in a simple editor, major portals rely on content management systems to automate the creation, editing, and maintenance of thousands or hundreds of thousands of web pages. You should consider content management for your organization, as it can have the biggest payoff of all your portal initiatives.

In many ways, content management is at the heart of a portal, whether it is an enterprise portal or an external portal, because so much content resides in web pages. The content management system is also an embodiment of the site taxonomy, and it governs the site navigation. It creates the consistent "look-and-feel" that is essential to giving users a positive experience in the portal. If all you did to implement a portal was to implement content management, migrate all pages to the system, and enable users to create their own fresh content, you would be providing quite an enhancement over what most web sites offer.

The first content management systems were created as custom solutions, and some served as the basis for what later became commercial content management systems. Content management systems consist of a repository where content is stored, one or more frontends for authoring and other management tasks such as review and approval, and additional components to enforce content management business rules and provide services such as notification to authors and reviewers of changes in the status of a page. The repository is typically a relational database, and the frontend systems are most often browser-based.

Measuring Return on Investment for Content Management

Automating content management is one of the portal initiatives with the highest return on investment. While portal content does not necessarily bring revenue in the door like the commerce section of a portal, organizations with large, complex web sites spend a great deal of time and money on maintaining that content, and a content management system (CMS) can result in significant cost savings.

The first value in the equation is to determine how much you are already spending on content management. How many hours of your web team's time are spent on creating or editing content? Is your webmaster responsible for fixing typographical errors in content? What is the cost of this time? What is the hourly rate or salary for the people engaged in content management? Don't forget to include the time of content authors who submit items to be posted on the web site. How much time do they spend on this activity?

Next, what is the lag time in posting content, from authoring to going live? The delay is often significant because the web team can be a bottleneck that slows down the process of updating and adding content. What is the value of more timely updates to your web site? Would improved communication on the web site increase customer satisfaction or make other constituents happier? How much would that improvement be worth to you?

Now calculate the cost of implementing a content management system. What would be the cost for hardware, software, maintenance, implementation, and conversion services? Over how many years should the investment be amortized?

This return on investment exercise may be enough to interest management in the development of your portal. By adding content management capabilities, you can significantly increase the growth of portal content, thereby leading to higher use of the portal.

Content Management Options

Content management products run the gamut from simple and inexpensive (or even free) to complex, powerful, and expensive. So it is within the

Microsoft product pantheon, which provides three choices for content management.

First, you can continue in the tradition of custom content management and create your own system by building .NET controls along with a database repository to store the underlying content. This is the best choice if you are being paid by the hour and have an unlimited budget and schedule. You can tailor the system to fit your unique requirements.

The downside to the custom CMS is the same as for any other custom solution. It requires a significant amount of resources to design, build, and maintain compared to an off-the-shelf solution. The blank slate offered by custom development may encourage users to be more creative in their requirements than the business case may warrant, or to ask for functionality that in the long run would be unnecessary or counterproductive. Custom software is only as good as the quality assurance process applied to it, and a surprising amount of work is required to bring software defects down to an acceptable level.

In short, building a custom CMS made sense only until commercial products were available to fill this niche. Now that the price of a CMS is dropping, the functionality of a custom system built with the same investment as a product purchase is dropping correspondingly, making only the simplest custom CMS worth building. For instance, Microsoft announced a small business edition of Microsoft Content Management Server that is only one-fourth the price of the full product (already competitively priced).

A second product option for content management has emerged. Share-Point Portal Server (SPS) has limited content management functionality built in, and with some creativity you can build an enterprise portal with a broad range of content and functionality without a full-bore CMS. For instance, SPS contains prebuilt pages with content management capability for such items as news, contact (name and address) listing, calendars, document libraries, threaded discussions, and others.

For most enterprise portals, you will need an industrial-strength content management solution. Fortunately for .NET portal developers, Microsoft has an off-the-shelf content management product built on .NET that is tightly integrated with .NET security, Visual Studio, ASP.NET, and web services. It is rather unimaginatively named Microsoft Content Management Server (MCMS).

This chapter provides an overview of how to plan content management for your portal, ways to implement that plan on the Microsoft platform, and the integration points for content management with other elements of the portal and .NET. I start by describing the planning and development process. The bulk of the chapter is devoted to implementation in MCMS, Microsoft's enterprise content management system. I also describe the content management features of SharePoint Portal Server 2003, as these are quite interesting for building internal portals. I discuss the option of a custom .NET content management solution. In every case, the place to begin is with a site framework.

Site Framework for Content Management

A web site or portal needs a foundation, and content management allows the developer or architect to lay a site framework that will ensure a solid site in the future. This section describes the approach for laying this foundation.

Our methodology is based on the Microsoft Solutions Framework (MSF) and the Rational Unified Process. MSF is a spiral process model. Over the course of a project, all the steps are carried out several times. Figure 9.1 shows the key steps in the development methodology, showing only one trip around the spiral. For more information on the Microsoft Solutions Framework, go to www.microsoft.com/business/services/mcsmsf.asp.

The MSF methodology consists of four broad phases:

1. *Inception*

   ■ Major Activities

      – Formulate the scope of the project, that is, capture the context and the most important requirements and constraints to derive acceptance criteria.
      – Plan and prepare a business case and evaluate alternatives for risk management, staffing, project plan, and trade-offs between cost, schedule, and features.
      – Synthesize a candidate architecture, evaluate trade-offs in design, and assess make/buy/reuse decisions so that cost, schedule, and resources can be estimated.

   ■ Work Products

      – Vision document containing a general vision of the core project's requirements, key features, and main constraints.
      – Initial project glossary.

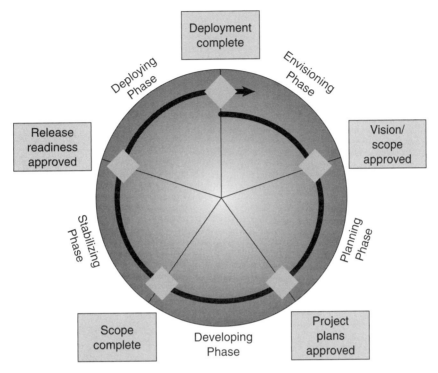

Figure 9.1 MSF Methodology Overview

- Initial business case that includes the business context and success criteria.
- Initial risk assessment.
- Project plan that shows the phases and iterations.

2. *Elaboration*

■ Major Activities

- Vision is elaborated, and a solid understanding is established of the most critical features that drive the architectural and planning issues.
- The process, infrastructure, and the development environments are elaborated, and the process, tools, and automation support are put into place.

- The architecture is elaborated and the components are put into place. Potential components are evaluated, and the make/buy/reuse decisions are sufficiently understood to determine the construction phase cost and schedule with confidence. The selected architectural components are integrated and assessed against the primary behavior scenarios.

- ■ Work Products

  - Requirements document that captures in detail functional, maintainability, extensibility, scalability, security, and usability requirements.
  - Software architecture description.
  - Revised business case.
  - Revised risk assessment.
  - A development plan for the overall project, including the coarse-grained project plan, which shows iterations and evaluation criteria for each criterion.

3. *Construction*

- ■ Major Activities

  - Resource management, resource control, and process optimization.
  - Complete component development and testing against the defined evaluation criteria.
  - Assessment of product releases against acceptance criteria for the vision.

- ■ Work Products

  - The software product integrated on the adequate platforms.
  - The user manuals.
  - A description of the current release.

4. *Transition*

- ■ Major Activities

  - Beta testing to validate the new system against user expectations.
  - Training of users and administrators.
  - Rollout of the product.

- ■ Work Products

  - Software acceptance and rollout.

All this methodology information may seem a bit much for a portal project, but it is quite important to manage a portal as you would manage any other significant development effort. Some customers have approached us to build portals without asking users about their requirements or verifying whether the capabilities the portal will provide will help users. This is a risky use of expensive resources.

Through the lens of our methodology, the MCMS portion of the portal project begins with review meetings and analysis to create a vision for the site in the inception phase. The elaboration or design phase calls for detailed functional specifications and design for elements including the templates and the navigation. The construction phase witnesses the implementation of channels, templates, and resources as well as supporting infrastructure implementation, including hardware and software installation. The transition phase involves putting the site into production, training, maintenance of the site, and preparation for the next round of development. The entire cycle may be iterated a number of times.

You may have your own methodology and want to map these activities accordingly. Having a solid methodology will reduce the risk of the project and improve the quality of the results. It also ensures continuity of a project when personnel change and safeguards against finger-pointing when schedule slips or scope changes.

MCMS lends itself to an iterative team development process much more than a typical page-at-a-time web site. You can approach the channels and templates in a modular fashion. While one team is fielding the templates and testing the workflow for the marketing department, another can be independently developing the human resources channel and integrating job application web pages with an existing PeopleSoft installation. When channels and templates pass user acceptance testing, the real work of cranking out or converting content begins, but developers have already been freed to focus on other development tasks.

Site Vision

The first step in planning the site is to hold a design review session to map the content and organization of the site with the stakeholders of the portal. Most portals start from existing web sites rather than from scratch, so it is essential to identify the pages in the web sites that will be converted to the CMS. Some dynamic content such as online stores or interfaces to databases and other applications will not be converted to MCMS; instead, this content will be integrated into the larger .NET Framework for the portal. A good place to start is with the static pages of the site, which typically constitute the vast majority by page count.

You can use the current site homepage as the baseline for a master template. Use it as the basis for suggestions during the design review meetings when graphic design and navigation decisions are made based on user input. During those meetings, participants provide graphic design and graphic elements for use in MCMS templates. The client freezes the graphic design at the conclusion of this phase. A storyboard, or static mockup of web pages, is a useful tool to capture this design.

Next, audit the existing web site to determine which components will run without modification in the new architecture, which will be migrated, and which will have to be rewritten entirely. At this time, measure the performance of the current site or sites as a benchmark for the new site. Include measures such as average response time for various operations.

> **TIP** *Microsoft Visio provides an excellent tool for this stage of designing your portal. Use the Conceptual Web Site Shapes under the Web Diagram provided with Visio to sketch out the general plan for the site.*

The deliverable from this phase is a site migration plan that enumerates the pages to be migrated, the target navigation, and the high-level template design. The site migration plan shows which pages will be migrated and how they map to sections in the new site. It also lists the templates to be created and describes the graphics and other elements to be used in the templates.

Taxonomy and Container Hierarchies

Once the overall vision for the site is set, you implement the site taxonomy using MCMS channels. A **taxonomy** is a hierarchy of categories under which content is organized. It helps users navigate and search in a portal. Chapter 10 provides guidance on how to create a taxonomy and some sample taxonomies. For the examples in this chapter, I use simple site taxonomies.

Microsoft recommends that you create channels before building and populating the other containers in MCMS because the channels are the vertebrae of your content management system. Later in this chapter I describe the steps in defining the channels. At this point you develop the template and resource galleries.

Security Implementation

This stage is a good time to choose the security implementation for the portal. Start by creating a simple login page to grant developers access to MCMS, and then add content creators and others as the site progresses.

Template Creation

You need to develop a base or skeleton template that includes shared page elements and navigation. It can be the basis of other templates for the site. Develop custom placeholders as required at this stage. You want to create the base templates as quickly as possible to allow the content creation and migration process to begin. Subsequent template development may be carried out in parallel to the content creation process.

Content Creation and Migration

The next step is to create content based on the templates and migrate existing content to the site. This is also the time to clean up the site by removing dated content, and editing and refreshing content as identified in the vision phase of the project. In the case of SharePoint Portal Server, this means migration of documents such as Office documents as well as the creation of HTML pages.

Site Testing

Site testing for functionality and performance is a continuous process that can be initiated once the framework is complete and content is being added to the site. Use whatever testing methodologies and automated tools you choose for the testing process.

Some vendors offer site-testing products integrated with MCMS. For instance, Coast (www.coast.com) provides testing and quality assurance tools for web sites during development and postdeployment. Their product becomes part of the MCMS routing and approval process, checking for errors such as broken links, inappropriate content, and compliance with accessibility guidelines such as Section 508 (http://www.section508.gov/). Section 508 is a U.S. government regulation which amended the Rehabilitation Act in 1998. It calls for Federal government agencies to make electronic and information technologies available to people with disabilities. HiSoftware (www.hisoftware.com) also integrates its solution with MCMS.

This package, called Solution for Online Accessibility, includes Content Management Server and HiSoftware products to help customers achieve Section 508 compliance (http://www.hisoftware.com/soa/).

Content Management Server Overview

Microsoft Content Management Server is designed to provide enhanced authoring and management of web sites of all sizes, including routing and approval processing of content, freshness dating for content, and tight integration with .NET. Therefore, in many ways it is the center of the overall .NET portal framework. For outward-facing portals, the bulk of content consists of web pages, and keeping those pages up to date is the most daunting task for a webmaster.

MCMS has evolved from a product called Resolution created by the nCompass, which was purchased by Microsoft in May 2001. The 2002 version of MCMS is the first major overhaul of the product since the acquisition, and this effort dramatically remolded nCompass into the .NET Framework and web services paradigm. The 2001 version was rebranded by Microsoft but was not very different from nCompass's product.

The following sections of this chapter introduce these MCMS features:

- Site framework
- Content creation and approval process
- Site navigation
- Site management
- Template creation
- .NET and web services integration

There is insufficient space here to provide a feature-by-feature tutorial on MCMS. Our goal is to introduce the key concepts and then go beyond the product help and documentation with practical guidance on how to use the product to achieve the overall goals of the portal.

MCMS Architecture

MCMS provides a repository to store content, along with content creation and site management tools as well as APIs to connect to other services in the portal. It consists of the following logical elements that make up its architecture:

- *Content Repository.* SQL Server is the database where content is stored for use in the site.
- *Site Manager.* Webmasters are provided a rich Windows client to manage many aspects of the MCMS site.
- *Authoring Connector.* This component allows authors to create content in Word XP and post it directly to MCMS. Note that this feature works only with Word and not with other Office programs.
- *Content Connector.* The Content Connector component allows programs to access content in MCMS without risking data corruption with a direct connection to the MCMS database tables.
- *Publishing API.* MCMS 2002 contains a number of APIs that are wrappers around COM (Component Object Model) APIs used in earlier versions, and also new APIs to be used within the managed .NET environment. The managed APIs in the Microsoft.Content-Management.Publishing namespace are known as the publishing API.
- *ISAPI.* The Internet Server API is the API for Internet Information Server. It provides one of the means of extending MCMS and also provides security services for HTTP requests by means of ISAPI filters.
- *APIs.* Programs can access the CMS content by means of APIs, such as the publishing API.
- *Word XP.* Users can publish directly from Microsoft Word XP without using the web user interface to MCMS. Developers can create authoring connectors to streamline this process. These are essentially wizards that define the format of the content and the location where it will be published. Once the user creates the content, it enters the standard MCMS routing and approval process.

Additional elements in the architecture (Figure 9.2) are outside of MCMS per se, but remain critical elements in the total portal picture:

- *Visual Studio.NET.* For developers, Visual Studio.NET is the integrated development environment for MCMS, and it is difficult to imagine implementing MCMS without Visual Studio. This is where templates are created, and .NET web services are created and

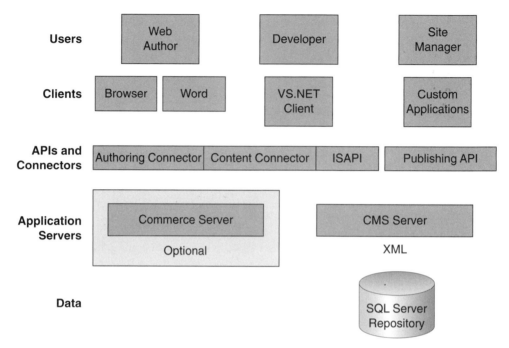

Figure 9.2 MCMS Architecture

maintained. With MCMS 2002, sites can be saved as Visual Studio projects. This means that .NET tools are used to directly manipulate every aspect of MCMS and extend it to provide new functionality.

- *Commerce Server.* While MCMS provides authorization-based personalization, it does not provide rule-based personalization capabilities, which are available in Commerce Server 2002. See Chapter 7, "User Profiles," and Chapter 8, "Personalization," for detailed information on how to implement personalization. As with MCMS 2002, Commerce Server 2002 sites can be saved as Visual Studio projects.

The MCMS architecture is extensible because it has been built on the .NET Framework and integrated with other Microsoft enterprise servers such as Commerce Server, SharePoint Portal Server, and BizTalk. In the next product generation, this integration will probably be even tighter, and code reuse will be even greater.

Site Framework for Content Management Server

A web site or portal needs a foundation, and MCMS allows the developer or architect to lay a site framework that will ensure a solid site in the future. The MCMS framework consists of three main elements. An MCMS site is stored in a hierarchical logical structure based on channels, template galleries, and resource galleries. The channels are used to organize content for site administration and also to create navigation. Channels should be based on the taxonomy you develop for your site, as explained in Chapter 10, "Developing a Taxonomy."

Channels

Channels are containers that can contain web pages or other channels (subchannels). For instance, a human resources site could have channels such as leave policy, benefits, health care, and salary history. The health care channel could have subchannels for medical, dental, and optical insurance.

One way that channels are revealed to users is in the navigation. Unfolding menus may belie underlying channels, as may left navigation with a tree structure. For instance, on the Information Strategies corporate web site, there is a page devoted to books written by the company's consultants (Figure 9.3). The left navigation shows that this page is in the Books subsection of the Resources section of the web site. Users appreciate as many navigational aids as you can provide to keep track of where they are, where they have been, and where they are headed.

You can expand and refine your channel structure as your project proceeds, but you will save time and effort by starting with a well-developed group of channels (Figure 9.4).

Do not use a root folder in the channels to store content. You should leave at least one level to store only child folders to make expansion of the site simpler. For instance, if you later choose to implement localization, you will want to create parallel channels for each of the languages you support, such as English, French, and Spanish channels.

> **TIP** *Do not use the Site Manager to move pages from one channel to another. This is better accomplished through the browser interface us one of the edit functions on a page menu.*

Figure 9.3 Taxonomy as Shown in Left Navigation

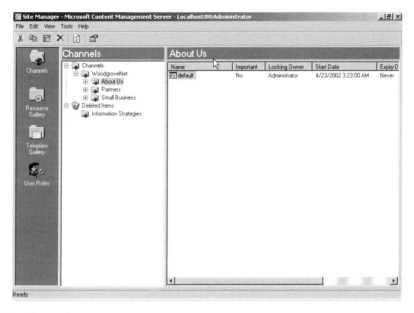

Figure 9.4 Channels

Template Galleries

Template galleries provide a place for site administrators to store the templates used for each section of the site. A channel is likely to have multiple templates associated with it. For an enterprise portal, the human resources channel would have templates for job postings, benefits, and policies such as leave. As with channels, template galleries may have subfolders and be arbitrarily deep. While the template gallery structure often mirrors the channels, it can be different from the channel structure because some templates are used across multiple channels.

You access template galleries from Site Manager and from Visual Studio.NET. Installing MCMS 2002 creates the Template Explorer in Visual Studio.NET, which displays the templates and their properties (Figure 9.5).

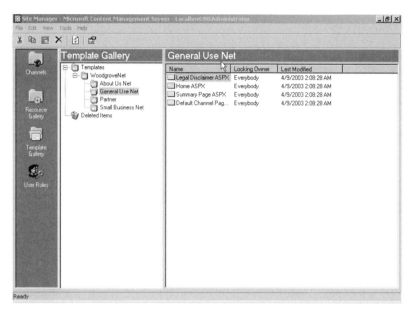

Figure 9.5 Template Gallery

In a typical web site, each template would have dozens or hundreds of pages associated with it. For instance, a product or service listing would be composed of many pages based on the same template. Each template might have several shared resources such as graphics or other design elements that would come from the resource gallery.

Resource Galleries

A resource gallery stores files used by the site, such as shared graphics, audio, or video files. Company logos and trademarks should be stored in a gallery to make them easily available to site editors and template creators. Like a template gallery, the resource galleries can contain subfolders (Figure 9.6). The resource gallery structure may reflect the structure of the template galleries, because the resources are typically used in the context of templates.

The resource gallery gives access to objects to many people in the organization. Therefore it is not the place to store files that must be secured or

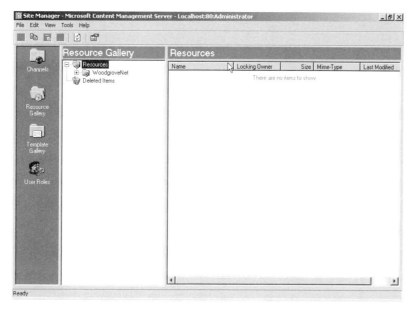

Figure 9.6 Resource Gallery

locked to prevent updates. It does not allow granular permissions for users to be managed in the same way as if the resources appeared on a single page in a channel.

Starting the Portal Site in MCMS

As with all .NET development, the starting point for MCMS is Visual Studio.NET. This is the tool you use to create templates for your site. To do so:

1. In Visual Studio .NET, select **Other Windows** from the View menu.
2. Click **MCMS Template Explorer** (Figure 9.7).

The Template Explorer reveals the template gallery structure of the site. To enhance maintainability, you should create an intelligible hierarchy of templates rather than lumping them all into a single folder.

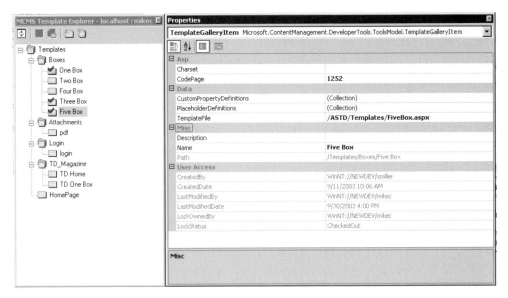

Figure 9.7 Template Explorer in Visual Studio.NET

Figure 9.7 displays two types of templates. First are generic templates with standard layout, labeled "One Box," "Two Box," and so on. These contain the standard page elements such as header, footer, and navigation, along with placeholders for content in single or multicolumn format. They are used throughout the site in many different channels. The second type of template is tailored for the special requirements of a subsite or section of the site. These special templates are used for one-off pages such as the login page or a page to list and view attached PDF files. The TD_Magazine template has a layout that is unique to that publication.

Users see the list of templates, organized in the template gallery, when they create new pages (Figure 9.8).

Selecting the gallery displays a list of templates. After a user chooses a template, he enters content in the content placeholders and saves the page. The page is stored in the appropriate channel based on where the user began in the authoring process.

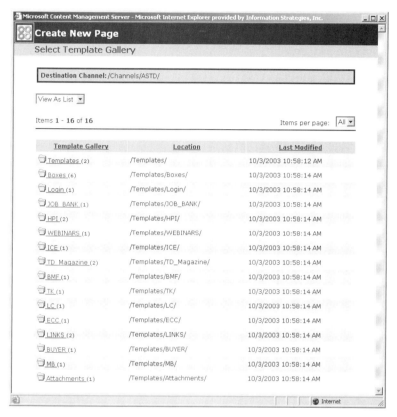

Figure 9.8 Template List

Creating Templates

Authors use templates to create new web pages. Templates consist of page elements such as text and graphics along with placeholders that are used to capture input from the authors. For instance, a press release template would have placeholders for the date, title, text, and contact information. The same template would be used for all press releases, so updating the template would update the appearance of all press release pages. One way to define a new template is to right-click the template gallery in MCMS Template Explorer, and select New Template. Another way is to create the template in Visual Studio. You can rename a template you have just created. In either case, you use Visual Studio.NET to edit templates.

In MCMS 2002, templates are stored in ASP.NET files. They are checked in and out of the template library by the developer. This functionality is important to coordinate the efforts of multiple developers working on the portal. All developers share a common MCMS repository, and they check out templates as they need to access them.

Placeholders are ASP.NET server controls. This tight integration with .NET gives developers close control over the behavior of the templates and the resulting web pages. It also means that template developers need to learn and master .NET programming. These skills carry over into other portal products. For instance, SharePoint Portal Server now uses the same .NET approach to creating web parts.

The standard placeholders that ship with MCMS are:

- *HTML placeholder.* Probably the most common placeholder; accepts HTML strings including text, formatting, and hyperlink tags.
- *XML placeholder.* Designed for data formatted as XML.
- *Attachment placeholder.* Allows user to insert a file as an attachment; displays resulting link to attachment.
- *Image placeholder.* Stores image file such as JPEG.
- *Office Attachment placeholder.* Contains Office file as an attachment.
- *Office HTML placeholder.* Stores HTML generated by an Office product such as Microsoft Word.

You can also create your own new placeholder definitions with the Custom Property Definition Collection Editor shown in Figure 9.9. You can change the properties of these placeholders or even create your own custom properties. The example in the figure shows a custom property called Roles. This property determines whether the page is visible to public users (anonymous users) or whether it requires authentication to get access to it. The value stored in this property is editable for page authors on the Page Properties page. Be careful about proliferating the placeholder definitions and check to see whether an appropriate placeholder already exists before you create your own. There is no reason to needlessly complicate maintenance of your templates by reinventing the placeholder.

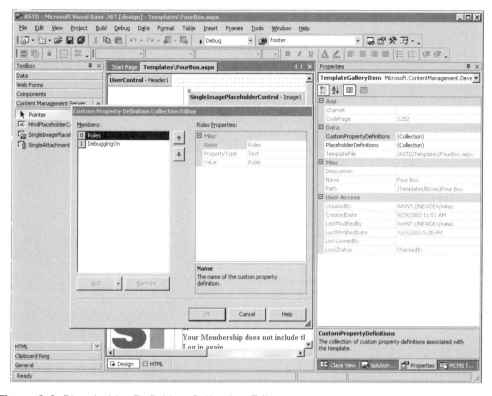

Figure 9.9 Placeholder Definition Collection Editor

MCMS offers quite a range of template design functionality and extensibility. A prerequisite for tapping this power is familiarity with Visual Studio .NET. You can create templates that use nearly anything you could build in a custom .NET web page.

Content Creation and Approval Process

In a mature web site, content goes through a process from creation to live publication, as shown in Figure 9.10. The process is iterative due to period

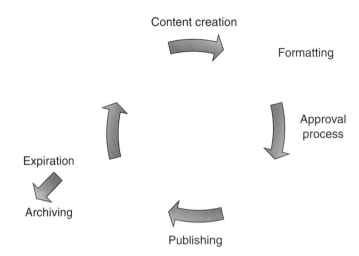

Figure 9.10 Content Management Cycle

updates. The first step is for an author to create the content, typically in a word processor such as Microsoft Word. Artwork may be created from digital cameras or illustration and graphics software. Content may originate in a database or a report that is generated from a line-of-business system such as accounting or customer relationship management. For this example, let's assume a content creator is using Word to write text that will appear on a web page.

In MCMS, content creation can be handled in one of two ways. Authors can continue to work in Word, with direct links between Word documents and the web pages where the content will be published. Creating or editing files puts them into MCMS version control and the approval process. The second approach is to use the browser client for MCMS to create the content. The editing controls on the template contain tools such as formatting, fonts, and spellchecking to make content creation as simple as possible. The template author determines how much control the content creator has over the page by, for example, determining whether HTML tags can be entered or leaving placeholders for photographs or other graphic elements.

The second step in the lifecycle is the formatting of the content into a web page that fits the look-and-feel of the site and incorporates the navigation and other shared elements of the site (such as copyright notice). Before content management, this step would have been handled by a web developer or webmaster who would have received an email with an attached Word document containing the text to be added. This content would have been cut and pasted into an HTML file with an HTML editor or a web-authoring tool.

With MCMS, the formatting step is accomplished by means of the page template. A graphic designer and web developer can create the container that holds the content, leaving the content creator with the job of creating the text itself.

Once the page is formatted, it is sent for one or more stages of approval. It might be sent back to the original author for feedback, to a supervisor, or to legal review. An accessibility review may be conducted to determine whether the page meets government accessibility guidelines such as those in Section 508 of the Disabilities Act. To learn more about Section 508, start with the official government site at www.section508.gov/. Microsoft is committed to making its products accessible to people with disabilities, and you can learn more about these efforts at www.microsoft.com/enable/. For a large number, perhaps the majority, of web sites, there is neither a review process nor a staging server where pages are placed before they go into production. Instead, the webmaster edits the live site directly. Approval processes may be simple or quite complex.

After approval, the page is either published or scheduled for publication. In MCMS, a page property determines the date that a page will go live (Figure 9.11). Embargoed content such as press releases can be prepared in advance and then displayed automatically when the publication date arrives.

When the end of the useful life of content is reached, the content disappears from the web site and is archived. MCMS allows content creators or web administrators to specify the shelf life of a page. Many web sites would benefit from freshness dating.

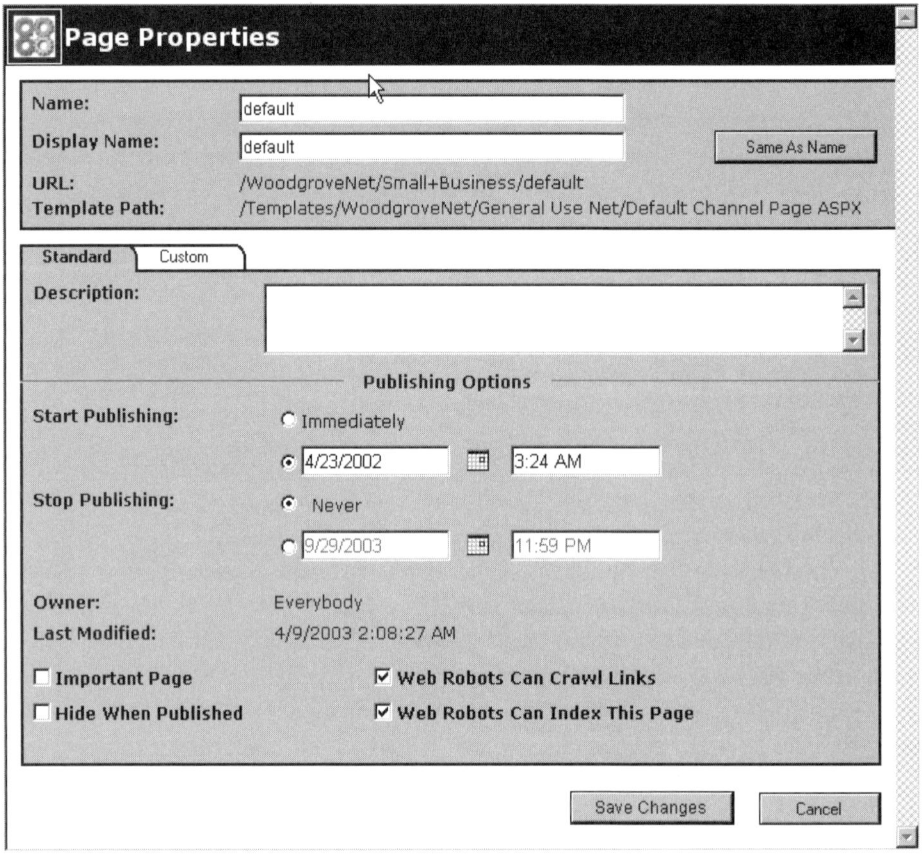

Figure 9.11 Page Properties Page

Defining Channels

Channels are defined in the MCMS Site Manager application. Once you have defined channels, you can start building templates and adding content to your site. For an example, I use the Woodgrove Bank sample site that ships with MCMS. This program is located in the MCMS program group on the Start menu. You will be instructed to log into the site. You can download a trial version of the software at www.microsoft.com/cmscrvcr/default.aspx?url=/cmserver/evaluation/trial/.

1. Select **Channels** in Site Manager.
2. Expand the Channels pane.
3. Right-click **WoodgroveNet** and select **New Channel**.
4. Fill in the information requested on the New Channel dialog box. Name the channel **LoanApplication**. Enter **Loan Application** as the display name and **Forms and background information for submitting loan applications** as the description.

Be sure to follow the naming rules for channels:

- Channel names must be unique and contain only US-ASCII characters (alphanumeric characters and dashes, underscores, commas, and quotation marks).
- Do not include #, &, %, +, /, or | symbols.
- Channel names are limited to 100 characters.
- Do not include spaces in channel names.
- Do not add the HTM extension to the channel name.

Once you have created the channel, you need to fill in the properties for the channel. Here are the steps to follow:

1. Add rights groups to the channel you have created. Start with the subscribers group, and then add another entry for authors.
2. Display the channel properties again by right-clicking the channel and choosing Properties from the menu, then click the **Publishing** tab.
3. In the Channel Rendering section of the channel properties, click **Use First Page** to make the first page the default for the channel.
4. Click **OK** to close the channel-rendering properties dialog box.
5. Set the publishing schedule for the channel. From the channel properties dialog box, click the **Publishing** tab, and then click **Set** in the Lifetime section of the tab. Click **Immediately** to make items published in the channel visible immediately.
6. Click **Never Stop Publishing** as the Stop Publishing entry.
7. Establish the web author default galleries, which are the template and resource galleries that are available to this channel. In the Channel properties, click the **Web Authoring** tab.
8. Browse to the desired locations in the template and resource galleries.

9. Set additional channel properties listed on the **Publishing** tab of the channel properties (Figures 9.12 and 9.13). These include designation as an important channel, hiding the channel, and allowing the channel to be crawled by web robots.

Repeat these steps for all the channels you need to create. You can always create new channels as your site evolves, and content may be moved from one channel to another.

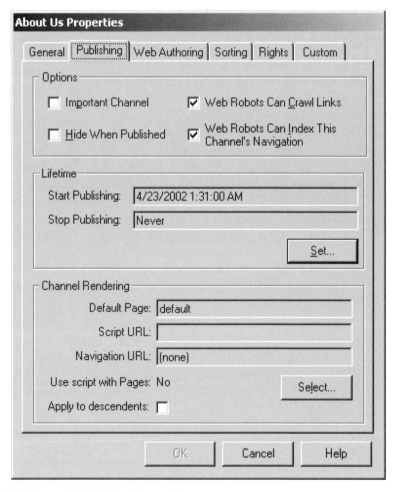

Figure 9.12 Channel Publishing Properties

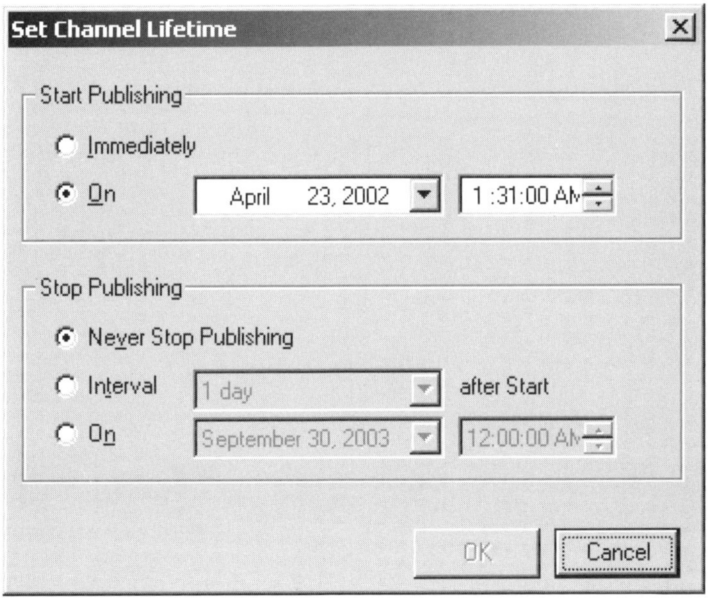

Figure 9.13 Channel Lifetime

The next step is to develop the templates identified in the design review session. You will reuse the templates as much as possible from one section of the site to another to simplify template and site maintenance. Developers must make trade-offs in template design between general use (fewer templates) and specific requirements (more templates). While it is possible to create a single master template that would handle nearly any contingency, this mother of all templates (MOAT) would be difficult to create and maintain, and its superset of page layout and functionality might be daunting to users. On the other hand, the more templates you build, the more templates you have to maintain (see the following box "One Template or Many?").

Multilingual Sites

MCMS 2002 allows you to develop multilingual sites to support the needs of your users. All languages that support the Unicode standard are supported in MCMS. To create a multilingual site, start by building the templates, channels, and pages for the primary language supported by the site. This work provides the site structure.

The second step is to translate resources used in your templates to the second target language. You do not want to have a Spanish site that uses images with English captions, nor a Lithuanian site with Russian page elements.

Next, create templates using the translated resources to map content from one language to another. MCMS uses a feature called connected pages that lets you link two or more pages that reference the same content source and use related templates. Therefore you could end up with an English press release template and connected Spanish and French pages.

One Template or Many?

Defining templates is the most challenging and time-consuming step in implementing a CMS. Programming, functional requirements, and graphic design converge here, often creating a long approval process or frequent revision. Nearly all web designers have experienced the phenomenon of five department representatives having six opinions on the color, font, or layout of a page.

Inexperienced CMS users are often tempted to allow templates to proliferate so each nook and cranny of the portal uses a different template. For instance, separate templates might be built for FAQs, articles, press releases, and product announcements.

Fight this instinct to create new templates and ask yourself whether a generic template might not be suitable in more than one section. Template discipline significantly reduces the maintenance burden of the site. The big payoff comes when users decide to change the colors, layout, and general appearance of the site. The fewer the number of templates you have, the quicker such changes, which are usually requested about one week before the site is scheduled to go into production, will be made.

Web Page Workflow Implementation

With the navigation and templates in place, the next step is to develop a workflow process for content based on information provided by the users at the design review. You may want to begin with a pilot to learn more about how your organization will choose to implement these new business processes. Start with just one section of the site, and identify the parties involved in the approval process. This workflow is based on standard CMS routing and approval functionality.

The task of the pilot is implementation of a sample workflow. For instance, a document may be routed from an author to a content editor and to an additional approval level such as a manager or legal review. I recommend that a representative workflow be chosen, as it may be copied and customized for subsequent workflows that are established.

Some routing and approval processes are better in theory than in practice. Complicated business rules can create content bottlenecks and delay content publication, thereby undermining the portal's raison d'être. This concept is not easy to explain but becomes quite apparent when a sample workflow is tested. People in the approval loop quickly learn how important it is to stay on top of their content responsibilities.

There are five levels in the MCMS approval process. You can omit some levels, but note that some levels have multiple steps. These levels are:

1. Template designer
2. Author
3. Editor
4. Moderator
5. Subscriber

Start by writing out the business rules for approval in plain English, also known as pseudocode. For instance, the press release section might have the following rules:

■ All press releases for the organization will be based on the press release template. This template has been created by the template designer and is available in the Press Releases channel.

- Authors for press releases include the offices of the president, chief operating officer, vice president of sales, marketing department, public affairs, and investor relations. Each of these offices has designated one or more users as authorized to create press releases. The press releases shall conform to the corporate style guide. After a press release is created, it is sent to the editor.
- The public affairs office is responsible for editing press releases. If a press release draft requires additional rewriting, it is returned to the originating office. If normal editing is sufficient, it is edited and forwarded to the web site moderator.
- The legal department and webmaster serve as moderators for press releases. They make a final check for substance and formatting. When they approve content, it is released into production.

Now let's take a closer look at how the steps are implemented in CMS.

Template Designer

The template designer is a web programmer with skills in graphic design and HTML programming. Using Visual Studio.NET, the template designer creates a template for a press release containing placeholder controls for content to be provided by the authors. The template contains standard elements such as masthead, copyright information, and navigation, as shown in Figure 9.14.

If multiple channels are supported, the designer may create multiple templates to match each of the channels. For instance, the default template could be for a browser on a computer or workstation, but a second template could be for a PDA or a cellular phone.

Each of the placeholders in a template has properties that determine the content that is allowed. For instance, a placeholder may restrict the author to enter plain text only without hyperlinks, graphics, or even a specific font. The appearance of the text entered is determined by the template itself. This approach would make sense for fields such as the press release title or date, for instance. On the other hand, a placeholder may allow images to be inserted, such as photographs, or file attachments. The power to insert such objects is one of the reasons why an approval process is needed, as these could create security or performance problems for users.

Templates have to be set up only once, so template building is intense at the beginning of projects and tapers off as the portal reaches maturity.

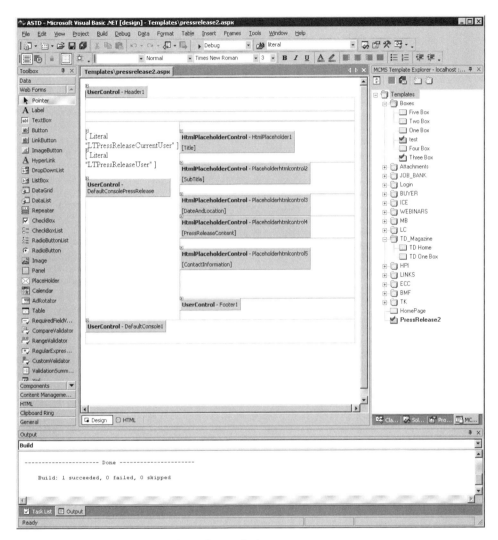

Figure 9.14 Template Design for a Press Release

Moreover, design elements are likely to be shared among templates by means of the resource library, so the tenth template is easier to create than the first.

If authoring will be performed in Word rather than in the browser interface to the template, the template designer must allow for this choice in the process and plan for how the Word authoring will map to the template, using the MCMS Content Connector wizard.

Author

With the template in place, the author fills in the placeholders in the template. For a press release, this would mean entering information such as the date, title, contact person, phone number, and body of the press release, as shown in Figure 9.15.

The placeholders are now rendered as fields of the appropriate type. Icons on the fields indicate the type of entry that is allowed, such as plain text, hyperlinks, formatted text, or attachments. If prompted, the user can upload graphics to reside on a page or documents to be stored as attachments to a page.

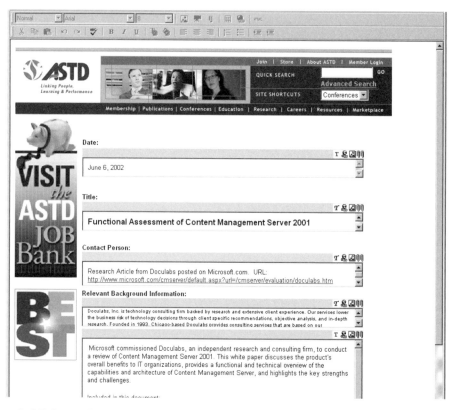

Figure 9.15 Press Release Template in Author View

Finally, the author specifies additional page properties such as the start and end date for publishing the content. Each time the page is saved, the old version is stored as well to allow rollback to a previous version. The author finally submits the finished page to the editor.

As soon as the page is submitted by the author, the editor is notified. She views the page by means of the web interface and edits the material directly. Again, each saved version is stored, so the author can review the editing marks and differences between the original and edited versions. Figure 9.16 shows the page status for a document that has been flagged by the author as complete and ready for editorial review.

If there are no editors or moderators, pages are automatically published when approved by the author. You may also have scenarios with editors or moderators or both. In the latter case, if the editor approves the page, it is forwarded to the moderator for final approval.

Editors and Moderators

The moderator checks the page and the publication date, and then approves or disapproves the page. The moderator can change the page or its properties. Moderators have special tools available in MCMS. The Production Manager is a web interface that allows moderators to see a list of

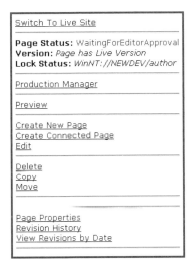

Figure 9.16 Editor Notification

pages in the product process, and then go from page to page to move it through the process (Figure 9.17).

If you want to publish pages without editor or moderator approval, you can simply not assign an editor or moderator to the channel where the page is published. This means that the author makes the decision on when the page is approved. The author can defer publishing by entering the start date in the page properties.

Subscriber

As soon as the publication date for an approved page arrives, it becomes visible to all the users of the site. Subscribers do not have access to any of the administrative features of MCMS. From their perspective, content management is invisible.

To define the approval process, go to the Channel Manager program. Select the channel on which you would like to define the approval process. If needed for your workflow, add editors and moderators to the process so they will receive the pages and approve them. Figure 9.18 shows the user rights assigned to a specific channel.

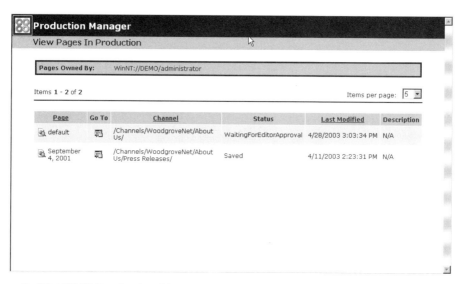

Figure 9.17 MCMS Production Manager Page

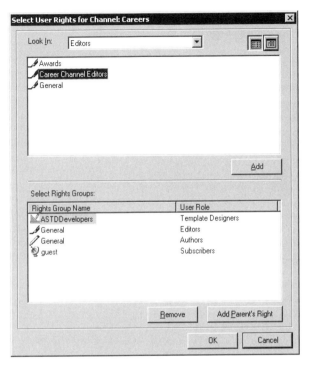

Figure 9.18 Adding an Approval to the Channel

Rights groups are assigned roles along with the permissions that are mapped to these roles. In the example shown in the figure, a group called ASTDDevelopers has the rights to design templates. A special group called Career Channel Editors has been created just for this channel to grant rights for maintaining a single channel without elevating the users to this status for the entire site.

Adding Workflow Email Notification

The out-of-the-box tools of MCMS provide web interfaces to monitor content management tasks, such as Production Manager and Approval Assistant. The problem with these tools is that they require users to go to a URL to see whether they have any pending web pages to approve. Your users will be thankful if you take this a step further and enable what MCMS calls

workflow email notification. This function advises reviewers of events as they occur in the approval cycle. The following code shows how to create email notification to reviewers when a page is submitted for approval. It uses the Microsoft Internet Information Services (IIS) Simple Mail Transfer Protocol (SMTP) service and Collaboration Data Object (CDO) COM components to send email programmatically.[1]

NOTE *Workflow email notification requires the ASP.NET version of Microsoft Content Management Server (MCMS 2002).*

To implement workflow email notification:

1. In the **global.asax** file, add a reference to **Microsoft.Content-Management.Publishing**.
2. At the top of the global.asax file, add the following **using** statements:

```
using System.Web.Mail;
using Microsoft.ContentManagement.Publishing;
using Microsoft.ContentManagement.Publishing.Events;
```

3. Within the **Global** class in the global.asax file, add the following event handler:

```
public void CmsPosting_Submitted( Object source, _
ChangedEventArgs e ) {
    MailMessage mail = new MailMessage();
    mail.From ="MCMS Web Author";
    Posting submittedPosting = (Posting)e.Target;
    mail.Subject = submittedPosting.Name & " has been _
    submitted for approval.";
    mail.Body = submittedPosting.Name & " has been _
    submitted for approval. ";
    foreach (User approver in _
    submittedPosting.Approvers)
    {
        mail.To = approver.ClientAccountName & _
        "@youknow.net";
        SmtpMail.Send(mail);
    }
}
```

---

[1]Microsoft, Content Management Server help file, "Implementing Workflow E-Mail Notification."

To register the event, follow the steps outlined in the help topic "Registering for Publishing Events Using HTTP Modules." Be sure to check the help file to get the code that matches your release of the product.

Enabling Security on MCMS

Because MCMS is so important for all types of portals, it is likely to be the first line of defense in your security scheme. The information and guidance offered in Chapter 6 apply here as well. This section provides special notes regarding security implications for MCMS. You must configure access in three locations: Internet Information Server (IIS), ASP.NET Web.config file, and the MCMS Server Configuration application. The entries you make in these locations depend on the usage scenario and your security preferences. These guidelines are for the most common scenarios.

Internet

A public web site should be available to anonymous users, with no authentication required. By default, a new MCMS site requires user authentication, even to view pages. To make your site visible to guests (anonymous users), you must change the configuration from the default as follows:

1. In the ASP.NET Web.config file, remove or comment out the following line:

```
<add type="Microsoft.ContentManagement.Web.Security. _
CmsAuthorizationModule, Microsoft.ContentManagement. _
Web, Version=5.0.1200.0, Culture=neutral, _
PublicKeyToken=31bf3856ad364e35" _
name="CmsAuthorizationModule" />
```

2. In the MCMS Site Manager, create an account to use as the guest account, and add this account to the subscribers rights group.
3. Go to the MCMS Server Configuration application in the MCMS program group and click Security.
4. In the Guest Visitors section of the Security Configuration dialog box, click the **Yes** radio button for **Allow Guests on Site**. Enter the name of the account to use as the guest account for the site.

If you want to provide some content exclusively to authenticated users, you can follow the guidelines in the following extranet section in addition to allowing anonymous users.

Intranet

Intranet sites use integrated Windows authentication. MCMS supports both Active Directory and Windows NT authentication. Integrated Windows authentication is suitable under the following conditions:

- All users have Windows NT or Active Directory accounts.
- The intranet is located inside the firewall.
- The entire site requires authentication and does not allow anonymous users.
- All users use Internet Explorer to access the intranet.

As you might imagine, Integrated Windows security is quite secure and even allows users to authenticate the servers that are attempting to authenticate them. It also spares the user from entering a username and password by using the current user information on the client computer for authentication. Of course integrated security also means one fewer username and password combination to manage for the user.

Extranet

Now that you know how to handle security for an intranet and an Internet site, the case of the extranet is simple, as it is nothing more than a combination of the two, with a portion of the site allowing anonymous access along with a private, secured channel that is accessed via the Internet.

The baseline configuration for the extranet is the same as for an Internet site. Handle all the pages that are unrestricted in the same way as you would for any public site. This part of the site should support multiple browsers and not be based on browser-specific technology such as ActiveX controls.

The restricted access sections should be protected with MCMS rights groups. This means that the administrator must grant access to the user of a particular channel, folder, or gallery using the MCMS Site Manager. For instance, you could grant author rights to the legal notices section of a site to the legal department.

> **TIP** *You may want to configure MCMS as an extranet to enable access for content managers. By doing so, you allow your site to be maintained from remote locations rather than just by users in your domain. For instance, content authors could create new pages and editors could participate in page review from home.*

There are three general approaches to authentication on an extranet: forms-based authentication, digital certificates, and custom authentication schemes. You can combine these approaches with one another (for more on choosing an approach, see Chapter 6). The following examples show how you can use these authentication approaches to grant access on an extranet to MCMS administrative functions.

> **NOTE** *Forms-based authentication uses a cookie that stores a ticket indicating that a user has been authenticated. The system checks the cookie first on subsequent access attempts. You should use secure sockets layer (SSL) to protect the contents of the cookie so users cannot falsify that they have been authenticated. Remember that SSL imposes a performance penalty, so don't apply it to pages where anonymous access is granted anyway.*

Forms-Based Authentication

Forms-based authentication routes unauthenticated users to an HTML form in which they enter their credentials. When authentication succeeds, a cookie is written and they are granted access to subsequent pages upon request. Chapter 6 provides examples of how to implement forms-based authentication. The basic steps are:

1. Design a logon page in Visual Studio.NET. Define fields for the username and password along with a Submit button. Be sure to use the Password field as the control to accept the password.
2. Right-click each of the controls dropped onto the page, and select **Run As Server Control**.

3. Add the following code to the **Submit1_ServerClick** event handler:

```
CmsAuthenticationTicket ticket;
ticket = _
CmsFormsAuthentication.AuthenticateAsUser _
(strServerAccount,
    strServerPassword,
    txtUserName.Text,
    "FirstName");
if( ticket != null )
{
    string strReturnUrl = _
    Request.QueryString["ReturnUrl"];
    CmsFormsAuthentication.SetAuthCookie(ticket, true, _
    false);
    StringBuilder strUrl = new StringBuilder();
    strUrl.Append("http://");
    strUrl.Append(Environment.MachineName);
    strUrl.Append(strReturnUrl);
    Response.Redirect(strUrl.ToString());
}
else
{
    Label1.Text = "Your username or password are _
    incorrect. Please re-enter your username and _
    password.";
}
```

4. Add the following code to the **Page_Load** handler:

```
if(!Request.IsSecureConnection)
{
    StringBuilder strSSL = new StringBuilder();
    strSSL.Append("https://");
    strSSL.Append(Environment.MachineName);
    strSSL.Append("/");
    strSSL.Append(Request.Url.PathAndQuery);
    Response.Redirect(strSSL.ToString());
}
```

5. Save your changes and build the solution.

Digital Certificates

Certificates are digital keys installed on a particular workstation. They contain information that uniquely identifies the user to applications accessed by the workstation. Certificates can be mapped to Active Directory or Windows domains. Users are issued certificates by a certificate-issuing authority, and these certificates are downloaded to their workstations. Windows 2000 comes with a certificate server so you can manage certificates.

The key difference between forms-based security and digital certificates is that certificate-based authentication does not require the user to enter authentication information on a login page. Authentication is more seamless and virtually invisible to the user. Therefore, certificates are more appropriate for processes that have no human user at all, such as the automation of the supply chain to post orders from a buyer to a seller.

You can set up your site so users without certificates are treated as anonymous users while those with certificates are mapped to the permissions and roles of the certificate user. You can establish unique certificates for each individual user or map many users to a single account. For more information on certificates and Windows security, see TechNet security how-tos at www.microsoft.com/technet/itsolutions/howto/sechow.asp and Michael Howard's book *Designing Secure Web-Based Applications for Microsoft Windows 2000* (Microsoft Press, 2000).

Custom Authentication

The third form of authentication for extranets is custom authentication. This approach uses another directory service and maps users back to related Active Directory accounts. For instance, user information might be stored in Commerce Server for means of site personalization. Users might be authenticated by a third party such as Microsoft Passport. The custom security scheme would then look up the appropriate Active Directory account and grant permissions based on that account.

Custom authentication is the least commonly used form of the authentication approaches discussed here. This approach may be selected when there is a limited amount of content or functionality to provide to authenticated users, and the site is therefore rather simple to administer.

Although it is technically possible, I do not recommend using databases to store authentication information. Active Directory and other directory servers are more hardened to security threats.

.NET and Web Services Integration

Up to this point, we have been implementing standard MCMS functionality, albeit in the larger context of our portal master plan. With .NET and web services integration, the true potential of the portal is realized. While MCMS is the heart of the portal platform, it is .NET that provides the overarching framework. Some services in the portal exist entirely outside MCMS, others are displayed within pages based on MCMS templates, and still others are web services either inside or outside the enterprise.

.NET integration means the use of the .NET Framework to extend functionality beyond MCMS to include additional server platform products such as SharePoint Portal Server, SQL Server, and Commerce Server, or non-Microsoft products based on the .NET platform. Not all .NET integration requires the use of web services. The fact that Microsoft has moved or is moving all its enterprise server products to a common application platform provides tremendous benefits in terms of your taking advantage of developer skills and component reuse.

With web services integration, you are free to connect to an even broader range of applications beyond the .NET world, such as Java, Web-Sphere, and any other service that jumps on the web services bandwagon. You now have the opportunity to syndicate content from news sources or tap into financial services for transactions, currency conversions, online marketplaces, and a host of other solutions.

> **NOTE** *I have omitted coverage of the Site Stager component of MCMS, as it is not compatible with ASP.NET-based sites. It is used to push static copies of HTML and ASP pages to other servers, including non-Windows servers.*

.NET Integration

MCMS provides a wealth of power with its out-of-the box user interface for content management and the Windows administrative clients for webmasters. You are likely to rely on these extensively in your implementation. They are not the only options for clever .NET programmers, however. You can create custom .NET applications that take advantage of all MCMS features, but with an interface of your choosing. For instance, you may find that some of the options available to users in the standard browser-based

Web Author are more (or less) than what your users need to accomplish their tasks. You can hide or simplify options. You can create specialized interfaces to run in an Office application that guide users through the steps of content creation. These are called MCMS web applications to distinguish them from MCMS web services. Within Visual Studio.NET, projects are stored in solutions, which are stored with the file extension .SLN.

Another way to extend MCMS is to customize the approval process discussed earlier in the chapter, providing email notification to users when an item awaits their approval. Similarly, you could implement more sophisticated routing rules for the approval process as a custom MCMS application.

MCMS provides several project templates in Visual Studio.NET (Table 9.1). You can use both Visual Basic and Visual C# to create these projects.

These three template types appear in the Templates list in Visual Studio.NET when you create a new project. The MCMS projects are like other project templates, except that they automatically run some preliminary steps to make MCMS components available in the project. The standard console is copied into the project as the basis for a custom console, changes are automatically made to the Web.config file, and users are authenticated against MCMS and their rights are checked.

MCMS projects provide additional toolbox items, the Template Explorer menu bar, and menu items on the Tools menu. The Content Management Server tab in the Toolbox window contains the placeholder controls you need to design MCMS templates. The Template Explorer window provides a hierarchical view of the templates along with the ability to view template properties. The Content Management Server menu item on the

Table 9.1 Visual Studio Content Management Projects

Project Template Name	Description
MCMS Web Application	Used to create an MCMS application with a web user interface
MCMS Web Service	Used to create MCMS XML web services that can be used from other applications
MCMS Empty Web Project	Used to create an empty project for an MCMS web application

Tools menu provides direct links to Site Manager, Database Configuration Application, Server Configuration Application, and Web Author.

You can convert an existing Visual Studio.NET project to an MCMS project. To do so, open the project and select Enable as CMS Project from the Project menu.

> **NOTE** *Do not remove references to MCMS components that have auto-matically been generated by Visual Studio.NET. Removing these references will produce unpredictable and undesirable results.*

Web Services Integration

Web services are probably the most widely touted benefit of the .NET platform because they provide the ability to integrate heterogeneous systems and even make Microsoft and Unix solutions talk to one another. MCMS 2002 brings web services into the fold in a content management product. Along with adopting Visual Studio.NET as the development environment for MCMS, you can create and consume web services with MCMS. Taking this approach results in new openness and the promise of even greater interoperability. It also raises many architectural and design options that require sorting through.

If you already know how to create web services, you know how to create them for MCMS. The big difference is that you must invest the time to learn the MCMS object model to get the most out of your web services.

> **NOTE** *Web services configured to directly access the MCMS publishing API create a potential security vulnerability, as they make it possible for the service to write changes to your MCMS repository, overriding a read-only configuration. Be sure to practice safe coding on your web service to prevent dangerous or malicious changes.*

Consuming Web Services

While MCMS may more commonly be used to provide a web service to another application, there are excellent opportunities to have MCMS play the other role and consume web services. This is the case for content syndication. MCMS can periodically retrieve news or other data from another web service.

It is possible to configure MCMS to consume a web service in real time. For instance, a user could view a web page with current weather information, prompting MCMS to request weather data in XML from a weather web service. MCMS would package the resulting data using the page template and display it for the user. In most cases, this is not the most attractive option. Users of your portal would be exposed to additional latency of the Internet and would be vulnerable to any outage or performance degradation of the web service. As usage rises, the load on the web service also rises, increasing the processing cost for the service and potentially increasing the financial cost depending on the revenue model. Real-time concurrency is not often worth this price.

Another problem with posting content directly from a web service is that you have fewer options for error-handling or human intervention to correct errors. You may expose your organization to legal liability by publishing incorrect information on your site, so you need a review process for content.

A better option is to take the data consumed by the service and store it in the CMS repository. This function can be performed on a scheduled basis to ensure a reasonable degree of concurrency. For instance, an hourly update of a four-day weather forecast might be acceptable, or an update on sports scores every minute. For even less volatile data, you could take the data from the web service and launch the content management routing and approval process.

Content Management in SharePoint

The SharePoint product family contains its own content management features, allowing users and webmasters to create new pages on their intranet by filling in web forms. These features were introduced in version 1 of SharePoint Portal Server and SharePoint Team Services and have been significantly enhanced in the current version. Although I am focusing on SharePoint Portal Server, many of the features are also available in Windows SharePoint Services, the successor to SharePoint Team Services. Figure 9.19 shows a portal home page in SharePoint. It consists of several elements called web parts. This example shows web parts such as News, Events, Links, and Topics. Some web parts include content management features.

Figure 9.19 SharePoint Portal Server Home Page

For instance, if you want to add a new event to the portal, you can click Add New Event to display the page shown in Figure 9.20.

When the record is saved, the new page is created. The event now appears in the Events web part on the home page of the portal and on the Events page, as shown in Figure 9.21.

This is virtually the simplest content management one can imagine. The user fills out a form with a handful of fields and then clicks Save to enter the content item. The data from the form is stored in the database repository for SharePoint (in this case, SQL Server). The web part controls the appearance of the content. You could build additional web parts based on the same data to present a different view of the user, such as a calendar view of events rather than a list view.

Several other web parts have equally simple content management capability. Others are enhanced to offer control over more properties of the content. For instance, the News Item web part offers much more flexibility than the Events web part. The first page is similar, with the addition of a text editor to control the appearance of the item such as its colors and fonts (Figure 9.22).

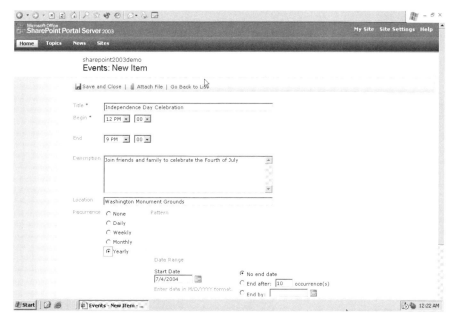

Figure 9.20 SharePoint Portal Server Events Form

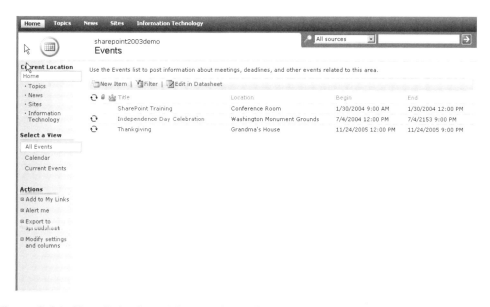

Figure 9.21 SharePoint Portal Server Home Events Page

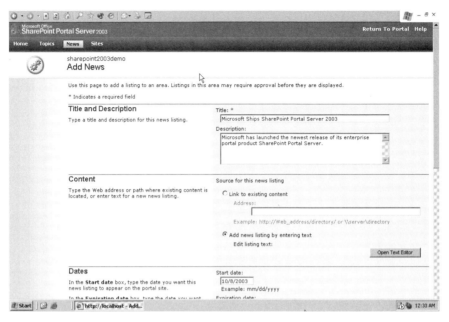

Figure 9.22 Add News Page

After you save an item, you can edit it at any time. This web page has tabs with more and different settings than those for a calendar entry (Figure 9.23).

The Publishing tab (Figure 9.24) controls the starting and ending dates for publication of an item. On this tab, users can also change the publishing status of an item to advance it through the approval process.

The next tab on the News Item page (Figure 9.25) allows an item to be assigned to a group, relates an image to an item, and grants permission to users for the item. The field that stores the filename of an image is used to display images or thumbnails that correspond to the page.

The final tab (Figure 9.26) controls whether the item is indexed by the SharePoint search engine. If the item is not included, it will not be included in search results.

SharePoint content management features are simple and direct, providing just enough to support the standard pages generated on SPS sites. They may be adapted and enhanced through custom web parts and custom site templates, both of which are discussed at greater length in Chapter 12. Compared to no content management, what SharePoint provides is a great leap forward.

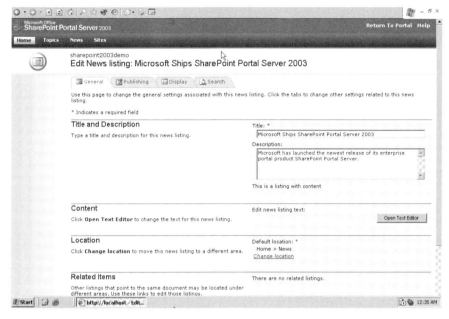

Figure 9.23 Edit News Item–General Tab

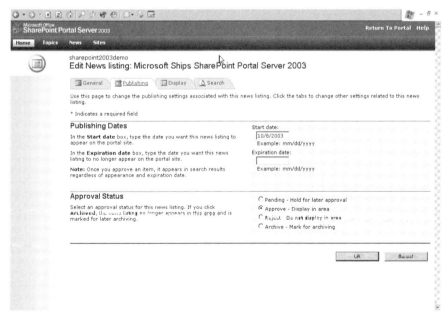

Figure 9.24 Edit News Item–Publishing Tab

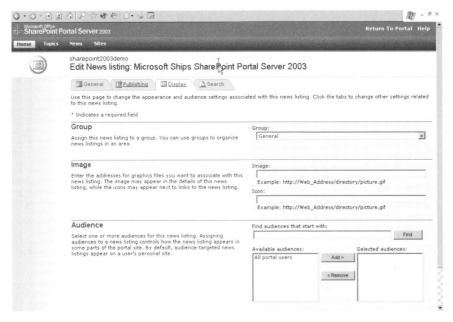

Figure 9.25 Edit News Item–Display Tab

Figure 9.26 Edit News–Search Tab

Integrating SharePoint with Microsoft Content Management Server

Now that we have examined content management both in Microsoft Content Management Server and SharePoint Portal Server, what about harnessing both at once for your site? Microsoft provides integration points that support at least four scenarios:

Using SharePoint portal search with CMS sites. SharePoint Portal Server offers Microsoft's most powerful web search technology, a vital asset for internal and external portal sites. MCMS lacks native search capability, and therefore wedding the two makes sense for many organizations. You can implement a SharePoint search and then add appropriate links in the MCMS templates to reach simple and advanced search capabilities.

Publishing WSS/SPS document libraries to CMS sites. SPS can augment CMS by providing document management capabilities by means of its document libraries. This functionality is similar to that offered in the connector between SPS 1.0 and CMS.

Publishing MCMS content within SPS sites. While SPS provides some rudimentary content management, you are likely to want to include rich content pages from MCMS within your SPS site.

Using MCMS authoring within SPS. Imagine that your public web site was implemented with MCMS and you have just implemented an intranet based on SharePoint Portal Server 2003. How do the twain meet? You can install web parts for MCMS in your intranet that connect to the content on your public web site. This step puts content management in a more visible place for users and integrates it with other line-of-business applications.

You may choose among these integration scenarios or implement features of more than one in your solution. Integration such as adding MCMS web parts to a SharePoint site does not really affect the underlying architecture of your CMS site, so the risk and impact are relatively low.

Custom Content Management

We have taken a look at two content management solutions in the Microsoft server family, MCMS and SPS. Another alternative is to create your own custom .NET content management solution. This approach is a throwback to the days before off-the-shelf content management existed. The value in products such as MCMS and SPS is such that it would be quite difficult to get anywhere near the same level of functionality, dependability, and support from a custom solution. For general-purpose content management, I discourage you from attempting to reinvent the CMS wheel.

On the other hand, a highly specialized content management solution might be better served with a custom approach. For instance, imagine that your entire web presence was constituted of pages dynamically generated from an existing database. Your site would essentially consist of forms for entering data and reports for extracting that data from the database. In such a case, your requirement is not really for content management at all, but rather for a custom application that happens to have a web user interface. In this scenario, a custom approach might be the quickest path to fulfilling the project requirements.

Conclusion

Nearly every portal needs content management; and the implementation of content management along with related page migration consumes a significant amount of time and labor, at least for large sites. Content management ultimately offers one of the strongest returns on investment for portal technology, as it places control over content in the hands of those who truly own it, freeing up webmasters, HTML programmers, and developers to turn their attention to more challenging tasks than coding static web pages.

The Microsoft .NET platform offers several content management options. SharePoint includes content management along with collaboration, a search engine, and document management. For most large portal sites, you need more content management than SharePoint alone can deliver. Including MCMS gives you tremendous control over the appearance of your web pages and supports a collaborative authoring environment so you can easily add new content and keep existing content fresh. The extensibility of the product along with its melding into the Visual Studio.NET integrated development environment means that you can build a significant amount of your portal solution in MCMS.

By starting with the taxonomy and the templates for static web pages, you can create a basis on which to hang not only static web content but the other applications that make your portal rich in functionality. Chapter 10 provides more detail on how to develop the taxonomy and make it concrete.

Developing Portal Taxonomy

This chapter introduces the fundamental principles of the taxonomy and offers practical hints about how to create a taxonomy for your portal. As discussed in Chapter 9 and further addressed in Chapter 12, the taxonomy is one of the keys to organizing your content, including site navigation, folder construction, and categories. It may be used for all types of portals, including outward-facing and enterprise portals.

You can think of taxonomy as an organizational map that is used to categorize information related to one or more areas of knowledge. A well-designed taxonomy helps a user locate information that would be difficult to find through a simple search process. The taxonomy provides a context or a knowledge map for documents.

In this chapter, I start by discussing the principal concepts of the taxonomy. I then apply these principles and illustrate several technical approaches toward developing taxonomy. Then I show how developing a corporate taxonomy can solve a real-world business problem. Next I discuss the business value of developing taxonomy, and finally I discuss the various methods for instantiating taxonomy.

What Is Taxonomy?

Though the concept of taxonomy may be new to you as it relates to managing information within a portal, the basic concept has been used widely for quite some time in a number of disciplines. Taxonomy provides a structure that serves to bring order to a particular area of knowledge.

In biology, arguably the king of taxonomies was devised by Carolus Linnaeus in 1858. He created a simplified system of classification of all living things (binomial nomenclature) that is still in use today. The classification begins with the most general groupings (kingdoms: Animalia, Plantae) to the most specific (species: rodentis, carnivora) (Figure 10.1).

This classification system includes all living things. For example, human beings fit within the following categories in the taxonomy, as shown in Figure 10.2.

Biologists use the attributes of a living thing to place it properly within this structure. This system has helped biologists in a number of areas by providing a structure within which theories, and eventually biological laws, can be deduced.

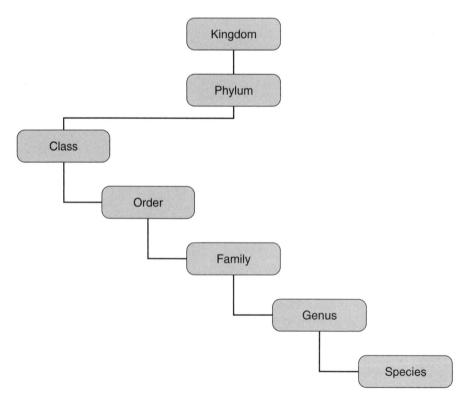

Figure 10.1 Binomial Nomenclature Used to Classify Plants and Animals

Kingdom: Animalia

Phylum: chordata

Class: mammalia

Order: primate

Family: pongidae

Subfamily: hominidae

Genus: homo

Species: sapiens

Figure 10.2 Humans in Binomial Nomenclature

People employ taxonomies in their everyday lives to help find things. If I were to ask you to get those crazy red socks that I've seen you wear to work, you would simply go into your bedroom to your chest of drawers, and open your sock drawer. Without knowing it, you have used your own organizational taxonomy to help you locate those red socks. You have many places to store things in your home, so how did you know to go to the bedroom and then the sock drawer?

Suppose that you have a living room and a bedroom in your home, and the living room contains two storage cabinets, a bookcase, and a TV cabinet. Moving on to your bedroom, you have a chest of drawers and a wardrobe in which you store most of your clothes. In your chest of drawers, you store socks and underwear in the top drawer and t shirts and sweaters in the bottom drawers. You also store items of clothing in the wardrobe, though you reserve the wardrobe for clothes that should be hung up, such as pants and dress shirts. As a result, you think of this piece of furniture as the hanging clothes wardrobe. To be more precise, you might decide to create a map to help you visualize this organizational scheme (see Figure 10.3). This figure is analogous to the knowledge map you create for a portal.

The vocabulary we have created is highly specific: The terms "clothes drawer" and "hanging clothes wardrobe" refer to items within your home. In other words, by developing this taxonomy, we are making the inherent assumption that you know what is meant by these terms. Taxonomy is a specialized view of content. As you searched for the socks in the sample scenario, you said to yourself that socks are an article of clothing and all articles of clothing are stored in your bedroom in either your closet or your drawer, and small objects belong in a drawer rather than hanging in a closet. In essence what we have done here is to create our own vocabulary to describe the organization of elements within your home.

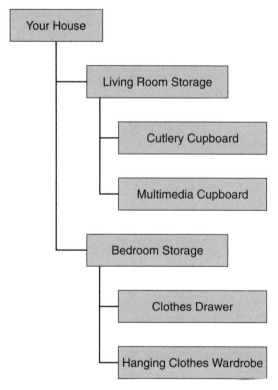

Figure 10.3 Sample Storage Taxonomy for a Home

Organizations that deal with different bodies of knowledge end up with different taxonomies. A manufacturer would have a different taxonomy than a reseller or a services company. Even companies in the same industry can end up with different taxonomies because their business models differ and the value they place on different kinds of information varies.

Applications for Taxonomy

Taxonomy structures can be used in a variety of ways, such as helping researchers find source materials, readers locate information in a book, or web site visitors locate information in an electronic journal. Taxonomies are used by buyers to locate products and services. They are employed by business decision makers to locate sources of expertise and to build communities of practice that include experts who are working on related research issues.

Taxonomy structures can also make automated processes more efficient. For example, taxonomy terms can be used in a search engine query to help users find information more easily or in a filtering program to personalize email alerts or web sites. Taxonomy applications have three key elements: people, tasks, and sources (of content). Note that the same taxonomy structure can serve multiple applications and can be applied to different kinds of content, including articles, books, videos, speeches, and so on.

A number of companies such as Inxight Software, Mohomine, and Metacode claim to interpret the semantic content of any textual document and automatically classify text on the fly. They use:

- Lists of standard terms (such as "maritime" instead of "ocean" as the standard term)
- Hierarchical relationships ("transportation" is subordinate to "industries")
- Cross-references (shipping via boat can be called "sea transport" or "maritime transportation")

Despite automated tools for this task, most analysts still develop taxonomy with no more than their wits. I follow this approach here to better understand the process.

Taxonomy Concepts

Let's explore the key concepts that relate to taxonomy and discuss its practicality in the context of managing large amounts of information within your business. A good place to start is to gain some insight into the nature of the data we are organizing. This data falls into two general categories: structured data and unstructured data.

Structured Data

Structured data is easier to understand than unstructured data, because it is more consistent and follows stricter rules. By understanding structured data, we will gain insights into unstructured data, which is a fundamental concept to taxonomy. Structured data resides within a database and contains well-defined tables, columns, and fields. Generally, a table represents some kind of entity, each row represents an instance of the entity, and each column represents a piece of data surrounding this entity. For example, we could represent the data surrounding a company's orders with Tables 10.1 and 10.2.

Table 10.1 Customer Data

Customers			
Customer number	**Name**	**Telephone no.**	**Credit limit**
1	Avis	0171 123 4567	$10,000
2	Boeing	0181 345 6789	$2,500
3	CA	0123 45678	$50,000
4	Dell	0134 56789	$21,000

Table 10.2 Order Data

Orders				
Order no	**Date**	**Customer number**	**Item**	**Quantity**
11234	2-Mar-99	1	A	150
11235	15-Mar-99	2	B	25
11236	21-Apr-99	3	C	1,000
11237	7-May-99	4	D	6,789

The first table represents data pertaining to customers, and the second table contains all information relating to orders. Furthermore, the association of which orders apply to which customers is tracked through the unique customer ID, which maps to an associated row in the Orders table.

The point is that a user can query the database on very specific questions and receive answers, provided that the questions can be answered by the data model. For example, for the relational data model described in Tables 10.1 and 10.2, we could ask questions such as:

- Who are your customers?
- How many customers do you have?
- Which customers have orders?
- What is the average number of orders per customer?

Unfortunately, unstructured information presents a situation that is not as straightforward because there is no well-defined model. Imagine trying to catalog the contents of your My Documents folder, which probably contains fax cover sheets, letters, work and personal documents, presentations, budget spreadsheets, family photos, downloaded software ready to install, and may other kinds of files.

Unstructured Data

Unstructured data is any electronic data that does not reside in a structured database (it is typically stored in documents). In contrast, structured data provides its own context: The data model itself describes what each field means. For instance, a field called Shipping Address in a table called Customers probably contains a physical address. A data field in the Invoices table probably stores the date that the invoice was created. Search techniques and rules for dealing with structured data are quite mature and generally understood. The mapping between data and metadata (data about data) is direct and straightforward. It is simple to generate a data dictionary in an automated fashion, even for a large database. Examples of unstructured information include Word documents, streaming audio and video, email, and PowerPoint presentations.

Unstructured information presents many challenges compared to structured data. It is relatively simple to produce a query in a relational database that shows all invoices created in a specified date range, because the structure of the data lends itself to the query. Adherence to the data model ensures that your answer will be unambiguous and complete, and the results will be consistent and replicable over time. You can be assured that an important field such as invoice date would be a required field and thus be included in all records. It would be validated to ensure that only valid values were present. Neither completeness nor consistency is guaranteed for unstructured data, on the other hand. To search for all new articles on a topic such as knowledge management on a web site you are counting on the date of the article being entered in a metatag, and consistent terms being used to identify the key topics of articles.

With unstructured data, you can search either data or metadata (or a combination of the two). The problem is that you cannot take much for granted in the quality of either. To find new articles, you could search for a date in the text of an article in a Word file or HTML, or in the metadata, such as in the HTML metatags or Word document properties. But how would you determine when the article was written? Does the file creation date mean the same thing as the date written? What if two conflicting dates were found? Which date formats should be considered? What about vague or incorrect date values?

Whereas a structured database encourages a fixed vocabulary of terms by means of dropdown lists, reference tables, and other means, unstructured data sources are by definition free of such constraints. Users cannot be sure that the same terms will be used in two different documents, even if both documents cover the same topic. On the other hand, the same word may be used in two unrelated documents. The richness of human language becomes the enemy of search accuracy.

Semantics

Semantics is the science of modeling the context and relationships of all the objects in a system for the purpose of attaching meaning to the information generated by the system. All information must be placed within a specific context in order to be useful. Although beyond the scope of this book, this is the crux of the work surrounding artificial intelligence and the study of human intelligence. For example, the information "two" has little meaning unless you know two of what. By attaching two to the object apples, you have an answer to the "what" of two; but you lack any knowledge of how "two apples" relates to other objects within the system. By adding the entity "Jim" with the relationship "have," you have a clear understanding that "Jim has two apples." So in fact the basic constructs used to model the semantics of a system are very similar to the basic constructs of any language—namely, subject-verb-object or entity-relationship-object, which is known as an associative model in the field of knowledge management.

Knowledge Representation/Ontology

A knowledge representation or ontology is a semantic representation of the objects within a specific domain of knowledge. The domain of knowledge could be sports, finance, insurance, and so on. The goal of the ontology would be to represent all the objects and relationships among objects within this domain. For example, suppose we chose to semantically model the same body of knowledge I described relationally earlier, namely, customer orders for a company. Within this knowledge space, only two objects exist—customers and orders. Furthermore, only one basic relationship exists: A customer "has" an order. All objects inherently possess the IS relationship indicating the entity (or class) to which the object belongs. We could begin to describe the relationship of the data in words in the following way:

- Knowledge space: All customers' orders
- Two entities: Customers, Orders
- Allowed relationship: Customers have (0 to N) orders, IS inherent

So we can start to talk about information that fits into this semantic model in the following way:

- Avis IS a customer
- Avis HAS a telephone number of 1234567
- Avis HAS a credit limit of $15,000
- #11234 IS an order number
- Avis HAS order #11234

Obviously, an area of knowledge such as sports or even orders contains many more objects, and the relationships between objects within this body of knowledge are far more complex, but the idea is the same. For example, for sports, we would define objects such as baseball, player, team, and so on. Next we would begin to define the relationship rules, such as a player is part of a specific team, a team belongs to one type of sport, and baseball is a type of sport. Next we would begin to instantiate the model with real-life information, such as the Blue Jays is a type of baseball team. Whenever we read through a document, we naturally bring our own ontology to bear that is modeled by individual neural pathways within our brains. For example, when we study a subject, we are in effect strengthening our ontological map through the creation of neural pathways, thereby strengthening the associations between various concepts within a particular subject.

What does this have to do with taxonomy? Well, unstructured documents are written using human languages. When someone reads a document, he is sifting through a large number of words that represent objects that are semantically related. By comparing our own internal ontological map to the information we read, we extract meaning. The goal of developing taxonomy is to make it easier for users to extract the meaning of content by providing a context.

Once the meaning is determined, the document can be appropriately classified within the categories defined by the taxonomy. For example, suppose you wanted to classify this book within your book collection. You would probably identify the area of knowledge covered as being related to the computer industry even though the word "computer" is not used within the book. As discussed later in the chapter, there are a number of tools that automate the process of classification; however, all require some human intervention because of the inherent complexity of human judgment.

Because the relationships that describe a whole body of knowledge are far more complex than the relationships represented through a relational model, we must use an associative model. The associative data model diagrams the semantics of the complex relationships of language using subject-verb-object terminology. While a database uses a relational model for describing the relationships between objects, a knowledge representation requires the associative model to model the concepts of a body of knowledge. The associative model represents the major technology used by the natural language query model.

Vocabulary

Within the context of the taxonomy, vocabulary represents a structured group of words that are used to define the main concepts used within the taxonomy. To enforce a system within your taxonomy, you must choose words carefully and consistently. Metadata tags content with words from your taxonomy.

Thesauri

A thesaurus keeps track of synonyms or words with the same or similar meanings. When we are dealing with unstructured information, the thesaurus creates a link between the words used to describe the same or similar concepts.

Taxonomy built on the thesaurus model (designating a preferred or authorized term with entry terms or variants) helps to link these different terms together. At search time, the term that the knowledge worker uses is associated with the preferred (or key) term for more precise searching, or the knowledge worker's term is expanded to include the variant forms of the term as well as the authorized term for a broader search. Taxonomies built on the thesaurus model do not force all work groups to use a common set of terminology.

Categories

A category represents a structured vocabulary that is decided upon by a specific concept within a body of knowledge. It is an individual node among a group of nodes that are related to one another. When defining categories, the terms used should be intuitive so people can deduce the information contained within. When categories are created with meaningful words, a context is automatically created for all documents and subcategories residing within the category. For example, in the biological plants and animals taxonomy example, a very specific category called Homo sapiens is used to categorize the last leaf in the classification of human beings. For this example, the category names used are unique; but with a portal taxonomy, the same category name can exist within different locations of the hierarchy. To understand why, we first need to realize that all categories have properties associated with them.

Attributes/Properties

Integral to the naming of the categories are the properties or characteristics associated with each category. The properties serve to describe where within the logical hierarchy of categories an individual category resides. All subcategories inherit the attributes describing the parent knowledge space, which means that the information contained in a subcategory represents a more specific area of the same knowledge space. For example, suppose we define a category called golf and a category called sports. Golf represents a specific area of knowledge within the parent category of sports. Like the data, attributes can be searched. Attributes can also be stored as metadata. For example, you may have used the properties associated with a Microsoft Word document to store data such as author, title, subject, and even categories (Figure 10.4).

Categorization Rules

You can devise rules that determine the categories in which an item belongs. For instance, the word "fly" could appear in items relating to civil aviation, bird watching, and trout fishing. You might have a rule that an item containing "trout," "rod," "reel," and "fly" pertains to fly fishing, while one containing "bird," "plumage," "habitat," and "binoculars" should be filed

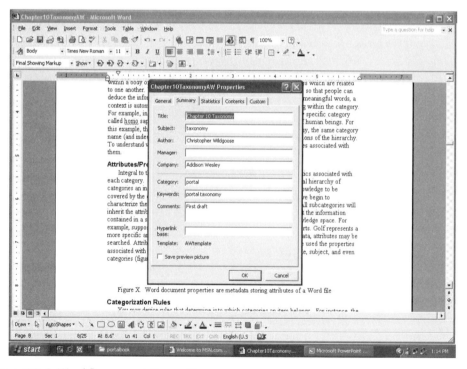

Figure 10.4 Word Document Properties

under "bird watching." SharePoint Portal Server offers categorization rules for its Audience feature.

Document Metadata

Metadata is information that describes another piece of information, object, or thing. Basically metadata makes finding a particular piece of information easier because moving through a stack of metadata takes much less time than moving through the data itself. For example, in the old days when you would thumb through a card catalog system in the library, you were using metadata to locate a book. The card catalog contained the necessary information for you to locate the physical book on the library shelf. Without the metadata located in the card catalog, you would have been forced to wade through all the books in the library to locate the book.

Document Card

A document card represents the metadata associated with a file, just as a paper card in a library card catalog contains information about a book it lists, such as author, title, publisher, and date. The document cards are indexed and made available for searching. The card contains a link to the original document.

Context Specificity of Taxonomy

Within an organization, a particular piece of information may have a number of different uses, and different knowledge workers may have a different perspective on the same piece of information. For example, let's suppose that a contract has been developed with a vendor. Where within the existing corporate taxonomy should this information reside? The answer depends on who is looking for the information. The legal department would say the contract should reside in the contracts category under that particular vendor. Because the contract represents revenue, the accounting department would suggest the accounts receivable category. Finally the sales department would see the document as a part of a client relationship.

Furthermore, many portals today support the ability of a user to create a personalized taxonomy. Remember that, although multiple views to the same document can be created, only one physical document exists. Generally, the portal stores only the document cards that store the metadata within your infrastructure. On the document card is stored the location of the physical document so the portal can locate that document when the user requests it. The actual document could reside anywhere within the infrastructure of the company. In other words, the document could reside on a file server, on the company's web site, or within a Lotus Notes database. As long as the taxonomy keeps track of the document cards in a local document repository, the user should have no problem locating the document.

Documents are partitioned into logical groupings that are easier to navigate. These allow users to locate information even if they start with a single-word search term. The categories within a taxonomy move from general to more specific. Taxonomies help avoid problems with common English language peculiarities of similar-sounding words or words with multiple meanings. Taxonomies facilitate iterative, drill-down searches that both advanced and beginning users can quickly traverse.

A taxonomy category can be used to limit the scope of a search, thus reducing the number of irrelevant documents returned. The category facilitates browsing of content, allowing a user to traverse a large number of related documents.

Information is filtered based on the attributes of each category. Think of the unstructured information within your business as water that is gushing out of a fire hydrant. The portal taxonomy is designed to catch hold of this information and place it into the appropriate places within the corporate taxonomy

Taxonomies provide flexibility in retrieving content. One of the central problems with finding information, as Humpty Dumpty said to Alice, is that words can mean so many different things. The inherent ambiguity of language makes searching more challenging because items are missed that are tagged with different, but related, terms or extraneous results are brought in because too broad a meaning has been assigned to a search term. For instance, a large Canadian systems integrator unfortunately shares its name, CGI, with the acronym for Common Gateway Interface, a widely used scripting tool for the web. Therefore, searching for "cgi" on a search engine returns thousands of results quite useful for CGI programmers and tens of thousands of pages that contain "CGI" in their URLs—and perhaps buried deep within the search results, a link or two to the company called CGI.

Taxonomy Best Practices

A few simple guidelines can steer your taxonomy development. While some may seem obvious, they bear repeating, much as soccer players must drill on passing, blocking, and shooting whether they are beginners or professionals.

Use Industry-Accepted Vocabulary

The taxonomy is all about the terms that you use. If you are not an expert on the subject matter of your portal, find someone who is to assist. You will want to use the correct terms and understand synonyms for those terms as well. Nearly every discipline has its share of jargon, as well as more precise meanings assigned to common words.

Be Consistent

Try to use a single classification approach. If it makes sense to combine approaches, keep the classification consistent on the sibling level. Use consistent vocabulary and thesauri. Maintain a consistent degree of generality in sibling categories.

Control Depth

A flat taxonomy ensures that a user will be able to locate information quickly. On the other hand, the information should be sufficiently segmented to make the taxonomy worthwhile. A flat taxonomy ensures that users can find information quickly with fewer clicks. A good rule of thumb is to go no more than 3–6 levels deep.

Control Breadth

A focused taxonomy ensures that users can easily digest the scope of information. Just as there is a limit to the patience of users in traversing a taxonomy from top to bottom, there is a limit to the width of the taxonomy. For most purposes, you should consider starting with 10–15 top-level categories. Assuming you restrict yourself to 15 categories at lower levels and are using no more than 3–6 levels, your taxonomy could then hold a maximum of 15^6 or 11,390,625 entries. A typist entering these terms at 100 words per minute would need about 80 days working 24 hours a day to complete the task. If you were more restrained and confined yourself to a 3-level taxonomy and a width of 15 entries, you would need to shoehorn your content into a mere 3,375 categories.

Divide and Conquer

Taxonomy development is much like spring cleaning at your house. It is a frightening prospect to tackle the entire project at one time, so you should start in one corner of your taxonomy house and complete a room at a time. You will have ample opportunity later to see your errors and refine your approach.

Keep Users in Mind

Be sure to consider the needs of your target users, and understand what they are trying to do on your portal and what mental baggage (or lack thereof) they bring with them. One of the frequent taxonomy mistakes is to assume outsiders have inside knowledge of your organization. Many taxonomies are built to reflect the bureaucratic structure of an organization rather than the functions of the departments. For instance, if a county government were to assign taxonomy development to each agency or office and then merge the results together, you would have a significant amount of overlap and duplication. Moreover, the taxonomy might contain "blind spots" for functions that didn't cleanly map to a particular office.

Implementing a Taxonomy

Now that we have shared more than you ever planned to learn about taxonomies, semantics, and artificial intelligence, it's time to tackle the implementation of your portal taxonomy. There are three general approaches to creating taxonomy:

- Automatic taxonomy creation and document categorization
- Human taxonomy creation
- Assisted taxonomy creation and document categorization

You may find that two or even all three approaches have value for your project. Bear in mind that taxonomies are never really complete as long as new content is being added. They grow and evolve over time in response to the changing demands of users.

The taxonomy industry has continued to grow and now offers a wide range of technology and products at various price points. Small to mid-sized companies are now also able to offer their employees and customers the same benefits formerly available only to corporate behemoths. In addition to public Internet and corporate portals, taxonomies are also finding their way into vertical portals, customer and partner extranet sites, and even to very specialized knowledge worker document repositories.

Automatic Taxonomy Creation and Document Categorization

Microsoft does not currently offer a product that automatically categorizes documents or creates taxonomy. Several other vendors have taken this approach, however, and you can use these third-party products to search and categorize your web pages, documents, and other content sources.

A number of algorithms have been developed to enable categorization of data repositories. In its taxonomy and content categorization study, the Delphi Group identified several basic algorithms, including:

- Linguistic analysis, which identifies the subject, verbs, and objects of a sentence and then analyzes them to extract meaning.
- Statistical text analysis and clustering, which measure word frequency, placement, and grouping and the distance between words in a document.
- Rule-based taxonomies, which classify documents based on specific rules created and maintained by experts using if-then statements that measure how well a document fits into a category.[1]

Even vendors of automated taxonomy tools (Table 10.3) concede that human judgment is essential to a finished taxonomy. Their tools can save time and money, however, and find patterns in data that would not be obvious to the analyst.

---

[1] A Delphi Group White Paper, "Taxonomy and Content Classification: Market Milestone Report," April 11, 2002, p. 16.

Table 10.3 Taxonomy and Categorization Tools

Product	Vendor	Notes	URL
BrainEKP (Enterprise Knowledge Platform)	The Brain Technologies	Despite the name, this is software; innovative visualization of taxonomy	www.thebrain.com
IDOL Server	Autonomy Corp		www.autonomy.com
Inxight Categorizer	Inxight	Uses linguistic and statistical analysis; includes visualization	www.inxight.com
LexisNexis Content Organizer	Verity Inc.	Prebuilt taxonomies from those used by LexisNexis; may be combined with custom taxonomy	www.verity.com
SemioTagger	Entrieva	Uses linguistic and statistical clustering techniques	www.entrieva.com
SemioTaxonomy	Entrieva	Collection of 27 prebuilt taxonomies	www.entrieva.com
Stratify Classification Server	Stratify Inc.	Linguistic and statistical analysis, statistical clustering techniques	www.stratify.com

Human Taxonomy Creation

The second approach discussed here is to unleash a specialist in taxonomy development to master the domain of your portal and formulate a taxonomy. This approach might be expensive and time consuming, but the taxonomy would benefit from the expertise and experience of the analyst. Many portal projects have taken this approach. One risk is that the taxonomy development might expand to soak up too many project resources and make it more challenging for the project to remain on schedule.

Assisted Taxonomy Creation and Document Categorization

This third approach is a hybrid of the first two. It involves human analysts in conjunction with automated taxonomy and search tools. There are many sources of data that can help with taxonomy development. Search query logs, analysis of library reference requests, focus group results, findings from in-person interviews of individual knowledge workers, and survey results are all indicators of what content each segment of employees needs, and on what schedule. These sources also tell you about the knowledge workers' information-seeking behavior, which in turn lets you know which access methods (such as searching and browsing) and access points (such as metadata elements) you need to use in schemas and in descriptive and navigational taxonomies.

Instantiating a Taxonomy

Now that you have defined the taxonomy, you need to implement it. This is the phase when content and documents are assigned to locations within the taxonomy. Once the taxonomy tree has been created, all the documents in the system are tagged as belonging to one or more taxonomy categories. This process is typically referred to as categorization, tagging, or profiling, depending on the vendor. Users can then browse and search within specific categories.

Creating Categories in Content Management Server

Content Management Server uses channels to store taxonomy information. The channels help organize the pages of a site along consistent patterns and facilitate navigation. Chapter 9 discusses how channels are created in Content Management Server. Channels are represented as a hierarchy much like the taxonomy.

Creating Categories in Commerce Server

Like Content Management Server, Commerce Server has no explicit functionality that is called taxonomy. It nonetheless uses taxonomy in its catalog hierarchies and categories. Therefore, the catalog is the place where the taxonomy is instantiated in a Commerce Server site. Figure 10.5 shows the catalog list. For instance, you could have a sporting goods store with catalogs for each sport.

Catalogs are related to product categories. The categories can be related as parents and children or as siblings. For instance, the golf category might have child categories of clubs, balls, apparel, and accessories. Golf apparel in turn might have shirts, trousers/pants, and footwear. Categories can be nested up to five levels deep in Commerce Server. Commerce Server has been designed for up to 10,000 catalogs, and each catalog can

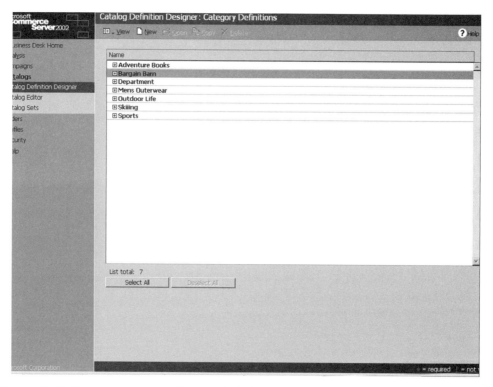

Figure 10.5 Commerce Server Catalog Definition Designer

contain up to 5 million items and 1,000 property definitions. When you create a category, you determine which properties are associated with items in that category, as shown in Figure 10.6.

You can assign catalog items to one or more categories, as shown in Figure 10.7.

Your taxonomy and hence categories will evolve during the life of your portal. If you monitor how users find content on your portal, you can shape the taxonomy to help them reach their destinations sooner.

Creating Areas in SharePoint

Areas are the means of instantiating your site taxonomy in SharePoint Portal Server. They are a hierarchy of terms used for three related purposes. First, areas provide a vocabulary of terms from the taxonomy that are used

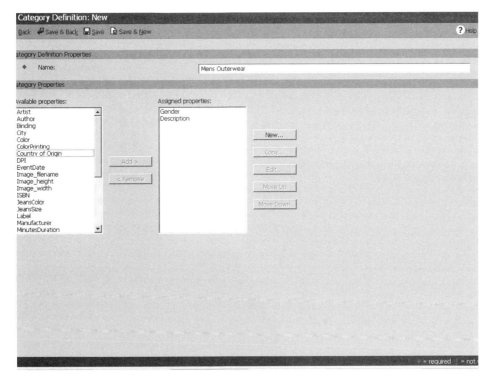

Figure 10.6 New Category Definition

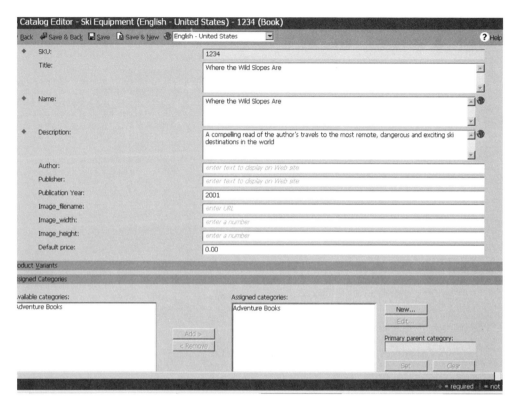

Figure 10.7 Catalog Editor

to categorize documents. Using areas simplifies and helps promote consistency in the categorization process. Users may be more willing to check a handful of areas than to spend the time to think up the keywords identified with a document.

Second, areas are used to organize the portal, as they are not only associated with documents but also with sites and people. You may want to use areas to show the expertise of your employees, and help establish networks among peers to share knowledge.

Finally, areas are used to streamline searching. They provide metadata that helps people find content even when the area itself is not included in the text of a document or other item. You can expose the areas as search terms in the search itself, or use them as links on the results to allow a user to browse area results.

SharePoint Portal Server takes areas so seriously that there is a special administrator role for maintaining them. The area manager maintains the areas, maps areas to users, and approves or rejects content requests. Areas are maintained in the site settings. They are also referenced in many other parts of the portal, such as content pages.

To create an area, follow these steps starting from the portal home page:

1. Click the **Site Settings** link in the top navigation to open the Site Settings page (Figure 10.8).
2. In the Portal Site Content section, click the **Manage portal site structure** link to open the Portal Site Map page (Figure 10.9).
3. Click **Create Area** in the Actions menu on the Portal Site Map page to open the Create Area page (Figure 10.10).

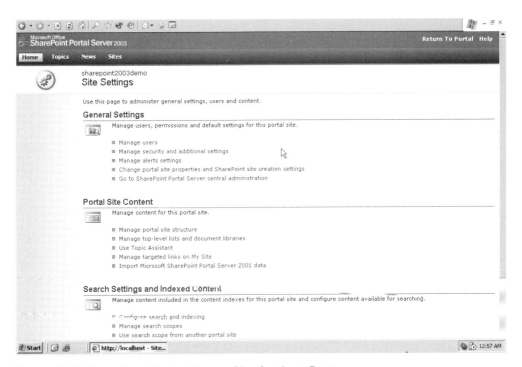

Figure 10.8 SharePoint Portal Server Site Settings Page

Figure 10.9 Portal Site Map Page

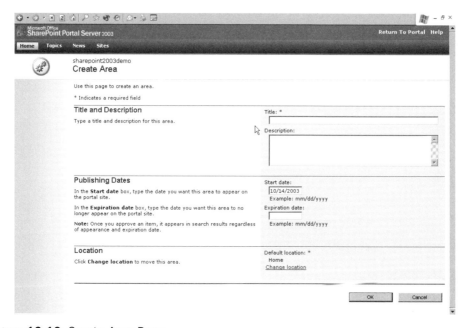

Figure 10.10 Create Area Page

4. Decide where the area fits in your overall hierarchy. For instance, the area MSF (Microsoft Solutions Framework) could be placed in the Methodology area within Topics.
5. Click **Change location** to select a location for the new area (Figure 10.11).
6. Click **OK** in the Change Location dialog box and then again on the Create Area page to save the new area.

TIP *If you place the area in the wrong location, you can always move it later from the Portal Site Map page.*

To delete an area, click the area name on the Portal Site Map page and select Delete from the dropdown menu (Figure 10.12).

In SharePoint, areas are the key to instantiating your taxonomy. If you used SharePoint Portal Server version 1, you can think of areas as the successors to categories.

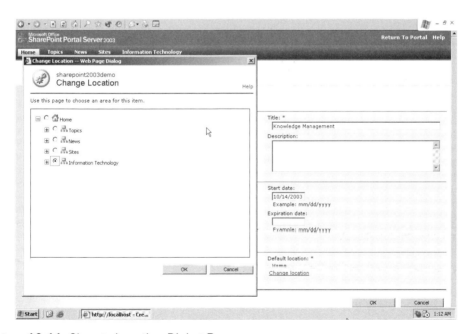

Figure 10.11 Change Location Dialog Box

Figure 10.12 Area Actions Menu

Using Topics

SharePoint Portal Server has a special area called Topics that is included in the default installation of the product. Topics is like other areas but is designed to highlight frequently used content and to be visible to the general population of portal users. Topics can contain web pages and objects such as news, calendar items, document libraries, people, and lists.

SharePoint includes a tool called the Topic Assistant to help you set up the topic structure. To use the Topic Assistant:

1. On the portal home page, click **Site Settings** in the top navigation.
2. On the Site Settings page, click **Use Topic Assistant** in the Portal Site Content section to open the Use Topic Assistant page (Figure 10.13).
3. The Area Assistant examines the areas that have been assigned to existing content and suggests areas for new content. Click the **Enable Topic Assistant** checkbox.

Figure 10.13 Use Topic Assistant Page

4. Click the **Train Now** link in the Training Status section of the page to launch the training process.

The Topic Assistant is trained by running searches and analyzing the contents of the documents that are found in the topic. The trained search engine is subsequently directed to organize more search results according to the structure of Topics.

Adding a Person to an Area

By associating people with areas, you can catalog the expertise of your organization and build communities of interest. To add a person to an area:

1. Navigate to the area by browsing or searching.
2. Click **Add Person** in the Select Action portion of the left pane of the page.
3. On the Add Person page (Figure 10.14), click the **Select person** link to find the person in the Active Directory.

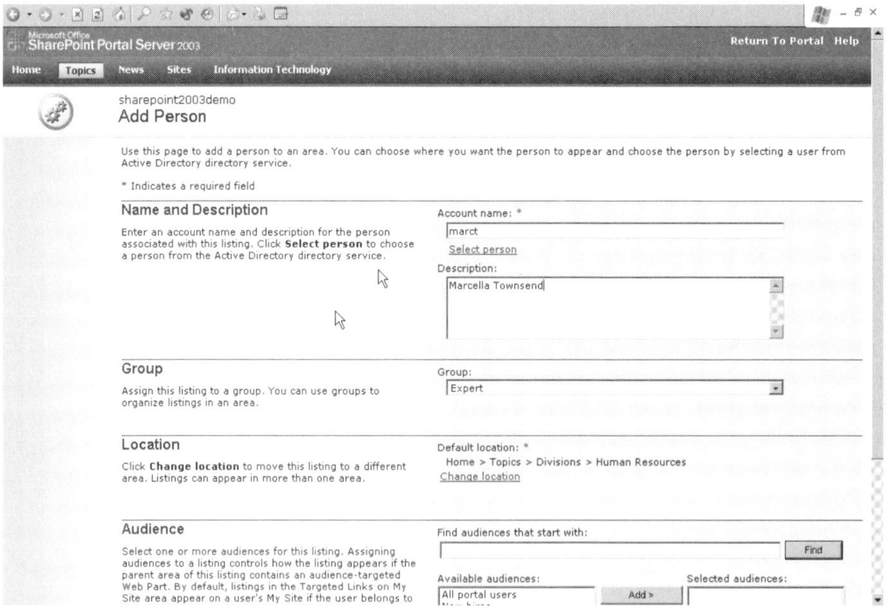

Figure 10.14 Add Person Page

4. On the Select a person page (Figure 10.15), fill in the person's name and click **Find** to search through the directory and find the account.
5. Choose the account from the Results list on the left and click **Add** to select it. You can also enter the name directly in the account list if you prefer. Click **OK**.

As you add a person to an area, you can map that entry to one or more audiences so the list for the person will be targeted to those audiences. This is a helpful way of encouraging people to find one another, such as developing a directory of specialists or experts in a field.

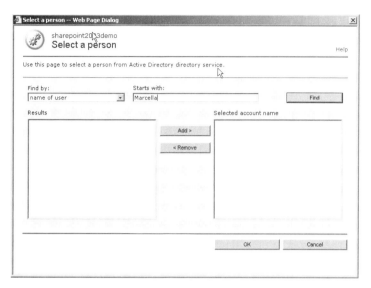

Figure 10.15 Select a Person Page

Conclusion: Business Value of the Taxonomy

The most important part of this chapter is a discussion of why taxonomy is so vital in today's organizations. Knowledge is power, and the organization with the right knowledge gains competitive advantage. I am familiar with the sales process within the IT industry, and I have learned firsthand the power of this principle. I am far more likely to be successful in selling my product when I am able to show superior knowledge of my product to my clients. Equally important is knowledge of my client's organization. This information is difficult to obtain; but before going into a sales call, I would want access to all previous presentations to this client, any recent news or press releases regarding the company, and specific information concerning the personalities involved. Armed with this kind of knowledge, I can more easily navigate through any obstacle to the sale to the best possible position against my competition.

The problem facing many corporations today isn't that the information doesn't exist; rather it is that they cannot locate the information quickly. Imagine that a salesperson leaves a company without handing over his notes on clients and prospects. Many organizations have learned from such experiences to keep a repository of employees' documents; but without an effective knowledge map, the right documents would be difficult to locate. Analysts estimate that over 80% of an organization's information exists in unstructured format, such as meeting notes. This information is accumulating at an accelerating rate as more and more organizations move to electronic records management and document management. Yet, data and information add little value to an organization because only knowledge gives an organization power and competitive advantage. Information requires context in order to become knowledge, and this knowledge must get to the hands of someone who can use it.

Knowledge management experts define data in its proper context as information. At the next higher rung of the knowledge ladder, information in its proper context is called knowledge. One could go one step higher and call information in its proper context wisdom, but for now most companies are content with extracting knowledge from their organization. So the big message is that successful organizations need to look toward moving up the pyramid by providing context to that which already exists within their organization. Over the last 50 years, businesses have invested trillions of dollars in IT in order to get and record information. Now businesses need to begin to shift their focus toward getting this information to the right people. Furthermore, because time is money, the faster an organization can impart knowledge to its employees and clients by supplying the correct information at the right time, the more money it will make. It really pays for an organization to invest in developing a well-designed taxonomy as a foundation for maximizing the potential of its people and, in turn, the organization. The downside, of course, is the considerable upfront cost involved, though the potential benefits are well worth the investment.

Chapter 11

Integrating Line-of-Business Applications

Thus far in this book we have focused on the frontend of the portal, examining the needs of human users working interactively through their web browsers. The most visible part of the portal, the frontend serves the business goals of the portal by helping organizations work together more closely, sharing information, creating transactions, and interacting in many ways. But a portal is much more than its frontend. The portal must consolidate information from multiple, disparate sources and provide ways for applications to interoperate. This chapter delves into addressing a different set of business goals: making applications talk to one another.

To really connect businesses, government, individuals, and nonprofit organizations, a portal must do more than serve human users. It must provide a similarly rich set of services to other computers as well. Just as a portal is used to standardize interfaces and facilitate data integration, it can support integration of heterogeneous systems through synchronous and asynchronous connections. This is called enterprise application integration (EAI). EAI solutions are distributed applications—that is, applications that run on multiple computers that communicate by means of standard protocols and interfaces. For instance, a retail distributed application runs on a cash register, the store's application servers, and the enterprise resource-planning system at corporate headquarters. Distributed applications meet similar business goals as other applications:

- Satisfy the functional requirements of business users.
- Include all necessary security mechanisms such as secure communication, authentication, and authorization.
- Provide performance that meets the needs of users.
- Be available when the users need the system.
- Allow management and monitoring by administrators.
- Be maintainable by using industry best practices for coding and documentation, and putting functions where they can be found by programmers.

In addition to meeting these goals, distributed applications must be suitable for long-running transactions and for loose coupling of systems in large, complex solutions and, as a result, they often cross organizational boundaries on multiple hardware and software platforms. Therefore, we must add some goals that are unique to distributed applications:[1]

- Build services rather than include all functionality in a single application.
- Use message-based techniques to provide robustness and scalability.
- Allow asynchronous as well as synchronous communication.
- Communicate with other services with the minimum amount of coupling.

Although services perform the same functions as other applications, they expose their functionality through a services interface. Because the implementation details of a service are irrelevant to an application that uses it, the dependence among components is reduced. You can have multiple development teams working on services independently, and they can choose the hardware and software platform that suits their needs best.

Unfortunately, the services architecture forces developers to factor in additional considerations that are not present in a homogeneous, synchronous application. They must be concerned about managing data concurrency, dealing with service failures or downtime, and communication issues such as protocol, data schema, and authentication.

These goals can be served by either developing a customer solution or embracing an EAI platform. EAI can be an enabling technology for building your portal. You can use it as the glue that binds legacy transactional systems together rather than rewrite them to conform to your latest enterprise architecture. For instance, if you are using SAP as your enterprise resource planning (ERP) solution, you may want to enable it for the portal. With EAI, you can build an alternative interface to the system that you make available via your web portal. Customers can inquire on order status, and suppliers on inventory levels. EAI products such as Microsoft BizTalk Server contain connectors for SAP that can access data in your ERP system. The philosophy behind this approach is "if it ain't broke, don't fix it." The

---

[1] Microsoft, Application Architecture for .NET: Designing Applications and Services. See Microsoft .NET Architecture Center at msdn.microsoft.com/architecture/.

result can be significant savings of development time and cost, as well as reduced technical risk. Another advantage of this approach is that it minimizes the additional performance burden on legacy systems by offloading much of the processing for these interfaces, which occurs on new servers provisioned for this purpose.

Another use of EAI in the portal is to create an online marketplace, or business-to-business (B2B) system. The same type of system is needed for business-to-government (B2G) and government-to-government (G2G) systems; but in this chapter, we use the B2B shorthand for all three. In a business-to-business portal, many types of transactions are supported. Suppliers must be able to check their inventory with a customer and initiate purchasing transactions to maintain optimum inventory levels. Distributors should be able to manage and orchestrate their transactions with suppliers and shipments to customers. Many of these transactions are automatically triggered by events, such as orders to maintain predetermined stock levels.

Nearly every organization has a need for integration outside its organizational boundaries. You can start by looking at the flow of money to and from an organization. Even small companies can have large numbers of customers and suppliers. An information technology reseller, for instance, may have 1,000 suppliers and offer 50,000 distinct products or services. Its customer list may be in the tens of thousands. While it is possible to establish each of these electronic trading relationships on a case-by-case basis, this effort can quickly become prohibitively expensive and time consuming for all concerned. Similarly, a manufacturer may have hundreds of companies in its sales channel. A government tax agency must deal with all tax-paying corporations and individuals, and of course these taxpayers spend a significant amount of time calculating their tax liability and making payments. Non-profit organizations need integration with suppliers for publications, event-planning companies, and with their members. What all parties need is an infrastructure that lends itself to quick and simple integration (Figure 11.1).

New technology provides a vital link for integration in the portal, especially web standards. The dominant approaches to integration in the past, such as Electronic Data Interface (EDI), were effective but were also costly to implement and maintain. As a result, only large players who could afford the integration investment used these technologies. With XML and web services, the same quality of service is available for a much larger group of users at a reasonable price.

This chapter shows how the Microsoft portal platform supports enterprise application integration, workflow, and orchestration. Our focus is on

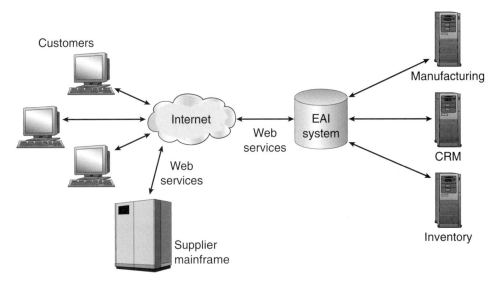

Figure 11.1 Business-to-Business Architecture

Office, InfoPath, and BizTalk. We examine how transactions are initiated, workflow is automated, and messaging traffic coordinated in an e-business portal.

There are essentially three elements in an integration scenario. First is some means of data entry to create the transaction. After defining some integration terms and concepts, we look at several options for capturing this data from users or systems. Second is the automation of workflow around the transaction, such as routing for approval. Third is a system for managing the transactions and ensuring their integrity.

Integration Concepts

We need to explore several new concepts in order to build a portal that can meet the integration needs of an organization. Our goal is to open the portal to support automated transactions. To do so, we need to set up automated business processes that conform to business process structures. The integration should support secure, one-time data entry and automate the response to the user.

You could build a custom system that handles transactions in this way from the ground up, which would be the old-fashioned way. A point-to-point connection might be the most direct and efficient approach to allow two systems to talk to one another. But even in the simplest instance, the code would grow more complex over time and ever more difficult to maintain. Furthermore, as you made more and more connections between systems, this dark cloud of bespoke code would become a dangerous thunderstorm. Investing in an underlying infrastructure to support transactions between systems reduces the effort for each new interface and simplifies management and maintenance.

Integration standards that have become widely adopted in the past five years make it more feasible to create an EAI architecture. Many services are already available as web services, from credit card processing to geographic information systems.

The rest of this chapter will be easier to digest if you preprocess a few acronyms and terms. The following are keys to understanding the integration puzzle:

- *Enterprise application integration (EAI).* The general term for linking applications with one another, particularly heterogeneous applications that cross network and organizational boundaries. You can find general information including EAI case studies at the EAI Industry Consortium (www.eaiindustry.org).
- *Electronic Data Interface (EDI).* A dominant standard for legacy EAI developed in the 1960s for the transportation industry. EDI has the reputation of being complicated and expensive to build and maintain. It is typically run over a private network called a value-added network (VAN).
- *Automated business processes.* Transactions that behave according to an agreed protocol and data model. An automated business process is designed to minimize errors and exceptions that require manual intervention.
- *Message-oriented middleware (MOM).* Software that supports the reliable exchange of data using asynchronous communication protocols and synchronous APIs.

- *Simple Object Access Protocol (SOAP).* This important standard dictates how structured documents (XML) are exchanged between peers in a decentralized, distributed environment. It is the fruit of the W3C XML Protocol Working Group and is now being updated from version 1.1 to 1.2. SOAP nodes send essentially one-way messages in a stateless environment, and they are combined in ways to handle more sophisticated transactions. They can also handle errors that arise. SOAP envelopes are the containers for messages; they can in turn hold zero or more header blocks and one or more body blocks. These blocks contain the data to be processed.
- *Web Services Description Language (WSDL).* The XML format that describes a web service, often used in conjunction with SOAP.
- *Extensible markup language (XML).* XML is a text language for representing data. It is self-describing, which means that it contains tags that explain the data model stored in the document. Therefore an XML document contains both data and metadata.
- *Multipurpose Internet Mail Extensions (MIME).* Messaging middleware that provides secure messaging to transmit and receive XML documents.
- *Extensible Stylesheet Language Transformation (XSLT).* The format in which an XML file is displayed.
- *XML schema.* Schema contains the underlying data structure for an XML file, including validation rules. The schema is used to generate the form definition file (.XSF) used by InfoPath.
- *Document Object Model (DOM).* The document object model is a platform- and language-neutral interface used to programmatically address the contents of a document such as an XML document.

To put it all together, an EAI system is composed of components that create data files, often in the form of XML documents; communicate with one another using technologies such as MIME; orchestrate the processing of the transactions; and map the data from the source to the target, including processes enforcing business rules during the transformation. The existence of these open standards and commonly used protocols allows heterogeneous EAI systems to communicate with one another.

An EAI system can also be made available to end users such as customers through web forms. The following section describes alternative approaches for developing these forms on the Microsoft platform.

Providing Intelligent Forms

The portal requires forms for many reasons, from registration and profiles to creating business transactions. Data should ideally be entered only once. You can choose among several tools to create web forms. This section discusses the pros and cons of these approaches, and the trade-offs in development, functionality, and deployment.

All of these approaches store data as XML. InfoPath was designed from the start as a tool for creating XML documents, Office has been migrating more and more to XML with each new version, and naturally data behind custom .NET forms is stored as XML. The trade-offs center around application functionality, development costs, and ease of maintenance.

Web Forms

As discussed in Chapters 4 and 5, the .NET Framework provides powerful development tools to capture data from users, store and manipulate it as XML, and send it to databases and other destinations. The framework has been the predominant tool selected for EAI implementations, especially when the approach has been chosen by IT consultants who are paid by the hour.

Building .NET web forms is a custom programming effort that offers virtually unlimited control over the look and behavior of the application (see Table 11.1). Forms can be tailored to precisely match the functional requirements for the application and to have the exact user interface you want. There are no extraneous features in custom forms, so less user training may be required.

Another significant advantage of custom web forms is that they can be deployed on multiple platforms such as workstations, handhelds, and mobile units. They are not tied to the Windows operating system so you can support Unix and Macintosh clients as well.

Table 11.1 Advantages and Disadvantages of Custom .NET Forms

Advantages	Disadvantages
Platform neutral	Development time and cost
No client footprint	No offline use
Easy to update centrally	Printing
Low dependence on versions of client software	Limited product support
No licensing cost	

On the other hand, you pay a price for custom web forms. The most obvious is the expense of developers building them in the first place. Before committing to this investment, you should ensure that your requirements cannot be met with an off-the-shelf system. In addition, typical custom web forms built with .NET do not support offline use; and like all browser-based applications, they may leave something to be desired in the printing department.

Office

With the introduction of native XML support in Microsoft Office XP and newer versions, organizations can take advantage of the familiar interface and rich functionality of these products to perform data entry for transactional systems. For instance, features such as the spellchecker can be handy in a form, and advanced formatting capability is useful in many scenarios.

Microsoft Office is ubiquitous in large and small organizations. You can almost take it for granted that users have Word and Excel, for instance, when sending documents via email. You do not need to conduct training to show users how to enter data in Office programs.

A retail web site could allow users to create orders offline via Excel (Figure 11.2). The company could create a spreadsheet that contained the order form, with fields such as customer name, address, and billing information, and a section for the items and quantities to be purchased. The user would download the spreadsheet from the company's portal. When the order form was complete, the user would click a submit button to execute a simple VBA script that would submit the XML data to a web service on

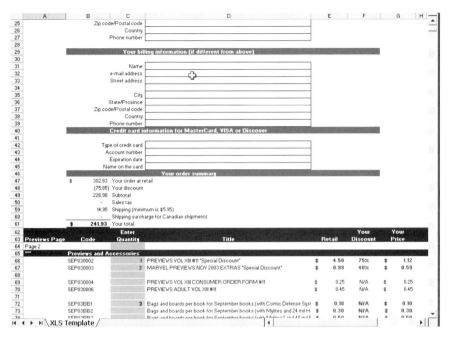

Figure 11.2 Product Order Form in Excel

the company's web site. If paying by check, the user could print the spreadsheet and enclose it with the payment.

For high-quality printed output and control over print attributes and printer settings, Office offers many advantages over a typical browser. Printing is in many ways antithetical to the hardware-neutral browser approach. The ability to print pixel-perfect forms is still needed in many industries, and paper forms are not expected to vanish overnight.

By using Office, users can work offline, which is often not possible with web-based browser applications. This can be a major advantage for mobile workers with no or slow network connections. Data entry speed is not affected by the latency of the network, so users are not frustrated by the pauses between screens that are typically experienced with a browser-based multipage form.

Office provides built in XML support. When saved as XML, the data in the spreadsheet in Figure 11.2 can be easily imported and manipulated. Figure 11.3 shows a portion of the spreadsheet as XML.

```
<Cell ss:StyleID="s102"><Data ss:Type="String">Previews Page</Data></Cell>
<Cell ss:StyleID="s102"><Data ss:Type="String">Code</Data></Cell>
<Cell ss:StyleID="s102"><Data ss:Type="String">Quantity</Data></Cell>
<Cell ss:StyleID="s102"><Data ss:Type="String">Title</Data></Cell>
<Cell ss:StyleID="s141"><Data ss:Type="String">Retail</Data></Cell>
<Cell ss:StyleID="s139"><Data ss:Type="String">Discount</Data></Cell>
<Cell ss:StyleID="s141"><Data ss:Type="String">Price</Data></Cell>
<Cell ss:StyleID="s102"/>
<Cell ss:StyleID="s102"><Data ss:Type="String">Retail</Data></Cell>
<Cell ss:StyleID="s102"><Data ss:Type="String">Total</Data><NamedCell
   ss:Name="_FilterDatabase"/></Cell>
</Row>
<Row ss:StyleID="Default">
<Cell><Data ss:Type="String">Page 2</Data></Cell>
<Cell ss:Index="3" ss:StyleID="s160"/>
<Cell ss:Index="5" ss:StyleID="s18"/>
<Cell ss:StyleID="s98"/>
<Cell ss:StyleID="s18"/>
<Cell ss:Index="9" ss:StyleID="s193"/>
<Cell ss:StyleID="s193"><NamedCell ss:Name="_FilterDatabase"/></Cell>
</Row>
<Row ss:StyleID="Default">
<Cell ss:StyleID="s100"><Data ss:Type="String">***</Data></Cell>
<Cell ss:StyleID="s100"><Data ss:Type="String">Previews and Accessories</Data></Cell>
<Cell ss:StyleID="s159"/>
<Cell ss:StyleID="s100"/>
<Cell ss:StyleID="s129"/>
<Cell ss:StyleID="s101"/>
<Cell ss:StyleID="s129"/>
<Cell ss:StyleID="s105"/>
<Cell ss:StyleID="s99"/>
<Cell ss:StyleID="s99"><NamedCell ss:Name="_FilterDatabase"/></Cell>
</Row>
<Row ss:StyleID="s152">
<Cell ss:Index="2" ss:StyleID="Default"><Data ss:Type="String">SEP030002</Data></Cell>
<Cell ss:StyleID="s168"><Data ss:Type="Number">1</Data></Cell>
<Cell ss:StyleID="Default"><Data ss:Type="String">PREVIEWS VOL XIII #11 *Special Discount*</Data></Cell>
<Cell ss:StyleID="s153"><Data ss:Type="Number">4.5</Data></Cell>
<Cell ss:StyleID="s154"><Data ss:Type="Number">0.75</Data></Cell>
<Cell ss:StyleID="s153"><Data ss:Type="Number">1.12</Data></Cell>
<Cell ss:Index="9" ss:StyleID="s153" ss:Formula="=RC[-6]*RC[-4]"><Data
   ss:Type="Number">4.5</Data></Cell>
<Cell ss:StyleID="s153" ss:Formula="=RC[-7]*RC[-3]"><Data ss:Type="Number">1.12</Data><NamedCell
   ss:Name="_FilterDatabase"/></Cell>
</Row>
<Row ss:StyleID="s152">
<Cell ss:Index="2" ss:StyleID="Default"><Data ss:Type="String">SEP030003</Data></Cell>
<Cell ss:StyleID="s168"><Data ss:Type="Number">2</Data></Cell>
<Cell ss:StyleID="Default"><Data ss:Type="String">MARVEL PREVIEWS NOV 2003 EXTRAS *Special Discount*</Data></Cell>
<Cell ss:StyleID="s153"><Data ss:Type="Number">0.99</Data></Cell>
<Cell ss:StyleID="s154"><Data ss:Type="Number">0.4</Data></Cell>
```

Figure 11.3 Product Order Spreadsheet as XML

Microsoft is increasing its emphasis on support for XML as a first-class file format for Office. FrontPage 2003 includes new support for building dynamic web sites based on XML, including live views on Word XML, Excel XML, and InfoPath XML documents. FrontPage has also been improved as the preferred customization tool for Windows SharePoint Services and SharePoint Portal Server to provide high-quality page design and manipulation of web part pages.

Office provides quite a different end-user experience from a typical web form. Depending on your requirements, it may be a good fit for your data entry needs. Table 11.2 summarizes the advantages and disadvantages of Office as a form frontend.

The advantages of Office are only conferred on users familiar with Office who have Office installed. The environment is quite rich, and the forms themselves are easily maintained. Printing is a trump card for Office

Table 11.2 Advantages and Disadvantages of Office Forms

Advantages	Disadvantages
Rich environment	Big client footprint
Widely installed	Version issues
Familiar to users	Future upgrades
Works offline	Maintenance of files
Printing	Licensing cost

applications, as they offer tremendous control over the look of printed documents. Offline use is a built-in feature with Office, and the richness of formatting and other helpful features is high.

While Office users are quite a large community, you may run into customers who do not have Office or do not want to use it. This is not a cross-platform solution for all operating systems. The Office client has a large footprint, and distributing updates and patches is a challenge. If you do not already own Microsoft Office, you must consider the licensing cost as part of the solution.

InfoPath

A new third option for data entry forms is InfoPath, a product added to the Office 2003 suite. InfoPath was designed from the ground up as a tool that assists with data entry through forms and that creates XML documents. It takes advantage of Office tools such as the spellchecker and advanced formatting, and it follows the task pane model so prominent in Office 2003 (Figure 11.4). A user navigating through the fields with the keyboard or mouse is presented with online help and editing tools as appropriate. For instance, in the Remarks field, users can choose fonts, colors, the spellchecker, alignment, text number—all the standard word-processing features they might expect.

This form has been designed to emulate the paper version. You can embed images and other objects in the form. This approach makes the form more familiar to long-term users, though it does not necessarily make the best use of screen real estate. As you wean your users from paper, you could design more streamlined versions of forms that would produce the same data.

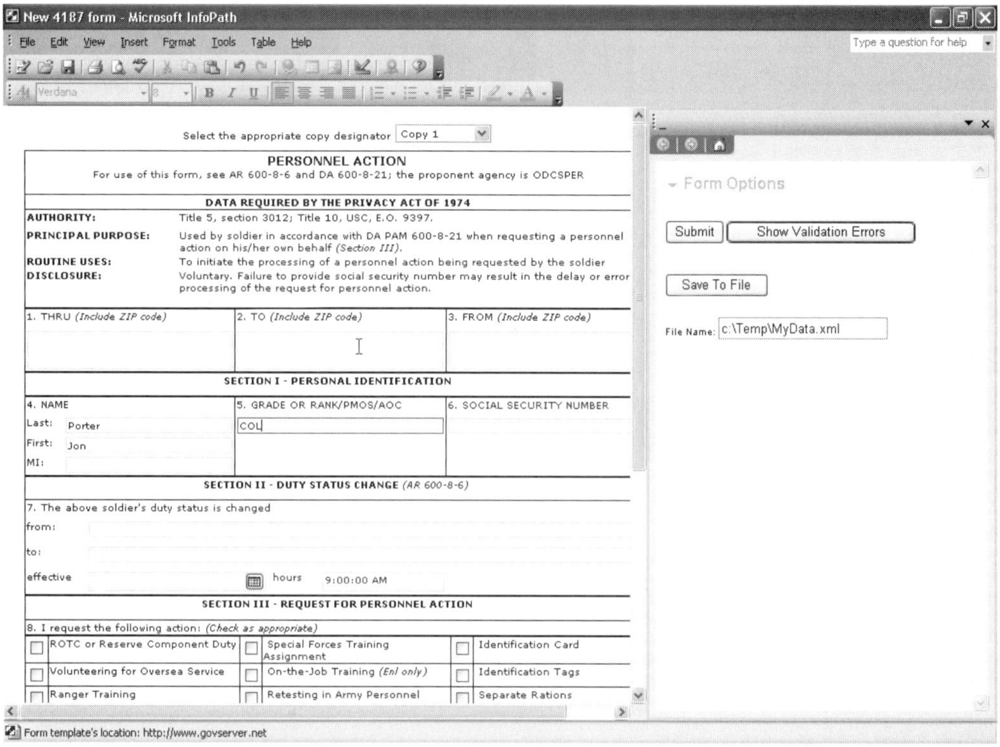

Figure 11.4 InfoPath Personnel Action Form

Validation is powerful and flexible. For example, the task pane in Figure 11.4 lets a user check the validation rules for the form. The user can save the contents of the form to an XML file for transmission or further processing.

Behind this form is the industrial strength of XML. If you were to save the contents of the form to a file and open that file with Notepad, you could plainly see the data model (see Figure 11.5).

InfoPath represents a halfway point between the custom form option and using Office itself for data entry (Table 11.3). Like Office, it is a rich client that can be used offline. It supports sophisticated field validation with features such as repeating areas used to enter a number of responses to a question. As with Office, it requires software licenses to be purchased and installation on each workstation. It is not a cross-platform tool, so your Macintosh and Unix users will need a different approach.

```
<?xml version="1.0" encoding="UTF-8"?><?mso-infoPathSolution solutionversion="1.0.0.26" href="http://www.govserver.net/sites/i
    <my:Thru></my:Thru>
    <my:To></my:To>
    <my:From></my:From>
    <my:DutyFrom>active</my:DutyFrom>
    <my:StatusTo>retired</my:StatusTo>
    <my:StatusChangeDate xmlns:xsi="http://www.w3.org/2001/XMLSchema-instance">2003-09-03</my:StatusChangeDate>
    <my:ChangeHours>09:00:00</my:ChangeHours>
    <my:ServiceSchool>false</my:ServiceSchool>
    <my:ROTC>false</my:ROTC>
    <my:Oversea>true</my:Oversea>
    <my:Ranger>false</my:Ranger>
    <my:FamilyProblems>false</my:FamilyProblems>
    <my:ExchangeReass>true</my:ExchangeReass>
    <my:Airborne>false</my:Airborne>
    <my:SpecialForces>false</my:SpecialForces>
    <my:OnTheJob>false</my:OnTheJob>
    <my:Retesting>false</my:Retesting>
    <my:MarriedCouples>true</my:MarriedCouples>
    <my:Reclassification>true</my:Reclassification>
    <my:officerCandidateSchool>false</my:officerCandidateSchool>
    <my:ExceptionalFamilyMembers>false</my:ExceptionalFamilyMembers>
    <my:IdentificationCard>false</my:IdentificationCard>
    <my:IdentificationTags>true</my:IdentificationTags>
    <my:SeparateRations>false</my:SeparateRations>
    <my:LeaveExcess>false</my:LeaveExcess>
    <my:NameChange>false</my:NameChange>
    <my:Other>false</my:Other>
    <my:OtherDesc></my:OtherDesc>
    <my:TodayDate>2003-09-16</my:TodayDate>
    <my:Remarks>lkjhasd <font face="Lucida Calligraphy" size="7" xmlns="http://www.w3.org/1999/xhtml">kaslkjh </font><fon
    <my:Certification>HAS BEEN VERIFIED</my:Certification>
    <my:Commander>Lt Jones</my:Commander>
    <my:ApprovalDate>2003-09-16</my:ApprovalDate>
    <my:CopyType>Copy 1</my:CopyType>
    <my:LastName>Porter</my:LastName>
    <my:FirstName>Jon</my:FirstName>
    <my:MI></my:MI>
    <my:Grade>COL</my:Grade>
    <my:SSN></my:SSN>
</my:da_4187>
```

Figure 11.5 Personnel Form Data Viewed as XML

Table 11.3 Advantages and Disadvantages of InfoPath Forms

Advantages	Disadvantages
Rich environment	Big client footprint
Optimized for form filling	Printing
Familiar to users	Future upgrades
Works offline	Distribution of files
Printing	Limited to Windows platform
	Not widely installed

You can publish InfoPath forms to shared folders, a web server, or SharePoint Portal Server. You can also send form data directly to a BizTalk server for additional processing, a topic covered later in this chapter. The form can be submitted via HTTP or through a web service. The wizard for publishing forms is extremely simple to use, requiring only the URL of the destination SharePoint site (see Figure 11.6). Forms published to a site cannot be edited there, but they can be overwritten with subsequent versions that are published.

Figure 11.6 An InfoPath Form Library in SharePoint Portal Server

Because InfoPath is a new product, there are few experienced InfoPath developers to be found. You can expect that this situation will change quickly and that Microsoft will make significant changes in the product after version 1.

Now that you have chosen one or more frontends for your portal forms, we turn to the EAI backend processing. We examine some options for building your EAI system. As with forms, we start with custom programming and then turn to the off-the-shelf programs.

SharePoint Portal Server and EAI

While BizTalk is undoubtedly the key to Microsoft's EAI offering, Share-Point Portal Server can be a potent combination with BizTalk or with other integration products. SharePoint is a natural starting point for integration of intranet applications because it is Microsoft's enterprise portal platform. The single sign-on capability is a key feature that makes it simpler for users to get to their applications. Most importantly, SharePoint Portal Server 2003 is based on the web services and .NET architecture that are at the core of integrating applications in the Microsoft paradigm.

SharePoint Portal Server presents the user interface through web parts residing in the portal. The portal consumes web services that are hosted on application servers. The web services, in turn, call on EAI layers that map data extracted from line-of-business applications. Figure 11.7 shows the entire process.

You can integrate web parts directly into the server application without the web services and other translation layers shown in Figure 11.7 in between. This approach is called **web clipping** or **screen scraping**. For instance, a web part could pass a parameter from a page to a query, which would then extract certain data from a manufacturing database. While effective, this practice can break down when the integration is more complex or when asynchronous connections are required.

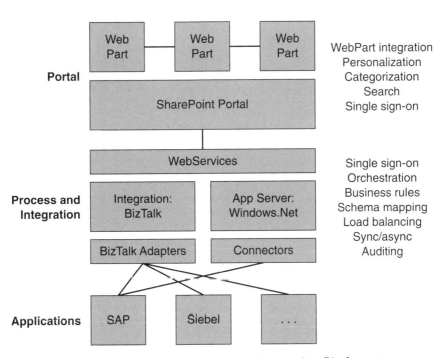

Figure 11.7 SharePoint Portal Server Application Integration Platform (Source: David Holladay, "Connecting Enterprise Applications to SharePoint Portal v2," PowerPoint presentation, March 2003.)

Similarly, SharePoint web parts could be used in a point-to-point integration scenario. Indeed, vendors of line-of-business solutions offer web parts to make it easier to connect to their systems from the portal. Like screen scraping, this approach can break down as complexity increases.

The richest form of EAI with SharePoint is to use it in conjunction with an EAI tool such as BizTalk Server so BizTalk manages the orchestration of transactions and other key EAI tasks. In this scenario, SharePoint is focused on the user interface and serving up content to users and not on the ultimate source of that content.

You can integrate SharePoint Portal Server with applications such as enterprise resource planning (ERP) and customer relationship management (CRM) tools using off-the-shelf connectors (also called adapters) from third-party software vendors. For instance, Actional (www.actional.com) offers PeopleSoft, SAP, and Siebel adaptors.

The Actional adapters connect users to APIs or metadata by exposing APIs as proxy web services. The Actional SOAPswitch software generates WSDL, maintains a service directory, and can publish to UDDI servers. When SOAP-based requests are received, they are translated to the native APIs for execution. The adaptors can be synchronous or asynchronous, and they are enabled for single sign-on (SSO).

Other connectors from Actional and other vendors are likely to follow the adoption of SPS 2003. Microsoft is also planning tighter integration with BizTalk Server in the 2004 version of that product.

SharePoint Portal Server 2003 ships with a sample application that demonstrates the EAI functionality you can have nearly out of the box. The sample shows how a human resources department can generate an electronic pay stub for its employees as part of a self-service intranet portal. Similarly, a corporate manager might want to create a dashboard of key reports and graphs that she could study on a daily basis. SharePoint can be the vehicle for this dashboard, with the data coming from an ERP system.

Integration with Custom Code

Now that we have XML documents as input, we need to create interfaces to our applications to automate the processing of transactions. We have three options here. The first is to write custom code and program the interface ourselves from scratch. Second is to create an infrastructure for supporting transactions and multiple interfaces using BizTalk Server. Third is to choose another off-the-shelf EAI product, which is an option I do not explore in this book.

If you choose a custom code approach, you can either focus on building a single point-to-point interface or on creating a more general-purpose infrastructure for integration. In essence, you would be building a lightweight version of what BizTalk offers, although probably without as sophisticated a user interface and administrative utilities.

Let's take a look at custom .NET interfaces. The interface must handle orchestration of transactions by preventing the same transaction from being entered multiple times and guaranteeing that no transactions are dropped.

You might guess that building an interface with custom programming would be more difficult and time consuming than using BizTalk. You would certainly be right if you were talking about creating lots of interfaces. For instance, a reseller dealing with many suppliers would easily recoup an investment in the BizTalk infrastructure. For a small number of interfaces, however, the case is more difficult to judge. Setting up BizTalk is not a small task or expense, and much of the analytical heavy lifting in terms of data modeling and business process automation is the same, regardless of the software tools involved. For all these reasons, you may find yourself building a custom interface. While you could use other languages and tools (such as C++ and COM+), we focus on .NET and its toolbox of languages to build the solution.

Figure 11.8 shows a typical legacy integration solution. This example is of a system that accepts data from a mainframe using flat files that are periodically generated by the mainframe. The task of creating the files is simple for a mainframe programmer, and they are placed in an FTP directory to be picked up. This task is scheduled (for example, data is written to the files every five minutes throughout the business day).

Microsoft Host Integration Server is another approach for integrating mainframe data. It provides the middleware to make a hierarchical or flat file mainframe data source appear as a relational data source to a consuming application.

The next step is to obtain the new files when they come in. While this step could be accomplished through polling, with a continuously running application periodically checking the FTP directory, a better approach would be to use the file change notification API, which triggers an event when a new file is written to a folder.

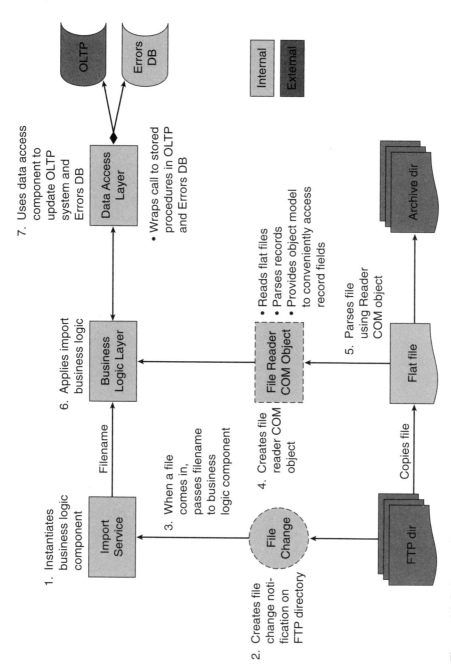

Figure 11.8 Legacy Integration Scenario

After the file change is detected, the file name is passed to the business logic component that will perform the import, and the file is copied to a directory on the receiving server. Next, the hard work of the import is performed: the file is read, the fields from the source are mapped to the destination, and the records are parsed. Because these flat files are fixed length, the field definitions are stored in the application and can be updated easily if the source file format changes. When files are successfully imported, they are transferred to the archive directory.

Imported files are entered into the online transaction processing (OLTP) database through application of the business logic rules. Here is another area in which the system differs from an interactive application. When data entry errors arise in an interactive system, the user is presented with an error message and given the opportunity to correct the error and attempt the data entry again. The system simply does not accept user data that is known to be invalid. Here there are no human users with whom to interact, and therefore errors must be handled differently. Erroneous records are written to an errors database for further processing, such as returning a batch of records to the originator.

The data access layer contains objects that enwrap calls to the relational database. It provides a higher level of abstraction for these data calls. This layer is responsible for adding, deleting, and updating records.

Building an interface to a legacy system is fundamentally just another instance of the n-tier application architecture. That is, the architecture consists of several components that can logically be divided into the data, business logic, and presentation layers. The bottom two layers, business logic and database, are also found in an interactive form-based application. Indeed, they are not aware of whether the data is coming from a web-form, an XML document, or a flat file generated by a mainframe. The difference lies in the user interface layer. For application integration, the user forms are replaced by objects that create records from files rather than from one page, field, or keystroke at a time.

BizTalk Concepts

BizTalk is Microsoft's entry into the EAI market. As with Microsoft's general approach to computing, BizTalk is designed to dramatically decrease the cost and time required to field EAI solutions and to automate processes that were formerly painstakingly performed by hand. This goal is accomplished by abstracting the process and developing software components that handle each step in an automated transaction.

BizTalk provides an integration platform that shields developers from the harsh world of communications protocols, data formats, and API details. It is based on the open standards of the Internet including HTTP, XML, SOAP, XSLT, and MIME. BizTalk supports both a loosely coupled asynchronous communications environment and a high-performance, optimized synchronous interface model. Asynchronous communications are preferred when poor network connectivity and a low number of transactions are present, while a synchronous approach often makes sense inside a corporate network with a predictably high volume of transactions. For instance, integrating dozens or hundreds of suppliers might call for the asynchronous approach, while connecting the factory to the shipping dock might lend itself better to synchronous communications.

BizTalk accepts messages with documents, and then processes them and sends them to the appropriate place (Figure 11.9). First, the incoming document is copied into BizTalk and then parsed and converted to XML (if it is not already an XML document). The source specification is a schema for the data model of the incoming document. It is created by the developer using the BizTalk Editor.

Next, the incoming document is mapped to the data schema, using the Extensible Stylesheet Language Transformation (XSLT) map. This mapping is created with the BizTalk Mapper. From this schema, the serializer converts data to the destination document format. Once again, the BizTalk Editor is the tool for creating the destination specification. BizTalk parsers and serializers can translate XML, EDI (X12 and EDIFACT), and flat files (delimited and fixed length).

While this transformation is at the heart of BizTalk, it has other components that manage the messaging traffic, orchestrate the transactions, and handle all other required functions. The BizTalk paradigm encompasses the following key elements: adapters, channels, and messaging ports.

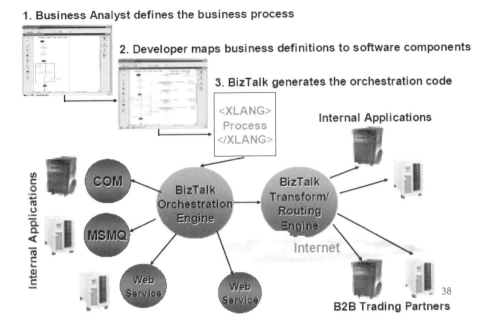

1. Business Analyst defines the business process

2. Developer maps business definitions to software components

3. BizTalk generates the orchestration code

Figure 11.9 BizTalk Document Processing (Source: Microsoft, "Using EDI with BizTalk Server 2002," February 2002.)

Adapters

BizTalk adapters are software components that link an application to BizTalk. The adapter provides two-way communication with BizTalk. It also defines the metadata and communicates changes to the metadata to BizTalk Server. The adapter is used for setup and maintenance of the interface between an application and BizTalk. As of this writing, there were more than 300 adapters available from Microsoft and third parties at www.microsoft.com/biztalk/evaluation/adapters/adapters.asp. If your company uses SAP for its manufacturing operations and PeopleSoft for human resources, for instance, you could use these adapters to make the systems talk to one another. Third-party vendors often certify the BizTalk adapters so you can be confident that they will be effective with your software installation.

Channels

Channels are dedicated to the processing of a particular type of incoming document. A channel is like an assembly line that is tailored to produce a certain product (Figure 11.10). The transaction is recorded in the log. The channel transforms the data, mapping the source to the destination using the XML schema. If the document is encrypted or digitally signed, the channel handles these functions.

Channels allow complex business processes to be broken down into manageable pieces that can be developed and maintained independently. A channel consists of functions and objects.

Messaging Ports

In all BizTalk implementations, messages are used as the means to move data from one system to another. These messages must be fast and reliable. A message contains the elements listed in Table 11.4.

Messaging ports are invoked by channels according to the business process described in the XLANG schedule. They can receive messages through multiple protocols, but most commonly HTTP is the protocol of choice (Figure 11.11).

Table 11.4 Elements of a BizTalk Message (Source: Adapted from Microsoft, "Adapter Developers' Guide White Paper," at www.microsoft.com/downloads/details.aspx?FamilyId=0F74B087-675E-4C8B-9921-49C986E345DC&displaylang=en.)

Element	Definition
Source Definition	The application that sends a message.
Destination Definition	The application that receives a message. The same application can be both the source and the destination.
Messaging Endpoint	Logical destination for message delivery. A source application sends messages to an endpoint and a target application consumes messages from an endpoint.
Messaging Services	The abstraction layer that supports the source application and endpoints.
Payload	The body of the message contains content or data to be sent to the endpoint of the message.
Acknowledgment	Acknowledgment of a message being received, stored, and/or processed that is sent to the sender by the receiver of the original message.

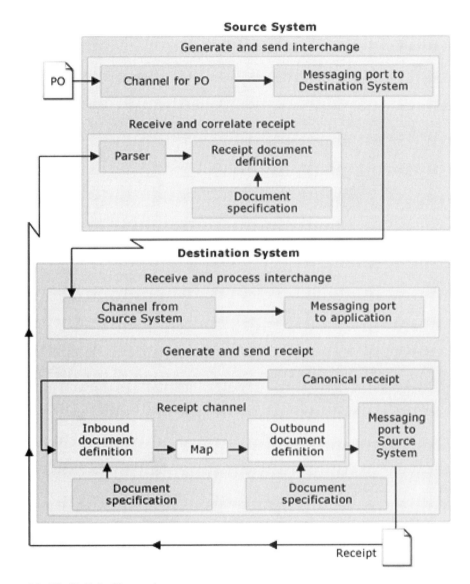

Figure 11.10 BizTalk Channels (Note: Directional arrows denote flow of data.)

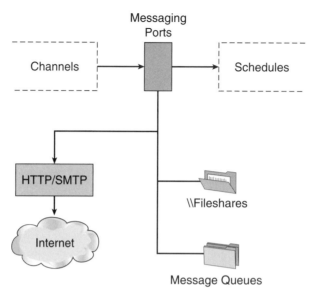

Figure 11.11 BizTalk Messaging Ports

BizTalk adapters automatically build messages for you. BizTalk Server monitors the messages as they move from one system to another. You can monitor the status of each message and visualize how your integration is working.

BizTalk Workflow

The functionality of BizTalk can be divided into five logical stages: receive functions, channels, messaging ports, scheduling, and administration. Receive functions accept incoming documents. Channels log the documents, manipulate them, and handle encryption and digital signature tasks. Messaging ports are used to communicate via messages and documents with trading partners. Scheduling is the transaction orchestration process. Administrative tools can be used to monitor and change the settings of BizTalk components. Each of these functions has a corresponding BizTalk tool.

A completed BizTalk solution therefore consists of many objects you have defined, connected by the workflow process (Figure 11.12).

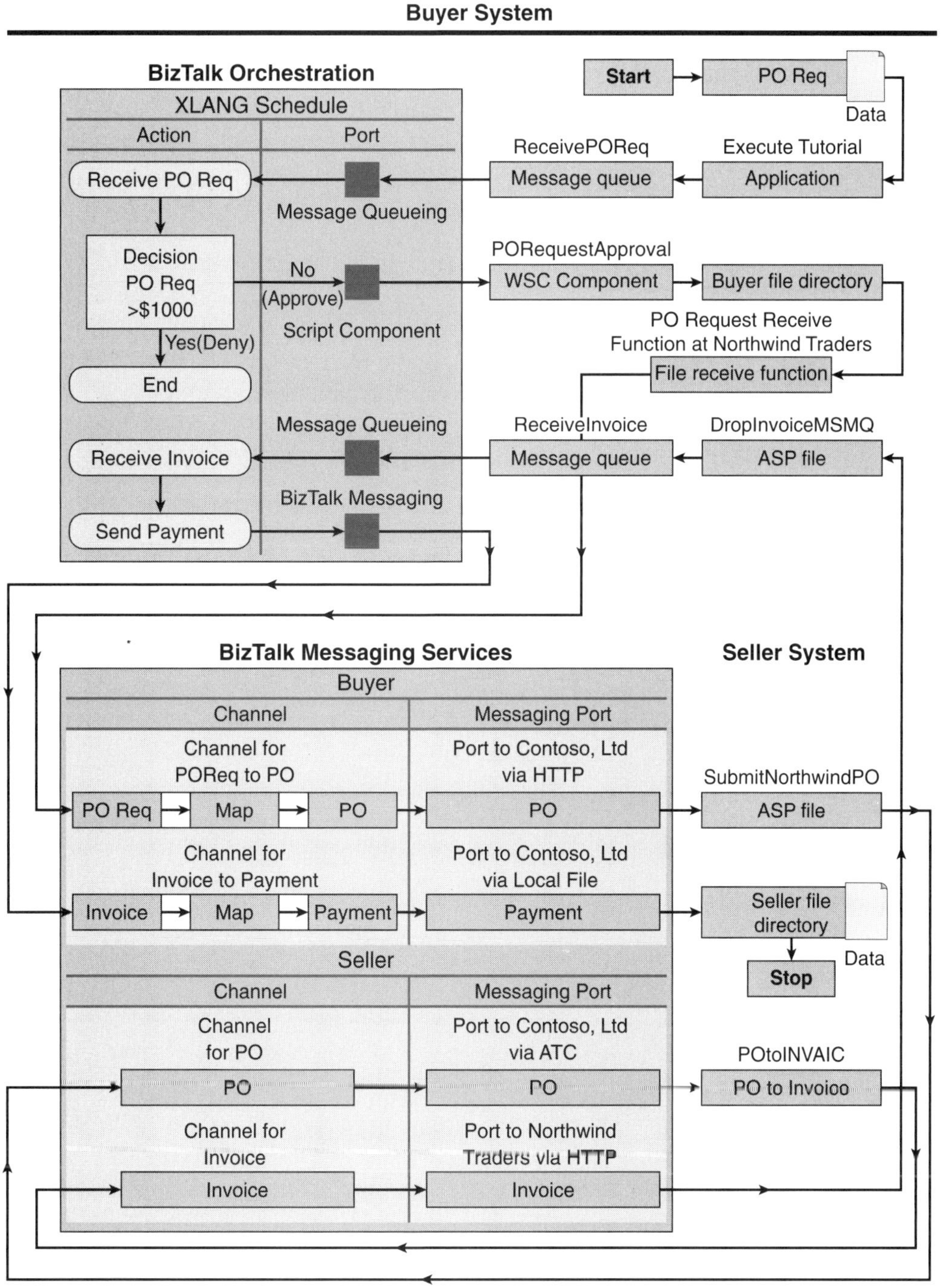

Buyer System

BizTalk Orchestration

| Start | → | PO Req | Data |

XLANG Schedule

| Action | Port |

| Receive PO Req | | ← | ReceivePOReq Message queue | ← | Execute Tutorial Application | ← |

Message Queueing

| Decision PO Req >$1000 | No (Approve) | → | PORequestApproval WSC Component | → | Buyer file directory |

Yes(Deny) — Script Component

PO Request Receive Function at Northwind Traders

| File receive function | ← |

| End |

Message Queueing

| Receive Invoice | | ← | ReceiveInvoice Message queue | ← | DropInvoiceMSMQ ASP file | ← |

BizTalk Messaging

| Send Payment | | → |

BizTalk Messaging Services   **Seller System**

Buyer

| Channel | Messaging Port |

Channel for POReq to PO | Port to Contoso, Ltd via HTTP

SubmitNorthwindPO

| PO Req | → | Map | → | PO | | PO | | ASP file |

Channel for Invoice to Payment | Port to Contoso, Ltd via Local File

| Invoice | → | Map | → | Payment | | Payment | | Seller file directory | Data |

Stop

Seller

| Channel | Messaging Port |

Channel for PO | Port to Contoso, Ltd via ATC

POtoINVAIC

| PO | | PO | | PO to Invoice |

Channel for Invoice | Port to Northwind Traders via HTTP

| Invoice | | Invoice |

Figure 11.12 BizTalk Workflow (Note: Directional arrows denote flow of data.)

Channels are used to logically define the processes and track the business rules that pertain to a particular group of documents. This architecture allows a number of developers to simultaneously tackle different business processes or different parts of the same process. The team may also specialize in different phases in the process. A developer, for example, may be assigned to the messaging ports for each channel.

BizTalk Editor

The BizTalk Editor (Figure 11.13) is the tool for creating source and destination document definitions. It is a graphical tool for building XML schemas. The BizTalk Editor can handle file types such as ASCII delimited or fixed-length data files, XML, and EDI, and it can also import and export XSD files.

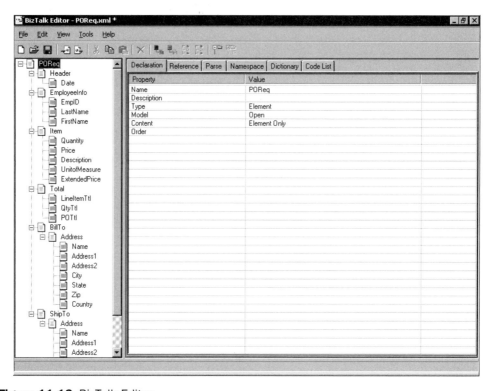

Figure 11.13 BizTalk Editor

The left pane of the BizTalk Editor displays the hierarchical structure of the document, and the right pane shows the properties for the selected node in the data hierarchy. The BizTalk Editor is a productive interface for defining XML schemas. You can also import XML, Excel, and other file formats to provide a rapid starting point for the new schema.

BizTalk Mapper

The BizTalk Mapper (Figure 11.14) creates the links between two XML schemas and saves them as an XSLT map. You can drag and drop to establish the connections between data elements in schemas, and you can perform functions to transform data during this process. This visual programming is much faster and easier to understand than line-by-line transformations in code.

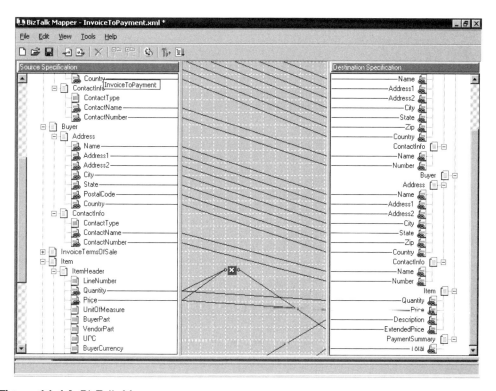

Figure 11.14 BizTalk Mapper

If the mapping of one source field to a destination field is one-to-one with no conversion required, these visual links suffice to map the data. In cases in which transformation is needed, BizTalk uses a **functoid**, which is a built-in data conversion function. These can perform parsing, concatenation, field type conversion, and other functions.

BizTalk Orchestration Designer

The BizTalk Orchestration Designer (Figure 11.15) is a graphic tool based on Visio that depicts business processes for developers and business analysts. BizTalk Orchestration allows design and execution of long-running transactions as well as creation of an executable XML representation of the transaction using a language known as XLANG. Typically a business analyst

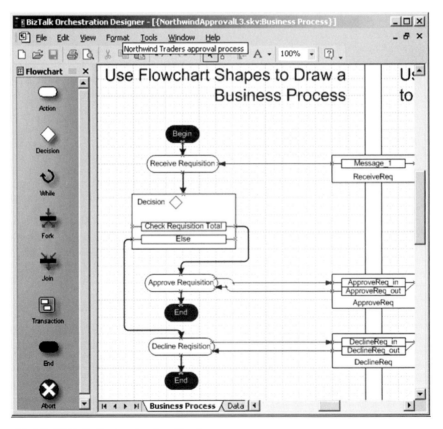

Figure 11.15 BizTalk Orchestration Designer

begins by creating a workflow process, consisting of steps such as the triggering of a product reorder from a supplier, the purchase order generation, and other steps.

BizTalk Orchestration Designer is a visual design environment that specifies the individual actions involved in a transaction. Actions are grouped into collections to provide a single unit of work that is either committed or rolled back as a whole. This approach is essential for long-running transactions, which consist of many actions spanning one or more services. BizTalk provides exception processing to handle transactions in the event of a processing error. Procedures can be developed for error processing using events such as On Failure.

Long-running transactions create a new challenge for the database. In a short-running transaction, affected rows are isolated while the transaction is running so no other user or process can update them at the same time and corrupt the data. While the transaction is running, it is not yet known whether the transaction will be committed or aborted so other programs cannot count on the integrity of the data. A second program seeking the same data must await the result of the transaction. For long-running transactions, this approach is a nonstarter. It would be impractical to isolate data for an indefinite period of time, and locks cannot be performed across databases in different organizations. Imagine a supplier dealing with lock requests on a product table from hundreds or thousands of customers at a time.

The solution to this riddle is to create a number of short-running transactions and embed them in a single long-running transaction. The short-running transactions are committed one at a time as the long-running transaction proceeds, so the data becomes available to other applications. If one of the transactions fails, however, the long-running transaction is aborted. This triggers rollbacks of all the short-running transactions that comprise the long-running transaction.

Server Administration

BizTalk provides a management console (Figure 11.16) to view the queues and monitor the number of message at each stage of the process. You can watch the messages flow through the system through this administrative user interface.

The event viewer is quite handy for debugging your BizTalk solution. It allows you to trace the events such as security activities and errors raised by the application.

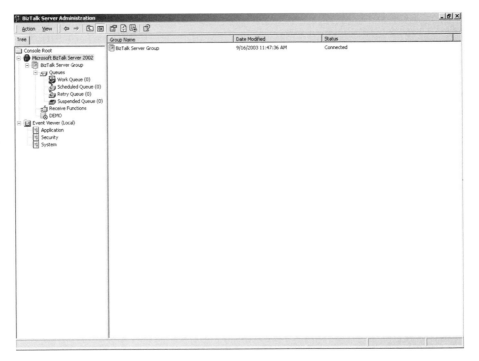

Figure 11.16 BizTalk Server Administration Console

Document Tracking

BizTalk relies on SQL Server as its database. The BizTalk repository stores all messaging and related BizTalk Orchestration metadata, as well as incoming and outgoing document instances. BizTalk provides a user interface for tracking its message and schedule activity and an API for programmatic access to tracking information. You can access the database directly and perform queries and data mining of BizTalk documents and metadata as well.

Accelerators and Third-Party Tools

The BizTalk foundation has led to the development of products for specific industries and third-party software to strengthen elements of the platform. For instance, Microsoft has developed accelerators for the healthcare industry (HIPAA) in the United States, electronics manufacturers (Rosettanet) and financial services (UCCnet, SWIFT financial messaging), and for suppliers. More information on the accelerators is at www.microsoft.com/biztalk/evaluation/accelerators/default.asp.

Several companies have developed add-on products that automate the workflow of transactions along with BizTalk. One of the most notable is Teamplate from Captaris. TeamPlate is built entirely on the .NET platform and offers a library of components and web services to simplify the building of workflow solutions. It integrates with the full range of Microsoft products, including not only BizTalk but also SharePoint, Office, InfoPath, Exchange, Visio, Content Management Server, and even Great Plains accounting software. For more information, see www.teamplate.com/internal/product/integration.asp.

Benefits of Business Integration

Aside from general computing infrastructure, one of the largest IT investments in nearly every organization is line-of-business (LOB) applications. These applications are at the heart of an organization's operations, embodying their unique way of doing business. They would be expensive and painful to rewrite, and such an endeavor would be disruptive to normal operations. Therefore such systems often outlast their underlying technology. They endure, often long after their authors have departed the company. Indeed, you know when you truly have a legacy system when there is no longer anyone around to support it. The core value of EAI is to add extra life to LOB systems, allowing them to work together more closely and enabling them for the Internet age.

EAI can reduce the time to market for new products and services. In a typical stovepipe enterprise, each application and business process stands alone. Integration is accomplished through manual, human intervention. Reports are generated from separate systems and passed to analysts, who reconcile the statistics they generate. Through EAI, new patterns are visible sooner, and the steps in creating new product and service offerings can be shortened.

Another benefit of EAI is easy to measure: the cost per transaction. Pennies quickly add up to millions of dollars when you are considering them in terms of cost per transaction. Nearly all ordering activity is expensive, whether it is customers purchasing your product or your employees buying travel, office supplies, or marketing support. Many businesses are following the lead of Microsoft in providing intranet e-commerce applications that dramatically streamline these processes. For instance, new employees can enter their orders for business cards, and these orders are automatically routed for approval and then placed with the supplier electronically. When you put all these benefits together, you derive increased business agility through faster communication with business partners and better linkages among internal systems.

Conclusion

Enterprise application integration is on the verge of significant growth as organizations move to standards such as XML and web services. EAI should be an integral part of your portal strategy, whether you are ready to integrate now or planning for the long term. Walls between proprietary applications are coming down, and enterprise architectures are shifting to a web-friendly model. Therefore, tools are making EAI far less painful and expensive than ever before. It remains a challenging endeavor and will require professional programmers and analysts for the foreseeable future, but the productivity of these individuals will continue to rise.

Your portal can be the starting point for EAI by providing a modern application architecture based on standards such as XML. It can go further than merely integrating the user interfaces of applications by integrating processes and bringing customers and suppliers to a common place where transactions may be conducted. The portal provides the opportunity to start from a new paradigm and technology base rather than merely paving the cowpaths of legacy line-of-business applications.

Chapter 12

Collaboration in the Enterprise Portal

In this chapter we turn our attention inward, to the corporate intranet or extranet. The portal is a natural place to provide collaborative tools for users. By including collaboration in our portal, we encourage users to adopt the technologies we have invested so much to purchase and deploy, and to realize the potential productivity gains that too often are untapped.

Collaboration and the related field of knowledge management are key enablers to allow organizations to achieve strategic advantage through information technology. Microsoft is making much of this fact in its marketing campaign around "the agile enterprise." The idea is that large enterprises have long since automated individual processes. Indeed, the fact that these processes are automated, along with the tremendous investment in current systems, may actually hinder an organization's ability to react to changes in its environment.

For an organization to be agile, it must respond to changes in its surroundings. These could be market forces, the regulatory environment, technological change, and new management, for instance. Collaboration can streamline the decision-making process and provide a communication channel for news to travel inside an organization. Most collaboration takes little advantage of technology, except perhaps the telephone.

Agility depends on management at least as much as, if not more than, it depends on technology. Organizations that will not or cannot use the knowledge gained through collaboration may be better off not opening Pandora's box. On the other hand, if you are planning to break down the barriers between your employees' application "islands" or "silos" and to increase the flow of information up and down the organizational hierarchy, this chapter may just be the most useful one in the book for you.

If the term "portal" is plagued by ambiguity and misuse, "collaboration" is not much better. There is no bright line dividing collaboration from other software tools. For the purposes of this chapter, we include the following collaboration features in the portal:

- *Collaborative authoring tools.* These include document management features such as version control, check in and check out, and routing and approval.
- *Automated workflow.* May relate to documents or to routing processes associated with electronic forms.
- *Threaded discussion.* Provides asynchronous messaging for a virtual community. May be related to a document or a standalone discussion.
- *Real-time collaboration (audio, video, application sharing).* There is a large return on investment possible here, as direct cost savings from travel expenses and downtime are readily measured.
- *Presence awareness.* Show users who is signed onto the portal and provide a means to reach them.
- *Instant messaging.* Complementary capability with presence awareness and real-time collaboration.
- *Project management.* Web-based access to project plans, project management data entry, and other related features.
- *Analysis tools.* Once you open the corporate data coffers, you need web-based tools to mine for useful data and smelt it into information or even knowledge.

This chapter shows how all these collaboration features can be implemented in the context of the portal. My examples take advantage of several Microsoft products, including SharePoint Portal Server, Windows SharePoint Services, Office, InfoPath, Live Meeting, Windows Messenger, Outlook XP, SQL Server, Exchange Server, and Project 2002. In some cases you are given the opportunity to choose among two or more tools that provide similar functionality.

Collaboration Checklist

An excellent place to start is to identify your options in providing collaboration functions and prioritize so you can start with the ones that will produce the greatest impact. Table 12.1 is a checklist of possible collaboration initiatives for your portal.

From this universe of choices, establish your priorities. Next, determine which ones come together as a package. For instance, SharePoint Portal Server offers team sites that provide document management,

Table 12.1 Collaboration Features Checklist

Feature	Description
Discussion groups	Asynchronous forum for posting messages. Users can subscribe to receive email notifications of new postings.
Document management	Shared and private document libraries that allow version control for documents of any kind.
Project web sites	Site that contains areas such as discussion groups, document libraries, shared links, shared calendar, and contacts.
Microsoft Project	Tool for advanced project management. Web-based with interface for data entry and reporting.
Chat	Online chat similar to Windows Messenger.
Presence detection	User interface that indicates people currently logged onto portal. Useful in conjunction with chat.
Audio and video conferencing	Real-time collaboration feature.
Whiteboard and application sharing	Window that shares viewing and control of software applications. Whiteboard allows notes and drawings to be shared online.
Team calendar	Group calendar maintained through web interface. SharePoint calendar is independent of Outlook and Exchange calendars.

discussion groups, shared calendar, shared contacts, and other features that may be enabled with a handful of keystrokes and mouse clicks. Figure 12.1 shows all the products that comprise the Microsoft collaboration platform.

Many organizations build enterprise portals that contain the following:

- Home page
- MyPage personalized for each user
- Search link on home page, and advanced search page
- Organizational listing (About Us section)
- Department subsites for collaboration
- Links to web-based internal applications or web parts that host these applications
- One or more shared calendars

This is a good place to start, and the rapid progress you will make with out-of-the-box products is bound to be impressive to users and management.

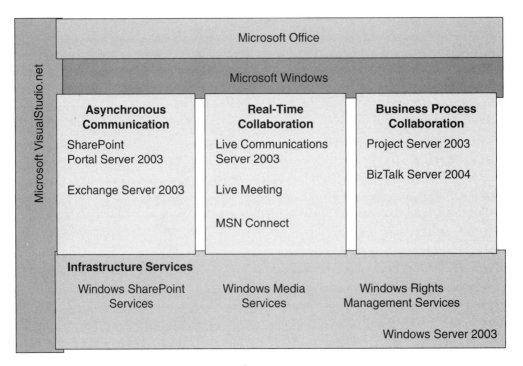

Figure 12.1 Microsoft Collaboration Platform (Source: Marc Sanders, "Enabling Enterprise Business Productivity—An Overview of Microsoft Office Live Communications Server 2003.")

The Human Side of Collaboration

The best-laid plans of knowledge management often beach themselves on the shoals of human behavior. In general, it is safe to assume that users fear change and will resist it whenever possible. I have seen many technically excellent knowledge management and collaboration systems designed, built, and deployed, only to sit idle while users continued with more familiar behaviors to get their jobs done.

You can make your portal much more successful by bringing users into the process early and often. Take serious heed of the pain felt by users, and understand their priorities. For instance, if traveling to remote locations is wearing people down, you may want to focus on real-time collaboration tools. One of the best technology solutions in this area is the ability to conduct software demos and training remotely through a combination of voice and application sharing. Video can be a nice touch, but they add surprisingly little to the content of many meetings.

If users are most frustrated with their inability to find the right versions of documents or collaborate on documents, you may want to put team web sites with document management at the top of your list. What incentive would encourage users to move documents from their laptop hard drives to a shared resource? Would simple document management features such as check-in and check-out paralyze any users?

Users adopt technology at different rates. Just as some people prefer online chat to telephone calls and others despise email, so it is with collaboration. Your user community spans a spectrum from early adopters to true Luddites who fight every innovation. Find ways to embrace your user community and bring people together who would otherwise not share with one another.

Technical barriers do not need to be high to effectively discourage users. Such issues as firewalls and VPNs or even browser security settings may be enough to stymie your users. Make sure that your test plan accounts for variations of infrastructure that could introduce these problems. What happens when a user is on the road? Can he access the portal from a public Internet terminal? Can he get to information he needs from a customer's machine? Does the portal require any software to be downloaded and installed on the desktop?

Whatever your priorities may be, follow the old adage of underpromising and overdelivering. Be conservative about your schedule estimates for rolling out new features and introduce nothing without the training that must go along with it. You would be far better off to have 100% adoption of a system that only has 40% of its full planned functionality than to have 40% adoption of a system with all of its functionality implemented.

The largest part of the collaboration functionality in the Microsoft portal platform is provided by SharePoint Portal Server, Windows SharePoint Services, and Office. These capabilities are the core of an enterprise portal. You can supplement them with additional advanced features, but you are likely to roll out this collaboration core first, as explained in the following section.

SharePoint Version 2 Paradigm

The core of the Microsoft collaboration suite is the SharePoint family, consisting of SharePoint Portal Server and Windows SharePoint Services. These products let you create dynamic workgroup sites and encourage such collaboration as document sharing, discussions, shared calendars, news events, and others.

SharePoint changed dramatically between versions 1 and 2, growing in capability, scalability, and programmability. In version 1, SharePoint Portal Server relied on ActiveX as the underlying technology for its web parts and used the web store as its repository. SharePoint Team Services and SharePoint Portal Server offered distinct technology and development models. As with version 1, SharePoint offers a host of collaboration features. With version 2, however, SharePoint is no longer the stepchild of the Microsoft server family but rather has entered the mainstream of .NET servers.

The other member of the SharePoint product family has changed its name. SharePoint Team Services has been replaced by Windows SharePoint Services. SharePoint Team Services was wildly popular within Microsoft. Microsoft ended up with around 80,000 Team Services sites, meaning an average of 1.6 sites for each of Microsoft's 50,000 employees. It allowed users to create ad hoc web sites with canned functionality for the myriad collaborative efforts under way at the company. In addition to its inherent features and benefits, SharePoint Team Services created consistency among project web sites. Users became familiar with how the sites functioned and where they should go to share documents, post calendars, and other functions.

The technology for both SharePoint products has now been merged, making Windows SharePoint Services the foundation for SharePoint Portal Server, which is now essentially a premium version of Windows SharePoint Services, including the advanced search engine and some other features lacking in Windows SharePoint Services. Windows SharePoint Services is a free component of Windows Server 2003. It is a free download and will be packaged with the server product in future releases.

Under the rubric of SharePoint Products and Technologies, SharePoint Portal Server and Windows SharePoint Services share a paradigm that needs an introduction. Microsoft has taken the web part concept from SharePoint Portal Server and migrated it to the .NET platform. At the same time, the quick and simple site generation of SharePoint Team Services has been extended and enriched. Figure 12.2 provides an architectural overview of the SharePoint platform.

New products need new jargon, and SharePoint is no exception. There are several key terms with special meanings in the context of SharePoint. Some of the terminology is different from that used in SharePoint version 1 and from that used by other Microsoft products.

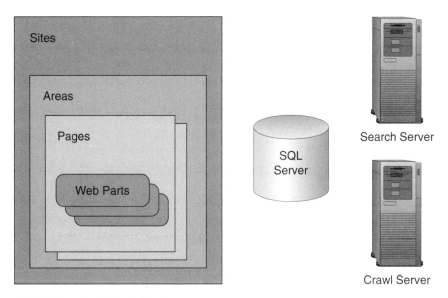

Figure 12.2 SharePoint Architecture

As you might expect, the main portal is called a **site**. SharePoint Portal Server lets you create subsites in a hierarchy that exists within the main site. For instance, you might create a site for each department in your company. A site consists of one or more **pages**. Pages can be content pages, web part pages, or other types of pages such as discussion groups and document libraries.

SharePoint uses the concept of **areas**, which are used to group content. A page can be associated with one or more areas, and an area in turn can relate to many web pages. Similarly documents can relate to multiple areas. Sites can also be associated with one or more areas. The term "area" replaces what was called a "category" in SharePoint Portal Server version 1. Areas are used as a feature for navigation and also for finding documents with the search engine. Documents related to an area are found even if the word used to describe the area is not in the document itself. Administrators and content managers maintain portal areas. They review content submissions, add and remove areas, and map areas to **audiences**, which are groups of users with interests in similar content.

SharePoint contains a number of off-the-shelf pages that are automatically generated when you create a new site. The pages that are included in a site are specified in a **template**. For instance, a meeting site would contain pages such as a list of attendees, a document library, and a discussion board. You can create your own custom templates as well as use the standard templates provided by Microsoft. Finally, pages can consist of one or more **web parts**. SharePoint offers a special type of page called a **web part page** that consolidates views into multiple data sources using web parts. The portal home page and MyPage are examples of web part pages. These are rectangular areas on a page that provide a user interface to an application or content. For instance, the News web part displays headlines and dates of news items. A couple of dozen web parts come with SharePoint, and many more can be downloaded from Microsoft. You can create your own web parts as needed.

SharePoint typically uses SQL Server or its variant MSDE as the repository for content, metadata, and site settings. This means that SharePoint is quite scalable to support large numbers of users and high transaction volume.

Windows SharePoint Services and SharePoint Portal Server

You can adopt SharePoint technology through two products, Windows SharePoint Services (WSS) and SharePoint Portal Server (SPS). The two are quite closely aligned and, unlike in their previous versions, based on the same technology foundation. The difference is that SharePoint Portal Server contains some features that are not part of Windows SharePoint Services.

Windows SharePoint Services includes:

- *Integration with Microsoft Office.* Integration is tightest with Office 2003 but earlier versions are supported to a lesser degree. For example, you can create a SharePoint document workspace from within Word 2003.
- *Web parts.* Both SPS and WSS are based on the web part architecture using building blocks developed for .NET. You can use Front-Page to edit SharePoint pages.
- *Document management.* WSS provides document libraries with features including check-in, check-out, version control, and collaborative authoring.
- *Presence awareness.* Users can see who is online from the team and contact them via email or instant messaging.
- *Alerts.* Users can subscribe to content and receive email notification of new postings and updates.
- *Threaded discussions.* Users can create discussion groups for asynchronous text discussions.
- *Inline discussions.* You can create discussions that are stored along with the documents in a document library.

SharePoint Portal Server provides features that build on the basis of WSS but take it much further. Microsoft offers a white paper on its web site to help users choose between WSS and SPS entitled "Deciding When to Deploy Microsoft Windows SharePoint Services and Microsoft Office

SharePoint Portal Server 2003," at www.microsoft.com/sharepoint/evaluationoverview.asp.

The following features are among those found in SPS but not in WSS:

- *SharePoint search engine.* Microsoft's most powerful search engine is found here, as described in Chapter 13.
- *News and topics areas for posting content.* These include several web parts for viewing summaries and complete items.
- *My Site personalization.* Users can customize their view of the portal, with public and private views of these pages.
- *Information targeting.* The audiences feature allows information to be mapped to groups of users.
- *Single sign-on for enterprise application integration.* This feature streamlines access to multiple applications.
- *Advanced alerts.* In addition to alerts on the document library, SPS contains alerts for people, news, lists, site directory, areas, and other portal elements.
- *Integration with BizTalk Server.* SPS offers third-party integration of leading CRM and ERP packages via BizTalk Server.
- *More advanced management features.* SPS includes more powerful administrative tools than WSS for creating and maintaining sites.

SharePoint Portal Server contains all the functionality of Windows SharePoint Services. Therefore, it is the focus of much of this chapter. If you do not need the features of SPS, you may want to consider the more limited power of WSS.

Creating a Basic Collaboration Site

One of the most common collaboration needs is a team web site, where members can post documents as they are developed, background information, contact information, and group calendars. At my company we use such web sites to develop responses to complex and lengthy requests for proposal.

These team web sites are simple virtual communities. Many are built like temporary shacks, with no intention to remain in operation for a long time. They allow disparate organizations, such as companies teaming on a contract bid, to bridge their incompatible messaging infrastructure, knowledge management programs, and databases. By being hosted in the demilitarized zone (DMZ) or at a third-party site, they allow users to work together who would not grant one another trust relationships within their individual domains (see Figure 12.3).

The most basic features of a team web site are:

- *Document library.* A place to post documents for download.
- *Threaded discussion.* Either standalone or relating to a particular document, the threaded discussion allows asynchronous collaboration.
- *List of members.* Profiles of members of the team, including contact information.

Figure 12.3 Sample Team Web site

- *Group calendar.* Facility to post team events and display and print the group calendar. This does not have to be connected to individual calendars in Outlook, for instance, but it is nice to display it in a conventional calendar format.
- *Ad hoc page creation.* A facility for creating new web pages as desired by the users.
- *Frequently asked questions.*

The project management functionality provided by SharePoint Portal Server is simple to use and rather basic. It provides a place for a project team to store files and share information such as schedules, contacts, and working files. It does not attempt to store structured information pertaining to a project. It would be impossible, for instance, to write a query against a SharePoint project site to determine whether a project is on budget or on schedule.

For a more structured approach to project management, you may want to consider Microsoft Project Server, the latest incarnation of Microsoft Project. This is an industrial-strength project management system that supports more structured data along with the detailed reporting that goes along with it.

Creating a Discussion Board

One of the most basic collaboration functions is the discussion board. SharePoint provides this capability with no programming required. Some site templates include discussion boards, or you can create a discussion board within a site you have already created, as shown in Figure 12.4.

Users create new discussions (Figure 12.5) by clicking the New discussion link on the Discussion Board page. They respond to discussions by clicking the dropdown menu on the discussion topic. The text editor provided allows rich text, including fonts, colors, and other formatting. You can embed linked documents to a discussion entry as attachments.

To keep tabs on your discussion board, you can sign up for an alert. When you create the alert, you are prompted to choose the interval in which to receive alerts, whether instantly, daily, or weekly (Figure 12.6). You will be notified via email when new items are posted on the discussion board.

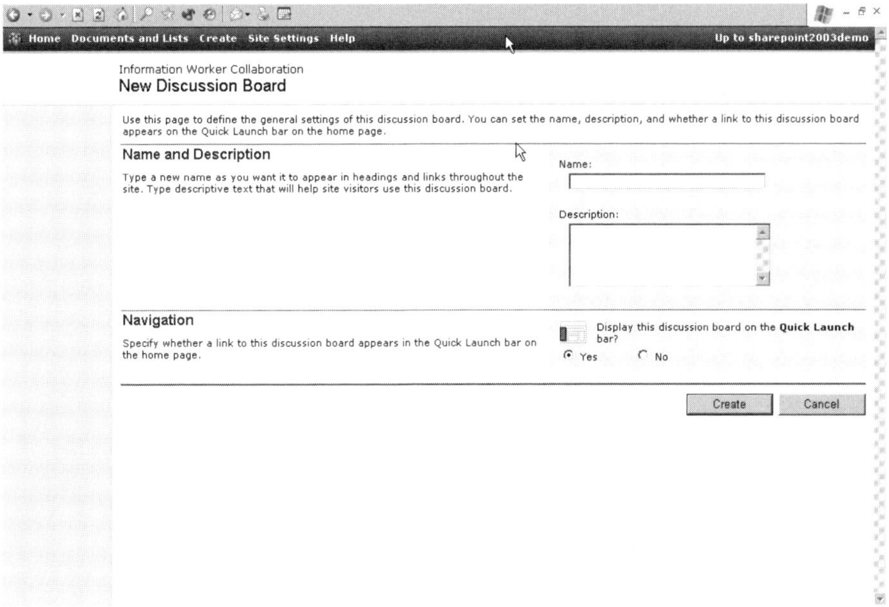

Figure 12.4 Creating a Discussion Board

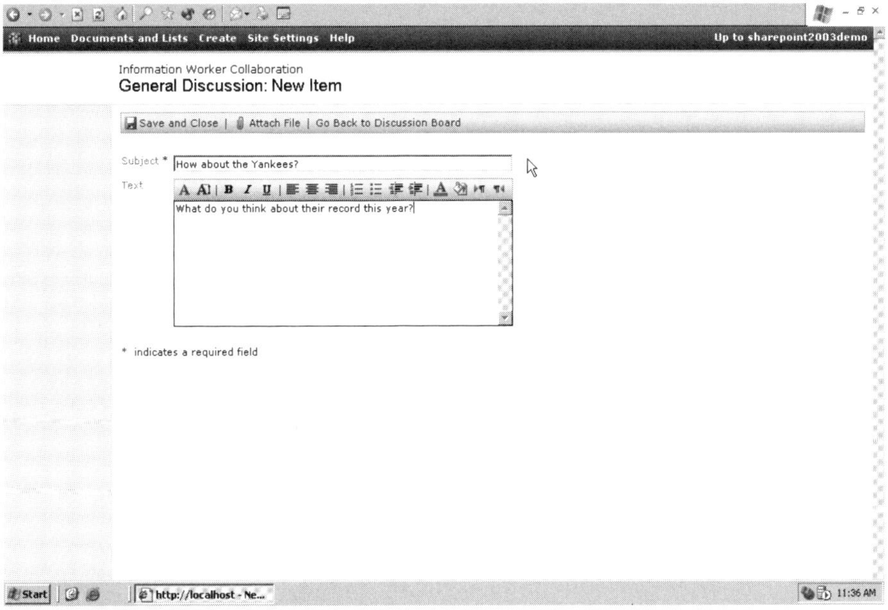

Figure 12.5 Sample Discussion

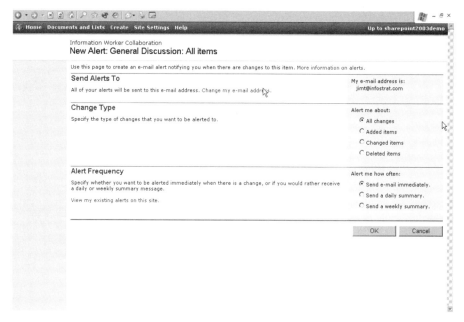

Figure 12.6 Subscribing to a Discussion

Discussions support multiple views. The user can choose the view from the left navigation bar. For example, you can view a hierarchy of the discussion or unfold it to a "flat" view.

Document Management

Document management provides authors, editors, and others involved with the production and publication for documents with advanced tools to maintain multiple versions of documents, track who is currently working on a document, publish documents to a targeted list of users, and establish an automated workflow for routing and approval.

SharePoint Portal Server provides these document management features at a price that is a fraction of competitive offerings. It is easy to learn and does not force users to radically change the way they work in order to adopt document management tools.

SharePoint uses SQL Server as the data repository for document management. This means it brings the same scalability, reliability, and high performance SQL Server has delivered to enterprise databases. It also puts SharePoint on a long-term path with other Microsoft server products that are moving toward SQL Server, such as Exchange. In version 1, SharePoint used the web store as its repository, the same information store used by Exchange 2000. The web store has been retained in version 2 as an optional component to allow backward compatibility for version 1 users who are upgrading.

Let's take a closer look at the document creation process and how to implement document management with SharePoint. The best place to begin is with the user who wishes to create a document.

User Roles

In most organizations, several people are involved in the process that brings a document from a brilliant idea to fruition as a published document. This book, for example, is a collaborative effort involving authors, editors, technical reviewers, an acquisition editor, a marketing department, and an editorial committee, to name a few. Similarly, corporate policy documents may begin with an author but must face peer review, legal review, and executive approval before they are made available to readers. SharePoint formalizes these roles into the following roles called **site groups** in SharePoint Portal Server version 2.

Table 12.2 SharePoint Site Groups

Site Group	Role and Rights
Reader	Read-only access to published documents. Search results show-only documents that the user can access.
Contributor	Reader rights and ability to submit content to categories to which they have been granted rights.
Web Designer	Ability to change layout and settings on a web page to which the web designer has been granted access.
Administrator	Full control of the site, including ability to administer users.
Content Manager	Administer settings and content in an area to which they have been granted rights.
Member	Profiled in site.

NOTE *Roles and the approval processes are different from default SharePoint version 2 behavior if you use the backward-compatible document library.*

You may notice that some of the SharePoint user roles resemble the roles in MCMS content authoring discussed in Chapter 9. In the current products the roles are different between SPS and MCMS. Perhaps in the future, the review processes as well as the user roles of SharePoint and Content Management Server will be integrated even more closely.

Managing Users

To grant users access to the portal, site administrators follow these steps:

1. Open the SharePoint Central Administration page (Figure 12.7). When you install SharePoint Portal Server, this page is installed in the SharePoint Portal Server program group.

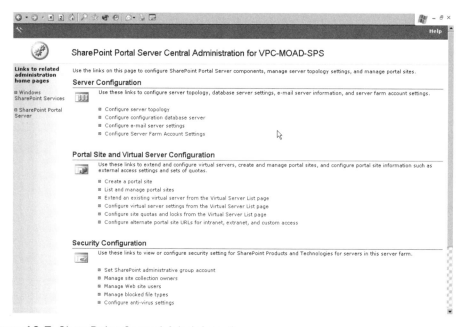

Figure 12.7 SharePoint Central Administration

2. Click **Manage Web site users** in the Security Configuration section of the page.
3. On the Manage Web Site Users page, enter the URL of the Share-Point site and click **View**. The page displays the fields you need to enter to create a new user in the portal (Figure 12.8).
4. Fill in the fields in the **New User** section.

   ■ Enter the username in the format domain/username.
   ■ Enter the name to be displayed for the user.
   ■ Enter the email address for the user in the format username@domain.com.
   ■ Choose the site group for the user.

5. Click **Add user**. The user is validated against Active Directory to ensure that the entry exists as a user and the Add Users page opens (Figure 12.9).
6. Click **Next** to display the second page of Add Users.

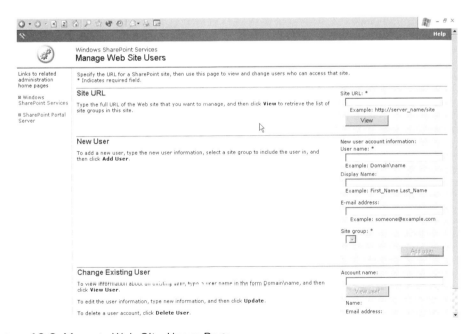

Figure 12.8 Manage Web Site Users Page

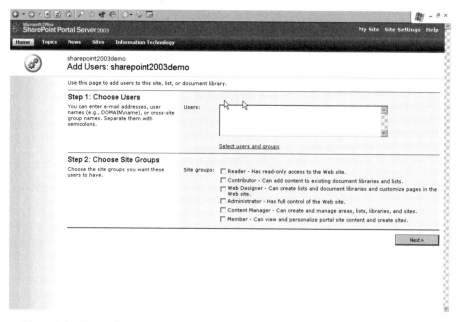

Figure 12.9 Add Users Page

7. To send an email to the user confirming that he has been granted access, click the checkbox **Send the following e-mail to let these users know they've been added** (Figure 12.10).
8. Customize the message as needed by typing in the Subject and Body fields, and click **Finish**.

Once users have been added, they can proceed with document authoring. First, they navigate to the document library in the portal. Next, they choose from the document management commands on the menu.

Document Management Process

The document library lists all the documents. Next to the document name is a dropdown menu with document management actions, as shown in Figure 12.11. Users can edit documents, check them out, check them in, view or edit document properties, and view the version history.

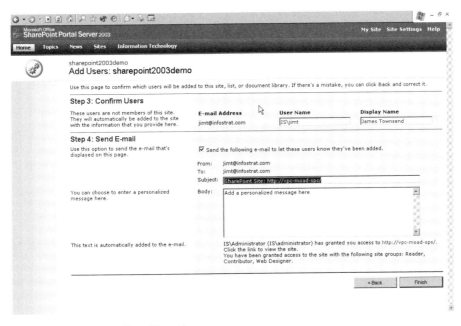

Figure 12.10 Send Email to New User

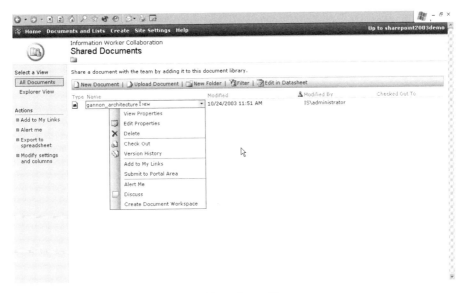

Figure 12.11 Document Management Dropdown Menu

A document can be either checked out or checked in. When an item is checked out, its status is changed so other users cannot check it out (though they can obtain a read-only copy). Users may want to check out a document and then take it offline for editing. As documents are opened, they are downloaded to the client workstation. When a document is checked in, the user can enter comments relating to that particular version, such as a list of the changes made to the document, as shown in Figure 12.12.

Only administrators can configure document library settings. To select these settings:

1. On the Shared Documents page, click **Modify settings and columns** in the Actions menu on the left to open the Customize Shared Documents page (Figure 12.13).
2. Click **Change general settings** in the General Settings section of the page.
3. On the Document Library Settings page, review the document library general settings (Figure 12.14). By default, document libraries

Figure 12.12 Checking In a Document

Figure 12.13 Customize Shared Documents Page

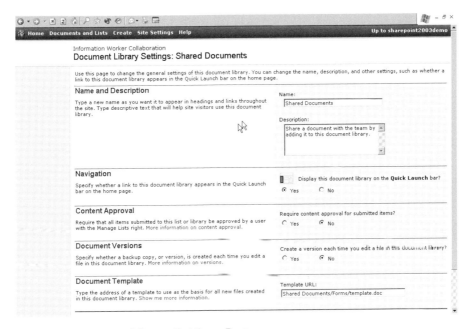

Figure 12.14 Document Library Settings Page

do not provide version control. A new document with the same name will overwrite the previous version. The settings on this page control the document management functionality, such as whether content approval is required and old versions are stored.

- Click **Yes** in the Document Versions section to enable version control.
- Click **Yes** in the Content Approval section to enable this function.

When version control is enabled, the previous version of a document is saved, not overwritten, when a new version is checked in. When you click the document menu (see Figure 12.11) and select Version History, a list of all the previous versions of the document is displayed, as in Figure 12.15. You can open previous versions or delete old versions from this page.

When document approval is enabled, the status of a document is set to Pending until it is reviewed. The reviewer selects **Approve/reject** from the document menu (Figure 12.16) and then approves or rejects the document. In either case, the reviewer can enter comments explaining the action

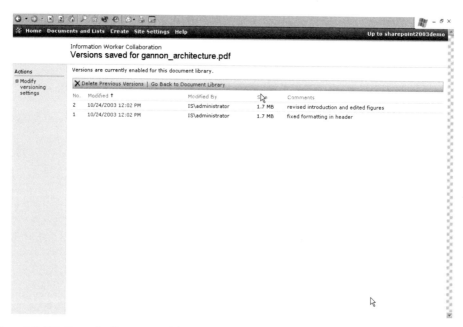

Figure 12.15 Sample Document Version History

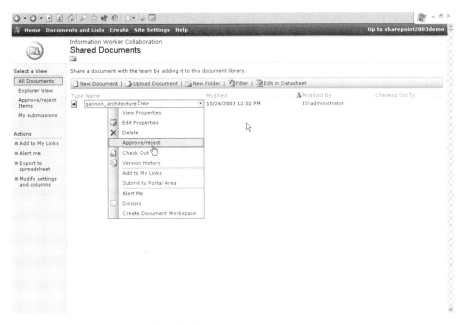

Figure 12.16 Approving or Rejecting Documents

(Figure 12.17). Approving a document makes it visible to readers. Rejecting a document notifies the author. Readers do not have access to rejected documents.

One of the handiest features of document libraries is the alert. Users can receive email notification whenever a document is added to or modified in a document library. As a result, moderators of a library can remain up to date about changes made by users. Similarly, reviewers can be notified when documents are pending. Figure 12.18 shows how to create an alert in a document library. The user can receive notification immediately or opt for daily or weekly summaries.

The alerts web part summarizes all the user's alerts. It can be placed on the home page, on the My Site home page, or any other web part page.

Document Discussions

Threaded discussions are especially potent collaboration tools in a document library. SharePoint allows users to insert discussions inside a document, as show in Figure 12.19.

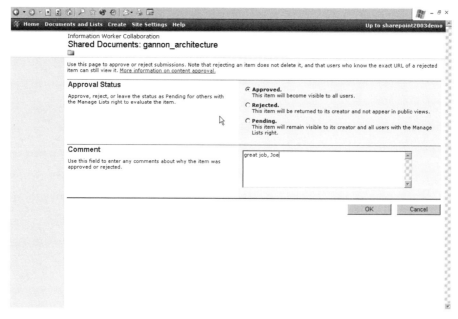

Figure 12.17 Approval Status and Comment

Figure 12.18 Document Library Alert

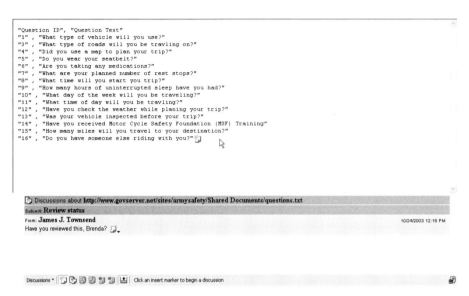

```
"Question ID", "Question Text"
"1" , "What type of vehicle will you use?"
"3" , "What type of roads will you be travling on?"
"4" , "Did you use a map to plan your trip?"
"5" , "Do you wear your seatbelt?"
"6" , "Are you taking any medications?"
"7" , "What are your planned number of rest stops?"
"8" , "What time will you start you trip?"
"9" , "How many hours of uninterrupted sleep have you had?"
"10" , "What day of the week will you be traveling?"
"11" , "What time of day will you be travling?"
"12" , "Have you check the weather while planing your trip?"
"13" , "Was your vehicle inspected before your trip?"
"14" , "Have you received Motor Cycle Safety Foundation (MSF) Training"
"15" , "How many miles will you travel to your destination?"
"16" , "Do you have someone else riding with you?"
```

Discussions about **http://www.govserver.net/sites/armysafety/Shared Documents/questions.txt**
Subject **Review status**
From: **James J. Townsend**   10/24/2003 12:18 PM
Have you reviewed this, Brenda?

Discussions ▾   Click an insert marker to begin a discussion

Figure 12.19 Document Discussion

You can discuss a document inside the document itself or around the document, as shown in Figure 12.19. When the discussion items are embedded inside the document, they remain with the text to which they relate. Discussions about the document stay together at the bottom of the window.

Project Teams

One of the key benefits of SharePoint over competitive portal products is the capability of users to create new ad hoc web sites without programming. These team sites are the focus of much collaborative activity. For most organizations, the smaller the organizational entity is, the greater the degree of collaboration. Most of the underlying features of these sites, such as the document library and discussions, have already been discussed in this chapter.

To create a team site:

1. On the Sites Directory page, click **Create Site** in the Select Action section to the left to open the Add Link to Site page (Figure 12.20).

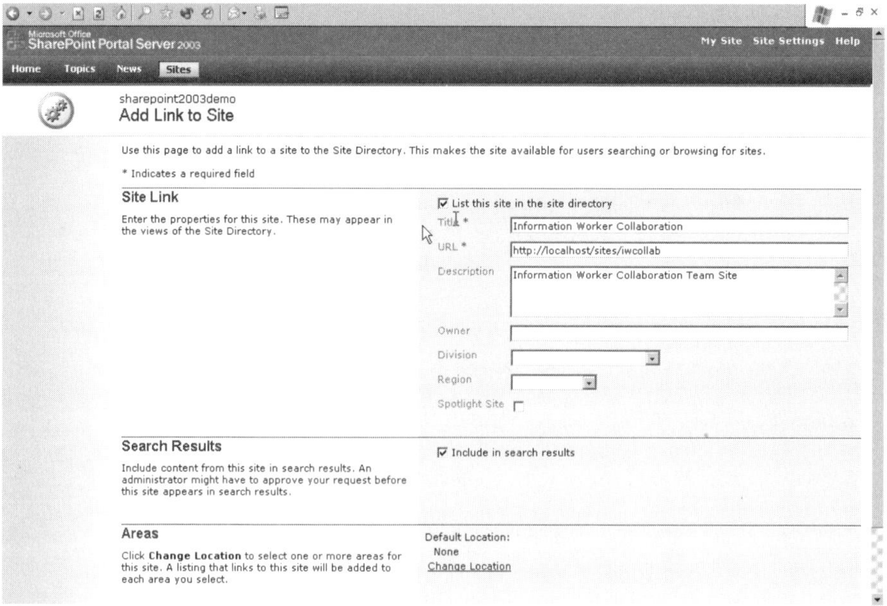

Figure 12.20 Add Link to Site Page

2. Fill in the title, description, URL, and contact email address for the site. Click **Create** to open the Add Link to Site page (Figure 12.21).
3. Choose whether the site will appear in search results, and associate the site with one or more appropriate categories.
4. Choose the site template to determine which pages are included on the new site (Figure 12.22).

After the site is created, you can add other pages that are not included in the template. You can also create your own templates or modify the existing site templates.

Types of SharePoint Sites

SharePoint Portal Server provides a number of site types for inclusion in your portal. They are designed to match the most common office collaboration scenarios. You can also customize the site by adding additional web parts to make it suit your requirements. Table 12.3 summarizes the site types and their characteristics, while Table 12.4 outlines team site features.

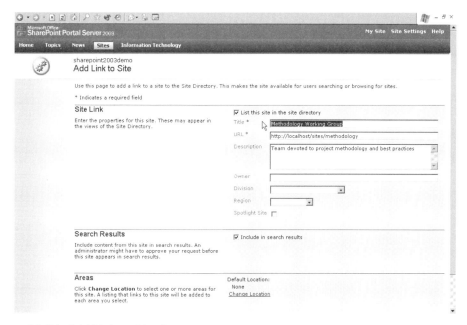

Figure 12.21 Add Link to Site Page

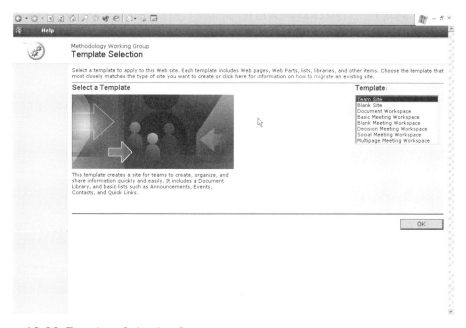

Figure 12.22 Template Selection Page

Table 12.3 SharePoint Site Types

Site Type	Description	Features
Team Site	A group of popular web parts for many scenarios. Contains places to "push" news to portal users as well as support for document collaboration.	Document Library Announcements Events Contacts Quick Links
Blank Site	Tabula rasa for adding your own web parts.	Blank Home Page
Document Work-space	Documents and related functions for creating documents.	Document Library Task List Quick Links Members Announcements
Basic Meeting Workspace	Content relating to a generic meeting.	Objectives Attendees Agenda
Blank Meeting Workspace	An empty site to which you can add new pages.	Blank Home Page
Decision Meeting Workspace	Includes basic meeting functions and also documents, tasks, and decisions.	Objectives Attendees Agenda Document Library Tasks and Decisions
Social Meeting Workspace	This is the template you might use for a company picnic.	Attendees Directions Weather Image/Logo Things to Bring Discussions Picture Library

Table 12.3 SharePoint Site Types (*Continued*)

Site Type	Description	Features
Multipage Meeting Workspace	Includes two additional pages in addition to basic meeting workspace.	Objectives Attendees Agenda Two Blank Pages
My Site	Personalized site. You can add additional pages to your personal site.	

Table 12.4 SharePoint Team Site Features

Feature	Description
Agenda	Place to list meeting agenda items.
Announcements	Post news to members of your group.
Attendees	Contact information for people.
Contacts	Contact information for people; may be dragged and dropped from Outlook.
Directions	Driving or other directions to a meeting location.
Document Library	Place to store shared documents. Includes check-in and check-out functions.
Events	Calendar of events.
Image/Logo	Placeholder for image file displayed on home page of site.
Members	Contact information for people.
Objectives	Meeting goals.
Picture Library	Place to upload and view photographs or other images.
Quick Links	Easy facility to share links to web pages.
Survey	Submit questions to users and tally results.
Task List	To Do list.
Things to Bring	Items to bring to social event.
Weather	Weather forecast or report for social event.

Most of the SharePoint team site features are self-explanatory, though the surveys feature bears more explanation. SharePoint lets you quickly generate opinion surveys and deliver them to your users. The surveys may be long or short, simple or complex. To create a survey on your team site:

1. Click **Create New** in the Actions menu to open the Create Page page (Figure 12.23).
2. Click **Surveys** in the left-hand navigation to open the New Survey page (Figure 12.24).
3. Name and describe the survey, and choose whether respondent names will be shown and whether people may respond more than once to the survey. Click **Next**.
4. Complete the series of pages for defining the questions in the survey (Figure 12.25). You can enter as many questions as you like. You can enter as many questions as you like. For each question, you specify the respond type along with the default value for the response. Validation for the field is provided depending on the data type for the response. For instance, you can set upper and lower limits for numeric values in responses.

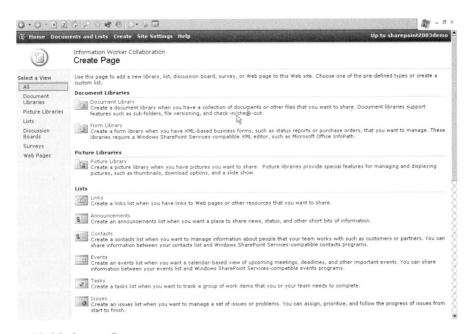

Figure 12.23 Create Page

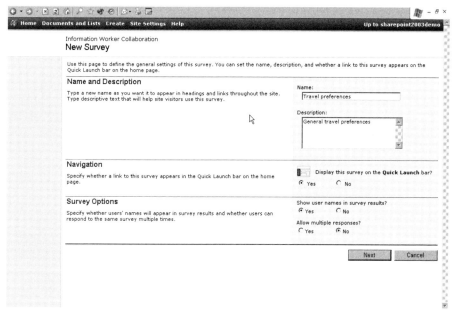

Figure 12.24 New Survey Page

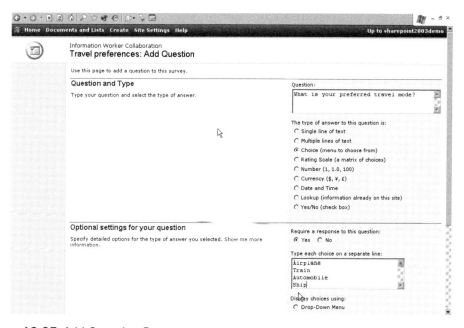

Figure 12.25 Add Question Page

5. Click **Finish** to open the Customize Survey page (Figure 12.26), on which you can review the survey or change settings. You can rearrange the order of the questions here, for instance.

The survey is saved and is ready for responses. Click **Home** to return to the homepage of the team site. The new survey appears in the left navigation under Surveys. Click the survey and then click **Respond to this Survey** on the survey page to respond to it, as shown in Figure 12.27.

When a user goes to a survey URL, he is prompted to respond to the questions in the survey. You may want to provide a link to the survey on your home page to encourage users to respond to it. By default, users are not allowed to respond more than once to a survey.

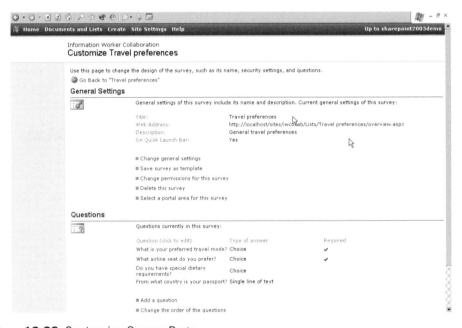

Figure 12.26 Customize Survey Page

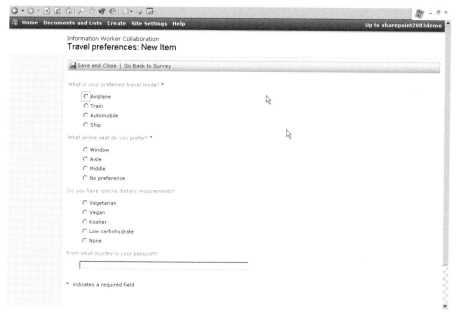

Figure 12.27 Responding to a Survey

Enabling Self-Service Site Creation

So far we discussed site creation from the point of view of a SharePoint administrator. Members of the SharePoint Administrator and Web Designer roles also have the power to create their own subsites. Users can even create subsites to MyPage. These subsites are complete SharePoint sites based on the site templates available to the user, containing home pages, news, announcements, and all the standard content provided by SharePoint. Subsites may have their own permissions established.

The Self-Service Site Creation feature takes this one step further, allowing users to create their own top-level SharePoint sites. By default, this feature is turned off. If you are in a multiple-server environment, you must enable the feature one server at a time. To create a site, users go to the signup page (scsignup.aspx) and fill in a few fields. When you enable self-service site creation, a notice containing this link is placed on the home page.

A site administrator can configure self-service site creation either from the command line or SharePoint Central Administration. From the command line, enter:

```
stsadm -o enablessc -url http://My_Server -require _
secondarycontact
```

In SharePoint Central Administration, follow these steps:

1. On the SharePoint Central Administration page, in the Virtual Server Configuration section, click **Configure virtual server settings from the Virtual Server List page**.
2. Click the virtual server you want to enable on the Virtual Server List page.
3. On the Virtual Server Settings page, under Automated Web Site Collection Management, click **Configure Self-Service Site Creation**.
4. In the Enable Self-Service Site Creation section, click **On** next to **Self-Service Site Creation is**.
5. Click the **Require secondary contact** checkbox to require two contacts for each site. By default only one contact is required.
6. Click **OK** to save your changes.

Self-service site creation is an empowering tool for users. It frees the IT staff from these routine tasks as well. Be sure to provide a support infrastructure for end users who create these sites so they don't feel abandoned by the IT department.

Online Conferencing

Next to having a place to share information and documents, conference capabilities are the most essential collaboration capabilities. Microsoft has provided several products to fulfill these requirements. The first was Net-Meeting. Later, Exchange incorporated conferencing technology and a separate effort produced Windows Messenger. Much of this technology was incorporated into Windows XP. Most recently, Microsoft purchased Placeware, a hosted conferencing service, to round out the offering.

Without online conferencing, users must choose between asynchronous communication via email and telephone conversations to communicate remotely. Both these are effective media, but online conferencing can augment both. For instance, email often ends up as a way of chatting with someone once you determine that they are online. It is relatively easy to click **reply** and post your response. The problem is that you may end up with overlapping messages and not see new items that pop into your inbox while you are still responding to a prior message. This type of conversation becomes confusing with more than two participants. Instant messaging displays all comments as they are posted and in the order that they are posted. You can invite several people to the same chat session. Instant messaging can also save time in wasted phone calls. Presence awareness in Windows Messenger, Outlook 2003, and SharePoint 2003 indicates whether a person is available before you pick up the phone. Otherwise, you may end up reaching voicemail. I often use instant messaging to ask a person whether she is available for a phone call and what phone number to use.

Microsoft offers several alternatives for online conferencing, most of which are compatible with the same clients. The key difference is whether you want to host these sessions inside or outside your enterprise.

Windows Messenger

The simplest and cheapest way to add real-time messaging to your collaboration environment is to encourage your user community to adopt Windows Messenger. Windows Messenger is part of Windows XP (Figure 12.28) and can be downloaded from www.microsoft.com/windows/messenger/default.asp. Windows Messenger is based on the Session Initiation Protocol, a standard used by MSN Messenger, Exchange, and other instant messaging (IM) servers.

Windows Messenger has the features you would expect from an IM client, such as displaying the presence information of others, exchanging text, images, file downloads and uploads, even accepting handwritten notes ("ink") from Tablet PCs participating in a discussion. Windows Messenger can be used to share control over your computer for remote troubleshooting. Application sharing includes running applications for remote software demonstrations and a whiteboard feature for sharing drawings online.

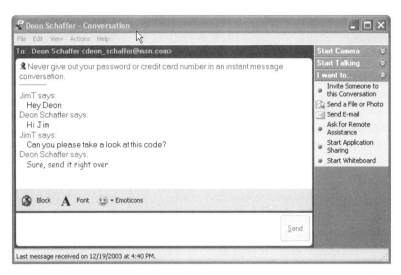

Figure 12.28 Windows Messenger

Best of all, Windows Messenger is available as a free download. Many of your users may have it installed already and may be using it for less official communications. You can broaden the hardware platforms support by Messenger with MSN Messenger. In addition to Windows, it is available for Macintosh, Pocket PCs, Smartphones, MSN TV, and the Microsoft TV set-top box.

For corporate use, MSN Messenger Connect for Enterprises is compatible with MSN Messenger as well as Microsoft Office Live Communications Server 2003. It contains security enhancements to protect your identity and your corporate data. MSN Messenger Connect for Enterprises allows you to log instant communications to ensure compliance with industry regulations such as those for the securities industry.

Live Communications Server 2003

Released simultaneously with Office 2003, Microsoft's Live Communications Server 2003 unbundles many of the collaboration features of Exchange 2000 and combines them with more advanced functionality and new collaboration standards. It combines instant messaging, presence awareness, and integration into the Office platform.

Live communications can augment other forms of collaboration. As with other tools discussed in this chapter, live communications help break down the geographic barriers that prevent in-person meetings. While asynchronous discussions and document libraries are excellent tools for bridging time zones and allowing collaboration to continue around the clock, synchronous communication is also vital to the enterprise. Instant messaging, for instance, can provide a "backchannel" of communications during a phone call.

Presence awareness, or knowing whether a person is online, is tremendously useful when you are trying to track down someone for help. A help desk can field more questions simultaneously using instant messaging than on the telephone, where such multitasking would be inefficient or impolite. Microsoft offers online immediate help for some of its web properties. For instance, I was seeking a graphics file for the Microsoft Gold Partner program to make a sign for a trade show. Despite my expert attempts to find it through browsing and searching, I was stumped on where the graphics file was located on the vast Microsoft partner site. I dreaded a call to the 800 number for help, fearing I would end up waiting on hold. Luckily, I saw a link offering real-time help. I followed the link, opening a session with the help desk on Microsoft Messenger. I entered my question, and a few seconds later was greeted with a response that the staffer was searching for the answer. After another 30 seconds, I had the link to the file I needed without ever interrupting my work to make the inquiry. The advantages of live communication make it a natural add-in for ERP and CRM systems. It also raises the prospect of ultimately augmenting or replacing support staff with software agents. Instant messages are already digital and expressed in human language that, unlike the spoken word, is easy to parse. Technical support questions follow predictable patterns, and many are quite repetitive, as witnessed by frequently asked questions (FAQs).

Live Communications Server lets you log conversations for further analysis later. For some businesses, such as the securities industry, this is a critical legal requirement that can simplify any investigations that may arise. The existence of the logs can also affect the behavior of the users online and encourage them to stay within prescribed regulations.

Live Communications Server is based on standards promulgated by the International Electrotechnical Commission (IEC). The most important of these standards are Session Initiation Protocol (SIP), SIP Instant Messaging and Presence Language Extensions (SIMPLE), and Real-time Transport Protocol (RTP). SIP is essentially the HTML of real-time communications. It is a text-based protocol much simpler than the standards such as H.323. In addition to supporting SIP and SIMPLE, Windows XP contains codecs that convert digital to analog as well as technologies to improve the quality of voice communication over packet-switched networks.

Microsoft Office Live Meeting

One of the key advantages of a hosted service is that someone else is responsible for making it work. Many companies rely on third parties to host conference calls, allowing participants to dial into an 800 number and connect in a chat room. While corporate PBX systems offer similar capabilities, the hosted offering can provide a toll-free number, offer support representatives, and provide an infrastructure that supports a large number of phone lines. Upgrading a corporate voice network to provide the same level of support is not usually a good investment. Microsoft Office Live Meeting (formerly Placeware) brings the same hosted quality of service and infrastructure to online conferences, as shown in Figure 12.29.

Office Live Meeting has a range of features too broad to discuss here. It allows flexible configuration to provide maximum control for the meeting organizer or to open it up to maximum collaboration. Users can be polled in real time, with graphical results displayed immediately to one or all participants. Control of the slide can be shared so people can make notes on it that are seen by the audience. Participants can ask questions that are queued up for review.

Microsoft Office Live Meeting is tightly linked with Outlook and other Office products. For instance, Outlook 2003 provides the option to start a Microsoft Office Live Meeting inside Outlook as NetMeeting was supported in earlier versions of Outlook.

One simple way to integrate your portal with Microsoft Office Live Meeting is to simply enter a link to the Live Meeting site (www.microsoft.com/meetnow) in the Links web part on your site home page. Users will then be directed to Microsoft Office Live Meeting to log in and join or schedule a meeting.

Microsoft Office Live Meeting can be purchased in several ways, from pay-as-you-go to all-you-can-eat, depending on the level of use you require. At this writing there was a free trial offer to use the service on a limited basis.

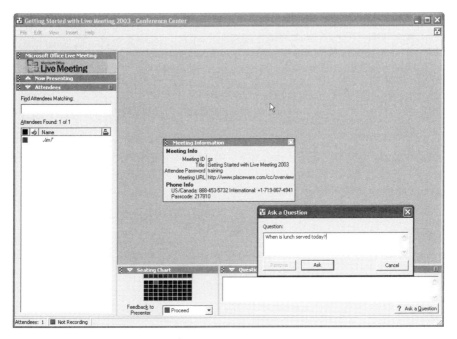

Figure 12.29 Office Live Meeting

Understanding Web Parts

Web parts are the fundamental building blocks of SharePoint. A web part consists of a title bar, a frame, and content. Web parts are stored in two files, a web part description file with the extension of .DWP and a web part assembly file with an extension of .DLL. The web part description file is an XML file defining the property settings for installing the web part. Table 12.5 shows the DWP file for the web parts that are based on .NET web custom controls.

The web part architecture is a subset of .NET, as discussed in Chapters 4 and 5. Web part pages are nothing more than ASP.NET web custom controls. As a result, they are as extensible as .NET itself and can be scaled out with large server farms.

You can extend SharePoint with third-party web parts and by creating your own.

Table 12.5 Standard Web Parts

Group/Web Part	Description
Windows Server	
HTML view of list	Simple listing of items
Content Editor	Controls for entering content on SharePoint web page
Page Viewer	Container for HTML page
DataView	Tabular view of data
XML/XSL	Viewer for XML data formatted with XSL
Office	
Web Capture	Display contents of web page
Spreadsheet	Viewer for Excel spreadsheet
PivotView	Viewer for Excel pivot table
ChartView	Viewer for Excel chart
Grid view of List	Format data rows in grid

Conclusion: Integrating SharePoint Portal Server with Content Management Server

Our portal architecture is based on the .NET Framework, with off-the-shelf products providing needed functionality in a modular fashion. For instance, our portal could use the document management features inherent in SharePoint Portal Server. Similarly, we could use Content Management Server for content management and navigation of web pages because it provides more control over the format of web pages with its templates.

How does CMS fit with SPS? Why do we need two products to manage two different forms of content, one for web pages and one for documents? Must users learn two different kinds of authoring?

In short, the answer is that CMS and SPS are designed to do quite different things, and they should be applied where they are most appropriate. For the sake of this discussion, we are focusing on the document management side of SPS rather than its search engine or portal (digital dashboard) capabilities.

The key question is whether the simple content management capabilities provided by SPS are sufficient for your enterprise portal. If the answer is yes, you can simplify your architecture by omitting CMS entirely. That means that you will use SPS to handle all site navigation as well as the content for web pages. You can adopt the standard SPS templates and create custom templates as necessary for the pages you wish to create.

On the other hand, you need CMS if you require any of the following content management capabilities:

- *Multiple templates for the same content,* such as having the same page served for different devices (PC with browser, Pocket PC). CMS supports this capability.
- *Localization of content (multilingual site).* CMS can maintain parallel pages in multiple languages with the same content.
- *Built-in routing and approval of content.* CMS offers more sophisticated user roles and greater built-in functionality. It also provides simpler ways for an editor to review content in the approval process.
- *Integration with Commerce Server.* CMS and Commerce Server are tailored to work together. This is important for e-commerce sites.
- *Sophisticated page layout.* CMS offers much greater control over the appearance and behavior of web pages.

Let's assume that you have determined that you need the capabilities of both CMS and SPS. Here is a way to divide the labor between the products. You can customize this approach to meet your specific requirements (Table 12.6).

Table 12.6 Functions Supported by SPS and CMS in the Integrated Portal

SharePoint Portal Server	Content Management Server
Handle all document management functionality.	Manage static pages.
Allow users self-service creation of ad hoc team web sites.	Handle overall site navigation through CMS channels.
Provide threaded discussion groups.	Routing and approval for content management.
Provide search engine for portal.	Integration with Commerce Server 2002.
Provide MyPage personalization features.	Manage user roles for content managers.

The main integration point between the products lies in navigational links. You can include links to SPS team sites in your CMS channels, for instance, and it is simple to link SPS sites to pages maintained in CMS.

The good news is that both products use SQL Server as their repositories for content and metadata. They also have their own rich tools for building and maintaining sites. Microsoft has hinted that all its server products will be more tightly integrated in the next product wave.

Additional Resources

SharePoint developers have many places to find additional information and help. The richest source is not surprisingly found at microsoft.com. The SharePoint site (www.microsoft.com/sharepoint/) contains technical information, evaluation tools, links to training, and other material. Within the MSDN site, go to msdn.microsoft.com/library/default.asp?url=/library/en-us/spptsdk/html/SPSDKWelcome.asp for SharePoint information. Microsoft hosts a community devoted to SharePoint at communities.microsoft.com/newsgroups/default.asp?icp=SharePoint. It contains up-to-date information from your peers and Microsoft staff to help you get the most from SharePoint.

For an independent perspective, check out www.spsfaq.com. This site is a rich source of news and links, and it even monitors Microsoft's web site for new downloads and articles on SharePoint. The New England SharePoint User Group hosts its web site at www.starit.com/sughome.htm. Finally, MSD2D.com has a section devoted to SharePoint at msd2d.com/Product_view.aspx?section=Sharepoint.

Chapter 13

Search Engine

Searching has become a serious challenge for the enterprise. Your portal by now contains a plethora of content, ranging from structured data in relational databases to unstructured data such as web content and documents. The data is stored in a number of formats and scattered across multiple locations. In most cases, the metadata is incomplete and inaccurate. For instance, how many users do you know who accurately fill in the title and author in the properties of Word documents? I confess that I often end up copying documents and moving sections around so much that I am surprised to see the contents of the document properties. With the increase in team collaboration online, critical documents may be located in collaboration sites, on file shares, and in email. In some enterprise architectures, each format requires a different search technique, making unified searches that cut across data sources impractical. A key challenge is to make this data accessible to all the categories of users of the portal.

This chapter shows how to plan, install, configure, and manage search capabilities for the portal. Most of these search technologies are full-text searches for unstructured data rather than structured queries in a relational database. Searches for both structured and unstructured data sources are needed for most portals.

Microsoft has developed full-text search technology that is implemented in several server products. It has made a significant investment in research and development for search (see Microsoft Researches Search Technology). For instance, full-text search capability is included in Indexing Service, SQL Server, Exchange Server, Office, and SharePoint Portal Server. The features of the individual products vary, but the core functionality is quite similar, and many of the search concepts carry over from one product to another. Indeed, the behavior of searches can be expected to converge as Microsoft makes better use of its research and development investment in search technology.

This chapter explains how full-text search can improve your portal and covers important concepts for search, a broad overview of the search engine architecture, and a comparison of the Microsoft server products that provide this feature. The primary emphasis in this chapter is on the search engine included in Microsoft SharePoint Portal Server because it is the most advanced search product that Microsoft offers. Windows SharePoint Services contains its own search feature as well, but it is not as powerful or flexible as SharePoint Portal Server. SharePoint Portal Server includes several features to make searches faster and more productive, including:

- Ability to search multiple information stores through a single search engine
- Search for not only documents but people (profiles), sites, and topics
- Scheduled index updates
- Full-text searches for documents and web pages
- Metadata searches for document properties
- Topic categories to browse search results
- Automatic categorization of documents
- Best Bet classification for highly relevant search results
- Multiple options for grouping and presenting search results by site, topic, author, and date
- Simple and advanced search
- Scalable indexing and searching architecture

Other SharePoint features that are discussed in other chapters complement search capabilities. For instance, alerts help portal users stay up to date on new search results, and taxonomies are important tools for searching and browsing (see Chapter 10). The white paper "Microsoft Full Text Search Technologies" (June 2001) provides an excellent overview of Microsoft search technologies. You can find it at www.microsoft.com/technet/prodtechnol/sppt/sharepoint/evaluate/featfunc/mssearch.asp.

Search Concepts

The purpose of full-text searching is to identify data sources, such as documents, that contain a specified search term. The search engine must quickly and accurately provide results to the user. It must handle a variety of file formats and storage locations. Finally, the search results should be sorted in a way to make the most useful documents most visible to the user.

We can differentiate between two large categories of searches: search against a well-defined source using SQL-type language and fuzzy search against weakly structured data sources like files, images, web sites, and so on. SQL Server, for example, employs both approaches through SQL queries (for example, `SELECT FirstName, LastName FROM tblPeople WHERE LastName LIKE 'SMIT%'`) and through its full-text search capabilities for performing searches within fields. Searches can also look at the metadata surrounding a document, such as the title, author, or keywords that are entered as document properties.

A sequential search of files for a character string is not a practical approach for any but the smallest number of documents. For instance, Windows XP and Outlook perform sequential searches by looking at files or messages one at a time. You probably have noticed how long these searches take for even a relatively small number of documents. Therefore, to solve the performance problem, much of the work of searching must be done in advance using inverted indexes—files that contain a list of all the words in a group of documents along with pointers to the documents that contain the words. A search does not result in a sequential read of any source files, but rather in an examination of the index file. Any matches can then be quickly identified.

The search engine consists of several architectural elements. At its most basic, a search engine must provide a means for creating an index of content, storing the index and providing search results based on user criteria from the index. Figure 13.1 shows key elements and concepts for search engines.

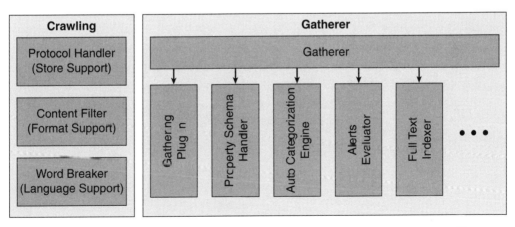

Figure 13.1 Search Engine Elements (Source: Uri Barash, "Enterprise Search with SharePoint Portal Server," Tech-Ed Israel, 2003.)

Microsoft Researches Search Technology

Microsoft has made a tremendous investment in computer science research relating to information retrieval through its Microsoft Research organization. The research findings are incorporated into products in order to make computing easier.

SharePoint Portal Server uses the advanced probabilistic ranking algorithm developed by Microsoft Researcher and City University Professor Stephen Robertson (research.microsoft.com/users/robertson/), winner of the prestigious Association for Computing Machinery Special Interest Group on Information Retrieval (ACM SIGIR) 2000 Salton Award.

The ranking formula uses the following factors to determine the relevance of a document:

- Length of the document
- Frequency of the query term in the entire collection of documents
- Number of documents containing the query term
- Number of documents in the entire collection of documents

For more information on Microsoft research in this area, see research.microsoft.com/research/ir/. There are a number of research papers on the Microsoft site of interest to students of information retrieval. For instance, "Inferring Informational Goals from Free-Text Queries: A Bayesian Approach" by David Heckerman and Eric Horvitz at research.microsoft.com/users/horvitz/aw.HTM and "Hierarchical Indexing and Flexible Element Retrieval for Structured Documents" by Hang Cui and Ji-Rong Wen at research.microsoft.com/users/jrwen/jrwen_files/publications/Hierarchical%20Indexing%20and%20Flexible%20Retrieval%20for%20Structured%20Document.doc.

The two main activities of the search engine are crawling and gathering. The crawling consists of reading content to be indexed, whether on the web, in file directories, or other content sources such as Exchange public folders or Lotus Notes databases. The crawler must understand the protocols used to access the content, such as HTTP for web content. Next, it must be able to read the file formats to be indexed. This software component is called a **filter**. It converts the source document to text that can be indexed. Finally, the crawler must process the text and perform conversions that make it more searchable, such as converting plural to singular or various verb forms to words that are easier to search. For instance, you would want a document containing the word "mice" to appear even if your search term were "mouse."

The gatherer takes the input from the crawler and organizes it to produce search results. The most common gatherer function in nearly all search engines is full-text indexing. All words found in the content are indexed along with pointers to the documents that contain them. The gatherer also may perform advanced search techniques such as binary file comparisons or automatic categorization of documents based on words contained therein. The gatherer alerts users who are subscribing to search results so they are made aware of new content as it is found. The following are elements that make up the crawling and the gatherer:

- *Content sources.* A repository of content to be indexed and therefore searched. SharePoint can crawl Exchange Server folders, file shares, web pages and sites, and Lotus Notes databases. Content sources can be located on multiple file servers in different domains, including public Internet web sites.
- *Protocol handlers.* A protocol handler is a component that accesses data over a particular protocol or from a particular store. Common protocol handlers include the file protocol, Hypertext Transfer Protocol (HTTP), Messaging Application Programming Interface (MAPI), and HTTP Distributed Authoring and Versioning (HTTPDAV). The gatherer passes URLs or URIs to the protocol handler.
- *Content indexes.* A full-text index of content sources specified by the SharePoint administrator. The indexes include file metadata as well as text in the target files. These are inverted indexes, which means that they contain entries for each word found in the content sources along with pointers to documents or pages that contain the word.
- *Search scopes.* Users can restrict their search to certain content sources based on a search scope. These are often displayed to the user in a dropdown list next to the search box. If you have many content sources that do not overlap, you can speed searches and provide

better search results for users by allowing them to target a specific content source. For instance, the Microsoft web site allows you to search only within the TechNet section when you are looking for technical information rather than bringing you results from their product marketing data or financial results.

■ *Index updating.* The process of indexing or crawling content and updating the index files. Indexes are usually updated periodically on a scheduled basis rather than continually.

■ *Best bets.* Highlighted search results that are most relevant to the user. Administrators may tag content as best bets so it will be placed higher in the search results than the ranking that would be ascribed to the document by the contents of the text alone. Users may suggest best bets for approval by administrators.

■ *Gatherer.* A software component that maintains the queue of files to be accessed. A gatherer uses techniques to optimize the efficiency of a web site crawl. For instance, some web sites restrict accesses to pages faster than they may be read by humans to curtail indexing activity. To overcome this, the gatherer interleaves URLs from one remote web location with URLs from other web locations, or with local file system documents or other stores. SharePoint also includes additional logic to improve crawl efficiency called **adaptive crawling**. Adaptive crawling balances the load imposed on crawled servers. When each document is accessed, the gatherer directs the stream of content from the protocol handler and passes it on to the appropriate filter.

■ *Filters.* Filters (also known as IFilters) extract textual information from a specific document format, such as Microsoft Word documents or text files. Microsoft provides filters for Microsoft Office that can extract terms from Word, Microsoft Excel, and Microsoft PowerPoint files. Other filters work with HTML or email messages. Adobe provides third-party filters to extract text from PDF files. The filter passes the stream of text to the indexing engine. All filters are written to an application programming interface (API), which is documented as part of the Microsoft Platform Software Development Kit (SDK).

■ *Word breakers and stemmers.* A word breaker determines where the word boundaries are in the stream of characters in the document being crawled. A stemmer extracts the root form of a word. For example, "go," "gone," and "going" are variants of the word "go." The word breakers are different for different human languages. The code for determining where words are broken is built into the Microsoft Search (MSSearch) service and cannot be changed.

■ *Indexing engine.* The indexing engine prepares an inverted index of content—that is, a data structure with a row for each term. The row contains information about the documents in which the term appears, the number of occurrences, and the relative position of the term within each document. The inverse index provides the ability to apply statistic and probabilistic formulas to quickly compute the relevance of documents. This means that the search engine can calculate the ranking of search results without looking at the source documents at all.

■ *Ranking.* In a search for unstructured data, ranking assists the user with prioritizing the search results based on their relevance. Ranking is not used for a structured, relational database search because structured data often lends itself to producing a single authoritative answer in response to a query. Full-text searches, on the other hand, tend to be less precise and often produce a large number of hits that must be sorted to maximize their value. The ranking algorithm is the "secret sauce" of the search engine. It makes the difference between mediocre and excellent search results. This is the reason why Internet users choose one search engine over another as their starting place to find new web pages and sites.

The search server naturally must be able to access and read a file in order to index it. In the case of password-protected files, this means that the account used by the server must have rights to the files that are to be indexed.

SharePoint reads files by means of software called an IFilter. SharePoint comes with IFilters for Office documents, Microsoft Publisher files, Visio, HTML, text, and Tagged Image File Format (TIFF) files. Third parties offer additional IFilters for other file formats. Adding an IFilter to your server expands the range of file formats that can be indexed. The IFilters only need to be present on the search server that crawls content. They do not provide viewing functionality to end users. Users must have software installed to open a file that they find in a search.

Microsoft Indexing Service

Indexing Service is the base search service for file servers and web services that is provided with Windows XP, Windows 2000, and Windows 2003. Formerly named Index Server for Windows NT 4.0, this search service was originally developed as an adjunct to Internet Information Server (IIS), the Microsoft web server that shipped with the server operating system. It has since been expanded to index documents in the file system as well as web pages.

Indexing Service extracts content from files by means of a software filter and constructs an index to speed up searching. It uses the IFilter interface, which it shares with SharePoint Portal Server.

The Search option in the Start menu uses Indexing Service as do search pages on IIS web sites. With the Microsoft Management Console (MMC), you can start, stop, and pause the service as well as define catalogs, as shown in Figure 13.2.

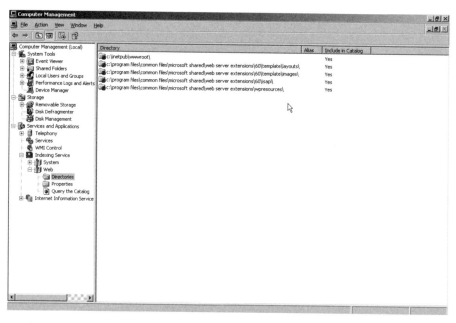

Figure 13.2 Indexing Service Management Console View

Indexing Service is powerful and highly programmable. It has its own software development kit with documentation that can be downloaded from msdn.microsoft.com/library/default.asp?url=/library/en-us/indexsrv/html/ixuwebov_4i0j.asp. The SDK includes numerous additional components for interacting with the Indexing Service, including ActiveX Data Objects (ADO) methods, ISAPI extensions, OLE DB Helper functions, and OLE DB provider for use with Visual C++.

By default, Indexing Service is not enabled when the operating system is installed. You must start the service manually. This is part of Microsoft's security effort to avoid use of unnecessary services on a server and therefore reduce the target area of servers for attacks.

Managing Search Settings in SharePoint Portal Server

When you install SharePoint Portal Server version 2, it includes search capability for content in your portal (the pages you create as well as documents in document libraries). This capability is also present in Windows SharePoint Services web sites. With SharePoint Portal Server, you can extend the data sources that you search.

Search settings are established in several places in SharePoint. As content is created, for instance, you can choose whether items are included or excluded from search results. Similarly, sites themselves can be included in search results. The central location for most search administration, however, is in the Manage Search Settings and Indexed Content section of site settings. You access these by clicking **Site Settings** in the top navigation of the portal home page. On these pages, you define most settings relating to searches. You can view a general status of indexing on the Configure Search and Indexing page (Figure 13.3). To open this page, click the **Configure** search and indexing link on the Site Settings page.

The Configure Search and Indexing page gives you access to many of the configuration settings that relate to search. From this page you can initiate crawls, manage search schedules, review error messages generated by the search engine, change search configuration such as which files are included and excluded, and see a high-level summary of the documents that have been crawled by the search engine.

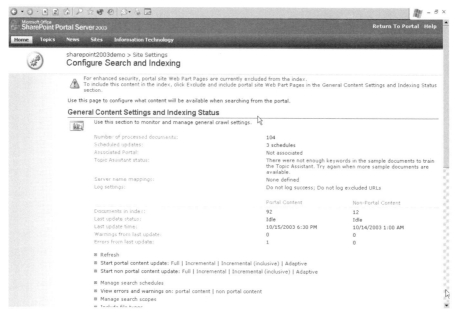

Figure 13.3 Configure Search and Indexing Page

Using the Topic Assistant

The Topic Assistant is a SharePoint feature that automates the process of content categorization. It is based on the areas to which content may be mapped. We have referred to this as your site taxonomy. For instance, you may have areas that are divided geographically, by functional areas, or by areas for each department in your organization. These taxonomy terms are stored as keywords in SharePoint. The quality of results from the Topic Assistant depends on the keywords you have created. The more keywords, and the more granular they are, the more accurate the Topic Assistant will be.

To use the Topic Assistant, you must first train it by providing sample content that relates to a specified area. Microsoft recommends that you create at least two areas with 10 documents each before you initiate the training process. The sample content should contain a reasonable number of your keywords in order to produce results. See Chapter 10 for more information on creating areas. The Topic Assistant is activated from the Use Topic Assistant page (Figure 13.4). Choose Use Topic Assistant from the Portal Content section of the Site Settings Page.

You can choose the level of precision with which the Topic Assistant is trained by raising or lowering the bar in terms of the relevance of search results. Higher precision means that a closer match will be required before the Topic Assistant suggests a content item belongs to an area.

After the Topic Assistant is trained, it suggests areas for new content that are then created. The Topic Assistant suggests areas to which content should be assigned, but these do not take effect until they are approved by an area manager.

Editing Properties of Crawled Content

Full-text searches can search not only the words within a web page or document but also the metadata, or properties of pages and documents. In HTML, metatags are vital for capturing indexing information and targeting search engines. Similarly, document properties are quite helpful for enterprise portals. Users often need to determine the author, date, and other document properties.

SharePoint lets you determine which properties of crawled content are used for a search. You can change the names of properties to make them

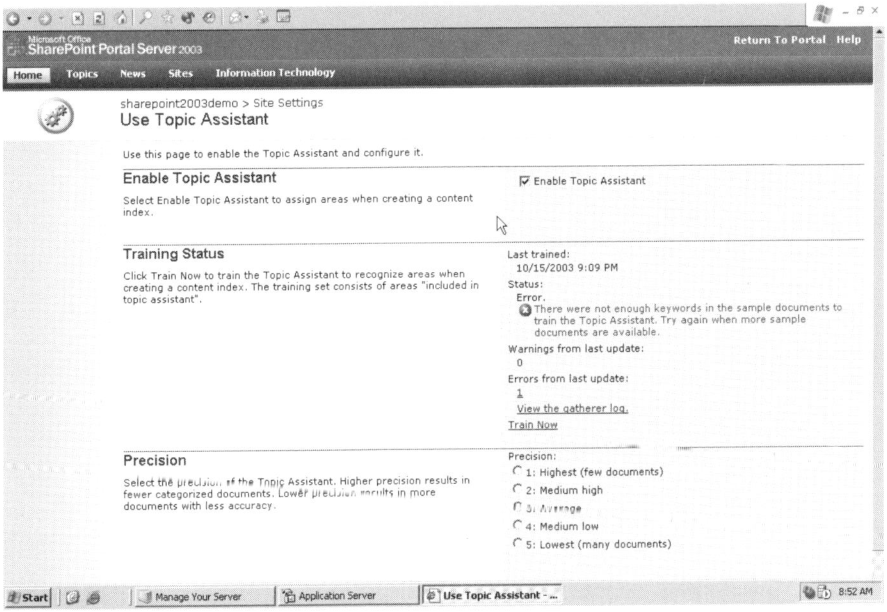

Figure 13.4 Use Topic Assistant Page

easier for users to understand and map properties to one another. For instance, two document types might use properties with different names to store the same data. These settings are controlled on the Manage Properties of Crawled Content page (Figure 13.5).

Different types of documents have different properties. For instance, while some file types have only a few properties, Microsoft Office documents have over 100 properties. Figure 13.5 shows some of these properties that have been selected to include in the search. You can edit an individual property by clicking its name in the list (Figure 13.6).

From this page you can see documents that include this property so you can view it in content. You can map this property to another property so the search engine treats the two as a single property. You can change the properties used in a search to help users search more productively. This step may be especially helpful if your users or programs are consistently entering data in these properties.

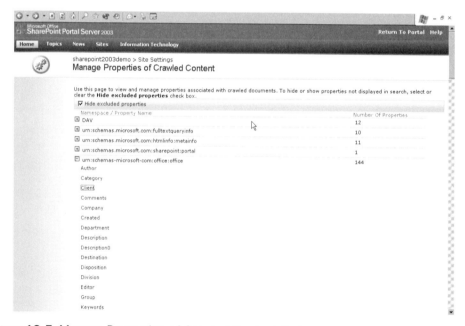

Figure 13.5 Manage Properties of Crawled Content Page

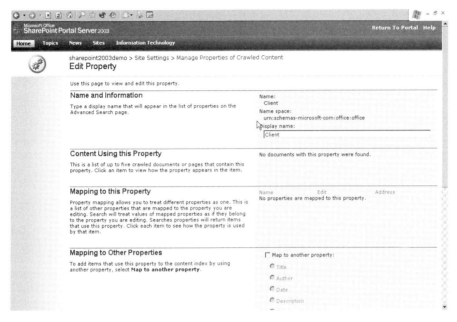

Figure 13.6 Edit Property Page

Managing File Types

You can configure SharePoint to include or exclude certain file types when building the index (Figure 13.7). You may elect, for instance, to exclude all documents with an extension of "txt" even though the search engine is capable of indexing such documents, because you know that they do not contain relevant information.

You may want to install third-party IFilters if your repository contains a large number of documents that cannot be indexed with the standard SharePoint filters. For instance, legal offices often have a large number of legacy files written in WordPerfect. Table 13.1 lists IFilters for popular file formats, including those that ship with SharePoint.

Figure 13.7 Exclude or Include File Types

Table 13.1 IFilters for Common File Formats

Filter Name	Files Filtered	Filter DLL	Company Web site
HTML filter	HTML 3.0 or earlier	Nlhtml.dll	www.microsoft.com
Microsoft Office Document Filter	Word, Excel, Microsoft PowerPoint	offfilt.dll	www.microsoft.com
Visio IFilter 2002	Visio versions 5.0, 5.0c, 2000 and 2002	Vistfilt.dll	www.microsoft.com
MIME Filter	Multipurpose Internet Mail Extensions	Mimefilt.dll	www.microsoft.com
XML Filter	XML documents	Xmlfilter.dll	www.microsoft.com
Default or plain text filter	Plain text files – Default Filter	query.dll	www.microsoft.com
Binary or null filter	Binary files – Null Filter	query.dll	www.microsoft.com
CGM IFilter	CAD files		www.imtechnical.com
DGN IFilter	CAD files		www.imtechnical.com
DWG IFilter	AutoCAD and other CAD files		www.imtechnical.com
StarOffice/Open Office	StarOffice and OpenOffice documents		www.ifiltershop.com

Table 13.1 IFilters for Common File Formats (*Continued*)

Filter Name	Files Filtered	Filter DLL	Company Web site
XMP IFilter	Image files including GIF, JPG, PNG, TIFF, PS, EPS, PSD, AI, and SVG		www.ifiltershop.com
Zip Filter	Zip archive files		www.ifiltershop.com
ZFilter	Zip archive files		www.4-share.com
Adobe PDF IFilter	Adobe Acrobat files		www.adobe.com
JPEG IFIlter	Metadata in JPEG files		www.aimingtech.com
FlashSeek	Flash Movies		www.imagiotech.com

The IFilters are installed on the server and help the search engine crawl all documents of that type in all the data sources that are crawled. Users must have the proper software registered on their workstation in order to open files found in a search.

Managing Rules That Include or Exclude Content

As if all the flexibility in indexing already discussed is not enough, Share-Point provides a feature that lets you create business rules that include or exclude content from searches. These rules are defined on the Exclude and Include Content page (Figure 13.8) accessed from the Configure Search and Indexing page of Site Settings.

Click Add Rule to define a new rule. On the Add Rule page (Figure 13.9), enter a path for content, and then specify whether content here is to be included or excluded. The rules are processed in the order in which they are displayed. You can move them up or down the hierarchy after you create them.

If the URL to be crawled requires authentication, you enter the credentials here. You can use multiple accounts to crawl various content sources.

Managing Content Sources

A content source is a location where indexed content is stored such as a web site, Exchange Server, file share, or the portal itself. SharePoint allows the

Figure 13.8 Exclude and Include Content Page

Figure 13.9 Edit Rule Page

administrator to define a number of content sources and individually configure indexes and other search options for each one. For instance, you might want to crawl certain external web sites every week rather than every day if they change infrequently or to avoid overtaking your indexing processing power and bandwidth. I have found from experience that it is not difficult to overwhelm a modest Internet connection by unleashing a server to crawl and index a massive web site.

Each SharePoint portal contains a built-in content source called "this portal" that cannot be deleted. This source represents content stored in SharePoint itself, such as news items, staff directories, and document libraries. When you create a new subsite, you can add it as a content source to be indexed as well. The Add Link to Site page includes an Include in Search Results option that controls whether you would like to include the site in the search results, as shown in Figure 13.10.

You can also control indexing behavior at the level of the individual item. For instance, Figure 13.11 shows a news item. By choosing whether to include it in the content index, you determine whether users can find the item through the search engine.

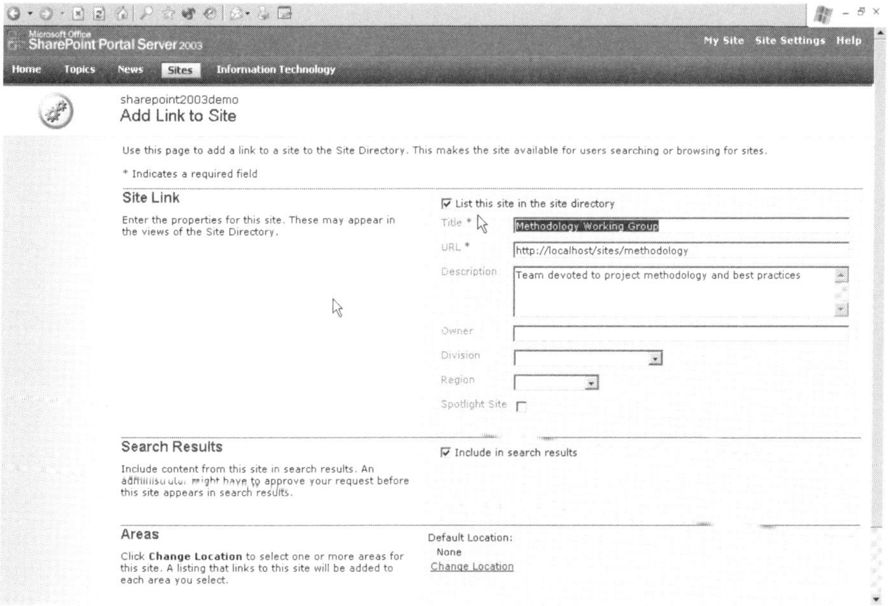

Figure 13.10 Add Link to Site Page

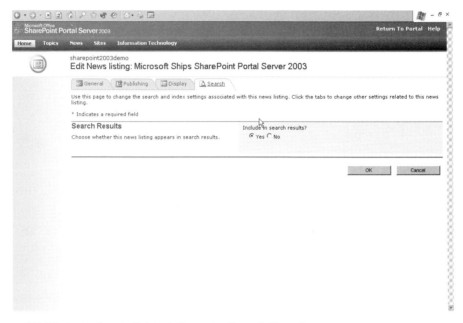

Figure 13.11 Including Individual Items in Search Results

The default setting for inclusion in content index is "yes." Even if you were to choose to include a subsite in the search results, it would only be displayed for users who have permissions to view that subsite.

Adding Content Sources

The most powerful tool for adding content sources is the Manage Content Sources page (Figure 13.12). This is only available to administrators, however, which is one of the reasons that other users have the ability to add content to the search or suggest that content be indexed. This is the only way to perform advanced functions such as crawling Lotus Notes databases and Exchange Server.

This page shows all the content sources that have been created in the portal. Some, such as This Portal and People, are automatically created. Others are added by the search administrator. To add a content source:

1. Click **Add Content Source** to open the Add Content Source page (Figure 13.13).
2. Complete the page, and click **Next**.

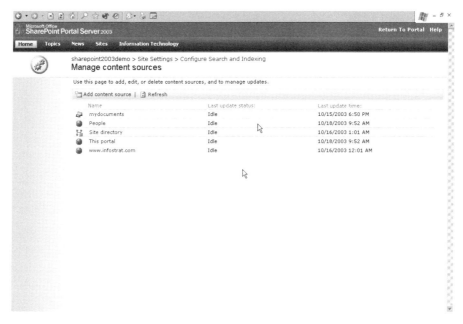

Figure 13.12 Managing Content Sources Page

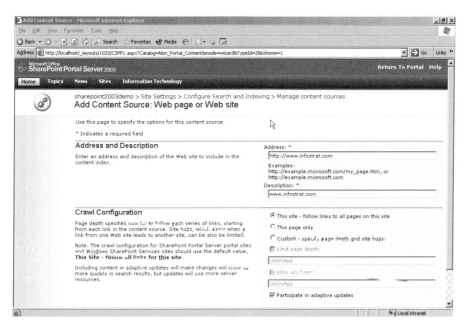

Figure 13.13 Add Content Source page

3. On the second page of the form (Figure 13.14), specify the URL and assign the content source to a group.

4. Click **Finish**. The Created Content Source page opens (Figure 13.15).

Another way to add new content to your indexes is to add a site to the site directory and include it in the search results. From Site Settings, click Approve and manage sites in the Sites Directory for searching in the Manage Search Settings and Indexed Content section. The Add Content Source page opens (Figure 13.16).

You can add sites created by users to the site directory so they appear in search results. For instance, you may want to include meeting sites, team sites, or departmental sites.

Figure 13.14 Web Content Source Page

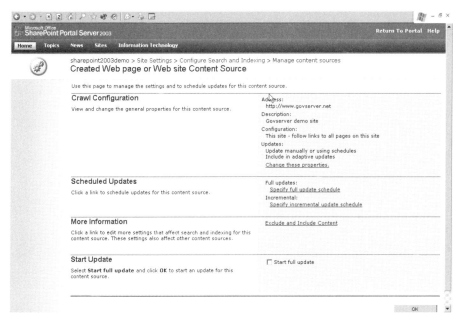

Figure 13.15 Created Web Page or Web Site Content Source Page

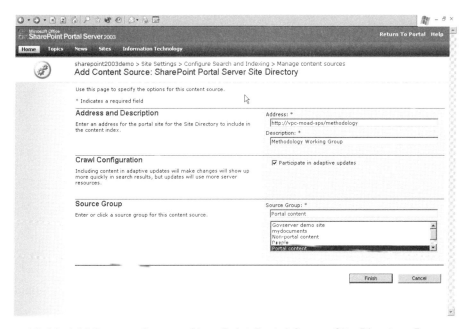

Figure 13.16 Add Content Source: SharePoint Portal Server Site Directory Page

Managing Search Schedules

The administrator schedules updates of content sources to provide timely updates while balancing workload of the server. In most cases, content outside the portal is crawled on a daily basis and scheduled for the least busy time of the business day. You can schedule more or less frequent updates to suit your requirements (Figure 13.17). A site that changes only infrequently might be indexed on a weekly rather than a daily basis, and internal portal sites may be crawled every 10 minutes (the default).

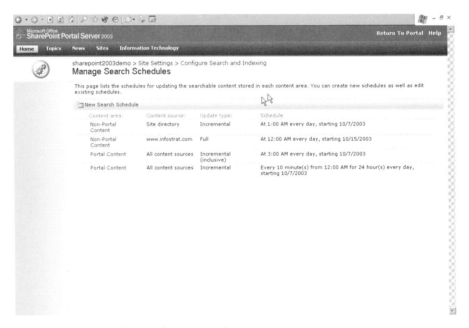

Figure 13.17 Manage Search Schedules Page

Managing Search Scopes

A search scope defines subsets of the portal data that can be searched by the user. The search scope usually appears as a dropdown list next to the search field on the home page and on the advanced search page. For instance, for your enterprise portal you might want to have search scopes such as "this site only," "competitor web sites," "news items," and "all portal content."

Search scopes can be limited by content sources, areas, and topics (Figure 13.18). For instance, the search scope "competitor web sites" would map to the content sources that crawl the web sites of your top 10 competitors. Similarly, "news items" might be mapped to the News area, which in turn consists of press releases, product announcements, and the corporate calendar.

Keep search scopes to a manageable number, as too many choices may confuse your users more than help them. If you feel the need to provide a large number of search scopes, you should confine them to the advanced search page rather than include them in the help option of your home page. The advanced search page provides more space to explain how these options work, and users who go to the advanced search page expect to see more options than the simple search on the portal home page.

Figure 13.18 Manage Search Scopes Page

Managing Keywords

In the land of search, not all words have equal value. At the bottom of the food chain are noise words that are ignored when documents are indexed. At the top of the food chain are words that have special meaning, called **keywords**. Keywords provide the opportunity for human analysts to make search results better than they would be with just the brute force of full-text searching. Keywords mark items as particularly relevant in search results so they will be more prominently placed.

Administrators create a list of keywords for common searches, defining a hierarchy of terms that can be used for browsing and searching information (Figure 13.19). Internet Information Server (IIS) logs searches so administrators can periodically review the most popular searches and determine whether new keywords should be created.

You can associate best bets with keywords so when a searcher enters a keyword in the search box, the best bets are featured with highest relevance and indicated with a keyword best bets icon.

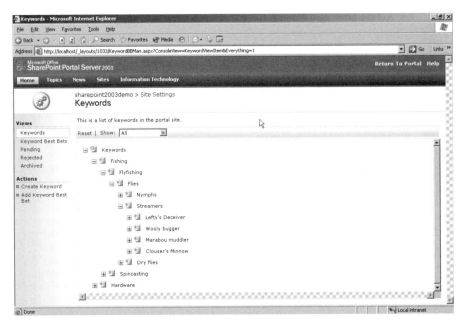

Figure 13.19 Keywords List

Site administrators can manage the keyword hierarchy or set up users with special roles as keyword managers. If desired, an approval process can be established for keyword management. If there is no keyword approval process, keyword best bets are approved automatically. If an approval process is required for keywords, they go through several stages in the process:

- *Pending*. Pending keyword best bets must be approved by someone with the correct rights before they are used by search. The status is reset to Pending if a rejected keyword best bet is resubmitted for approval. To change the status of an item to Pending, click the item and then click **Undo Approval**. This makes the keyword best bet Pending, and allows users with the proper rights to approve or reject the keyword best bet.
- *Approved*. Approved keyword best bets have been submitted for approval and subsequently approved by someone with the appropriate rights. To approve a keyword best bet, click the item and then click **Approve**. An archived or expired keyword best bet can also be changed to Approved to reactivate it.
- *Rejected*. Rejected keyword best bets have been submitted for approval and rejected by a user with the appropriate rights. To reject a previously approved item or an item that is Pending, click the item and then click **Reject**.
- *Expired*. Expired keyword best bets are those that are past their expiration date, regardless of whether they were approved. Keyword best bets expire automatically after their expiration date. To change the status of an expired keyword best bet, change its expiration date. You can delete those items that won't be used again or archive those that you may want to use later.
- *Archived*. Archived keyword best bets are those that are not currently in use, but that you want reserved for the future. Expired items are often archived. To archive a keyword best bet, click the keyword best bet and then click **Archive**.

To manage keywords, click Site Settings from the portal home page, then Manage Keywords under the Manage Search Settings and Indexed Content section. A list of keywords is displayed (Figure 13.20).

There are six different views of this page that you can choose from the left navigation pane. The default view lists all keywords. The page also lists keywords that are pending, rejected, expired, and archived.

Figure 13.20 Keywords Page

Clicking Keyword Best Bets in the left navigation opens the Keyword Best Bets page (Figure 13.21), which shows items that have been selected as keyword best bets grouped under their parent keywords. Keyword best bets are flagged with icons that show their status. To hide keyword best bets, you can apply a filter or choose keywords only in the toolbar. The second view shows only keyword best bets, and the final four show keyword best bets filtered by their approval status, as discussed above. Here an administrator can check on pending keyword requests and approve or reject proposed keywords.

To add a new keyword best bet:

1. Click **Keyword Best Bets** in the left navigation to show the list of keyword best bets.
2. Click **New** in the list toolbar to open the Add Keyword Best Bet page (Figure 13.22).
3. Fill in the name and description of the new keyword best bet.
4. Select the parent keyword or keywords for the keyword best bet, and enter the URL for the page or document.

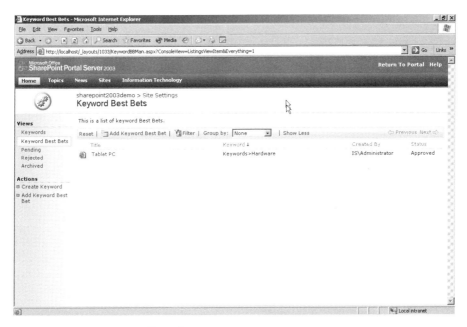

Figure 13.21 Keyword Best Bets Page

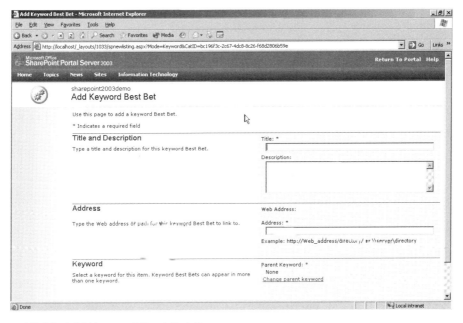

Figure 13.22 Add Keyword Best Bet Page

5. Click **OK** to save the new keyword best bet. The keyword best bet is now displayed on the Keyword Best Bets screen. If you choose more than one keyword parent for the keyword best bet, it will be listed multiple times.

Creating, Editing, and Deleting Keywords

Keywords are used to mark items of high relevance for a search. They are most important when the text of the document does not directly convey the topic to which it is related. For instance, abstract concepts might not be explicitly mentioned in a document, but the entire document might apply to the keyword. A speech by the chairman of the Federal Reserve might be quite relevant to "economic forecast" or "interest rates," but it might use other terms to discuss these issues. Without keywords, such an item would be missing from the search results. You should create keywords before you create keyword best bets, as the keywords provide the hierarchy in which the keyword best bets exist.

To create keywords, perform the following steps:

1. Click **Manage keywords** in Site Settings under the Manage Search Settings and Indexed Content section.
2. Click **Create Keyword** under Select Action in the left navigation pane. You may also select a parent keyword in the keyword list and then click **Create Keyword** in the action pane.
3. On the Create Keyword page (Figure 13.23), enter a title and description for the new keyword. The title is the word typed in the search box that triggers the keyword best bets for this keyword to be displayed in search results.
4. Enter a start date and expiration date for this keyword. To create a keyword that doesn't expire, leave the expiration date blank.
5. In the Synonyms section, type potential search words for which you want the keyword best bets for this keyword to appear, separated by semicolons.
6. Click **Change parent keyword.** In the Keyword Chooser, select the keyword under which to create this keyword, and then click **Save**.
7. Click **OK**.

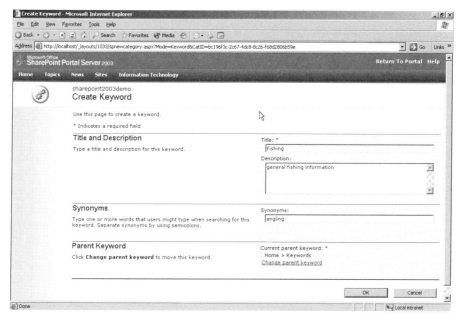

Figure 13.23 Create Keyword Page

Note that deleting a keyword also deletes the keyword best bets associated with that keyword. Do not delete a keyword unless you also intend to delete its keywords and keyword best bets.

Scaling Up Your Search Solution

The most sophisticated search functionality in the world is no good if it cannot support the number of users and the intensity of the searching and indexing activity that you throw at it. Microsoft has addressed these scalability concerns with the latest generation of its search products in Windows 2003, Content Management Server, and SharePoint Portal Server 2003.

One of the design goals of SharePoint 2003 was to support one million users of a portal. For searching, the goal was to perform 95% of all queries in less than two seconds, and index up to 20 million documents (up from

5 million in version 1). This performance requires fast loading of thesaurus files and rapid crawling and indexing. SharePoint version 2 achieves at least double the indexing rate of version 1 in terms of documents per second. You can accomplish high availability and scalability by using a number of servers to perform different roles in the portal. Indeed, you may need multiple servers for the search function alone.

SharePoint lets you assign multiple servers to roles as web servers, search servers, and index servers. For instance, if you had a small number of users but a vast amount of data to index, you would propagate many index servers but only require a small number or perhaps a single search server. Figure 13.24 shows the notional architecture for SharePoint search.

A search starts with a user request that hits one of the portal web servers. Search requests are balanced across search servers from the web servers and therefore directed to an appropriate search server. All search servers have identical copies of each index through index propagation.

Each indexing server is devoted to crawling and indexing up to four content indexes. For instance, you could devote an indexing server to

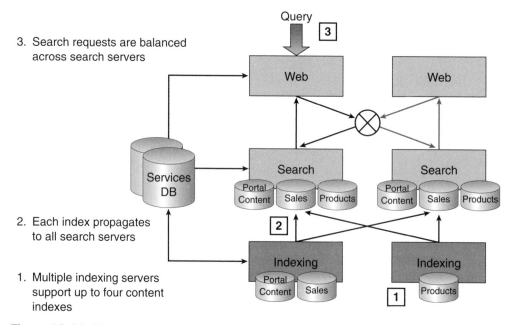

Figure 13.24 SharePoint Search Architecture (Source: Steve Tullis, "Enterprise Search with SharePoint Portal Server V2.")

competitive company web sites, and another to file shares within your organization. Separating the indexing from the search service means that the performance of searches will not be hindered by indexing activity, or vice versa.

Extending Search

We have discussed implementing search and scaling the search engine to support a large number of users, but what about extending the functionality of search? SharePoint provides APIs, web parts, and other components that make it possible to add new functionality or modify existing search functionality.

You can customize the user interface to search by modifying the search web parts. For instance, some users need more than the simple search provides but are confused by all the options in advanced search. By customizing the search web part, you could create a streamlined version of advanced search that displays or hides fields as you desire. Similarly, you could reorganize the search results web part if you wanted to highlight different elements of the search results.

SharePoint Portal Server provides an Advanced Search Administration mode. This provides additional settings that are not available by default to the SharePoint administrator. For instance, you can create as many search scopes as you like, and group together crawled sites for simpler administration.

Editing a Noise Word File

Some common words are ignored during the indexing process in order to reduce the size of the index and improve meaningful search results. For instance, a search on "the" or "an" would not likely return meaningful hits. SharePoint stores a list of noise words in a text file that you can modify. SharePoint comes with 20 noise files for 18 languages. By default SharePoint uses the neutral noise file noiseneu.txt in the server directory \Program Files\SharePoint Portal Server\DATA\Config.

The noise word file can produce some interesting results. For instance, users who abbreviate information technology to "IT" will be disappointed that no hits are returned, because "it" is included in the standard noise word file (Figure 13.25). All single character words are similarly excluded.

Figure 13.25 Default SharePoint Noise Word File

To include all words in indexes, delete all entries from the noise word list. Do not delete the file, as this will result in all single characters being treated as noise words.

You can edit the noise word file in any Unicode editor, such as Notepad. If you change the contents of the noise word file, be sure to run a full update of the index. Otherwise, the search engine may accept search terms as valid but produce no results because the term was ignored during the indexing process or reject terms that should be valid because you deleted them from the noise word file.

Microsoft SQL Server uses a noise word list of its own that is maintained independently of SharePoint. You may want to consider whether changes in the noise word list of one system should be reflected in the other.

Search Feature Comparison

The portal has many needs for search capability, and you face several options for how to implement them. You may find that an integrated approach that uses more than one product or technology works best for you. Table 13.2 summarizes the search capabilities of several Microsoft products.

Table 13.2 Search Technology Feature Comparison (Source: Adapted and updated from white paper "Microsoft Full Text Search Technologies," June 2001.)

	SharePoint Portal Server 2003	Indexing Service	SQL Server 2000	Exchange 2000 Server	Office XP on Windows XP
Crawls:					
File system	✓	✓			✓ Local only
Web sites	✓	✓ Local only, through file system			
Lotus Notes	✓				
Exchange 5.5	✓ Public folders				
Exchange 2000	✓ Public folders			✓ Public folders and private mail boxes	
SQL tables	✓ Through ASP		✓		
SharePoint Portal Server workspaces	✓				✓

Continues

Table 13.2 Search Technology Feature Comparison (*Continued*)

	SharePoint Portal Server 2003	Indexing Service	SQL Server 2000	Exchange 2000 Server	Office XP on Windows XP
Third-party protocols	✓				
Best Bets	✓				
Categories	✓				
End user UI	Dashboard site	Windows Explorer on Windows 2000 and custom	Custom	Outlook through Advanced Find, custom	Office search task pane

While SharePoint is clearly the most advanced search engine offered by Microsoft, you may want to consider how it fits with the other search products in the family. Most importantly, give your users what they need to bring them to the rich content you offer in the portal.

Conclusion

A portal really isn't a portal without search capabilities that can handle unstructured as well as structured information. That means we need full-text search capability. Because the portal contains many kinds of data in multiple repositories, we need search tools that can integrate these sources and provide results from all of them from a single query.

Microsoft has developed advanced and easy-to-use search capabilities that have been implemented in various ways throughout its software products. Ranging from file searching in Windows XP to catalog searching in Commerce Server and document searches in SharePoint Portal Server, you have several options for search engines.

For the enterprise portal, SharePoint Portal Server is the hands-down winner for most organizations. It is the most advanced search product offered by Microsoft, and it is capable of indexing the greatest variety of data sources. As shown in this chapter, it has a rich, yet relatively easy, administrative user interface. Your software licensing for SharePoint in the enterprise already includes the search capability, and you would be remiss not to include it in your portal.

An external portal, on the other hand, may be better served with other search engines. Index Services for Windows can adequately index your web pages and provide both simple and advanced search for your users. Best of all is the price, as it is included in Windows Server.

Whatever search engine you choose, be sure to spend the time it takes to catalog and index data that will be helpful to your users. This effort will be rewarded by helping users find the content they need in your portal, making it a more productive experience.

Chapter 14

Scalability and the Portal

What happens if you build the best portal ever, and hundreds, thousands, or millions of people flock to it day after day to get the information for which they hunger? This is precisely the problem we all seek, the reason this book was written, and the motivation for your making it all the way to the final chapter. If the portal cannot support the volume of its users or provide the performance they expect, it will fail. **Scalability** is a way to describe the impact of rising traffic, users, data volume, transactions, and other metrics on the performance of the portal.

High availability is the close companion of scalability. An infrastructure that supports a large number of users and high volume of transactions cannot be so brittle that it fails frequently. Fortunately, the same technologies and architecture that support scalability lend themselves to improving availability, such as clustering, fault-tolerant hardware, and distributed systems.

To achieve the highest levels of availability, you need three things:

- *The right technology.* Hardware and software components are the building blocks of your architecture. They should be of the correct performance category and be compatible with one another. It makes no sense to hire a crew of construction workers to build a skyscraper out of straw. Spend your resources according to your business priorities and invest adequately where failure of a system is not an option.
- *The right architecture.* Quality building materials do not guarantee a comfortable, habitable space. Emulate the successful architectures of others that achieve goals similar to yours. Microsoft, for instance, shares many details of its information technology infrastructure, as do other vendors such as Dell and Hewlett-Packard. These are great case studies for large organizations.
- *The right operations.* Maintenance procedures must match the quality of the materials and the plan to achieve greatness. This is the area most likely to be shortchanged. Money may have already been spent

on gee-whiz hardware and the high-priced architect consultants when it comes time to operate and maintain the network or server farm. High availability is every bit as much a function of the vigilance of the people who monitor the network as of the underlying hardware and software.

Failure in any one of these portal infrastructure pillars will cause the entire structure to wobble or perhaps topple. Be sure to pay equal attention to all three, as they are interdependent. A great architecture with top-drawer hardware does little good if no one is trained on how to operate it, and you don't have to look far to find people who have employed today's technology with yesterday's architecture to produce underwhelming results.

In this chapter we take a look at the scalability and availability goals for a portal and options for scaling. We also survey hardware, software, and network techniques and best practices for achieving the performance you need. Special attention is paid to .NET scalability and the unique requirements of different servers in the Microsoft portal platform. An approach that produces optimal performance with Content Management Server, for instance, may not be appropriate for beefing up the search engine, or making catalog order transactions quicker.

The best this chapter can do is to scratch the surface of the topic, as scalability and related issues are both broad and deep. Volumes have been written on each of the areas discussed here, including entire books devoted to scalability of a single Microsoft product such as SQL Server or Windows 2000.

Planning for Scalability

Before deploying your portal, you need to make preparations for its growth. You need to ask some serious questions, and catalog your current and proposed infrastructure. Let's assume that you do not have a portal in place, but that you have an existing IT infrastructure.

The first step in the process is to understand the baseline. You should assess the current infrastructure, cataloging your assets, capacity, and usage. Determine current availability statistics, maximum loads, and performance parameters. Do you have excess capacity or a shortfall? How much are you spending on the current infrastructure?

For each component of a solution, performance is a function of factors including:

- Amount of information retrieved from and sent to the browser
- Complexity and resulting time required to process requests
- Resources allocated per user (memory, data connections)
- Location of processing (client, server, or both)

The less work a component has to do, the quicker it can do it. The closer the processing occurs to the user, the better, in terms of reducing communication time and taking advantage of distributed computing power. A t-shirt popular at university physics departments reads "186,000 miles per second isn't just a good idea. It's the law." The more electrons have to move and the farther they travel, the more you need to be concerned about performance. If you can locate related components close to one another, performance will benefit.

Identify the business and functional goals for your future architecture. Do you have a target for response time, throughput, or some other metric? Must your portal be available to outside business partners such as trading partners, banks, or others? What is the impact of this new group of users? What degree of availability do you require?

What is the budget for your project? Which resources could be upgraded or replaced and which must remain as they are? What are your schedule constraints?

Next, create an architecture for the portal you are building. This chapter contains some guidelines and resources for understanding the architecture of the portal. Be sure to factor in any anticipated growth in users or transactions. Will the portal create new demands for certain groups of users, such as content authors, discussion moderators, or site visitors? Will the storage requirements expand dramatically for new content? Are you planning separate environments for development, testing, staging, and production?

Develop a migration plan to get from your current architecture to the bold new portal. What is the business impact of the migration? How can you mitigate disruption to employees and other users? What risks should you consider?

Test the new architecture, using pilots and labs as necessary to guarantee that the actual performance will measure up to theoretical performance. Feed the testing results back into the design and make changes as needed.

Deploy the new portal environment, developing management and maintenance procedures along the way. Next, migrate data and users to the new environment. Finally, go on vacation to a beach far away from Internet access and cell phones.

Microsoft offers these steps to scalability as a nine-step program in a slightly different context at www.microsoft.com/business/reducecosts/ efficiency/consolidate/steps.mspx.

Scaling Up and Out

Scaling is the process of adding resources to a system so it can handle increased workloads. In the n-tier architecture we have described throughout this volume, an application is divided into logical units (tiers) organized into layers for user interface, business rules, and database access. These tiers do not necessarily map to servers on a one-to-one basis. When it comes to scaling a solution, we have options on which tier to bolster in order to provide the needed performance and availability. While there are many approaches to achieving scalability, they may be divided into two broad categories: scaling up and scaling out. The first approach is to create bigger and bigger boxes (such as servers) and the second is to set up many smaller, often inexpensive ones.

Scaling Up

Scaling up (or vertical scaling) means adding more resources to a server to meet growing demand. These resources include storage, memory, processors, and network adapters, or even replacing the entire server. If response time of your email degrades over time, for instance, adding memory and processors to your Exchange Server will probably improve performance for all users. In its early days, large-scale computing achieved scalability strictly through scaling up. With mainframes, computing power was a scarce resource that was centrally controlled and managed. When new users or heavier loads were added, the mainframe was upgraded to accommodate them. Because it was centrally managed, mainframe configuration changes only needed to be performed once if they were done correctly, and users could do little to disrupt the performance of the system.

Figure 14.1 Scaling Up and Scaling Out

Windows operating systems support scaling up by supporting multiple processors, large amounts of memory, and other resources. Windows Server 2003 (like its predecessor) supports multiple processors with the symmetric multiprocessing standard (SMP). The operating system allocates threads to run on the available processors, achieving performance boosts over single-processor systems.

The Windows Server 2003 family represents the latest generation of Microsoft operating systems and therefore the highest performance and scalability. A system can move from a single-processor all the way to a 64-way Itanium box that would make any network administrator chuckle with glee.

Windows 2003 supports a range of storage options, offered by many manufacturers. Windows Storage Server 2003 is based on the NTFS (NT file system) and supports capacities from 320 gigabytes (GB) to over 60 terabytes. The NTFS has no upper limits on the number of files on a volume (over four billion have been tested), and each volume can be up to 256 terabytes.

The most important advantage of scaling up is that adding memory or other hardware does not add to your administrative or management burden. Troubleshooting a single server is simpler than handling multiple servers. The disadvantage is that scaling up only takes you so far, and you may need more performance than a single server can offer. Performance gains from scaling up are not usually as dramatic as those from scaling out. Scaling up also runs the risk of creating user contention for shared resources, while scaling out essentially segments users into groups with their own resources that they do not share with the entire user community. Scaling up creates fewer points of failure; but when a failure occurs, it can be catastrophic. It can also present a security liability, as application components with external exposure may end up hosted side-by-side with sensitive internal information. Scaling out allows a physical separation of data in such a case and provides more architectural options.

Another advantage of scaling up is that it is easy to measure your success. By monitoring server utilization statistics, you can determine when it is time to add more resources. For instance, if the CPU capacity exceeds 80%, it may be time to add additional CPUs. If disk queue length averages more than one, or if disk I/O utilization approaches 100%, go write a check for additional physical disks. You can set up an early warning system with a performance monitor and establish alerts in SQL Server to notify the administrator when performance problems are coming.

Scaling Out

Scaling out (or horizontal scaling) means adding additional resources by adding one or more additional computers, or nodes, to the system. In some cases the new servers are essentially clones of one another. The traffic generated by the largest web sites creates processing and communications loads that exceed the capacity of large individual servers. In these cases, scaling out may be the best option for increasing the processing capacity of the system, as increasing the memory or other resources for a single server will produce limited gains. For instance, if static page hits represent the bulk of your web traffic, you can achieve performance benefits from spreading the workload across multiple servers. When communications bandwidth is the bottleneck, performance can be improved by moving the web servers as close to the users as possible to reduce network traffic. If the largest traffic volume for your site comes from the United States and the Philippines, deploying servers to both regions would likely improve performance.

Microsoft Windows Server products (2000 and 2003) are designed to support scaling out. You can use software components in clusters of Windows 2000 application servers to form a clustered business services tier. Each server can be configured with identical sets of components, and Windows 2000 balances the cluster processing load by sending new requests to the server that has the least processing load. New servers can be easily added to this cluster to meet scalability needs. The cluster is relatively easy to administer regardless of the number of servers employed.

Several portal products can take advantage of clustering and load balancing. For instance, Commerce Server, SharePoint Portal Server 2003, and Microsoft Content Management Server components use network load balancing on the web tier. Load balancing across the web tier is particularly suitable for stateless data such as static web pages or streaming media. A web cluster using network load balancing typically consists of multiple servers called **cluster members**, each an independent web server that does not share data with other cluster members. When an HTTP request is received, it is routed to an available web server, which handles the request. In the event of failure, the cluster member can be removed from the cluster so incoming client requests are directed to other cluster members. You can add new servers to a cluster relatively easily and often without halting the operation of the cluster.

Clustering lets you optimize the site architecture to increase performance and availability. It also simplifies maintenance as you can remove a node from a cluster for scheduled or unscheduled maintenance without disrupting the overall operation of the portal. Management of clusters is nearly as simple as managing single servers, and the clusters can be mapped to the logical architecture of your application to further streamline management. For instance, you may have a business process that accepts certain files from other organizations, and then performs extensive manipulation of the files—parsing them, checking for errors, and generating messages to many systems. This process can create bottlenecks for your operation. By creating a cluster of servers to perform these tasks, you can allocate resources as necessary and monitor the process easily. This approach is important for

BizTalk Server, which deals with such scenarios frequently in enterprise application integration.

Clustering is also an effective technique for databases such as SQL Server. Combined with shared storage, clustered SQL Servers can overcome hardware bottlenecks by handling a large volume of read and write requests. This technique is explained further in the following section on SQL Server.

We have encountered clients who take scaling out to its extreme. One such client had built a web application with a database backend based on Microsoft FoxPro. FoxPro is known to produce excellent performance for a single user on a PC, and even for a workgroup of users on a local area network. In this case, new users kept coming until the user population had grown to over a million. From time to time, performance would deteriorate sharply, and new users would not be allowed to connect to the database. Brought in for a consultation, we met with the development team to help define the best course of action. On the table was the option of migrating the data to SQL Server on a powerful server and building an *n*-tier architecture for the application. A member of the development team objected, pointing out that this option would require a significant rewrite of the existing FoxPro code base. Because FoxPro works well for a small number of users, he reasoned, why not segment the application into 26 servers, one for each letter of the alphabet. As users logged in, they would be routed to the correct server based on the first letters of their last names.

Despite this cautionary tale, scaling out is an important tool for achieving high performance. It is likely that you will adopt this approach at a minimum for your web servers, and possibly for additional servers in your infrastructure.

Hybrid Approach

In the end, you are likely to arrive at an architecture that combines scaling up with scaling out. You will find that different elements of your portal architecture respond to different scalability and availability prescriptions. Figure 14.2 shows how a complete portal architecture might look for all the server products addressed in this book.

Each implementation varies depending on the business requirements and the performance characteristics desired as well as the hardware and software on hand. A widely dispersed organization would consider spreading this infrastructure around the world, for instance, and many large portal

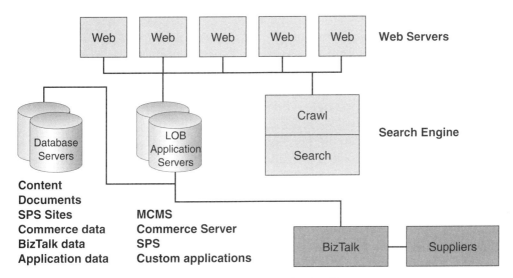

Figure 14.2 Microsoft Portal Architecture Hybrid Scalability

infrastructures would include servers and systems that are not from Microsoft, such as Oracle databases or Documentum document management systems. Your implementation will probably use hardware you have on hand or the fantastic bargain you found on an eight-way server and disk storage subsystem on eBay.

Most of the Microsoft server products lend themselves to the hybrid scalability approach. Microsoft Content Management Server (MCMS), SharePoint Portal Server, BizTalk Server, and Commerce Server all consist of several components that respond to different scaling techniques. Beefing up the SQL Server repository for content, commerce catalogs, and transaction tracking benefits all these servers. You may also need to scale out servers, such as adding a new server dedicated to crawling indexed content (SharePoint), managing the queue of transactions (BizTalk), or serving up web page content (MCMS).

The goal of performance optimization is to achieve maximum throughput and to reduce response time. While optimizing a complex system has many possible adjustments and configurations, using a systematic approach leads to better optimization.

The first step in optimization is collecting data on the system, such as current performance under various load conditions. When a performance issue is identified, the remediation alternatives are analyzed. One of the alternatives is chosen, implemented, and tested. The modification is accepted or rejected, depending on the results of testing as well as cost and other factors. Following the change, the testing process begins anew.

A systematic approach to optimization requires a top-down methodology, starting with system optimization followed by application optimization. For instance, there is little point in tweaking the code of a server component when you do not have adequate performance from your SQL Server database. These larger system components and network performance must be tackled first. A consultant I work with was once troubleshooting a document management system that was taking an inordinate amount of time to check in files. In the course of upgrading some components, he noticed that a particular server was requiring a long time to download any file at all. It turned out that a network port had been configured as half duplex rather than full duplex, bringing this particular server to its knees in terms of file input and output. Once this system flaw was detected and fixed, he could move on to application issues.

To understand how your portal can grow and scale, let's examine the key elements that make up the platform and how they respond to vertical and horizontal scaling techniques.

Server Operating System

The Windows 2000 generation of server products marked a significant milestone in Microsoft's quest for true enterprise-scale products. With the prior NT 4.0 generation, there were still general-purpose business solutions that were beyond the reach of Microsoft's operating systems. The operating system also constrained the performance of SQL Server, preventing it from contending as the most powerful relational database. Nonetheless, SQL Server 7 was able to deliver excellent marks for cost effectiveness and manageability, even if it left a certain low percentage of potential users untouched.

With Windows 2000 and the concurrent growth in hardware to accompany it, Windows can scale to meet virtually any business need. It runs on much more powerful servers than NT 4.0, addresses more memory, and scales through symmetric multiprocessing and clustering.

Windows 2000 offers three levels of the server operating system. Windows 2000 Server is for department and small business use. Windows 2000 Advanced Server is designed for higher availability, while Windows 2000 Datacenter Server meets the most demanding needs for large-scale computing. The latter versions of Windows 2000 break the former limit on addressable memory of 4 GB of RAM.

The directory component of Windows 2000 and Windows 2003 is Active Directory, and it is a key for scalability. Prior versions of Windows could only store 3,000 to 40,000 objects, creating a barrier for large organizations and certainly for portals. Active Directory is highly scalable, robust, and secure. Tests indicate the performance degradation with Active Directory (caused by replication among the Active Directory instances) begins at about one million users in a domain. The global catalog replication overhead creates a practical limitation of approximately five domains with one million users in each domain. Therefore a configuration of five Active Directory domains per forest equates to a practical limit of five million accounts.

Microsoft provides the excellent article "Active Directory in the Outward-facing Role" at www.microsoft.com/downloads/details.aspx?displaylang=en&familyid=e95b2d36-d746-4f57-ae79-e2adba31ec95, but you will find it easier to search for it by name. This document explains how to use AD as a single sign-on architecture for your portal, using a tight consistency model of directory replication.

Application Servers

Once you have established your network, web server, and file server architecture, it is time to examine the application servers you need for the enterprise. These servers are responsible for the middle tiers of your applications, such as BizTalk orchestration and SharePoint indexing and search. Your architectural choices are no less critical here than the choices you have already made for your server room.

Microsoft Content Management Server 2002

Microsoft Content Management Server 2002 has been tested to serve over 100 million dynamic pages per day. By adding processors to a computer,

Content Management Server 2002 scales up to continue to provide superior performance with high web site traffic demands. By adding additional computers running Content Management Server 2002 into a load balanced environment, Content Management Server 2002 scales out to meet the highest traffic demands and provide failover support, ensuring maximum uptime. Go to www.microsoft.com/cmserver/default.aspx?url=/cmserver/evaluation/overview/ for additional details on CMS scalability.

You can integrate Content Management Server 2002 with Microsoft Application Center, making it easier to deploy additional web servers. This integration also provides an open deployment API for building customized deployment scenarios. For instance, Application Center enables customers to schedule automatic or incremental deployments, and it helps with registration of server control components.

Commerce Server 2002

A Commerce Server site consists of two main elements that must achieve acceptable performance. First are the web pages, including the product catalog, which are likely to receive a great deal of user traffic. The second and related element is the SQL Server database that stores the catalog, accepts the transactions, and maintains some or all of the user profile information.

SQL Server 2000 has been designed for high scalability and stability. It supports the highly dynamic data typical for an e-commerce site, with read/write balances approaching 50/50 with no significant performance degradation. Commerce Server stores have been successfully tested for up to 10 million users in the store. To optimize a Commerce Server site, you must follow all the best practices relating to SQL Server configuration and management. There are many sources for this information, including the online help file and TechNet. A good place to begin is the Microsoft Reference Architecture for Commerce at msdn.microsoft.com/library/default.asp?url=/library/en-us/dnrac/html/mracv2_ch00.asp. You should also read a fictional case study called Duwamish VB 7.0 Beta 2 at www.microsoft.com/downloads/details.aspx?displaylang=en&familyid=32dbda05-b5de-45b9-a626-55fc20203cb4 or Duwamish 7 C# at www.microsoft.com/downloads/details.aspx?displaylang=en&familyid=132e17b9-d241-4400-b744-54134cbc1b88.

In addition to standard SQL Server configuration, you may need to scale the database out for best performance. You can subdivide the database function by allocating additional database servers for each Commerce

Server database. For instance, you may want to move the Commerce Server data warehouse to its own server so its operation does not degrade transaction processing on your store. Similarly, you could segment profile information from the catalog by putting the catalog and user profiles on separate servers. The Commerce Server Manager lets you move databases after the site is deployed, or you can assign them as desired during the initial site configuration.

As discussed in Chapter 7, you can store user profiles in SQL Server, in Active Directory, or in a combination of the two. For an external commerce site, you are likely to use SQL Server profiles alone or store a minimum of account information in Active Directory, such as username and password, with the remaining attributes (address, payment information, site visits, and so on) in SQL Server.

Much of the performance optimization for Commerce Server depends on SQL Server. Many large commerce sites use clustering for the SQL database. For a detailed example, see "Commerce Server 2000 High Availability Reference Architecture: Compaq-Microsoft High Availability Reference Architecture Validation," available at go.microsoft.com/fwlink/?LinkId=6687. Moving to a clustered environment will affect your Commerce Server installation. For information about installing Direct Mailer and Predictor on a cluster, see "Installing Commerce Server 2002 Resources as Clustered Resources" in your Commerce Server online help.

SharePoint Portal Server 2003

The architecture of the prior version of SharePoint Portal Server (version 1) was not suitable to scale beyond the needs of workgroups and medium-sized organizations. Microsoft has taken a new approach with SharePoint Portal Server 2003, moving the repository to a relational database and allowing components of the product, such as indexing and search, to be moved to separate servers. You can use a server farm for frontend web servers, which would have a large impact on performance for pages served.

SharePoint Portal Server 2003 lets you choose the storage engine. The default storage for a single-user installation uses the Microsoft SQL Server Desktop Engine (Windows) 2000 (WMSDE) for your databases. This is adequate for development or for operating in a small-scale environment. To support hundreds of sites, you may need the performance advantages of Microsoft SQL Server 2000 Service Pack 3 (SP3) as your database backend.

Once you move to SQL Server as your database engine for SharePoint Portal Server or Windows SharePoint Services, you can follow the architectural guidance to scale SQL Server as high as you need to accommodate your requirements.

A large-scale SharePoint Server deployment might therefore consist of:

- 3–5 web servers as the frontend to the portal
- 1–2 search servers to serve up search results to users
- 1–2 index servers to crawl content and maintain indices
- 1 large, clustered SQL Server installation for the repository

The model and configuration of the servers would be tailored to these roles. Relatively inexpensive commodity servers lend themselves to the web server, search, and index server roles.

Scaling Up Your Search Solution

The most sophisticated search functionality in the world is no good if it cannot support the number of users and the intensity of the search and indexing activity that you throw at it. Microsoft has addressed these scalability concerns with the latest generation of its search products in Windows 2003, Content Management Server, and SharePoint Portal Server version 2.

One of the design goals of SharePoint version 2 was to support one million users of a portal. For searching, the goal was to perform 95% of all queries in less than two seconds, and index up to 20 million documents (up from five million in version 1). This performance requires fast loading of thesaurus files and rapid crawling and indexing. SharePoint version 2 achieves at least double the indexing rate of version 1 in terms of documents per second. High availability and scalability may optimally be accomplished by using a number of servers to perform different roles in the portal. Indeed, you may need multiple servers for the search function alone.

SharePoint lets you assign multiple servers to roles as web servers, search servers, and index servers. For instance, if you had a small number of users but a vast amount of data to index, you would propagate many index servers but only require a small number or perhaps a single search server. Figure 14.3 shows the notional architecture for SharePoint search.

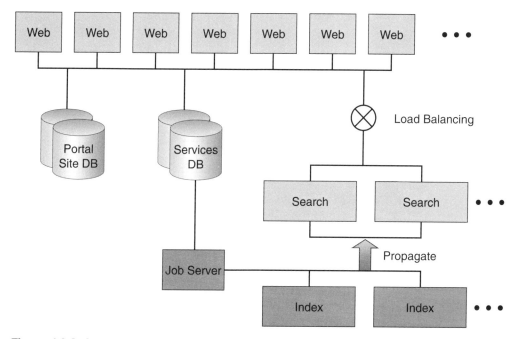

Figure 14.3 SharePoint Search Architecture (Source: Microsoft Corporation, Steve Tullis, "Enterprise Search With SharePoint Portal Server V2.")

A search starts with a user request that hits one of the portal web servers. Search requests are balanced across search servers from the web servers and therefore directed to an appropriate search server. All search servers have identical copies of each index through index propagation.

Each indexing server is devoted to crawling and indexing up to four content indexes. For instance, you could devote an indexing server to competitive company web sites, and another to file shares within your organization. Separating the indexing from the search service means that the performance of searches is not hindered by indexing activity, or vice versa.

BizTalk Server

Sometimes scalability presents obvious solutions to the analyst. Web servers, for instance, are generally scaled out to spread communications bandwidth and I/O (input-output) across a broader surface, while database servers are generally scaled up and maintained centrally. BizTalk presents no such pat answer, as its components can be scaled out and scaled up, depending on the pressure points that affect your system. Only by understanding the components of BizTalk Server and the business problems that can be created by potential bottlenecks and latency can you achieve an optimal solution for your budget. Therefore we look at both scaling up and scaling out options in this section.

One of the best sources for BizTalk scalability is in the MSDN article "Enhancing Performance and Scalability" at msdn.microsoft.com/library/default.asp?url=/library/en-us/bts_2002/htm/lat_perfscale_intro_fakz.asp.

BizTalk contains many components that can become bottlenecks in the system. In addition to the BizTalk server load and the multiple SQL Server databases required to track the messages and transactions, BizTalk depends on four transport services: HTTP/HTTPS, File, SMTP, and Message Queuing. Each of these can be scaled if necessary to support the desired transaction volume. The good news about this granularity of BizTalk configuration is that it offers so many options for scaling a solution, and it provides employment to analysts and network engineers as well as selling new hardware and software.

If you are starting with a single dedicated BizTalk Server, you can scale up by adding processors and memory. This approach keeps site management simple, but may be more costly than scaling a system horizontally or improving software architecture. Once the maximum capacity of the existing server is achieved, you must look elsewhere for further performance improvements.

The following steps are recommended to scale up a BizTalk Server:

1. Increase the processor size (such as the Pentium III and its Xeon derivatives with large level II caches).
2. Use symmetric multiprocessing (SMP) servers that accommodate up to eight CPUs.
3. Use a faster disk system.
4. Decrease file I/O and network bottlenecks.

As of late 2003, the following specific hardware and configurations are recommended for BizTalk Server:

- A multiprocessor PIII Xeon MHz processor system (the highest MHz possible for maximum performance), capable of being upgraded to eight CPUs.

- A 1- to 2-MB L2 processor cache (increases parsing performance).
- 1 GB of RAM (more if an organization is processing multiple-megabyte documents).
- Multiple 100-Mbps (megabits per second), or greater, network cards connected to 100-Mbps switch ports to increase network I/O throughput.
- Multiple disks and controllers for message queuing and distributed transaction coordinator (DTC) file and log operations. Write DTC log operations to a central remote server to offload file I/O contention on the local BizTalk Server.
- RAID 0 and RAID 1 disk configuration for better performance on the Shared Queue database and message queuing.
- Multihomed network interface cards (NICs) in the BizTalk Servers to separate HTTP processes from the dedicated Microsoft SQL Server processes of the Shared Queue and BizTalk Messaging Management databases. Also, consider using a switch network to reduce the traffic to the network card.

These recommendations assume that BizTalk Server is running on a dedicated server. If the BizTalk Services are sharing the server with other application services, additional hardware is recommended, or you may want to move BizTalk to a dedicated server.

Scaling up is often the preferred approach for the BizTalk database server. See the section on scaling SQL Server in this chapter for general database performance information. Microsoft recommends that the BizTalk Messaging Management, Shared Queue, Tracking, and Orchestration Persistence databases be on separate disk channels, as this improves access to each of the databases. Consider the following as a minimum for acceptable performance of BizTalk Server databases: A multiprocessor PIII Xeon MHz processor system (the highest megahertz possible for maximum performance), capable of being upgraded to eight CPUs, with 1 GB of RAM (more if an organization is processing multiple-megabyte documents).

Optimize the underlying Microsoft SQL Server databases and logs based on standard database best practices. If you initially plan to complete only a few transactions, you can install the databases on the same disk I/O channel. As more transactions are being processed, add disks and/or controllers to a server and move the databases to these new disk I/O channels. Additionally, an individual database can be moved to a new server.

To optimize the BizTalk Messaging Management database, the greatest benefit can come from installation of each of the databases on its own server or on its own disk channel. This prevents the Messaging Management database from hindering the performance of the Shared Queue or the Tracking databases.

The Tracking database should have more physical disks and additional disk space than the Shared Queue database, as the tracking database will end up with multiple copies of each message in the queue. To size the Tracking database, estimate the average document size for a single transaction and multiply the document size by the number of times the document will be logged to the Tracking database. Multiply the document storage space value by the estimated throughput requirement to determine the amount of space needed for the Tracking database.

Install the Tracking database on its own disk I/O channel due to the high volume of data that is written to it. A separate disk I/O channel is particularly important in heavy transaction environments. Follow similar optimization techniques for the Orchestration Persistence database.

Scaling BizTalk Server Horizontally

BizTalk Server 2002 implementation can benefit greatly from scaling out. While scaling up simplifies maintenance by minimizing the number of servers required, scaling horizontally provides the following benefits:

- *Cost effectiveness.* At current prices, multiple inexpensive servers can produce higher return on investment for application performance.
- *Server fault-tolerance.* When multiple servers share the workload, if one server fails, the other servers in the group can pick up the load.
- *Separation and optimization of the different components.* Performance of BizTalk Services, the databases, and the transport services can be increased, and the administrator is allowed more control over how each of the services is configured.
- *Hardware optimization for each server and service.* Servers can be optimized for the services they are running, so memory is allocated to servers where it is most needed, and I/O optimized throughout the server farm.

The downside of scaling out is some growth in the management and administrative burden, although Windows Server and related products greatly assist in this effort. You must also allow for server room space, air conditioning, and power to support the proliferation of servers, as well as including them in your backup and disaster recovery planning.

Database Repository—SQL Server

Aside from the operating systems, when it comes to scalability, SQL Server is the champion of Microsoft servers for scalability. As the data store for nearly all the enterprise servers with the exception of Exchange, Microsoft depends on SQL Server as the center for its offensive line.

SQL Server 2000 introduced a host of features to boost scalability and availability, including:

- Large memory support
- Support for large Windows 2000 Data Center Server clusters
- Multiple instances of SQL Server 2000 on a single server
- Integration with Active Directory to provide location transparent access to SQL Servers
- Log shipping for hot standby servers
- Updateable partitioned views among cluster nodes
- Improved parallelism in data and database management operations
- Indexed views and snowflake schema to support large-scale data warehouses
- Native XML support for Internet and data interchange operations

SQL Server 2000 has achieved impressive performance on a single server, and even more stellar results in a clustered environment. A single eight-processor SQL Server node can support more than 40,000 concurrent users accessing billions of records on a 4-terabyte (TB) disk array. This server can process more than 50 million business transactions per day, according to "Microsoft SQL Server MegaServers: Achieving Software Scale-Out" (msdn.microsoft.com/library/default.asp?url=/library/en-us/dnsql2k/html/megasrvs.asp). Although 2-way, 4-way, and 8-way processors are most common, SQL Server 2000 and Windows 2000 run on 32-way SMP hardware with up to 32 GB of memory for 32-bit Intel architecture and up to 4 terabytes of RAM with Intel's 64-bit Itanium architecture.

When 40,000 users and 50 million transactions per day are simply not enough, clustering takes SQL Server up to the stratosphere. Servers configured using Cluster Service share common data and work as a single system, while servers can operate independently of other servers in the cluster. This means that if one server fails, another server takes over its functions.

Each node has its own independent resources, including memory, system disk, operating system, and a subset of the shared resources in the cluster. If one node fails, another one takes ownership of the resources of the failed node. The cluster service then registers the network address for the resource on the new node so client traffic is routed to the new server. When the failed server is brought back online, the cluster service can be configured to redistribute resources and client requests.

You may consider several other server clustering techniques, including shared disks and mirrored disks. Servers can be configured as active/active, in which each server runs applications while also serving as a backup for the other server; or active/passive, in which one server runs applications while the other one serves as a backup. Table 14.1 lists three techniques you can use to share disk data in a server cluster.

The *Microsoft Windows 2000 Server Deployment Planning Guide* provides additional information on planning your clusters. The Windows Cluster Service Configuration wizard can help you create and configure your server cluster. For prescriptive information on installing Cluster Service, see the "Step-by-Step Guide to Installing Cluster Service" at www.microsoft.com/windows2000/techinfo/planning/server/clustersteps.asp.

Table 14.1 SQL Server Data-Sharing Techniques

Technique	Description
Shared disk	This technique requires specially modified applications using software called a distributed lock manager (DLM).
Mirrored disk	In the mirrored-disk technique, each server has its own disks and mirrors every write from one server to a copy of the data on another server.
Shared nothing	Each server owns its own disk resources. In the event of a failure, a shared-nothing cluster transfers ownership of a disk from one server to another. This technique avoids the potential bottleneck of a DLM.

Whether or not you cluster your servers, you face the decision among several disk configuration options, as shown in Table 14.2. To achieve optimal performance and fault tolerance, we recommend that you use a redundant array of independent disks (RAID) controller. There are several levels of RAID with different performance characteristics.

Higher RAID numbers do not imply that the controller is better or more advanced than one with a lower number. In fact, you can also combine multiple RAID levels to optimize performance. While RAID 0 provides the best performance, it does not provide fault tolerance. On the other hand, RAID 1 provides the best fault tolerance, at the cost of performance. The number of available disk controllers and disk channels also impacts performance. A one-to-one ratio of controllers to disks outperforms a one-to-five ratio, all other things being equal.

For a look at a sample SQL Server hardware configuration for the enterprise, see the Unisys ES7000 at www.unisys.com/datacenter/msa/. For the Microsoft Enterprise Systems Architecture, the database server was configured as follows:

A Unisys ES7000 was set up as a 24-processor production partition and an 8-processor development/test partition. These two partitions were

Table 14.2 Disk Configuration Options

RAID Level	Cost Effectiveness	Disk Utilization Percentage	Speed	Fault Tolerance
0 (Striping)	Low	100	Fast	Low
1 (Mirroring)	High	50	Medium	High
5 (Striping with parity)	Moderate	Effective disk space is the total space of all disks in the array combined minus 1 (for parity)	Slow	Moderate (only because performance degrades with a failed disk)
0 + 1 (Mirroring an array of striped disks)	High	50	Fast	High

clustered so the 8-processor development partition acted as the standby for the production environment. Each node ran Windows 2000 Datacenter and SQL Server 2000 Enterprise Edition.

The 24-way production partition included the following hardware:

- *Processor*: 24 x Intel Xeon 700 MHz
- *Memory*: 24 GB
- *Internal disk (for operating system)*: Four 18 GB
- *Host bus adaptors*: Six Emulex LP8000
- *Network interface cards*: Six Intel Ethernet Server NICs, teamed in pairs
- *Hardware management*: Unisys Integrated Management System
- *Operating system*: Windows 2000 Datacenter

The 8-way development/test partition included the following hardware:

- *Processor*: 8 x Intel Xeon 700 MHz
- *Memory*: 8 GB
- *Internal disk (for operating system)*: Four 18 GB
- *Host bus adaptors*: Two Emulex LP8000
- *Network interface cards*: Six Intel Ethernet Server NICs, teamed in pairs
- *Hardware management*: Unisys Integrated Management System
- *Operating system*: Windows 2000 Datacenter

Source: www.microsoft.com/technet/treeview/default.asp?url=/technet/itsolutions/edc/pak/ pag/edcpag03.asp[1]

You can view benchmarks for SQL Server on the ES7000 at the Microsoft and Unisys web sites. The tested configuration was designed to illustrate a high-end enterprise configuration, but is not the maximum scalability that can be achieved on the platform. Unisys can support up to a 4-node cluster with 32 processors each for larger data services capacity and performance requirements.

---

[1] Microsoft, Prescriptive Architecture Guide Version 1.5, Chapter 3, www.microsoft.com/technet/treeview/ default.asp?url=/technet/itsolutions/edc/pak/pag/edcpag03.asp

The performance of the Unisys ES7000 is an illustration of the kind of horsepower that can be brought to bear with SQL Server. Other vendors offer similar capabilities, and there are many possible server configurations that yield high database throughput.

Scaling Out with SQL Server

Scaling up is usually the most productive approach with SQL Server. Unlike with web servers, it is difficult to produce a high-performance SQL Server cluster with small, inexpensive servers. If you ultimately end up scaling out with SQL Server, it will likely be with servers that are also scaled up to a rather high level.

New features in SQL Server 2000 help with scaling out by simplifying administration of partitioned data. The servers that share partitioned data are called a **federation**. Each server is administered separately but shares a portion of the database workload. More resources can be applied to the database access than on a single server. For instance, if your application supports orders from customers who are distributed around the world, and you ship from regional warehouses close to the customers, you might want to partition the database geographically. This approach might result in one server handling Latin American transactions and another covering Europe. In cases in which queries need data from both geographies, SQL Server could look across the federation and pull together the appropriate results.

The techniques for scaling out include:

- Distributed partitioned views
- Data-dependent routing
- Replication
- Message queuing

You can combine these techniques in many different ways, depending on your requirements. A common scenario calls for distributed partitioned views with data-dependent routing, along with some form of replication.

When data is partitioned, SQL Server creates a view across multiple tables with identical structures and treats them as a single entity. Data-dependent routing is a method of accessing partitioned data that programmatically determines where data is located and routes the connections to the appropriate server. The developer determines how data is distributed with the goal of optimizing use of the computing and network resources at hand.

While this approach yields benefits, these must be considered against the costs. For instance, maintenance of the application becomes more complicated when data-dependent routing is employed. If the use of the database is quite dynamic, it may be difficult to predict which partitioning scheme will produce the desired load balancing.

For more information on scaling out with SQL Server, see "Designing Applications to Use Federated Database Servers" in SQL Server Books Online (msdn.microsoft.com/library/default.asp?url=/library/en-us/acdata/ac_8_qd_10_48oj.asp).

ASP.NET Optimization

Nearly all the solutions we have discussed in this book are built on .NET. Some special considerations apply to optimizing .NET applications. Some of these are common to many programming architectures, while others are especially important for .NET.

- *Cache data and output wherever possible.* With luck, your portal receives millions of hits per day. This translates into many times as many millions of disk accesses. If each hit means a new database query, the database server bears the entire load. The integrated cache included in .NET can dramatically reduce the time required to serve these pages by caching entire web pages, fragments of pages, or other objects. The ASP.NET programming model lets you design your pages with caching in mind to optimize performance of high-traffic areas of your portal. Appropriate use of caching is the single most important technique you can use to boost performance of your site.
- *Manage session state provider carefully.* ASP.NET provides three distinct ways to store session data for your application: in-process session state, out-of-process session state as a Windows service, and out-of-process session state in a SQL database. Each has its advantages, but in-process session state offers the best performance by far. For small amounts of volatile data in session state, use the in-process provider. The out-of-process solutions are primarily useful in web garden and web farm scenarios when you cannot lose data in the event of a server/process restart.

- *Disable session state when not in use.* Managing session state requires server resources. When applications or pages do not require per-user session state, disable it.
- *Avoid excessive round trips to the server.* As with caching, design to get the most out of each time a user moves from one page to another, or fills out a new form.
- *Avoid excessive server control view state.* Automatic state management can hurt performance although it is a convenient feature. Be conscious of when you really need ViewState and when you do not.
- *Use server controls sparingly.* Don't use server controls when another rendering or data-binding approach would work better and offer superior performance.
- *Use web gardening for multiprocessor computers.* Web gardening is a technique for distributing the work to several processes on a multiprocessor machine, one for each CPU, each with processor affinity set to its CPU. Some applications can achieve significant performance boosts with this technique.
- *Do not rely on exceptions in your code.* Because exceptions are very expensive in terms of performance, they should rarely occur in your code.
- *Port call-intensive COM components to managed code.* While the .NET Framework allows interoperability with traditional COM components, be sure that you are not paying too high a price in performance. If so, manage these components to managed code.
- *Use SQL stored procedures for data access.* The n-tier application architecture provides the most scalable web applications. This means using stored procedures in SQL to generate data, which is passed to middle-tier objects.

Performance Testing with the Web Application Center Test

All this talk about scalability is good in theory, and it's not hard to find hardware and software that produce impressive benchmarks. Theories and benchmarks don't guarantee adequate performance of your portal. You have to prove it yourself by either putting the system into production and hoping for the best or testing. For most of us, life is too short not to perform performance testing.

You can test the performance of your portal by standing it up in a test environment and unleashing a large number of users, or simulated users, to monitor how it responds to a load. You need dozens or hundreds of human users to get your portal to break a sweat. This type of testing is expensive and difficult to coordinate. On the other hand, you should tap into testing by human beings if possible, as you may uncover not only performance problems but usability or even training problems. Sooner or later, you need to allow humans to use the system, and getting bad news sooner is usually preferable.

For serious performance testing, however, automated testing tools can take you much higher than you can go with human testers alone. Coordination of automated testing is much simpler, and you do not have to worry about testers being pulled away from their mission by phone calls or carpools. You can perform automated testing any time of day or night, and you can strictly control the behavior of the test by means of a test script.

You can choose from a large number of testing products on the market. Here we focus on a single one to illustrate scalability testing: Microsoft Application Center Test (ACT). One reason is that it comes from Microsoft, and the second powerful reason is the price. The product is a free download from www.microsoft.com/applicationcenter/. You can view information on the tool at this site and read the documentation on MSDN. The link for the documentation is at msdn.microsoft.com/library/default.asp?url=/library/en-us/act/htm/actml_main.asp.

ACT is designed for Visual Studio .NET. It lets you record a Microsoft Internet Explorer browser session as the basis for testing or code the script from scratch. Test scripts are written in VBScript or JavaScript. The tool stores data generated during the test for subsequent analysis.

Hosting for Scalability

Once you have completed your requirements analysis, functional requirements, network architecture, application architecture, server architecture, and capacity planning, you may come to an unhappy conclusion. Your expectations for performance might exceed your ability to buy, configure, and maintain the necessary server farm. Luckily, you have another option: turn to a managed services company to host all or part of your portal.

Managed services offer compelling advantages for providing high-scale portal solutions. You can take advantage of the huge investments made by hosting companies in bandwidth, physical infrastructure, redundancy, disaster planning, maintenance, and monitoring of servers. Rather than make your own mistakes in buying and provisioning hardware, you can turn to someone who has already made and corrected their own mistakes.

The collapse of the dotcom era has left a trail of empty data centers around the country just looking for customers like you. As of this writing, it is a buyer's market in hosted services, and nearly every pricing offer you receive has room for negotiation. Hosting companies are an excellent reality check for your scalability plans. Working through the proposal process will help you better understand the needs of your data center and the real costs associated with it. You may find that the monthly subscription would be less than you would spend on services to maintain the infrastructure yourself, and you would be spared the capital investment in products that depreciate rapidly and become the building blocks for artificial reefs all too soon.

Best of all, if you have a problem with a hosted solution, there is someone else to blame and a service level agreement to force that someone to deal with the problem. All these factors point to outside hosting as a solution worth considering for many public or even enterprise portals.

Additional Scalability Information

You already have tremendous research materials on scalability at your fingertips if you have access to the web and the Microsoft products discussed in this book. Some of the best sources are to be found in white papers published on the Microsoft Developers Network (MSDN), the online help that accompanies each product, and in books and magazines devoted to Microsoft products. The online help for administrators is often most helpful when it comes to scalability hints.

We find the definitive source for architectural guidance on designing and building .NET solutions is in Patterns and Practices (msdn.microsoft.com/practices). This is a treasure trove of thousands of pages of information distilled from technical support, Microsoft consulting, partners, and customers. Not only are these prescriptive architectures created and approved by Microsoft, but they are supported by Product Support Services. Following these recommendations reduces technical risk for your implementation and is a simple form of insurance against the unknown incompatibilities you may discover on your independent integration efforts.

Patterns and Practices is available for download and on CD. Some content from it is also printed in book form. A great place to start is the Microsoft Systems Architecture–Enterprise Data Center. This resource is the foundation for Windows 2000/2003 servers including file/print services, Exchange, and SQL Server. The Microsoft Systems Architecture illustrates the principles it covers with specific hardware configurations, from Compaq (now HP) Proliant DL360 servers all the way to Unisys ES7000 servers.

Conclusion

Achieving highly scalable and available systems is a challenging endeavor that calls for study of complex hardware and software interactions. The diverse needs of the portal make it even more challenging than traditional applications, because the portal combines requirements for fast service of static web content, real-time interaction, transaction processing, server-to-server integration, data warehousing—in short, nearly every feature that could be demanded of today's computing environment. You may end up calling on an interdisciplinary team of experts to arrive at a solution that works for you. It takes even longer to come up with a solution that is affordable that will work.

The rewards of building a successful portal for nearly every type of organization are tangible and achievable. I hope that the information and ideas presented here have helped smooth the road for you in reaching your goals.

Index

Also from Addison-Wesley

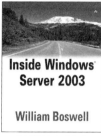
0-7357-1158-5

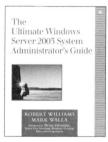
0-201-79106-4

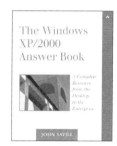
0-321-11357-8

0-321-13345-5

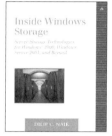
0-321-12698-X

0-201-61621-1

0-321-19444-6

0-201-77574-3

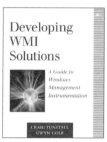
0-201-61613-0

0-7357-1192-5

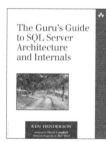
0-201-70047-6

0-201-61576-2

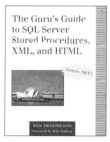
0-201-70046-8

0-201-74203-9

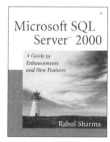
0-201-75283-2

For more information on these and all our titles go to www.awprofessional.com